Y0-DJM-918

Organized Crime in America

ORGANIZED CRIME IN AMERICA

A Book of Readings

BY
GUS TYLER

Introduction by Senator Estes Kefauver

Ann Arbor Paperbacks
The University of Michigan Press

LOURDES HIGH SCHOOL LIBRARY
4034 W. 56TH STREET
CHICAGO, ILLINOIS 60629

83-14667

FOURTH PRINTING 1977
FIRST EDITION AS AN ANN ARBOR PAPERBACK 1967
COPYRIGHT © BY THE UNIVERSITY OF MICHIGAN 1962
ALL RIGHTS RESERVED
ISBN 0-472-06127-5
PUBLISHED IN THE UNITED STATES OF AMERICA BY
THE UNIVERSITY OF MICHIGAN PRESS AND SIMULTANEOUSLY
IN REXDALE, CANADA, BY JOHN WILEY & SONS CANADA, LIMITED
MANUFACTURED IN THE UNITED STATES OF AMERICA

52517

36 4.1
TYL

Permissions and Acknowledgments

Section

1. From *Only Saps Work* by Courtenay Terrett: Vanguard Press, Inc., © 1930.
2. From the Third Interim Report, Special Committee to Investigate Organized Crime in Interstate Commerce, May 1, 1951.
3. From "The Big Fix" by Gus Tyler, *ADA World*, Sept. 1951.
4. From the Final Report, Select Committee on Improper Activities in the Labor or Management Field, U.S. Senate, March 28, 1960.
5. From "20th Century Crime" by G. L. Hostetter and T. Q. Beesley, *The Political Quarterly*, Vol. 14, No. 3, 1933.
6. From "The Underworld as Servant" by Walter Lippmann, *Forum*, Jan. 1931 and Feb. 1931.
7. From *Paths to the Present* by Arthur M. Schlesinger: The Macmillan Co.
8. From "Crime in a Competitive Society" by M. Ploscowe, *The Annals of the Amer. Acad. of Political and Social Science*, Vol. 217, 1941.
9. From *America as a Civilization* by Max Lerner, © 1957 Max Lerner: Simon and Schuster, Inc., and Jonathan Cape, Ltd.
10. From *The Gangs of New York* by Herbert Asbury: Alfred A. Knopf, Inc., © 1927.
11. From *The Barbary Coast* by Herbert Asbury: Alfred A. Knopf, Inc., © 1933.
12. From *King Crime* by H. Collinson Owen: © 1932, © 1959 by Holt, Rinehart and Winston, Inc.
13. From *Fighting the Underworld* by P. S. VanCise: Houghton Mifflin Co., 1936.
14. From *The Gangs of New York* by Herbert Asbury: Alfred A. Knopf, Inc., © 1927.
15. From *Syndicate City* by Alson J. Smith: © 1954 Henry Regnery Co.
16. From *The Barbarians in Our Midst* by Virgil Peterson: Little, Brown & Co.
17. From *Chicago Surrenders* by Edward Dean Sullivan: Vanguard Press, Inc., © 1930.
18. From *The End of Ideology* by Daniel Bell: The Free Press of Glencoe, Illinois, 1960.
19. From a statement submitted by Harry E. Barnes to the "Racket" Subcommittee of the Committee on Commerce, U.S. Senate, 1933.

20. From "Racketeering" by Murray I. Gurfein, *Encyclopaedia of the Social Sciences:* The Macmillan Co.

21. From a statement by Steve Sumner at a hearing before a subcommittee of the Committee on Commerce, U.S. Senate, 1933.

22. From *The Stolen Years* by Roger Touhy and Ray Brennan: Pennington Press.

23. From *Crime on the Labor Front* by Malcolm Johnson: McGraw-Hill Book Co., Inc.

24. From *Treasury Agent* by Andrew Tully, © 1958 Andrew Tully: Simon and Schuster, Inc.

25. From *Murder Inc.* by Burton B. Turkus and Sid Feder, © 1951 by Burton B. Turkus and Sid Feder: Farrar, Straus and Cudahy, Inc., and Bertha Klausner.

26. From *The Mob's Man* by James D. Horan: © 1959 Crown Publishers, Inc.

27. From the statement of Federal Judge Irving R. Kaufman: *The New York Times,* January 14, 1960.

28. From *The Man Who Rocked the Boat,* © 1956 by William J. Keating and Richard Carter: Harper and Brothers, and Victor Gollancz, Ltd.

29. From *Underworld U.S.A.* by Joseph F. Dinneen: © 1955 by The Curtis Publishing Co., © 1956 by Joseph Dinneen.

30. From "The Numbers Racket" by Ted Poston: © 1960 New York Post Corporation, *New York Post,* Feb. 29–March 10, 1960.

31. From *The D.A.'s Man* by Harold R. Danforth and James D. Horan: © 1957 Crown Publishers, Inc.

32. From *Crime in America* by Estes Kefauver, © 1951 by Estes Kefauver: Doubleday and Co., Inc.

33. From "The New Surge" by Robert F. Kennedy: © 1959 *Nation's Business,* May 1959.

34. From a Kansas City Grand Jury report, May 4, 1961.

35. From "On Wall Street" by Sylvia Porter, *New York Post,* Aug. 3–7, 1959: Hall Syndicate, Inc., all rights reserved.

36. From *Brotherhood of Evil* by Frederic Sondern, Jr., © 1959 by Frederic Sondern, Jr.: Farrar, Straus and Cudahy, Inc., and Victor Gollancz, Ltd.

37. From *Waterfront Priest* by Allen Raymond: © 1955 by Holt, Rinehart and Winston, Inc.

38. From Third Interim Report, Special Committee to Investigate Organized Crime in Interstate Commerce, 82d Cong., 1st Sess.

39. From "Mafia" by Gaetano Mosca, *Encyclopaedia of the Social Sciences:* The Macmillan Co.

40. From the *Encyclopaedia Britannica.*

41. From *The End of Ideology* by Daniel Bell: The Free Press of Glencoe, Illinois, 1960.

42. From Final Report, Special Crime Study Commission on Organized Crime, California, May 11, 1953.

43. From *Murder Inc.* by Burton B. Turkus and Sid Feder, © 1951 by Burton B. Turkus and Sid Feder: Farrar, Straus and Cudahy, Inc., and Bertha Klausner.

44. From "The Idle Boy" by George K. Turner: *McClure's*, July 1913.
45. From *The New York Times*, Aug. 11, 1960.
46. From *The New York Times*, July 25, 1960.
47. From "A Youth Looks at Gangs" by Gay Talese: *The New York Times*, Oct. 2, 1959.
48. From *America as a Civilization* by Max Lerner, © 1957 Max Lerner: Simon and Schuster, Inc., and Jonathan Cape, Ltd.
49. From *Street Corner Society* by William Foote Whyte: © 1943 The University of Chicago Press.
50. From *Delinquent Boys* by Albert K. Cohen: The Free Press of Glencoe, Illinois, 1955.
51. From "The Puerto Ricans" by Rev. Joseph P. Fitzpatrick, S.J.: *Catholic Mind*, May–June, 1960.

For Rick

For Ruth

One of the most important and most frustrating problems confronting our society today is organized crime.

Unfortunately, the coverage of its activities is usually superficial. Crusading and courageous newspapers and other communication media have always been important in fighting and exposing crime and corruption. But we must recognize that crime does make for sensational reading, and too often this is what the public gets. In television and motion pictures, crime is likewise a staple commodity. Night after night, through these channels, Americans are fed mixtures of violence and vice that may be exciting for the moment but that seldom lead to greater public understanding or remedy.

It is therefore with great pleasure that I welcome this volume by an astute observer of our social scene. There are many books on crime; some of them are significant. But this study is unique. It goes beyond simply dramatizing the criminal in "human interest" terms. More importantly, it adds to our knowledge of crime and the criminal personality by putting at our disposal a great amount of material hitherto unavailable or difficult to find. It gives us the background of organized crime, including its historical roots, its development into a flourishing business and its relationship to American society. And it concludes with a penetrating look at the place of juvenile delinquency in our culture. All of this is bound together into a unified whole by a series of perceptive and illuminating introductions by the author. We are thereby doubly indebted to Mr. Tyler—for his excellent selection of writings by experts in various aspects of the problem, and for his interpretive essays which are so written that they can almost stand by themselves.

Yet, this is far from being a cold, clinical dissertation on crime. It is, rather, as exciting as any whodunit on television. The principal difference is that whereas in crime fiction the culprit is ultimately identified, the responsibility for the existence of real crime is more difficult to pinpoint. One cannot point out any individual or any group and say, "This is the guilty party." We know that this responsibility must be shared by many elements in our society, beginning with the criminal himself and including certain forces in government, in business, in the unions and in other groups in the American mosaic. Mr. Tyler's study gives us a deep and penetrating insight into all the ramifications of organized crime and all the elements which sustain its growth.

I commend Attorney General Robert F. Kennedy for the anticrime bills he has offered the Congress and the fight he has made to obtain passage of some of them; they will serve as real deterrents against organized crime. But I feel that we need, in addition, a National Crime Commission.

During the investigations conducted a decade ago by the Senate Crime Committee, it became clear to me as chairman that crime does not end at the county or state line and that the only way to deal successfully with the problem is in some nationally co-ordinated way. Events in the intervening years have strengthened this belief and the studies in this book help to confirm it.

Another personal word: As a member and onetime chairman of the Senate Juvenile Delinquency Subcommittee and also as a father, I find the final section of this book of particular interest. I agree fully with the conclusions of these experts that the best way to cure a criminal is to stop him from becoming one, in his youth.

I am convinced that this book, if widely read (and it should be), will make a significant contribution to public understanding of and public action against organized crime.

Preface

This reader on *Organized Crime in America* is the by-product of a study commissioned by the Fund for the Republic (now the Center for the Study of Democratic Institutions) on the impact of organized crime on our democratic institutions.

The study flows from a discussion at Arden House on trade unionism, at which I maintained that trade unions faced the problem of "how to perpetuate a moral labor movement in an immoral community" (A New Philosophy for Labor, The Fund for the Republic).

The American underworld—the organized expression of this "immoral community"—does not issue from the trade unions, nor from the business community, nor from government—although it has penetrated all these basic institutions. Nor is organized crime the child of the Italians, or Irish, or Jews, or the Puerto Ricans—although it has drawn recruits from all these, and other, ethnic groups.

Organized crime is a product and reflection of our national culture.

In undertaking this study I found that the evidence for this conclusion was available at many sources. But the testimony was scattered and disorganized. This volume is an attempt to collate and organize the argument.

My views and conclusions are expressed in the introductory essays to the seven parts. The readings that follow do not necessarily reflect the same point of view, but they are all written by people whose standing is sufficiently serious and responsible to deserve a hearing in a comprehensive and many-sided study of this subject.

I should like to express my thanks to the Fund for the Republic for having helped to make this first step in the examination of organized crime possible (the second step is to be a paper on Organized Crime in our Democracy), to the various authors and commissions for the valuable material they gathered and the penetrating observations they have made, to the publishers who so generously granted permission to reprint, and to the University of Michigan Press for indulgence in granting time for quality.

GUS TYLER

CONTENTS

PART I
THE EXTENT OF THE UNDERWORLD

IN THE LAST QUARTER CENTURY a new class has risen to a position of power and prestige in America. That new class is the American underworld.

This underworld is not some vague and misty cellar of our civilization peopled by free-lancing desperadoes and delinquents committing acts of vice and violence against men and property. This underworld is a well-organized national cartel, with international ties. Its origins, its methods, its morality, its code, its culture are criminal. Its inner urge, however, is to end the typically parasitic life of criminality by "taking over" the institutions on which the professional criminal traditionally preys.

During the last decades the hand of the underworld has been exposed in a number of American institutions: in politics and government, in business and labor, in sports and entertainment, in transport and communication, in finance and insurance. The exposures have been made by Congressional and state committees, by private and public crime commissions, by grand juries and crusading district attorneys, by crime reporters and roving columnists, by magazine writers and book-length authors. Repeatedly, the nation is shocked. Following the shock there is a flurry of action: arrests, legislative proposals, deportations, and sometimes even capital punishment. And then a few years later, or perhaps a few days later, there is a new exposé, a revelation of the same disease on some other portion of the body politic—or maybe even in the same portion.

In these repetitive exposés and reforms the public focus is far less on the underworld than on the institution victimized by the organized criminal. When sports-loving America is shocked by the discovery that a World Series has been fixed by a kingpin of the underworld, the nation demands action —not to tear the underworld out of our culture by its roots, but to put a great new czar over baseball to keep it clean. When almost a generation later a New York district attorney proves that American boxing has been ruled by a well-known leader of the Syndicate, a distinguished sports columnist suggests that we get rid of boxing altogether as an arena beyond reform. When a Senate investigating committee in the early thirties reveals organized rings engaged in the kidnaping business, a statute is enacted to make kidnaping a federal offense—compelling the professional kidnapers to turn to other forms of criminal income. When the Volstead Act evolves into a guarantee of superprofits for great bootlegging combines, the nation repeals the Prohibition Amendment—compelling the separate combines to meet in national convention to explore new fields of endeavor: business and labor. When the Senate Crime Investigating Committee digs deeply into government only to find the underworld gnawing away close to the very heart of our national politics, the nation clucks a thunderous tongue about the evil ways of politicians—a chronic frailty fit for stale jokes. When another Senate committee investigates improper labor-management practices and the hand of the underworld is once more revealed, Congress enacts legislation to "curb" and "reform" unions. When corporations—publishers, auto manufacturers, chain stores—are found using the underworld to curb labor, to "guarantee" uninterrupted delivery of their wares, to charm customers and conventioners, public indignation rises to extort a promise from these entrepreneurs not to do it again. Always the focus is on the institution or the individual infected with the disease, on the host and not the parasite.

Probably the reason we concentrate on the host rather than the parasite is our notion that each of the infested institutions, in an hour of sinfulness, spawns its own breed of underworld. Hence, we berate the institution rather than the organized criminal in it. This is a normal tendency until such time as we discover that the underworld boss of boxing, and the underworld boss of newspaper distribution, and the underworld boss of a city's politics and government, and the underworld boss of a union, and the underworld boss of an automobile delivery business, and the underworld boss of a retail association are not separate entities without previous ties but old buddies, cradled in the same neighborhoods, blood brethren of commonly planned and executed theft and murder, who happen to be in their present separate fields because that is the way the jurisdictions were carved. The discovery of this ancient nexus—The Underworld—with a life of its own outside any of these aforementioned pursuits introduces a new level, a new depth of inquiry and concern. We can no longer confine ourselves to the weakness in the accepted social institution that permitted the infestation; we must now examine the underworld itself as a distinct, independent force and power, as something *sui generis*.

The material is at hand for such analysis. The separate investigations and revelations of the scattered institutions that have been enmeshed with the underworld have made available a mass of data. We have names and cases available for public use because they are on the public records. We have "inside" stories on the methodology of the underworld. We have sociologic studies on the origins of the underworld. We have a mountain of information: scandalous and scientific, lurid and pedestrian, primitive and refined. We have the raw material, begging for assimilation, codification, and analysis. It is now possible to do a dissection: to study the anatomy of the American underworld.

Some of the above-mentioned materials are collected in this volume.

Part I deals with the extent of organized crime in America. For the past fifty years there have been repeated warnings against the growth of the underworld in American life.

The concept of *institutionalized* crime—the criminal as an organization man—was voiced as early as 1915 by a Chicago crime commission.

"While the criminal group is not by any means completely organized, it has many of the characteristics of a system. It has its own language; it has its own laws; its own history; its tradition and customs; its own method and techniques; its highly specialized machinery for attacks upon persons and property; its own highly specialized modes of defense. These professionals have interurban, interstate, and sometimes international connections."

In 1923 the Associated Press reported from Philadelphia that "by banding together and aiding each other in case of trouble, by obtaining lawyers and advancing funds, the criminal element has strengthened its position, not only in this city, but in almost every large city in the country. The ring leaders in the movement are old offenders and from their former experiences have a wider knowledge of the law than many policemen."

"Unless I am woefully mistaken," wrote Courtenay Terrett in 1930 in the closing sentence of a book on the gangster-racketeer, "there is an excellent chance that racketeering will some day be not an industry, but industry itself."

In 1931, Arthur B. Reeve, in his *Golden Age of Crime,* predicted: "More racketeers—bigger and better rackets; a refinement of the racketeer—a standardization of the racket." That same year the *Saturday Evening Post* cried out in anguish: "Before we can settle any other question, before any other question is worth settling, we must get a decision on who is the Big Shot in the United States—the criminal or the Government."

In 1932 the Committee on Mercenary Crime reported to the section of Criminal Law and Criminology of the American Bar Association that "the gangster flourishes because of the conditions, laws, and customs which make his business profitable, and because of a large popular demand for the products of his illegal business. He will doubtless continue to flourish as long as crime continues to pay such large dividends and there is such a remarkable demand for his wares."

That same year Dennis Tilden Lynch reported in his "Criminals and Politicians" that "In the last ten years an aristocracy has arisen in this country. Its leaders, in the main, are the spawn of the brothels, the gambling dens and the corrupt political machines of the big cities, and the prisons. Their followers are drawn from all walks of life. Its law is the law of terrorism—the law of the club, the torch, the bomb and the machine gun."

In 1933, Gordon L. Hostetter, executive director of the Employers Association of Chicago, with Thomas Quinn Beesley, in the *British Political Quarterly*, said that "if rackets continue to grow at their present pace, they will completely blanket industrial United States in another ten years. What is more, there will be established a new aristocracy in business, traceable in its beginning to a criminal class. . . . The ascendency of this class will also sound the death knell of organized labor, as labor organization is constructed and carried forward today."

"America's chamber of crime commerce," wrote Martin Mooney in 1935, "exceeds in smoothness and effectiveness of organization anything ever known in the world. 'Why then,' asks someone, 'hasn't this all-powerful organization actually taken over the whole country?' The answer is: 'It practically has. Only the people don't know it.'" On the flyleaf of this book, entitled *Crime Incorporated,* appears a letter from J. Edgar Hoover, director, FBI, endorsing the expertness of Mooney and declaring that "racketeering is a problem which, if not determinedly and intelligently met and solved, will destroy eventually the security of American industrial life and the faith of our people in American institutions."

"You may definitely assume that crime, too, is incorporated," Thomas E. Dewey told the Citizens' Committee on the Control of Crime in New York in 1937.

"Early in 1940, while digging into the sources of local felony, the DA's office in Brooklyn ran head on into an unbelievable industry," recalls Burton Turkus, the assistant district attorney who discovered the business. "This organization was doing business in assassination and general crime across the entire nation, along the same corporate lines as a chain of grocery stores. The ensuing investigation exposed a vast network dealing in every known form of rackets and extortion, with murder as a by-product to that 'business' —an incident to the maintenance of trade. The disclosures, in fact, uncovered a national syndicate with coast-to-coast ramifications."

Although headlines in the early 1940's spoke of the liquidation of the syndicate, in 1949 the California Crime Study Commission on Organized Crime reported: "The great and truly dangerous criminals of the present are the directing heads of the syndicates . . . men who are almost unknown to the public and whose names never appear currently on any police blotter. . . . They live peacefully and luxuriously, enjoying a full sense of security, and with complete confidence that they will not be disturbed in their criminal activities."

Two years later Senator Estes Kefauver told the nation, still in shock as a result of one whole year of televised probing into organized crime, that "a nationwide crime syndicate does exist in the United States of America, despite the protestations of a strangely assorted company of criminals, self-serving politicians, plain blind fools, and others who may be honestly misguided, that there is no such combine."

Following the Kefauver report, the Assembly of the American Bar Association was told by the chairman of its Commission on Organized Crime, Robert P. Patterson, that "a hundred years ago, fifty years ago, no one would have foreseen a criminal combination of the power the Senate Committee has turned the lime-light on. . . . Crime has become big business, with a structure of chief executives, fiscal departments, legal departments, public relations and the rest."

In 1958, addressing the New York University Law Alumni Association, the U. S. attorney for the Southern District of New York, Paul W. Williams, in his description of "The Invisible Government," stated that "in this country today, we have a second government extending throughout the entire country and in its parasitic way it is eating at the democratic and moral foundation of our society. This invisible government has millions of dollars at its disposal. It issues its own edicts. It enforces its own decrees. It carries out its own executions. It collects its own revenues. It includes the major criminals of the country, and it has as its allies some public officials tempted by the lure of money and power, as well as short-sighted business and labor leaders. It is a rotten and vicious empire built on greed, murder and violence."

The four excerpts that follow were chosen because they approach the same problem from different angles and at different times.

The first of these was written in 1930. It is a fantasy, a piece of science fiction, written in the vein of Orwell's *1984*. It reads like a lighthearted nightmare, yet when reread against the background of all the supporting evidence in this volume, this projection of the future society, run by gangsters, appears no less real than a trip to the moon.

The second piece is an excerpt from the findings of the Senate Crime Investigating Committee headed by Senator Estes Kefauver and made public in 1951. It relates conclusions drawn from months of hearings that shocked America. Indeed, nothing in our times has done more to awaken the nation to the brazen and subtle power of the American underworld than the Kefauver hearings, televised before an unbelieving nation.

The third piece was written shortly after the Kefauver hearings when its chief counsel, Rudolph Halley, ran for public office in New York City. It was an argument directed to "liberals" who, while fully aware of the importance of carrying through economic reforms and of preserving civil liberties, were above the struggle against the underworld.

The fourth piece is the most recent, excerpted from the Final Report of the Select Committee on Improper Activities in the Labor or Management Field. The excerpt deals with the underworld convention at Apalachin, New York, in the fall of 1957.

Section 1 **THE GANGSTER STATE**

From *Only Saps Work* by Courtenay Terrett, 1930.

The pistol, short of barrel and with simple wooden grips which age and the sweat of long-dead palms had made a rich smooth brown, was the very one, the curator of the American Museum of Criminal History had declared, with which Scarface Capone had been killed. The platinum belt buckle upon which the initials "A. C." were paved in diamonds had been taken from the body of that almost fabulous Chicago Robin Hood, that twentieth-century Cid Campeador. And toying with them as he sat at his desk—a quaint old thing, all shining steel rods and ebony planks which the Baron of Antiques had unearthed to complete this Hoover Period office on the sixty-eighth floor of the New Hampshire summer palace—the Main Guy ruminated upon the past, the past which was so definitely bygone, though scarce a hundred years had elapsed.

With an unspoken and almost surreptitious pride, he reflected that his great-grandfather Pagani—his mother's grandfather, that was—had cast three votes apiece for President Hoover and Governor Al Smith in 1928, and he nothing more than a young immigrant who scarcely knew his district leader's first name.

He was not one to boast of blood and breed, but it was pleasant to be able to remember that one's forbears had helped to make America what it was today. And wouldn't the old gentleman—he smiled, and the six men who waited for him to speak were puzzled to see that strange grimace—wouldn't he be astounded to see the vast structure that his seed had reared upon those little dry-cleaning and broccoli rackets of which he had been so proud.

Abruptly he swept the buckle and the old revolver aside and glanced, stared almost, at the six men upon the far side of the desk.

"Gentlemen," he said, "I asked you to come here today in regard to some changes which must be made."

Though the facial muscles never twitched, there somehow appeared a look of apprehension on each of the broad, smooth-shaven countenances. He recognized it.

"Not that," he said with a grim smile. ". . . although you have noticed, I suppose, that Joe Flaherty is not here. Joe died suddenly this morning"— he stared at them levelly—"of heart disease, I believe they said.

"No," he went on, with an almost visible mental shrug, "what I called you in to tell you is that we've got to tighten things up. In the present state of affairs there is inexcusable waste—in duplication of overhead and equipment, in a purely traditional competition between essentially non-competitive industries, in a conflict of industrial jurisdictions. We must stop that."

He paused for a moment and let his gaze rest upon the cluster of Modigliani Drawings on the wall between the two tall poison gas-proof casements; they'd cost him $875,000, and very likely they were a bargain at the price, but he was damned if he saw what made them great art.

He jerked his mind back to its orderly path. "Gentlemen, we have made great progress, tremendous progress. The American tradition has been entrusted to the safe-keeping of our generation, and I believe we may boast truly that we have not only been faithful to that trust, but that we have made immeasurable advances.

"In you six are vested the control of every American endeavor and function, and I flatter myself that I have picked good men for the jobs. The Food King"—he bowed formally in the direction of Paddy Spinelli—"knows food from the seed store to the garbage pail. The Clothing King"—again he bowed, this time to Maxie Rabinowitz—"deserves the highest honors if for nothing more than that one flash of genius, the order that all American suckers above the age of four must wear silk hats. The long and able services of the Housing and Building King and the King of Transportation, Communications, and Power are familiar to the world, and the King of Recreation and Education has discovered methods of realizing undreamed-of profits from his rackets. And I am sure," he concluded with a kindly note of welcome to the burly young man who seemed less at ease than the others, "that Jerry O'Brien, who has succeeded Joe Flaherty as King of Public Health, Morals and Procreation, will prove an able administrator in that still somewhat undeveloped field.

"I might add," he interrupted himself, "that the reason Joe died of heart trouble was that he'd been doing a bit of outside racketeering in the Procreation License Bureau. I found out that he'd not only been cutting in on Harry's racket in the Recreation Department by selling contraceptives, but that he'd actually been bootlegging licenses to couples whose classification cards didn't match.

"Well, that's in strict confidence," he plunged on. "What I was about to say is that we're going to merge everything. You fellows are going to keep your jobs, of course, but we're going to start tearing the whole country down and rebuilding it. We'll stick up new buildings, all over. 'Every city a building, and every building a city.' How do you like that for a motto? I thought it was pretty good myself. When we get through people will be born and live and die in the same building, and we'll have increased the productive area of the United States by something like two million square miles.

"Why, gentlemen," he said, and his eyes blazed, "we'll make so much money that we'll be able to buy Europe outright, which will be several billions cheaper than taking it by force."

Abruptly he dismissed them. "I'll send you your orders in a few days."

He was staring out over the timbered hilltops when his secretary entered the room half an hour later. He was obviously annoyed at the intrusion.

"I'm sorry, sir," the young man said, "But I thought you might like to know. That President fellow sneaked out of Washington last night and has turned up in Russia. He's putting up a frightful howl about the racketeer despotism in America—says a man can't even breathe here without paying for the privilege."

"The damned fool," snorted the Main Guy, "if he'd stuck around he'd have been in the plush. I was going to put him in charge of the Propaganda and Patriotism Bureau of the Department of Education and Recreation. But say, make a note, will you, about what he said about breathing. There may be an idea in that."

Section 2   THE SYNDICATE AT MID-CENTURY

From the Third Interim Report, Special Committee to Investigate Organized Crime in Interstate Commerce, 1951.

1. Organized criminal gangs operating in interstate commerce are firmly entrenched in our large cities in the operation of many different gambling enterprises such as bookmaking, policy, slot machines, as well as in other rackets such as the sale and distribution of narcotics and commercialized prostitution. They are the survivors of the murderous underworld wars of the prohibition era. After the repeal of the prohibition laws, these groups and syndicates shifted their major criminal activities to gambling. However,

many of the crime syndicates continued to take an interest in other rackets such as narcotics, prostitution, labor and business racketeering, black marketing, etc.

2. Criminal syndicates in this country make tremendous profits and are due primarily to the ability of such gangs and syndicates to secure monopolies in the illegal operations in which they are engaged. These monopolies are secured by persuasion, intimidation, violence, and murder. The committee found in some cities that law-enforcement officials aided and protected gangsters and racketeers to maintain their monopolistic position in particular rackets. Mobsters who attempted to compete with these entrenched criminal groups found that they and their followers were being subjected to arrest and prosecution while protected gang operations were left untouched.

3. Crime is on a syndicated basis to a substantial extent in many cities. The two major crime syndicates in this country are the Accardo-Guzik-Fischetti syndicate, whose headquarters are Chicago; and the Costello-Adonis-Lansky syndicate based in New York. Evidence of the operations of the Accardo-Guzik-Fischetti syndicate was found by the committee in such places as Chicago, Kansas City, Dallas, Miami, Las Vegas, Nev., and the west coast. Evidence of the Costello-Adonis-Lansky operations was found in New York City, Saratoga, Bergen County, N. J., New Orleans, Miami, Las Vegas, the west coast, and Havana, Cuba. These syndicates, as well as other criminal gangs throughout the country, enter profitable relationships with each other. There is also a close personal, financial and social relationship between top-level mobsters in different areas of the country.

4. There is a sinister criminal organization known as the Mafia operating throughout the country with ties in other nations, in the opinion of the committee. The Mafia is the direct descendant of a criminal organization of the same name originating in the island of Sicily. In this country, the Mafia has also been known as the Black Hand and the Unione Siciliano. The membership of the Mafia today is not confined to persons of Sicilian origin. The Mafia is a loose-knit organization specializing in the sale and distribution of narcotics, the conduct of various gambling enterprises, prostitution, and other rackets based on extortion and violence. The Mafia is the binder which ties together the two major criminal syndicates as well as numerous other criminal groups throughout the country. The power of the Mafia is based on a ruthless enforcement of its edicts and its own law of vengeance, to which have been creditably attributed literally hundreds of murders throughout the country.

5. Despite known arrest records and well-documented criminal reputations, the leading hoodlums in the country remain, for the most part, immune from prosecution and punishment, although underlings of their gangs may, on occasion, be prosecuted and punished. This quasi-immunity of top-

level mobsters can be ascribed to what is popularly known as the "fix." The fix is not always the direct payment of money to law-enforcement officials, although the committee has run across considerable evidence of such bribery. The fix may also come about through the acquisition of political power by contributions to political organizations or otherwise, by creating economic ties with apparently respectable and reputable businessmen and lawyers, and by buying public good will through charitable contributions and press relations.

6. Gambling profits are the principal support of big-time racketeering and gangsterism. These profits provide the financial resources whereby ordinary criminals are converted into big-time racketeers, political bosses, pseudo businessmen, and alleged philanthropists. Thus, the $2 horse bettor and the 5-cent numbers player are not only suckers because they are gambling against hopeless odds, but they also provide the moneys which enable underworld characters to undermine our institutions.

The legalization of gambling would not terminate the widespread predatory activities of criminal gangs and syndicates. The history of legalized gambling in Nevada and in other parts of the country gives no assurance that mobsters and racketeers can be converted into responsible businessmen through the simple process of obtaining State and local licenses for their gambling enterprises. Gambling, moreover, historically has been associated with cheating and corruption.

The committee has not seen any workable proposal for controlled gambling which would eliminate the gangsters or the corruption.

7. Rapid transmission of racing information and gambling information about other sporting events is indispensable to big-time bookmaking operations. This information is presently being provided by a monopoly operated by the Continental Press Service. The Continental Press Service, at critical times and in crucial places where monopoly of bookmaking is at stake, yields to the domination and control of the Accardo-Guzik-Fischetti crime syndicate, to which it is beholden for its own monopoly in the wire-service field. The wire service is so vital to large bookmakers that they are compelled to pay what the traffic will bear to the Continental Press Service. This makes it possible for the Accardo-Guzik-Fischetti crime syndicate to participate in the profits of bookmaking operations throughout the country.

8. The backbone of the wire service which provides gambling information to bookmakers is the leased wires of the Western Union Telegraph Co. This company, in many parts of the country has not been fully co-operative with law-enforcement officials who have been trying to suppress organized criminal rackets which make use of telegraph facilities. By permitting its facilities to be used by bookmakers, Western Union has given aid and comfort to those engaged in violation of gambling laws. In some cases, Western

Union officials and employees actually participated in bookmaking con-spiracies by accepting bets and transmitting them to bookmakers. It should be noted that during the latter months of the committee's investigation, Western Union has taken steps to prevent this practice and has been more co-operative with the committee.

In many areas, of which New York is a notable example, the telephone companies have co-operated fully with law-enforcement officials. However, in still other areas, telephone companies have been much less co-operative. Local legislation is apparently necessary in many States to require telephone company officials to refuse facilities and remove existing facilities of sus-pected bookmakers and to call to the attention of local law-enforcement officials the use of telephone facilities by bookmakers.

9. Crime is largely a local problem. It must be attacked primarily at the local level, with supplementary aid, where appropriate, from State and Federal authorities. The conduct of various forms of gambling enterprises, houses of prostitution, the distribution of narcotics, the use of intimidation, violence, and murder to achieve gang objectives are all violations of State laws. The public must insist upon local and State law-enforcement agencies meeting this challenge, and must not be deceived by the aura of romanticism and respectability, deliberately cultivated by the communities' top mobsters.

10. The Federal Government has the basic responsibility of helping the States and local governments in eliminating the interstate activities and interstate aspects of organized crime, and in facilitating exchange of infor-mation with appropriate safeguards between the Federal Government and local and State law-enforcement agencies as well as between law-enforce-ment agencies in the various States.

The task of dealing with organized crime is so great that the public must insist upon the fullest measure of co-operation between law-enforcement agencies at all levels of Government without buck-passing. The committee feels that it has fully demonstrated the need for such co-operation. The time for action has arrived.

11. Wide-open gambling operations and racketeering conditions are supported by out-and-out corruption in many places. The wide-open condi-tions which were found in these localities can easily be cleaned up by vigor-ous law enforcement. This has been demonstrated in the past in many differ-ent communities and has received added demonstration during the life of our committee. The outstanding example is Saratoga, N. Y., which ran wide-open through the racing season of 1949 but was closed down tight in 1950.

12. Venal public officials have had the effrontery to testify before the committee that they were elected on "liberal" platforms calling for wide-open towns. The committee believes that these officials were put in office by gamblers and with gamblers' money, and that in the few cases where the

public was convinced that gambling is good for business, this myth was deliberately propagated by the paid publicists of the gambling interests. In many wide-open communities, so-called political leaders and law-enforcement officials have sabotaged efforts of civic-minded citizens to combat such wide-open conditions and the crime and corruption that they entailed.

13. The Treasury of the United States has been defrauded of huge sums of money in tax revenues by racketeers and gangsters engaged in organized criminal activities. Huge sums in cash handled by racketeers and gangsters are not reflected in their income tax returns. Income tax returns filed with the Federal Government have been inadequate since, as a rule, they contained no listing of the sources of income nor any itemization of the expenses. Gangsters and racketeers, moreover, do not keep books and records from which it might be possible to check tax returns.

14. Mobsters and racketeers have been assisted by some tax accountants and tax lawyers in defrauding the Government. These accountants and lawyers have prepared and defended income tax returns which they knew to be inadequate. At the very least, those who are guilty of such practices could be convicted of a misdemeanor and sent to jail for a year for every year in which they have failed to comply with the law.

The Bureau of Internal Revenue states that it has, to the best of its ability, considering its limited manpower, been investigating these returns. It states further that when it pursues the case of one of these individuals, it prefers to set up against him a case of criminal tax evasion which is a felony, rather than the lesser offense of failing to keep proper books and records, which is a misdemeanor.

Despite this, the committee believes that the Bureau of Internal Revenue could, and should, make more frequent use of the sanctions provided for failure to keep proper books and records than it has heretofore. In any event, the Bureau of Internal Revenue should insist on adequate returns and proper books.

While the great majority of agents of the Bureau of Internal Revenue are honest and efficient, there have been relatively few instances in different parts of the country of lack of vigorous and effective action to collect income taxes from gangsters and racketeers.

15. A major question of legal ethics has arisen in that there are a number of lawyers in different parts of the country whose relations to organized criminal gangs and individual mobsters pass the line of reasonable representation. Such lawyers become true "mouthpieces" for the mob. In individual cases, they have become integral parts of the criminal conspiracy of their clients.

16. Evidence of the infiltration by organized criminals into legitimate business has been found, particularly in connection with the sale and dis-

tribution of liquor, real-estate operations, night clubs, hotels, automobile agencies, restaurants, taverns, cigarette-vending companies, juke-box concerns, laundries, the manufacture of clothing, and the transmission of racing and sport news. In some areas of legitimate activity, the committee has found evidence of the use by gangsters of the same methods of intimidation and violence as are used to secure monopolies in criminal enterprise. Gangster infiltration into business also aggravates the possibility of black markets during a period of national emergency such as we are now experiencing. Racketeers also have used labor unions as fronts to enable them to exploit legitimate businessmen.

17. In some instances legitimate businessmen have aided the interests of the underworld by awarding lucrative contracts to gangsters and mobsters in return for help in handling employees, defeating attempts at organization, and in breaking strikes. And the committee has had testimony showing that unions are used in the aid of racketeers and gangsters, particularly on the New York water front.

Section 3 **THE BIG FIX**

From "The Big Fix" by Gus Tyler, 1951.

Once upon a time, any candidate who stood up to announce that he was opposed to sin was our standard laughing stock. Nowadays, however, our political morals have fallen so low that if a candidate declares his opposition to sin and means it, he is not only taking a very definite stand on a very definite issue, he is being downright outspoken on THE dominant issue in the many municipal elections across our country this November.

America is running a referendum on sin. The most dramatic, though not the only such, referendum is being run in New York City where Frank Costello, "Prime Minister of the Underworld," still holds sway; where ex-mayor and present Ambassador William O'Dwyer rose to fame; where Rudolph Halley, Chief Counsel of the Senate Crime Investigating Committee, is the Liberal-City Fusion-Independent Party candidate for President of the City Council. Similar referenda are being run in Philadelphia, Boston and dozens of smaller communities.

Several weeks ago, the cities of America were stripped naked before the television cameras for all the nation to see the shame. Faced by our shame, we should turn Election Day into a Day of Atonement!

Money, Muscle or Murder

The basic fact is a crime syndicate, running a business worth 22 billion dollars. Murder is a tool of the syndicate to enforce law and order within its underworld, to soften up clients for extortion, to silence witnesses. But murder is not the main business of the syndicate. Its multi-billion dollar take comes out of gambling, prostitution, white-slavery, dope, loan-sharking, extortion, waterfront racketeering—plus a number of "legitimate businesses" picked up with money, muscle or murder!

The syndicate is a near monopoly with the finance capitalist elements of the underworld—the gamblers—at the top. The syndicate is held together through a complex of interlocking directorates and hierarchies. The few smaller entrepreneurs operate only with the sufferance of the big boys and, in most instances, must pay for the license to exist.

The underworld is an economic system within our economic system; a law within our law, a state within our state.

How does this extra-legal, illegal anti-society escape the long arm of the law? Especially how does it escape the law at this time when the contours of its banditry and the profiles of its outlaws are known to millions of Americans?

The underworld does not escape the law by bribery. There's some of that, but it is not a basic operating method because it is too slipshod. The underworld does not escape the law through intimidation. Honest officials, backed by honest agencies, do not back down before the hoods.

The underworld wins its immunity through political action: through non-partisan political action.

When Abner (Longy) Zwillman appeared before the Kefauver Committee, he was asked whether he was head of a political club. He nodded assent. He was asked the party affiliation of the club. Longy said it was strictly non-partisan. When Frank Hague recently charged that Zwillman is the real boss of the Democratic Party of New Jersey, Hague was wrong. Zwillman's influence reaches into both the Democratic and Republican Party of New Jersey.

The underworld offers a candidate two of the most indispensable elements for the conduct of a campaign: manpower and money. The manpower is the mob, their families, relatives and friends who can get a job with the rackets or on the city payroll, looked upon as just another kind of racket. The money is cold cash: millions in crisp greenbacks for which no accounting need ever be made. To quote the inimitable O'Dwyer: "Whether it's a banker, a businessman or a gangster, his bankroll is always attractive."

After the election, millions are paid out in small—and, as in the case of payments from New York bookies to the police, not so small—bribes. But this is the little fix. The BIG FIX is the selection and election of public officials who know that they owe their elevated position in government to the underworld.

In New York City, the top man in crime is the top man in politics: Frank Costello. The Kefauver Committee proved this to the hilt.

ITEM: A New York judge called Costello the morning after the former's nomination to thank "Francesco" and to pledge "undying gratitude" to the boss of crime.

ITEM: When Mike Kennedy, boss of Tammany, stalled at a particularly nasty nomination, Costello called Kennedy to ask the latter whether he was a "man or a mouse." Kennedy proved he was a man by doing exactly as Costello ordered!

ITEM: When a Manhattan Borough President was elected, he followed the victory by paying his respects to Costello in the latter's apartment.

CLASSIC ITEM: William O'Dwyer, between his defeat in 1941 and his election in 1945, visited Costello's apartment. O'D says it was on war contract business. Present in the apartment were Irving Sherman (identified at the Kefauver hearings as a racketeer), Mike Kennedy (boss of Tammany), James Moran (very close pal of O'D and presently convicted of perjury), O'Dwyer and Costello himself. Rudolph Halley referred to this family portrait as "the picture of crime in politics."

The BIG FIX means the syndicate's man in City Hall—if they can get it. The BIG FIX means the syndicate's very own DA, its very own Police Chief. Failing that, the syndicate seeks to buy an assistant DA, an inspector, a deputy treasurer, a toadie in the tax assessor's office. Failing that, the syndicate seeks to buy a witness or a judge. Failing that, the syndicate intimidates a witness, or, failing that, the syndicate kills. (The above paragraph can be substantiated sentence by sentence, phrase by phrase, from the Kefauver Hearings.)

The BIG FIX is the system whereby the outlaw becomes the law. The system operates through political action. The system can only be broken through political action!

Liberals belong in the van of this fight, the municipal elections this November, the crusade against crime-in-politics: the referendum on sin. In a recent report to the National Executive Committee, Vi Gunther reported to ADA that the most virile chapters across the country were those that were genuinely involved in *local* issues. The successful realism of these chapters should be an object lesson to other liberals who refuse to wrestle with municipal corruption because they are either too supercilious or supercynical. The supercilious school is so concerned with world peace, national affairs, civil liberties that it will not stoop to gangbusting. Result? Many futile motions by people of good will while political power, real power in the precincts, rests in the hands of bums. The supercynical school, assuming sin to be a constant in the political equation, courts the machine for election to some lowly legislative post. Result? Bright lads with once shining faces become stuffed shirts to hide the shame of our cities. Being ideologues, American liberals might gain new strength by taking one long look at crime-in-politics against our total social philosophy.

1. Crime-in-politics is a direct challenge to the *moral* basis of American liberalism. The Soviet Union is frightening proof that collectivity in economics does not necessarily mean freedom in politics or fraternity in human relations. Restated in American terms: The growth of the welfare state, as an economic phenomenon, is no proof that the people will be free or unoppressed. Restated in general terms: economic reform in an immoral society can mean a smooth machine, worked by slaves and directed by tyrants. Restated in homely terms: Jersey City under Hague sent a New Dealer to Congress, backed FDR, instituted many local welfare set-ups, yet properly remained anathema to the American liberal. A homelier case was Huey Long!

Economic liberalism, plus political immorality, add up to Haguedom run by a Kingfish!

2. Crime-in-politics is a direct challenge to the *economic* philosophy of liberalism. And this on three counts:

a) Crime-in-politics means a farce of the welfare state, especially at the local level. The American municipality is a great dispenser of services: schools, health, sanitation, fire and smoke control, traffic, transit, housing, highways, hospitals, bridges, beaches, playgrounds, markets, airports, docks. The city, in America, is the germ of the welfare state idea. Crime-in-politics shakes faith in government, any government, as a creator of commodities or a dispenser of services. Municipal corruption means waste, inefficiency, dishonesty, Joe Citizen is gypped—and he knows it.

b) Crime in politics means a higher cost of living. Waste means higher sales taxes. Waste means higher property taxes and hence higher rentals. But, above all, the rackets impose a hidden tax—the gang levy—on millions of commodities, especially in coastal cities whose waterfronts are overrun with the hungry rats of the underworld.

c) Crime-in-politics IS big business, with all the evils of monopoly and none of its advantages. The Kefauver investigation proves that the relationship between business, politics and crime today is not the relationship of Lincoln Steffens' day. When the great muckraker wrote his *"Shame of the Cities,"* the businessman was the source of pollution. He bought the politician. Jointly, they used the muscle-man for bit parts in nasty scenes. Today, crime IS a big business, as big and arrogant and powerful as the best of them. It bows to no known capitalist overlord; it does force thousands of capitalists to bow to the syndicate. The criminal is no flunkey of the district leader, mussing up a few voters Election Day. The district leader is more apt to be the flunkey of the criminal.

The model modern muscle-man is versatile: gangster, businessman, politician. As he reaches out for more and more power, the modern overlord of the underworld becomes political boss and economic royalist as well. Which means that—

3. Crime-in-politics is a direct challenge to the *political* basis of liberalism.

Without alarmism or dogmatism, I would suggest a closer look at the crime syndicate as the shock troops for an American brand of fascism. I would suggest that we are not apt to ape the brown or black or silver shirts of Europe. We have our own fashions. Our future shock troops can wear nylon shirts, pin-stripe suits, and patent leather shoes.

Look at it closely: a nationwide organization with a fixed hierarchy, changed only occasionally and then by assassination; a standing army, well armed and disciplined; a contempt for democracy; a stunning political influence in hundreds of cities; billions of dollars in ready cash, more in holdings, and ever more billions as the underworld reaches out to buy real estate, hotels, oil wells, garment factories.

If Fascism is the politics of gangsterism then I would suggest that gangsterism in politics is the first step toward Fascism.

In the fight against the gangster society, the liberal can not be neutral. He dares not seek refuge either in the ivory tower or the sewer. The referendum on sin is on! No liberal can be above it—and, surely, none below it!

Section 4   **AN UNDERWORLD CONVENTION**

From the Final Report, Select Committee on Improper Activities in the Labor or Management Field, U. S. Senate, 1960.

During much of 1958 the committee looked into the extensive infiltration of gangsters and racketeers into legitimate trade union and business activity. This phase of the committee's hearings was given a preliminary study in June and July when hearings were held on the background of a number of the men who attended the gangland meeting at Apalachin, N. Y., on November 14, 1957.

The Apalachin meeting was the latest in a series of underworld gatherings which have occurred down through the years and by far the biggest known assemblage of top racketeers. Only alert work by the New York State Police resulted in unmasking the participants.

There were 58 known hoodlums in attendance at the Apalachin meeting, and law-enforcement officials are convinced that others were present and escaped the dragnet which was placed around the home of Joseph Barbara, after the existence of the meeting was first discovered by Edgar D. Crosswell of the New York State Police on the morning of November 14, 1957. To show the extensive infiltration of gangsters into legitimate trade union and business and trade activities, committee investigators made a survey into the irregular and illegal activities with which the men at Apalachin were connected. From this survey a great deal of valuable background material on these men was established. For instance, of the 58, 50 had arrest records; 35 had records of convictions, and 23 had spent time in prisons or jails as a result of these convictions; 18 of these men had been either arrested or questioned at one time in connection with murder cases. Other illegal activity noted in the survey included narcotics (for which 15 had been arrested or convicted); gambling (for which 30 had been arrested or convicted), and the illegal use of firearms (for which 23 had been arrested or convicted).

As to legitimate business activities, a study of the men who attended the Apalachin meeting showed: 9 were or had been in the coin-operated machine business; 16 were involved in garment manufacturing or trucking; 10 owned grocery stores or markets; 17 owned taverns or restaurants; 11 were in the olive oil-cheese importing or exporting business; 9 were in the construction business. Others were involved in automotive agencies, coal companies, entertainment, funeral homes, ownership of horses and racetracks, linen and laundry enterprises, trucking, waterfront activities and bakeries, and one was a conductor of a dance band.

There were several other significant facts produced by a study of these men at Apalachin: (1) They maintained extensive communication between themselves, even though they came from widely separated areas of the country; (2) there was an extensive blood line and marital relationship among these men, as well as between them and others who were not present at the Apalachin meeting. Thus, while certain key sections of the country appeared on the surface to be unrepresented at the Apalachin meeting, there is little doubt that the interests of those underworld figures were represented by others who were in attendance. For example, one of the largest unrepresented areas at the Apalachin meeting was the Detroit, Mich., underworld.

Yet a study of the telephone communications between those who were at Apalachin and persons living in Detroit showed extensive interchange of calls. Other areas of the country were also in touch with members of the Apalachin group. For example, John Ormento, a major trafficker in narcotics, who is currently a fugitive from an indictment in the southern district of New York, and who attended the Apalachin meeting, had been in communication with such parties as Joe Salardino in Canon City, Colo., Joe Civello in Dallas, and Michael Polizzi in Detroit.

The same type of extensive telephone communications to various parts of the country was maintained by other bigwigs who attended the Apalachin meeting, such as Joseph Profaci and Vito Genovese.

A study of blood-line ties also provides interesting examples: Two of the big-time hoodlums in the Detroit area are William "Black Bill" Tocco and Joseph Zerilli. Although neither of these men was present at Apalachin, they were related by marriage to men who were there. For example, Anthony Tocco, the son of "Black Bill" Tocco, is married to Carmela Profaci. Their New York wedding in 1955 was attended by leading hoodlums from all over the Nation. Joseph Zerilli's son, Anthony Zerilli, is also married to a daughter of Joseph Profaci—Rosalie Profaci. Angelo Meli, another top Detroit hoodlum, had a son, Salvatore Meli, who was married to Dolores Livorsi, the daughter of Frank Livorsi. Livorsi, in turn, is related by marriage to the aforementioned John Ormento.

The background of the problem of criminal infiltration was voiced by the chairman as the committee hearings got underway:

> There exists in America today what appears to be a close-knit, clandestine, criminal syndicate. This group has made fortunes in the illegal liquor traffic during prohibition, and later in narcotics, vice and gambling. These illicit profits present the syndicate with a financial problem, which they solve through investment in legitimate business. These legitimate businesses also provide convenient cover for their continued illegal activities.
>
> ❖   ❖   ❖   ❖   ❖   ❖
>
> It is important to understand from the outset that this criminal syndicate operation is not a localized one, but national in scope. The fact that the gangland meeting took place in Apalachin, N. Y., does not in any way make this a localized New York problem. Similar gangland meetings, known to authorities, have been held in Cleveland, Ohio, and on the Florida Keys. There is no telling how many other meetings, in other parts of the country, have been undetected by authorities (pp. 12192–12193).

The physical history of what took place on November 14, 1957, was provided to the committee by Sgt. Edgar Crosswell of the Bureau of Criminal Investigation of the New York State Police, headquartered at Vestal, N. Y. Sergeant Crosswell said he first became interested in Joseph Barbara in 1944 when a man was arrested for stealing gasoline from one of Barbara's plants. Barbara was the operator of the Canada Dry Bottling Co. in Apalachin, N. Y. Crosswell said that Barbara seemed reluctant to prosecute the man who had been arrested for stealing the gas, and it was further found that when he (Barbara.) appeared at police headquarters he was carrying a gun. Crosswell said that this piqued his curiosity and that thereafter he spent some time delving into Barbara's background. He found, for instance, that Barbara had been arrested for the murder of a man in Pittston, Pa. The murdered man's name was Calomero Calogare, who was shot down in Pittston on January 4, 1931. The victim made a deathbed statement accusing one Tony Merreale of shooting him. Merreale, however, said that at the time he was working at a still for Joseph Barbara. Barbara was arrested on suspicion of being the second man, but witnesses failed to identify him, and he was discharged. Again in 1933 Barbara was arrested by police in Scranton, Pa., on suspicion and for investigation as a result of the murder of a racketeer named Samuel Wichner. The information which police obtained was that Wichner was lured to the home of Barbara on the belief that he would have a conference with Barbara, Santo Volpe, and Angelo Valente, who were to be his silent partners in a new bootlegging venture. Barbara's record also shows that on June 13, 1946, Barbara was convicted in the U. S. district court at Utica, N. Y., of illegal acquisition of 300,000 pounds of sugar. On this charge he received a $5,000 fine. The committee was interested to note that Barbara held a pistol permit in New York State until after the Apalachin meeting was exposed. Such a permit must be obtained on an application which must include four or five character witnesses. Sergeant Crosswell said that investigation of the subjects who apply for pistol permits is very much guided by the people who are listed as references.

> Senator Goldwater. Did you ever see his application?
> Mr. Crosswell. Yes, sir; I have.
> Senator Goldwater. What kind of character witnesses did he give?
> Mr. Crosswell. He had the very best.
> Senator Goldwater. In New York State?
> Mr. Crosswell. Yes, sir (p. 12207).

Sergeant Crosswell said that during 1957 a number of hoodlums went to visit Barbara. He named them as Russell Bufalino of Pittston, Pa. (who is currently under order of deportation by the Bureau of Immigration), Emanuel Zicari, and Anthony Guarnieri, both of whom have long criminal records. Another visitor at the Barbara home was Patsy Turrigiano.

Sergeant Crosswell also said his investigation disclosed that there was a meeting of hoodlums in the Arlington Hotel in Binghamton, N. Y., in 1956. He named some of those he found to have attended as Joseph Barbara, Frank Garofalo, John Bonoventure, and Joseph Bonanna, also known as "Joe Bananas." All of these men have extensive criminal records; Bonnana, for example, had once been arrested for transporting machine guns to the Capone mob in Chicago. Galente was picked up after he left the city of Binghamton in the company of Frank Garofalo. He has an extensive police record going back to 1921, including terms in Sing Sing for grand larceny, assault, robbery. In 1930 he was sent to the penitentiary for shooting his parole officer. The expenses at the hotel during this meeting were paid for by Barbara.

The discovery of the Apalachin meeting came quite by accident. Sergeant Crosswell said he and his partner, Trooper Vasuko, were investigating a bad check charge in a motel in Vestal. As they were talking to the motel owner, they noticed the son of Joseph Barbara, Joseph Barbara, Jr., approaching the motel. Crosswell and his partner said they hid in the living room behind the motel owner's office and heard young Barbara engage three rooms for the nights of November 13 and 14, 1957. He said he wanted the rooms charged to the Canada Dry Bottling Co., and wanted to take the keys with him. The owner's wife asked young Barbara to register the names of the persons coming and he said he did not know who they would be and he would register them the following day. Crosswell said he checked around that night and found two cars parked near Barbara's home. One was registered in the name of Patsy Turrigiano and the other in the name of James V. LaDuca, an official of the Hotel and Restaurant Workers Union in Buffalo, N. Y. A third car with a New Jersey registration was found to have belonged to one Alfred Angelicola of Paterson, N. J. This was at 9 p.m. on the night of November 13. At 9:30, Crosswell said, he checked the motel and found a car registered to the Buckeye Cigarette Service of Cleveland, Ohio, operated by a man named John Scalish:

> Sergeant Crosswell. We asked the proprietor about that car and he said two men had driven in and went into one of the rooms that Barbara had reserved and so we sent him out with a couple of registration cards to get the men to register. He came back and he said that they had refused to register and said that "Joe" would take care of it the next day (p. 12213).

The motel owner wanted to evict these men, but Crosswell told him to leave them alone. At 2:30 in the morning a further check was made, and the only new item noticed was that LaDuca's car had moved from in front of the Barbara home to the motel. At 8:30 the following morning Crosswell checked the motel again and found that in the three rooms reserved by Joseph Barbara, Jr., six beds had been occupied, indicating that four men had come with LaDuca. He then notified the senior inspector of his district that it appeared that another meeting was underway at Barbara's home. Crosswell drove by the Canada Dry plant and found nothing going on there. He then headed for Barbara's home, and that is when, in his own words, the "stuff hit the fan. We drove in and everybody started running in all directions." As Crosswell and his men came up the long road leading to Barbara's home, "a lot of men ran from around the barbecue pit * * * and some ran for the house and some came out of the house and ran the other way and everybody got all excited and all worked up." The road on which Crosswell drove toward Barbara's home was the only entrance and exit road to and from the estate. Another road, which was a potential escape route, had a washed-out bridge. However, Crosswell said, as he and his men set up the road block, they saw 10 or 12 men running from the direction of Barbara's house into the pine woods behind the house. Crosswell said, however, that even after going through these woods the men would have to escape down a road called McFaddin Road. Crosswell said he set up an additional road block on this road so that they could pick up the men coming out of the woods. Crosswell said the men were all dressed for the most part in silk suits and white-on-white shirts, highly polished pointed shoes and broad-brimmed hats. Some of the men who took the woods route, however, appeared a bit bedraggled when picked up by the police. "Some of them lost their hats and they were full of cockle burrs and their shoes were scuffed up."

Of all the persons ensnared by the police dragnet, however, by far the most interesting from many aspects was John Charles Montana, who in 1956 had been voted "Man of the Year" in Buffalo, N. Y., for his civic good works. According to Crosswell, Montana was one of the men who chose to go through the woods on the approach of the police. He was found near Mc-Faddin Road caught on a barbed-wire fence.

> Mr. Crosswell. He called me over to the house and he sent a man over and said he wanted to see me and I went over and he told me he was very embarrassed being there, and he had just stopped in to see Barbara, and did not know that there was going to be any such gang of characters as he found up there, and if I would let him go up and get his car and get out of there he could probably do something for me.
>
> He started mentioning a lot of prominent people that

he knew in Buffalo and that area and one of the officials of our department that he knew very well. He mentioned no specific that he could do for me, but that he could do something for me if I would let him go and get his car.

Senator Ives. How was he attired? Did he have the George Raft attire, too?

Mr. Crosswell. Yes, sir; topcoat and all.

Senator Ives. Pointed shoes and all?

Mr. Crosswell. Yes, sir.

Senator Ives. Large hat?

Mr. Crosswell. Yes, sir.

Senator Ives. He had all of that on to have a cup of tea?

Mr. Crosswell. That is his story (p. 12215).

Montana's story of how he arrived at the home of Joseph Barbara on November 14, 1957, was one of sheer amazement to members of the committee. According to Montana, he had known Barbara for a number of years, going back to 1934 when Barbara became a distributor for one of Mr. Montana's farflung enterprises, the Empire State Brewery Corp. Montana said that when he left Buffalo he had an appointment in New York City with a man named Frank Sawyer to discuss matters affecting the taxicab industry. He said that he had also decided to make a stop in Pittston, Pa., to see William Medico, the head of Medico Industries. Montana said that in 1956 he had sold a compressor to William Medico but that he had never received any pay from Medico for this. "I was going to find out whether I would get paid for it or ship it back."

Mr. Kennedy. Weren't the phones working at that time? Couldn't you just telephone down to Pittston?

Mr. Montana. Well, telephones didn't do any good. As long as I was going to New York, I thought I may as well get it over with, stop there and find out and ship it back if I couldn't get the money.

Mr. Kennedy. Just go down there and find out about the compressor yourself?

Mr. Montana. That is right (p. 12298).

Montana said that he left Buffalo on Thursday morning, November 14, 1957, at 8:45 a.m. Traveling with Montana was Anthony Maggadino, whom Montana described as "an uncle through marriage to my nephew." Maggadino has an extensive criminal record, including arrest for falsifying passports in Italy, homicide, extortion, rape and violation of the U. S. immigration laws. Montana said he was completely unaware of Maggadino's record. Montana said he had gone up to Niagara Falls on Wednesday, November 13, to see one of his older brothers. "He is the father of a girl that married Maggadino's nephew." He said Maggadino was at his brother's house and asked him if he could go to New York with him so that he could see his sister. Thus, Montana and Maggadino left Buffalo on Thursday morning, November 14. It was raining, and when Montana got 15 or 20 miles out of Buffalo he started having trouble with his windshield wiper. Montana said he stopped the car on the thruway and fixed it in the rain.

Montana said that when he got 10 miles west of Endicott, N. Y., he started having trouble with his brakes.

> * * * On that road there is no service stations of any kind, and I could not drive the car more than 15 or 20 miles an hour. Of course, to my own sorrow, I know that Joe Barbara lived there (p. 12302).

Montana said the trouble actually occurred just before he drove into Owego. Senator Irving Ives, vice chairman of the committee, who lives in upstate New York said he had been in Owego many times and that there were several garages there. Mr. Montana said he did not stop in any of these garages because they "don't know how to take care of a set of brakes." Montana said he drove to Barbara's home because he said he felt Barbara would get one of his mechanics to fix the brakes. He said he parked at the entrance of the house and went in to look for Joe Barbara, leaving Maggadino sitting in the automobile. He said he met Mrs. Barbara in the house and asked her if she would give him a cup of tea. Montana said to his best judgment he arrived at the Barbara home about 2 p.m. Sergeant Crosswell said that when he went up to the Barbara home at 12:40 Montana's car was not parked where he said he parked it. Further, he said that the roadblock was set up immediately following this and that no cars went in or out of the Barbara estate after 12:40 p.m., November 14, 1957, without his knowledge.

Montana said that after he had been sipping tea for a few minutes, Joe Barbara came into the room and told him that he would get a mechanic to fix the car.

> Mr. Kennedy. In the meantime, Mr. Maggadino was still sitting in the car?
>
> Mr. Montana. Still sitting in the car.
>
> Mr. Kennedy. Wasn't he hungry?
>
> Mr. Montana. I didn't ask him if he was hungry. I just went in to get this car business taken care of, and I told him to wait.

Mr. Kennedy. But you were in there having tea.

Mr. Montana. That is right.

Mr. Kennedy. You were eating.

Mr. Montana. That is right.

Mr. Kennedy. It was after the lunch period. Wasn't he also anxious to eat?

Mr. Montana. Well, he didn't discuss anything about eating (p. 12306).

Montana said that the tea party was broken up when Joe Barbara suddenly exclaimed that there was a roadblock. Montana said that when he saw the commotion "I was no part of it and I thought I would walk away from it." It was this walk that took Montana into the woods behind the Barbara estate and out toward McFaddin Road, where he was ultimately apprehended by the police.

Mr. Kennedy. Would you explain to the committee why you thought it was necessary to go to the woods?

Mr. Montana. Well, I was no part of it.

Mr. Kennedy. Did you feel it was gangsters who were establishing a roadblock and you would have to run from them, or what?

Mr. Montana. I wouldn't know, Mr. Kennedy. It could have been gangsters. I didn't think they were. Those people were eating when I was there. My best judgment was to leave, and I did (p. 12308).

Mr. Montana was asked about others who were at the meeting at Barbara's home. He said he knew Salvatore Falcone, Joseph Falcone, Russell Bufalino, and James LaDuca. Montana insisted, however, that he saw none of them at the Barbara home on that day. As to Anthony Maggadino, Montana said that he faithfully sat in the car until he came out of the house and then walked into the woods with him. As peculiar as Montana's story seemed to the members of the committee, he was the only person who attended the Apalachin gathering who appeared before the committee who did not invoke the fifth amendment. Others who attended the meeting at Barbara's home who appeared before the committee were Russell J. Bufalino, Vito Genovese, James LaDuca, Louis Anthony Larasso, Rosario Mancuso, Mike Miranda, Joseph Profaci, and John Scalish. (Further background on these individuals will follow in this report.)

The operations of the criminal underworld were outlined to the committee by a number of expert witnesses who have had experience in the racket field. These included Martin F. Pera, special agent for the U. S. Bureau of Narcotics; Capt. James E. Hamilton, head of the Intelligence

Division of the Los Angeles Police Department; Daniel P. Sullivan, operating director of the Miami Crime Commission; and Sherman S. Willse, committee staff investigator who served for 20 years as a member of the Narcotics Squad of the New York Police Department. Pera, an agent for the Narcotics Bureau for 10 years, had performed special investigative assignments in Turkey, Greece, Italy, France, and Portugal. He said that the Bureau of Narcotics has established that the major traffic of narcotics into the United States has gone "through the hoods of the organization that we term to be the Mafia." He said the organization was originally established in Sicily in the late 18th century to combat the exploitation by the Bourbon overlords of Sicily at that time. During the late 1800's and early 1900's many Sicilians immigrated to the United States. Agent Pera said that among the early immigrants some were members of a criminal syndicate. He said their first criminal activity was to extort money from the more successful of their group and from the more successful Italian merchants that had immigrated to the United States. He said the group became particularly active in the prohibition era.

> Mr. Pera.* * * The prohibition era found tremendous opportunity for them. This organization was a secret organization. It was dedicated to work contrary to the laws of the United States, and local laws, and with the tremendous profits inherent in the production and distribution of bootleg liquor it offered an opportunity that these people took advantage of. We have some of the group that attended Apalachin that became wealthy during that time.
>
> There were men like Barbara, for instance, who was found with a tremendous load of sugar. Well, sugar, of course, is used in the fermentation process, with yeast, and is one of the raw materials with which bootleg alcohol is made.
>
> Of course, the Falcones. Among the many, of course, was Capone that made his mark in the prohibition days (p. 12221).

Pera said that in 1928 a meeting of the Mafia was observed in Cleveland, Ohio. Among this group were two who also attended the Apalachin meeting, Joe Profaci and Joe Magliocco. Pera outlined for the committee the methods by which heroin is smuggled into the United States.

> Mr. Pera.* * * The smuggling of heroin into the United States has taken place through different routes during dif-

ferent years, but generally, predominantly, most of the heroin smuggled, let's say, within the last 10 years, has taken place in the following manner:

The opium was produced in the Balkan countries, such as Turkey, in the Near East, in Turkey and Iran, and perhaps in Yugoslavia, and is processed into morphine base. Let's say Turkish opium that is purchased by traders in Istanbul outside of the government monopoly. There is a government monopoly in the trading of opium in Turkey, and the controls are very strict.

On the other hand, there is what is called the black market in opium where individual businessmen will go and purchase outside of the Government monopoly, quantities of opium from the farmers.

This opium is processed into morphine base, after it is transported across Syria into Lebanon. From Beirut, Lebanon, or perhaps Aleppo, Syria, this morphine base is shipped to clandestine laboratories in France for conversion into heroin. In the laboratories in France and this is in the last, say, 7 to 10 years, they are operated by Corsican traffickers, and we might point out there that the Corsican underworld element are cousins to the Sicilians. They call each other cousins. They speak Italian. Many of them immigrated originally to Corsica from the Italian islands.

They understand one another thoroughly, and even though they might come from separate disciplines at the top level, they have an efficient interchange in criminal activity.

The laboratories in France are operated by Corsican violators who, in turn, arrange for the smuggling of these drugs, of heroin, into the United States, via French seamen smugglers, couriers, as it were, or else in some instances the heroin is sent back to the traffickers in Sicily or in Italy, and it is brought over here by means of concealment in trunks or the personal effects of immigrants (pp. 12222–12223).

Pera also emphasized the point which was made by the staff survey, that there is a tremendous family tie-in between groups in various parts of the country.

* * * The intermarriages are significant in that oftentimes you wonder whether these people want to marry each other. Yet the marriages take place. Let's say two people of a prominent status within the Mafia if they have children, you will find that their sons and daughters get married. They don't marry on unequal terms, too often (p. 12228).

Pera said that investigation by the Bureau of Narcotics had convinced him that this organization has made a concerted effort to "penetrate into the broad field of labor-management relations." As an example, Pera cited the Greater Cartmen's Association in New York, which was controlled by Vincent J. Squillante. This situation was the subject of committee hearings during 1957. Pera said that Pasquale Pagano, also known as Patsy Pagano, who is known by the Narcotics Bureau as a key distributor of heroin, had been active in gang efforts to gain control of longshoremen activities in Hoboken, N. J. In this activity, Pera said, Pagano was the contact man for Anthony Strollo, also known as Tony Bender. Pera said that in his longshore activities Pagano was aided by Joseph Gurney, who had been a close associate of Elmer "Trigger" Burke, a New York racketeer who was electrocuted. The New York State Anti-Crime Commission focused attention on Tony Bender's activities, which forced him to withdraw Pagano and Gurney from the Claremont Terminal. After leaving the longshore activities, Pagano became a business agent for local 59 of the International Hod Carriers, Building and Common Laborers Union in East Harlem, New York. Three other Hod Carriers officials, Rosario Mancuso of local 186 in Plattsburgh, N. Y., and Louis Anthony Larasso and Frank Majuri of local 394 in Elizabeth, N. J., attended the meeting at Apalachin. Pera also said that Carlo Gambino, who attended the Apalachin meeting, runs a labor relations consultant service in New York. Pera was asked by committee members to name the persons he considered important in the top structure of criminal syndicates in various sections of the United States. He said that in Chicago the important figures were Anthony Accardo and Paul DeLucia, also known as Paul Ricca. (Accardo was a witness before the committee in its investigation of gangster infiltration into the Chicago restaurant industry. A section of this report deals with that hearing. Paul Ricca was a committee witness concerning the sale of his home in Indiana to the Teamster locals in Detroit headed by James R. Hoffa and Owen Bert Brennan. Both Accardo and DeLucia invoked the fifth amendment.)

Pera says that an important figure in Detroit was Raffaele Quasarano, who he said was involved in the distribution of narcotics. (The committee also heard testimony about the relationship between Quasarano and Owen Bert Brennan and James R. Hoffa. This testimony is covered in the section of this report on Hoffa.)

Other important figures named by Pera were Anthony Giardano, Anthony Lopiparo, and John Vitale in St. Louis, and Santos Trafficante in Florida and Cuba. Pera said that there was no doubt that this was a national problem.

> Mr. Pera. * * * I would say that you could never appreciate the total activity of this group if you dissect it from one area and focus your attention only on one particular area. I don't think that enforcement agencies that observe their activities in one particular city can appreciate the network involved in this criminal conspiracy. I don't think that they could appreciate the extent or the ramifications or what it costs the public, the loss of money to the public and the extent of their criminal activity unless attention was focused on them from a national or interstate point of view (p. 12246).

Daniel P. Sullivan, operating director of the Crime Commission of Greater Miami, testified the Miami area is a well-known meeting place for some of the Nation's top racketeers. Some of those who have congregated in Miami have been Frank Costello, Joe Adonis, Abner "Longy" Zwillman, Gerardo Catena, and Joe Massei. Sullivan also said there was substantial contact between the Miami group and a group of American racketeers who have entrenched themselves in Havana, Cuba. Santos Trafficante, who Sullivan said was the key figure in criminal circles in Tampa, Fla., is the operator of the Sans Souci Casino in Havana. Trafficante was one of those present at the Apalachin meeting. It should be noted that on the day that Albert Anastasia was shot down in the barbershop of the Park-Sheraton Hotel in New York City, Santos Trafficante was occupying a room in the Warwick Hotel in New York City which had been reserved by Anastasia. Trafficante moved out of the room an hour or two after Anastasia was murdered.

Sullivan said that a number of hoodlums who had moved into the Miami area had made inroads or attempted to make inroads into the labor field. For instance, he said an ex-convict named Charles Karpf attempted to organize the jukebox business in Miami with the assistance of a Cleveland racketeer named Anthony Randazzo. Another member of the group interested in the jukebox enterprise was Joseph Indellicato, also known as Joe Scootch. Sullivan said that through the assistance of representatives of the International Brotherhood of Electrical Workers, the scheme of Karpf was exposed and brought to an end.

Sullivan also bore out the testimony of Pera that the American underworld is highly organized.

Mr. Sullivan.* * * Nobody, for instance, like [Joe] Massei, could control the apparently tremendous lottery operations that he has in Detroit and be able to sit outside a barber shop in Miami Beach day after day, week in and week out, and month in and month out, and not have a tremendous organization behind him.

Certainly, we find this: When these people come there, they are very close. For instance, Massei arranged to have a boat slip back about 7 or 8 years ago for Tony Accardo, who is a top man of the Capone mob in Chicago. He was intimately acquainted with Charley Vicetti, who is now dead, of the Capone mob. He is very close to the Cleveland crowd,* * * All of these people are very intimately associated with one another, and there is no question in my mind that they are operating on a national level, and that they are highly organized (pp. 12434–12435).

Sullivan gave the following reason as to why gangsters found it profitable to move into the labor union field.

Mr. Sullivan.* * * We had a representative of one of the Senate committees attend one of our annual conventions, and he spoke about a man who moved into the union welfare business. They asked this man who had been in some other type of business why he had moved into this type of business, and he said: "Well, first of all, when you have a checkoff system, you have a foolproof system of collections. It doesn't cost you any money to operate. Secondly, if you run into one of these insurance companies or welfare outfits, you don't pay any money out and you take it all in. And thirdly, you have no inspection on the local, county, State, or Federal level. So your funds are not audited." What it amounts to here is that you have a kind of vacuum in our political economy whereby a great mass of money can flow into the hands of individuals where [there is] no accounting and no inspection of any kind (p. 12438).

Capt. James E. Hamilton, commander of the Intelligence Division of the Los Angeles Police Department, also reported to the committee on infiltration of gangsters into union and business enterprises. For example, Hamilton said that a dress-importing company, Rose Marie of California, was controlled by the late Jack Dragna, who was reputed to be the top gangster leader in southern California, along with Sam Scozzari and Frank DeSimone. Scozzari and DeSimone both attended the Apalachin meeting.

52517

Hamilton said that a gangster named James Iannone, also known as Danny Wilson, was found to be acting as a "labor adjuster" in the Los Angeles shoulder pad industry. Los Angeles shoulder pad manufacturers noticed that the Custom Made Shoulder Pad Co. had no labor troubles as long as Iannone was on their payroll. It was found that shoulder pad companies which incurred picket lines could have the picket lines removed by the simple expedient of hiring Iannone. Hamilton said that Iannone also operated on the management side of the street. He said there was a small company called the Buy-Rite Disposal Co. which manufactured commercial garbage disposal units.

> Two or 3 years ago Danny Wilson and Joe Sica first started hanging around the office of the Buy-Rite Disposal; which was out in county territory. There was a man by the name of Sam Eglit, who was the principal of Buy-Rite at that time. It was a small concern. Today Mr. Eglit is gone. Danny Wilson is the man at Buy-Rite Disposal. This isn't the first time we have seen this happen. We have seen it tried in other places. When this type of individual moves into a legitimate business, the legitimate people get pushed out (p. 12330).

Backing up the testimony on the intermarriage of top racket figures and their children, Hamilton told the story of Carlo Licata, the son of Nick Licata, one of the top leaders of criminal groups in California. Hamilton said that Carlo Licata was a bartender at the Five O'Clock Club in Burbank, Calif. Sometime in 1951 or early 1952 he disappeared from his usual haunts. Hamilton said the next he heard about Carlo Licata was a letter from a law-enforcement official in Michigan, notifying him that Licata had married the daughter of William "Black Bill" Tocco, one of the top racket figures in the Detroit area. Licata is now secretary-treasurer of the Melrose Linen Supply Co. in Detroit.

83-14667

Staff Investigator Sherman S. Willse outlined for the committee the reasons why gangsters and hoodlums enter into certain types of business activities. For example, he said that trucking operations in some instances give gangsters access to the waterfront, where they can facilitate smuggling of narcotics. The importation of narcotics is also sometimes covered through import-export businesses. Willse said that narcotics are sometimes sealed in barrels of olive oil or in the heart of huge cheeses. Such businesses as jukebox, linen, laundry, and bar provide a method by which large amounts of cash can be concealed or transferred. Willse said that acetic anhydride, which is used by garment manufacturers in connection with the treatment of rayon, can also be used to convert raw opium into a morphine base from which it

LOURDES HIGH SCHOOL LIBRARY
4034 W. 56TH STREET
CHICAGO, ILLINOIS 60629

can be made into heroin. While a member of the New York Police Department, Willse made a study of a bar in lower Manhattan called the Alto Knights. This bar was a notorious hangout for hoodlums. From a vantage point near the Alto Knights, Willse was able to photograph frequent meetings held in front of the Alto Knights showing the close association between some of the top New York underworld figures. Pictures introduced into evidence included a number of top gangland figures, such as Vito Genovese, Michael Miranda, Pasquale Normando, Peter DeFeo, Frank Tieri, Joseph Stracci, Joe Tortorici, Lorenzo Brescia, Gregory Ardito, Alfonso Criscuolo, and Joseph Gorgone.

Of this list a standout figure in the American underworld is Vito Genovese. Agent Pera of the Narcotics Bureau testified the Bureau has information that Genovese has amassed a fortune of $30 million. He was present at the Apalachin meeting and since the committee hearing was indicted on a narcotics charge by a Federal grand jury in New York. One of the most interesting cases related to the committee concerning Vito Genovese involves the 1934 murder of Ferdinand "Shadow" Boccia. Willse said that the murder occurred ostensibly for two reasons. One was that Vito Genovese and Mike Miranda had set up a rigged card game and money machine swindle, in which they obtained around $150,000. Boccia had been promised $65,000, and when he did not get the full amount he started to complain about it. In addition, Boccia had reputedly held up the liquor headquarters of Anthony Strollo, alias Tony Bender. Bender was a very close friend of Vito Genovese and in fact had acted as best man at Genovese's wedding, a favor which Genovese returned when Bender got married. At any rate, for 10 years following Boccia's death his murder remained unsolved. In 1944 a man known as Ernest "The Hawk" Rupolo, facing a prison term in a shooting case, started to talk about the Boccia killing. Rupolo said he was first approached by Mike Miranda, who told him that "Boccia has to go." Rupolo said that Miranda wanted Boccia "cowboyed." This meant that they wanted Boccia killed whenever Rupolo ran into him. Rupolo said he was to take a man named Willie Gallo with him when he went to kill Boccia, and after killing Boccia he was to also kill Gallo. The following night there was a meeting between Rupolo, Mike Miranda, Vito Genovese and Pete DeFeo. On the night of September 9, 1934, after receiving two pistols from DeFeo, Rupolo, Gallo and another man known as Sal Palmira went to a movie in Brooklyn with the intention of killing Boccia later that evening. However, before the movie ended Palmira got word that Boccia had already been killed. The three men left the movie, and as they walked down the street, Rupolo pulled out a gun, aimed it at Gallo's head and pulled the trigger. The gun, however, misfired. "He made a joke out of the thing and pacified Gallo and they walked a few more minutes." (p. 12367). They went to the home of a mutual friend, where Rupolo presumably oiled the gun and fixed it, and they continued walking again with Gallo. Again Rupolo pulled out the gun and fired at Gallo, this time successfully, but Gallo did not die. Rupolo told police that Mike Miranda was very angry at him for failing to successfully dispatch Gallo. Gallo was able to testify against Rupolo, who was sentenced to prison from 9 to 20 years. It was on emerging from this sentence that he began to talk about the Boccia murder.

As a result of Rupolo's statements, Vito Genovese, Mike Miranda, Gus Frasca, and George Smurra were all indicted for the murder of Boccia. Before he could be arrested on the indictment, Genovese disappeared and later turned up in Italy, where he was working as an unofficial adviser to the American Military Government. While in Italy, one of the key witnesses against Miranda, and Genovese, was murdered; a second died under the most mysterious circumstances. He was Pete LaTempa, known as Petey Spats. LaTempa had been placed in jail as a material witness. While in jail he had to take regular medication for a stomach ailment. One day he asked for his medicine and was handed a glass with a liquid, which he consumed. He died soon after, and an autopsy disclosed that LaTempa had taken enough poison to kill eight horses.

The activities of Genovese in Italy were outlined to the committee by Orange C. Dickey, a former special agent for Military Intelligence in Italy. Dickey said he was conducting an investigation into black market activities in Italy when he ran across the trail of Vito Genovese. Dickey said that the black market was largely in Army supplies: sugar, blankets, clothing, and food, some of which had been stolen from the Army and some of which had been illegally sold. The track of the black marketeers eventually led to an Italian civilian who, Dickey said, was a leader in these illegal activities in the Naples and Nola area of Italy. In questioning this individual, Dickey said he told him that he had been interviewed by many Criminal Investigation Division agents and that nothing ever came of the cases because he had friends in the Italian courts and in the Allied Military Government. This man indicated that one of his contacts was Vito Genovese, who, he claimed, was an interpreter for the Allied Military Government at Nola. This information was of interest to Dickey, particularly since he had discovered the fact that Genovese was a strong supporter of Mussolini and had contributed heavily to the Fascist Party. For his activities on behalf of the Mussolini government he was made a Commendatore del Re, which is supposedly the highest Italian honor a civilian can receive. Dickey said that other informants that he developed in Italy also told him that Genovese was a top leader of criminal syndicates both in the United States and in Italy. Dickey said that with his case completed he was finally able to move against Genovese and arrest him, which he did on August 27, 1944, to May 14, 1945, at which time the Army

agent brought Genovese back to the United States to face the charges growing out of the Boccia killing. During the time Genovese was in jail Dickey
was offered $250,000 to let the gangster go free. Dickey said that as he was
preparing to put Genovese on the boat, he objected violently; but once the
ship had left the port Genovese's attitude changed radically, and he told
Dickey, "You are doing me the biggest favor anyone has ever done to me.
You are taking me home." During the boat ride from Italy to the United
States Dickey and Genovese occupied the same cabin, and Dickey said that
Genovese talked rather freely to him about a number of subjects. In one
instance, he talked to him about the fact that he had done work in strikes
and that he had been responsible for bringing in workers to break strikes.
Genovese also told Dickey that he could make money by working for both
sides in labor-management disputes.

As mentioned previously in the report, the Bureau of Narcotics and
other agencies have identified a large segment of the criminal underworld
as the Mafia. Whether it goes by this or any other name, there is no doubt
there is a highly organized criminal group, related by nationality, marriage,
and other ties. Top hoodlums like Frank "Buster" Wortman, Meyer Lansky,
and Abner "Longy" Zwillman, have found it expedient to mesh their operations with this group. The Apalachin meeting is historic because it did more
to open the eyes of the public to the seriousness of the criminal conspiracy
than almost any other event in the past 20 years.

In closing the hearing, the chairman declared:

> The testimony we have heard can leave no doubt that
> there has been a concerted effort by members of the Ameri-
> can criminal syndicate to achieve legitimacy through as-
> sociation and control of labor unions and business firms.
> The extent of this infiltration poses a serious threat to the
> very economy of our country.
>
> The criminal syndicate which we have identified here
> as the Mafia has revealed an arrogant challenge to the
> Government and to the decent people of this country. The
> contempt with which the leaders of the underworld, as
> they have displayed it here on the witness stand, regard
> both their Government and the citizens of this country
> has been demonstrated repeatedly during this past week
> by their refusal to cooperate, even in the slightest degree,
> with this committee, which has a mandate to carry out an
> important function of this Government.
>
> The lack of regard which these racketeers and gang-
> sters have for their country can be amply demonstrated by

their extensive police records since arriving in the United States. In addition, it has been demonstrated in the case of Vito Genovese that he actively collaborated with the Italian Government after receiving his American citizenship and while the United States was actively at war with Italy (pp. 12478–12488).

PART II

THE MATRIX OF ORGANIZED CRIME

ORGANIZED CRIME IN AMERICA is not the result of any one fault in our national character. The underworld is the end product of many forces: some bad, some good, and some both. The modern criminal is not the child of our shame, but springs as well from acts and attitudes that we proclaim to the world with pride. Indeed, the very strength of organized crime arises from the fact that it is a complex counterpoint to our complex civilization, an ironic image in a mocking glass.

"American criminal activity," wrote Frank Tannenbaum in his *Crime and the Community* (1938), "must be related to the total social complex. The United States has as much crime as it generates. The criminals are themselves part of the community, in its deeper sense, and are as much its products as are its philosophers, poets, inventors, businessmen and scientists, reformers and saints."

This view takes some of the mystery and myticism out of the French bon mot about every civilization getting the kind of criminal it deserves. We agree that any culture at a given time gets the music, literature, or practicing ethic it deserves. Why not the criminals it deserves?

"The community has given [the criminal] not merely his ideals and ends, not merely his relationships with the world that make the kind of career he lives a possibility. The community has given him his *methods* too, whether these be graft, political pull or the use of the machine gun. The distinction between the criminal and the community drawn in sharp contrast—a distinction between good and evil—is a false distinction and obscures the issues" (Tannenbaum, p. 25).

To relate the organized criminal to the culture does not wipe out the distinction between good and evil, but it does help to show how both good and evil are siblings of the same culture: blood brethren of the same womb.

Society has always tended to make the criminal something "different"—an outsider, an outcast, a foreign element to the society. The criminal has a different-shaped head, a faulty intellect, a demon inside him. The criminal is obsessed or possessed. The criminal can resemble anything except our normal selves. The search for the criminal is a manhunt *outside* our own skins, the yearning for a scapegoat.

This tendency to draw a hard, sharp line between the normal and the abnormal is probably as old as man. To act otherwise would invite an inquiry into ourselves to uncover the tight relationship between the "irrational" and the "rational"—a most disquieting bit of introspection, to say the least. And so when confronted by the face of evil, madness, or simple nonconformity, we have always looked upon it as the face of a stranger.

When we do summon up the courage occasionally to face inward, we do so to find the faults, the cracks, in our character. We look for the unfortunate moments of trauma: the bang on the head, the lost love, the ugly hour that tipped the scale of sanity. Thus, in trying to reveal the origins of organized crime in our own culture, we seize on Prohibition, some wave of immigration, World War I or II. We try to ferret out the exciting experience that produced the evil within us.

This is a limited view, although it contains an element of truth. Just as the Mafia spirit contributed to the development of our underworld, so can specific traumas in our national life—war, economic crises, the Eighteenth Amendment—create widespread social disorders expressed in group criminality. But these are limited views because organized crime—like crime itself—is not simply derived from evil institutions and events but, ironically, from social forces usually viewed as "good." Organized crime is the nightmare lurking in the shadows of the American dream!

What is this American dream? Riches and rights available to all! Someday, anybody may become somebody, such as president of U.S. Steel or the U.S.A.

We are a self-made nation bearing self-made sons. We are independent, free, and equal, conceived in bloody revolution. No document is more basic to our national aspirations than the Declaration of Independence, a clear, ringing statement that we have the right to take up arms—to resort to force—for what we believe is right. If any document takes second place, it is not the Constitution with its established chain of authority, but the Bill of Rights with its repetitive checks on authority. This is a basic component of the American dream: inalienable rights!

Yet precisely this concept of inalienable rights—the right of a man or group of men to deny authority—is the original matrix of a lawless spirit in America. This spirit runs from Lexington and Concord, where yeomen took the law into their own hands, to the Connecticut Turnpike, where motorists whiz past traffic signs to set their own speed limits.

Our history drips with tales of men, bands, gangs, and states who took the law into their own hands. Indeed, even a president of the United States could say to the Supreme Court: you made the decision, now you carry it out! And a mayor of one of America's greatest cities could define the difference between "statute" and "law," the former being what you are supposed to do and the latter being what you really do. This is a tradition of which we are both proud and ashamed, depending on who you are, what you did, and whether you got caught. At times we identify this lawless tradition with the spirit of liberty, the right of every fellow and his companions to take up arms against intolerable oppression, the right to revolution. At other times we identify this same lawless spirit with a return to tyranny when it appears as a night rider under a bed sheet with rope in hand. And at other times, as when several states proclaim their independence, the self-same event is viewed as the day of liberty by one side and the night of slavery by the other, and the dispute is resolved by force! But, for good or evil, better or worse, Americans have for centuries been contemptuous of law, mixing democracy with anarchy, liberty with license, and freedom of the individual with freedom from society.

American historians, concentrating not on crime but on our culture, have long noted this lawless streak.

The American's "individualistic bias sometimes assumed forms that defied government," observed Arthur M. Schlesinger (*Paths to the Present*, p. 15) in 1949. "The colonists in their relations with the mother country evaded unwelcome regulations and, prompted by their theologians and lawyers, insisted that acts of Parliament contrary to their 'unalienable rights' were void. Within the colonies those who dwelt remote from centers of law and order adopted a like attitude toward the provincial authorities. The Scotch-Irish who illegally occupied Pennsylvania soil in the early eighteenth century contended 'it was against the laws of God and nature that so much land should be idle while so many Christians wanted it to labor on and to raise their bread.' As a substitute for constituted authority the settlers sometimes created their own unofficial tribunals, which adjudicated property titles and punished offenders against the public peace. In other instances they resorted to the swifter retribution of individual gunplay, or of mob action and lynch law, for from taking the law into one's hands when it could not function, it was but a step to taking the law into one's hands when it did not function as one wanted it to."

Writing in 1949, this historian insisted that "the tendency to violence so generated has continued to condition the national mentality to the present time."

Another historian, James Truslow Adams (*Our Business Civilization*, p. 101), writing in 1929, referred to Americans as a "population already the most lawless in spirit of any in the great modern civilized countries. Lawlessness," he continued, "has been and is one of the most distinctive American traits."

Aware of the tendency to blame it on the "foreigner," Adams argued that it "is impossible to blame the situation on the 'foreigners.' The overwhelming mass of them were law-abiding in their native lands. If they become lawless here, it must be largely due to the American atmosphere and conditions."

To recount the long tale of this lawless spirit is to recite a repetitive catalogue of riots, rebellions, and revolutions finding their legitimacy in the struggle for "rights." The heroes of this drama are not criminals. There stands Thoreau, the kindly anarchist, advising Americans to be "men first, and subjects afterward," who should not "ever for a moment, or in the least degree, resign conscience to the legislator." There stands John Hancock, smuggler and signator of the Declaration of Independence: a dual distinction struck from one medal. There stand the worthies of New England who signed the Hartford Convention to give moral force to their nullification of federal law during the War of 1812. There stand the statesmen of chivalric South Carolina, speaking through the refined brain and golden tongue of John Calhoun, making nullification the very basis for our national existence. There stands William H. Seward in 1850 advising the slave senators that there "is a higher law than the Constitution." There stand the pillars of the Northern churches, defying the Fugitive Slave Act with their Underground Railway.

While the great names in this drama found grounds of conscience on which to justify their defiance of "law," Schlesinger notes rather sadly and soberly that "generally it has been self-interest and convenience, rather than conscience, that has provided the incentive to law-breaking." Out of this complex issue the "wrongs" sprung from our American ideal of "inalienable rights!"

Rights and riches are the American dream. Indeed, for many Americans this is one and the same thing: the right to be rich! In this land of almost unbounded resources—or at least so it seemed during the past three centuries—there arose flesh and blood giants—real life Paul Bunyans—to harness and exploit the land and its people to amass empires of wealth. Moguls of industry and finance put together companies strong enough to wrestle with the land leviathan, America. Starting with nothing but their two fists and a sharp turn of mind, these roughhewn men gathered riches fit for a king.

They and their children's children—Astors, Vanderbilts, Goulds, Rockefellers, Harrimans, Lorrilards—were the economic examples of their times and the social fashion plates for future generations. They built a productive society without parallel in the history of mankind. They and their deeds became part of the American dream, immortalized by Horatio Alger and all those who sang the saga of rags to riches.

In the literature of later decades these worthies of wealth became known as "robber barons," a title derived from the methods of the primitive plutocrats.

Land grants, covering the acreage of full states, were gained by bribery of colonial legislatures and governors. Original accumulations of capital were amassed in tripartite deals among pirates, governors, and brokers. Fur fortunes were piled up alongside the drunk and dead bodies of our noble savages, the Indians. Small settlers were driven from their lands or turned into tenants by big ranchers employing rustlers, guns, outlaws—and the law. In the great railroad and shipping wars, enterprising capitalists used extortion, blackmail, violence, bribery, and private armies with muskets and cannons to wreck a competitor and to become the sole boss of a trade. In time these "robber barons" became the very models of a modern major gentleman, writing laws and appointing law-enforcers to establish legal dominion over their illegally won gains. Very few, if any, of society's "four hundred" had any other origin, thereby establishing it as high fashion that compliance with the law is obviously subordinate to the swashbuckling life of liberty and the pursuit of property.

This sordid history need not be spelled out again, for it has been done repeatedly by such brilliant researchers as Gustavus Myers (*Story of Great American Fortunes*), Matthew Josephson (*Robber Barons*), and Stewart Holbrook (*Age of the Moguls*). The parallel between these empire-builders and the criminal, however, was never delineated more clearly nor more fiercely than in Henry Demarest Lloyd's searing *Wealth Against Commonwealth*, written in the closing years of the nineteenth century.

"Our fanatic of wealth," cried out Lloyd, "reverses the rule that serving mankind is the end and wealth an incident, and has made wealth the end and the service an accident, until he can finally justify crime itself if it is a means to the end—wealth—which has come to be the supreme good; and we follow him.

"It is an adjudicated fact of the business and social life of America that to receive the profits of crime and cherish the agents who commit it does not disqualify [one] for fellowship in the 'most solid' circles—financial, commercial, religious, or social. It illustrates what Ruskin calls the 'morbid' character of modern business that the history of its most brilliant episodes must be studied in the vestibules of the penitentiary. . . . Property to the extent of uncounted millions has been changed from the possession of the many who owned it to the few who hold it:

1. Without the knowledge of the real owners.
2. Without their consent.
3. With no compensation to them for the value taken.
4. By falsehood, often under oath.
5. In violation of the law."

Fearful for our civilization, Lloyd saw in the plutocrat a new barbarian threat. Just as Virgil Peterson parodied Inge to find that the organized criminal was the "barbarian in our midst," so did Lloyd paraphrase Macaulay: "If our civilization is destroyed, as Macaulay predicted, it will not be by his barbarians from below. Our barbarians come from above."

In protest against the pillage of property and people by the "vested interests," countermovements arose. Untutored in the ways of the law, these "lower classes" knew no better than to imitate their superiors. From the ranks of the simple agrarians came Bacon, and Shays, and Mehitabel Wing, and the Kentucky tobacco growers burning the crops of those who were underselling, and the angry yeomanry of the Midwest threatening judges and auctioneers with lynching if they foreclosed a farm during the Great Depression of the 1930's. From the ranks of the industrial proletariat came "dynamite": the bombings of the McNamaras, the sabotage of the Wobblies, the terrorism of the Molly Maguires, the revenge of Don Magregor as he led impromptu armies to capture three mountain states in protest against the Ludlow Massacre. Class conflict in America is violent, almost without peer. The "lower classes" blame it on the "upper," and the "upper" on the "lower," and, to tell the truth, they are both sprung from the same matrix of "direct action"—the habit of carrying the law around in one's fist.

From the lawless matrix there also came forth our minions of the law: police and courts, governor and legislature. The process whereby these minions reach their station is called "politics," in itself a dirty word in the American culture. To call a man a "politician" in the United States is to fling a flattering insult: scorn for his method and praise for his success. Around the politician there has clustered a specialized glossary: graft, fix, pull, or—in the ever-creative argot of Chicago—clout. All these words mean something slightly different, nuances on a synonym, suggesting that when dealing with the law the most effective means for getting things done is to operate outside the law—under, over, and around the official channels. In our law schools a young man soon learns that "it's not what you know but who you know." And as he rises in the law, he soon discovers why, here at least, intimacy breeds contempt. He soon loses his childish notion that cops and robbers are always at war as he looks at several giant cities where the cops are the robbers. He learns about lawless judges. He notes how legislation is bought and sold, how enforcement and nonenforcement are arranged. After a lifetime he will conclude that law as law is only a sometime thing, a sanctuary in a jungle where the big decisions are made with club and fang. From the universal matrix arises our lawless law.

Law, like civilization, is "a plant of slow growth." It needs a settled environment, a culture of consent where opposing parties bow graciously to their opponents. It thrives on homogeneity and accepted authority. It refuses, however, to be hurried in its maturity and is easily retarded and set back by inner social conflict, clashes of heterogeneous cultures, economic insecurity, new rulers, and new subjects.

This normally slow grower was further slowed down in America by the continual presence of the frontier. For three hundred years—from 1600 to 1900—America lived on the frontier. This frontier influence runs deep in our life and wide in our literature. In our movies and television the eternal struggle between good and evil, between God and the Devil, is depicted as the weekly battle between Wyatt Earp, Bat Masterson, Yancy Derringer, and their perennial foes. Our knight-errant, with the head of a horse as his coat of arms, inscribes on his card the noble parole: "Have Gun, Will Travel." Out of the frontier came the egalitarian spirit and with it came the great "equalizer"—the gun. Out of the frontier came gangs, amateur and professional killers, sometimes representing no one but themselves as entrepreneurs of violence, sometimes representing social classes locked in fierce combat. The long frontier gave a new dimension in time to both our democracy and our lawless spirit, constantly refreshing our civilization with the egalitarian views and pistol guns of the West.

The spirit of the open frontier—the wild and woolly way of the wide open spaces—was mimicked on the internal frontier—in the dankness of the dingy slums. Here there evolved subcultures where law and order came to represent a foreign foe. Geographically buried in the midst of great cities, these subcultures were culturally planets apart from the surrounding civilization. A few experiences with the "law" of the superculture—if they ever dared venture that far—persuaded dwellers on the inner frontier that it would be better to make their own law. Out of these slums arose great gangs—violent, antisocial, the direct ancestor of modern Crime Inc.

Out of this internal frontier come the juvenile troops for the aging gangs, the cadets of crime. Hostile to the superculture he would like to imitate, clanned around the subculture he would like to escape, the juvenile is torn between cultures and within himself. Each youngster tries to resolve the dilemma according to his own lights, seeking an avenue in his own culture to provide access to the privileges and rights of the superculture. Some become comedians, delighting the nation with dialect stories of their own people. Some become singers, providing a melodic variation on the same theme. Others turn to boxing. Some become trade union leaders or seek political office, depending on the organized strength of their own people to break into the total culture. Some move into trades and industries with ease of entry. Still others find all the joys and rewards of a total civilization by establishing a little world of their own: the gang. Here is loyalty, fealty, acclaim, warmth, love, courage, sacrifice, sharing—physical and emotional security. And here, too, is a means for voicing anger: anger with the oldster, anger with the stranger, anger against the cold and distant superculture called "society." Out of the juvenile gangs, their loves and hates, their frustrations and aggressions, have come the recruits for the organized underworld for more than a century—and the process is still on its way!

Challenging the animalistic mode of life in America stands an enshrined puritanism, forbidding, illegalizing, censoring, reforming. Its purist ethic is the public face of our schizoid civilization. All except the underworld make visible homage to this prophylactic code, and even the underworld bows down before the official morality when one of its number rises into "society." Yet, ironically, even this puritanism is grist to the mills of organized crime.

Our puritanism creates a whole range of illegal commodities and services, for which there is a widespread demand. Into the gap between what people want and what people can legally get leaps the underworld as purveyor and pimp, with gaming tables, narcotics, and women. Puritanism gives the underworld a monopoly on a market with an almost insatiable demand, a market in which it can operate without controls, without license, without taxes, without guarantees or rebates, outside the jurisdiction of federal commissions or the Better Business Bureau. The underworld still remembers the day that our nation, in a burst of righteous indignation, amended its Constitution to illegalize fermentation and still regrets the day when the same nation amended the amendment to legalize the illegal. To the underworld the word *prohibition*, scribbled on any commodity or service, is translated to read *profits*, whether the item is "alky," smut, scab-herding, bombing, or murder.

The efforts of "law and order" to check the underworld by the honest and diligent use of legal procedures have been frustrated by multiple archaisms. Our government is fragmented into federal and state units. In many cases police jurisdiction ends at the city line. By developing expertise on the interstices of the law at police and judicial levels, a well-informed and well-counseled underworld can operate safely in the legal gaps. Under high-paid legal direction, moreover, the underworld can ferret out the loopholes in "due process" and in agency jurisdictions. While the arm of the law, therefore, is restrained by the strait jacket of geography, jurisdictions, due process, the underworld can move freely, mocking and taunting even the most honest and efficient police systems.

The interplay of all these forces produced our modern underworld. Arisen out of an antisocial milieu, this underworld has come to mimic, as well as mock, the society against which it warred. As our nation tied itself more tightly with modern means of transport and communication, the underworld learned to utilize and organize the instruments of modern trade, commerce, and intercourse. As our nation moved toward business consolidation, so did the underworld. As we developed a national consciousness, so did the underworld; and as we developed an international awareness, so did the underworld. As capital, labor, farmer, Democrat and Republican all learned to conceal their basic animosities under a mask of verbal niceties, so did the underworld.

For American civilization, our underworld is the "dear enemy," our menace and mimic, our oedipal son whom we damn and nourish daily!

The following excerpts are by scholars, none of whose specialties is "crime," but all of whom looked upon crime, especially organized crime, as a revealing symptom of our civilization.

These essays, written within the last three decades, are the works of men of many parts: the head of a Chicago businessmen's organization, a newspaper columnist without peer, a creative historian, a distinguished lawyer, and a journalist-sociologist.

They all dig for the roots of crime in our noncriminal culture.

Section 5 **TWENTIETH-CENTURY CRIME**

From "20th Century Crime" by G. L. Hostetter and T. Q. Beesley, 1933.

Racketeering is beginning to emerge as the distinct contribution of the twentieth century to crime. Conspiracies of a strictly business character, employing even hired assassins to gain their ends, are common to the political and economic history of every nation whose records have survived. Environment, social system, and method of government have merely varied these conspiracies from age to age and people to people. Superficially, in that they were conspiracies, they resemble modern rackets, but in reality they were simply sporadic forms of organised larceny, attesting how ancient and universal greed is, as a vice.

Racketeering, unfortunately, cannot be classified as a present-day form of standard larceny and thus become a matter for routine police work. Racketeering is an established philosophy of business, criminal in its ethics, and subversive in its economic and political programme.

Its first appearance in legal records is on the docket of the Municipal Courts of Chicago in 1890, when an embattled Irish widow named Mary G. Hennessy brought action in damages against the Chicago Laundrymen's Association for unlawful competition in the form of malicious interference with her business. The case was bitterly contested and carried to the Supreme Court of the State of Illinois which, in December, 1898, ruled in her favour in a lengthy decision that contains the following significant sentences:

> "No persons, individually or by combination, have the right directly or indirectly to interfere with or disturb

another in his lawful business or occupation, or to threaten to do so, for the sake of compelling him to do some act, which, in his judgment, his own interest does not require . . . If a wrongful act is done to the detriment of the right of another it is malicious, and an act maliciously done, with the intent and purpose of injuring another, is not lawful competition."

This decision is of multiple interest, quite apart from the fact that it is the first ruling on racketeering in a court of last resort. The decision is, in effect, a complete description of the methods, ethics, and results of racketeering, as viewed in the very beginning. It considers racketeering in the light of a politico-economical philosophy, thereby establishing for it a criminal category of its own. It restrains and punishes racketeering as an invasion of inalienable human rights. It invokes State and Federal constitutional guarantees in protection of the common citizen.

Racketeering in the United States had its political beginning also as long ago as 1890, with the enactment by Congress of a Federal statute known as the Sherman Anti-Trust Law. In brief this law was designed to prohibit the formation of trusts or combinations or agreements that would operate to restrain the free flow of trade between the States or tend toward the creation of great trade monopolies. In 1914 this law was supplemented by the Clayton Act, another Federal measure designed to strengthen the Sherman Law, but more especially to free combinations of labour (labour unions) from the strictures of the Sherman Law. By reason of this liberation the organisation of labour went forward with a speed not hitherto possible. The American Federation of Labor did not come to full flower until the benign provisions of the Clayton Act made that possible. Constitutent labour bodies were established throughout the forty-eight States. These in turn set up local constituents of their own and thus on down to the smallest local units. In their efforts at orgnisation the then leaders of labour converted the liberty vouchsafed by the Clayton Act into licence. The history of that conversion is largely a history of felony and folly. The leadership of local unions of labour was largely determined by brawn rather than brain. Leaders were not considered such unless they were in constant trouble with the authorities or had to their credit a jail or penitentiary record. It is not the purpose of this article to indict the whole labour unionisation movement, nor indict the employer organisation movement which followed closely on the heels of the former as a corrective (but sometimes retaliative and equally destructive) step. Each group has accomplished much that is good, but each has also made its distinctive contribution to racketeering as the inevitable development of wrong policies wrongly pursued.

While this organisation of labour and business was going speedily forward, commerce was developing with amazing swiftness. The tremendous growth of the automotive industry, with all its connotations to the field of business generally; the advent of the radio and a thousand other fields of manufacturing and commercial activity that spread the commerce of the United States to every corner of the globe, brought about the concentration of great aggregations of capital. These great industries, in their turn, brought about the establishing of thousands of other and smaller businesses, until there was created a vast framework of trade and commerce, all interdependent, and beset with economic, social and political problems of the first magnitude. Not the least of these problems were the restrictions of the Sherman Law prohibiting pools, trusts, combinations, and price-fixing arrangements.

Business found the cut-throat competitor a continuing factor. The price reductionist was for the most part without responsibility, and as an individual did not last, but, despite his coming and going, he was always present in sufficient numbers to be a problem of first importance. The Sherman Law, a counterpart of which in state statute existed in nearly every industrial state, operated to keep otherwise responsible businesses from joining legally with still other businesses to fight the menace of the irresponsible. Out of this inability came the fully developed present type of racket.

Racketeering might briefly be described as a *method for control of business competition, and commodity price regulation, otherwise illegal by the provisions of the Sherman Anti-Trust Law and the Clayton Act.* This definition would be accurate only in part, however, because racketeering has gone quite beyond a rationalised control of competition, and has become organised conspiracy for exploitation. Moreover, such a definition would be in derogation of these two statutes, which in many minds are looked upon as "Liberty Laws," and as entirely in consonance with the Constitution of the United States in its guarantees of individual freedom. It is a fact, however, that many sections of business, being unable under the law to organise themselves for rational control of competition, have developed a positively criminal philosophy, and have created an economic monstrosity the acts of which have run the whole scale of crime.

Five distinct but interdependent elements comprise the structure of any racket. These are:

> Business men
> Leaders of Organised Labour
> Politicians
> Criminals
> Lawyers

Racketeering in short is a combination of business, labour unionism, politics, lawyers and the criminal underworld, the purpose of which is exploitation of commerce and the public through circumscribing the right to work and do business; the product of an age of ruthless business competition and lax or corrupt law enforcement; the latter being in turn the outgrowth of individual and collective indifference and of absorption in purely material affairs.

Accepting this as the definition of racketeering let us examine each unit of the racket structure and see what each hopes to derive from participation in it.

1. The business man seeks to create and maintain for himself and a favoured few a monopoly in his particular field of service or trade. He seeks, through the pressure that can be brought by politicians in the misapplication or thwarting of the law, and through the withdrawal or withholding of labour by union leaders, to embarrass his competitors to the point where they will either recognise and abide by racket rules and edicts or quit the field of competition. He seeks to maintain an arbitrary and usually artificial price for his commodity or service, through forcing universal recognition of his particular notion of what constitutes a satisfactory price. He seeks even to dictate the enactment or application of laws that govern his business.

2. The leader of organised labour who betrays his trust and lends himself to a racket seeks first a monopoly of control over the workmen engaged in a given trade. This insures to his treasury the dues of all men of that trade, or creates a situation by which he may dispense the right to work under the "permit" system, at so much per man per day. Moreover, it enables him to manipulate his man forces to the advantage of his co-conspirators, the business man or the politician or both, and to the discomfiture and disadvantage of businessmen who dare to assert independence of the racket.

3. The politician by paralysing the hand of the law is, of course, looking to campaign contributions, organisation work, and votes at election time, and frequently also to participation in the profits of the conspiracy.

4. The criminal underworld finds lucrative employment to bomb; to commit arson; to slug, maim and kill; to terrorise an entire community into staying away from the poll at election time, and to organise fraudulent voting and terroristic practices at the polls, and latterly to control racketeering in its entirety.

5. The importance of the lawyer in the racket set-up is not so quickly and easily dismissed. True it is, he guides and protects the racketeers in the matter of counsel, before the courts, in the realm of politics, and often is to be found exercising the powers of an actual officer in the racket structure. It is true also he is paid large fees or salaries for his services, but his peculiar relation to society makes any contact with the racket reprehensible. He is or should be grounded in a tradition of ethical conduct stretching beyond the recorded memory of man. Yet we find the lawyer, or a certain type of him, probably the most important cog in the machinery of crime. He has twisted

and distorted the law to suit the purposes of a criminal clientele. He has subverted the dignity of *habeas corpus*. He has made the "continuance" in criminal cases anathema to complainants and a solace to the criminals. He is the godfather of every criminal gang worthy of mention in America. He devises the clever legal instruments that constitute the charters of rackets. In themselves these charters are not illegal, in the main, but the lawyer knows that they are inoperative except as they are applied with the rule of force. They are, however, providing a respectable façade to fool the public. Some rackets have had their very genesis in legal quarters, and yet the profession of lawyers appears to be without facilities of inquiry and discipline for such members, or if such facilities exist they seem to have atrophied long ago.

If all, or the majority, of these five elements are not present in the conspiracy, there is no racket in the true sense of the term. When one or more is absent the racket project is doomed to failure, for it cannot exist for long without the ministrations of all. Moreover, no racket has ever been known to present itself as having other than worthy economic or social purposes, and because it can show active participation or tacit acceptance by some persons high in the councils of business, social or political life, it is difficult to convince the average citizen of its iniquity. Herein lies the secret of the mighty growth of the racket as a philosophy of business, especially during the past decade. If this philosophy is not destroyed, or considerably checked, and rackets continue to grow at their present pace, they will completely blanket industrial United States in another ten years. What is more, there will be established a new aristocracy in business, traceable in its beginnings to a criminal class who obtained their training in business administration through organised violation of the National Prohibition Act.

The ascendancy of this class will also sound the death knell of organised labour, as labour organisation is constructed and carried forward today. Already more than half of the labour unions of Chicago and New York are controlled directly or indirectly, by criminals who formerly confined their activities to the sale and distribution of illegal liquor. This control is not at all surprising. Rather it is a logical outcome of resort to the hired forces of such criminals by union labour, and by associations of employers, for the commission of criminal acts designed to discipline recalcitrant employers and non-members of the unions, i.e., force them to join, and to observe the monstrous rules of the rackets.

Readers of newspapers everywhere were profoundly shocked when on February 14th, 1929, the bulletin was flashed around the earth that seven men had been lined up against the inner wall of a garage in Chicago, and mowed down by machine guns in the hands of rival gangsters. The press of the world pointed with scorn at Chicago and that city's law enforcement officials. Chicago was openly characterised as the outlaw of American cities.

By inference, at least, the Federal government at Washington was importuned by a section of the press to declare the city under martial law, and bring it immediately under the police control of the United States army. Some editorials even went so far as to suggest complete isolation of the state of Illinois from the Federation of States, until the people of that commonwealth should become sufficiently aroused about racketeering to put out of office a group of politicians who, by their corrupt alliances with professional criminals, had brought the entire nation as well as the state and city into world derision.

Only a part of this happened, of course. The Federal government could not invade the State of Illinois, and take over a function of government belonging peculiarly to that state as well as to all other states of the American Union. The problem of governmental cleansing was the state's very own, and even the state itself could not encroach too far upon certain definite municipal rights belonging to Chicago, and guaranteed to it by the state constitution. In its relation to the State of Illinois, Chicago occupied and does occupy approximately the same position that the state in turn occupies to the Federal government. Each is autonomous within the limits of definite constitutional guarantees.

The job of housecleaning belonged to the people of Chicago, and to some extent that job has been done. With the defeat of William Hale Thompson for mayor in 1931 began the destruction of probably the most corrupt political machine that ever infested the politics of an American municipality, a political machine whose ramifications extended to the entire state and to a certain extent to the national capital itself. It was a political oligarchy, drunk with power, corrupt almost in its every fibre, and openly contemptuous of any voice of protest. The "St. Valentine Day Massacre" was only one episode in a long chain of incidents in Chicago arising out of racketeering and other forms of organised crime. Business was levied upon at will by racketeers, and woe to the business man who dared assert independence. He would find himself the victim of all manner of visitations designed to teach him that his welfare lay in the direction of "going along" with the municipal and underworld powers.

Gangsters ruled their various realms like despots. They set up and dispensed their own law through their "Kangaroo" courts in which men were tried, sentenced to death, and executed. They appeared to be, and indeed in many instances were, absolutely without fear of prosecution by the authorities. If prosecution was attempted it became a farce. Witnesses were intimidated or killed; juries were bribed; judges were influenced by threat of defeat at the elections. Indeed, candidates for public office, having definite alliances with professional gangsters were elected by a system of fraudulent control of the people's votes, not only to minor offices, but to the state legislative assembly, to the municipal council and places of similar power.

Such is the background of racketeering in any city. Chicago was a large-scale development, and therefore, is chosen as a complete example. Any city in any country living under a modern form of industrial civilisation, will inevitably reach this same development of racketeering, if it tolerates the same type of officeholders and misrule. The way out is to overturn the political machine responsible for the misrule. Most law enforcement offices in Chicago today are in the control of men recently voted in and pledged definitely to the proposition of destroying crime at its source and restoring the city to the confidence of the nation and the world.

This awakening of the people of the city, and their elected representatives, has not come of a sudden nor has the process of awakening been easy. It has come over the opposition of strong business, legal, and other non-political as well as political forces, who were mesmerised by the absurd notion that evil will work its own cure if left alone. These forces decried the publicity to which the city was being subjected, and openly denounced the brave few who persisted in the attempt to get the facts of Chicago's crime problem to the people. The few have had their vindication. The electorate of any American community is by nature lethargic, but once aroused it moves with incredible force and destroys everything in its path which it believes to be oppressive, incompetent, or corrupt. Nowhere in the world can be found such a thoroughgoing dethronement of political oligarchy as took place in Illinois in the recent elections of 1932.

A bad political situation, expressing itself in lax or corrupt law enforcement may be a cause of crime. Again, corruption in politics may be an effect of indifference or conscious disregard of law on the part of the people themselves. Either condition presents a rich field of opportunity to the criminally minded. It is not a coincidence that opportunism, with all that it denotes, constitutes the essential framework of racketeering. Racketeering is, therefore, swiftly becoming the most lucrative field of crime and the most difficult to eradicate in modern industrial society. Moreover it strikes deeper toward the foundations of fundamental liberty because it attacks the individual in his weakest spot—job or occupation.

With the advent of the economic depression there occurred a sharp and continuing decline in the sale of illicit liquor. Bootleggers found themselves unable to obtain the fabulous prices for their products they had formerly enjoyed. Their patrons fell away or resorted to cheaper stimulants such as synthetic gin, or contented themselves perforce with beer, all of the ingredients of which they could buy cheaply, and brew in the basements of their homes or apartments. This set up a definite economic problem for the leaders of bootlegging gangs. They had great armies of young men in their organisations. Men chiefly between the ages of eighteen and thirty to whom they were paying weekly salaries ranging from $100 to $500 per week; men who had entered the employment of gangster chiefs upon leaving high school or the grades, and who had never known the feel of an honest day's work in legitimate enterprise. If this great army of criminals, or its more important nucleus, was to be maintained, a new field of activity must be found.

Criminals are positive in their actions whether in executing a traitor, an enemy, or moving upon new fields of endeavour. The new field toward which they cast their covetous eyes, three years ago, was racketeering. Possession was not immediate, of course, because the leaders of crime in the United States are astute and lay their plans with a shrewd cunning worthy of more legitimate undertakings. They began laying the groundwork for control of racketeering in Chicago, for example, by the very simple device of sending for one of the most powerful leaders of Chicago unionism, who, being already beholden to them, could not refuse to obey their summons. They told him of their new plans for taking over control of his unions, and, through these unions, of many associations of business men. He was advised that he could continue in nominal and titular control if he desired. He asked time to think the matter over. He was told he would return his answer before leaving The Presence, and if his answer by any chance should be in the negative, he could withdraw immediately from any control whatsoever of his unions. They would seize them anyway. He elected to "go along."

From that beginning has grown a vast system of criminal racket control of labour unionism and business, which in this one city alone is estimated to cost the people of the city more than one hundred millions of dollars per year in artificial prices for services and commodities, unnecessary overhead costs of doing business, high insurance rates, property damage, costly police protection and legal services. It is a veritable racketeering strangle-hold, because basically, the racket network controls the transportation of goods and commodities within the city, and now threatens to extend itself to motorised transportation throughout the state. The following lines are known to be under such domination, and others are being added with alarming swiftness:

Laundry.	Dairy products (partial).
Cleaning and dyeing.	Building wreckage.
Linen supply.	Produce (perishable).
Carbonated beverages.	Long-distance hauling.
Barbers.	Circular distribution.
Bakers.	Ice cream.
Coal.	Furniture storage.
Sausage mfrs. (Kosher).	Meats (Kosher).
Building material.	Ash and garbage removal.
Paving.	Machinery moving.
Excavating.	Railway express.
Flour.	Lumber, box and shavings.
Tobacco.	Florists.

Ice.	Baggage delivery.
Beauty culture.	Janitors.
Roofing material.	Window washers (commercial).
Municipal teamsters.	cial).
Sanitary, cinder and sprinkler	Oil wagon drivers.
Workers (city).	Electrotyping.
Garages.	Motion picture (operators).

Many of these were rackets or conspiracies before the coming of purely criminal domination. Some have been converted to that status since, but all present a problem of distinct importance to community life. It is tragic, but true, that as this article is being written there resides in one man the power, and he a notorious criminal, to paralyse the city by a single order stopping the labour of the unions under his control. Such autocratic power is not possessed by any other individual in the country, not excepting the President of the United States. Only as one envisions the robber barons of an earlier Europe can he find a counterpart of such a situation. In fact, stoppage of work in some lines is taking place regularly as a means of coercing agreements, compelling observance of price regulations, and extortion of tribute. Perhaps it would be a good thing if this man would become so drunk with power that he would undertake such a diabolical task as a general and complete stoppage. Perhaps then the people would at last realise what racketeering means to the individual citizen.

The wresting of control of the rackets by criminals has made no essential changes in the structural make-up of these organisations. Business men, labour leaders, criminal mercenaries and lawyers still constitute the framework of racketeering, the change being only in the personnel in control. The purpose of racketeering, however, has undergone considerable enlargement. From control of competition and prices, racketeering has broadened into a vast system of exploitation for the enrichment of a criminal class.

Peculiar as it may seem, racketeering, even with criminal domination, is acceptable to an astonishingly large number of business men, particularly those engaged in the service trades, and who are constantly beset with the problem of the ever-present price reductionist. They appear to see in racketeering the answer to the age-old question of business regulation—a sort of lifting of oneself by one's economic boot straps, a system by which all units of a tottering industry may be kept stable regardless of overcrowding and the very obvious unfitness of some to remain in business at all. "All units," in this sense, of course, describes only the favoured ones who are constituents of the racket.

What this class fails utterly to see is the extent to which they undermine the political principles of freedom of opportunity that originally made possible their entrance to the field of business; and the extent also to which they destroy freedom by contributing to the creation of a criminal overlordship and the final breakdown of ordered security. To them it does not matter that they trample upon human rights which have been established step by bitter step through the centuries in the common man's emergence from serfdom. In fact, after a period they become serfs indeed in the harshest sense of the word, because once a part of the racket, they are beyond the pale of help. Being equally culpable, with the criminal, before the law, they can do nothing but bear the impositions the racket places upon them.

With the coming of this criminal domination of rackets, there have been unmistakable evidences of an attempt at syndication of racketeering efforts. It is known that Chicago racketeers have working arrangements with racketeers in New York, Philadelphia, Cleveland, Detroit, and elsewhere throughout the country. It is not demonstrated that these racketeers, separated so widely geographically, function as one machine, but sympathetic and co-operative effort has been discovered. From this it is now but a step to organisation on a national basis. Racketeers of one city are frequently to be found in another assisting in the building of rackets within an industry, or working alone to that end except for the assistance accorded them by business men beguiled by successful racket practice in another locality. The movement of gangsters from one city to another for the commission of crimes of violence is, of course, standard practice and a fact known to every schoolboy. This mobility of the armies of crime introduces serious difficulties in the matter of apprehending criminals. With excellent highways, powerful and swift automobiles, and short-wave radio sets at their command, they move across the country from state to state with a facility that almost, if not completely, defies apprehension by policing methods which have been obsolescent for at least twenty-five years.

Section 6   **THE UNDERWORLD AS SERVANT**

From "The Underworld as Servant" by Walter Lippmann, 1931.

In the large urban areas, the American capacity for self-government is put to its severest test. For they are the focuses of modernity: it is here that applied science works the most drastic and far-reaching effects upon the lives of men. Here simultaneously the issues are increasingly novel and complex, the power of decision is continually diluted by the swelling size of the electorates, standards of judgment are disrupted by the erosion of accepted ways of thinking. The region of the modern city is thus the place where the older American polity, its premises, its purposes, and its methods, is confronted with the newer American civilization.

Among the phenomena which certainly accompany, and, as I think, are caused by our maladjustment to the new social order, there is the growth of a powerful underworld. It is necessary to fix clearly in mind just what we are to mean by the term. I shall make a distinction between mere crime on the one hand and the activities of the underworld on the other.

The distinction turns upon this fact: that the criminal as such is wholly predatory, whereas the underworld offers something in return to the respectable members of society. Thus, for example, burglars are lawbreakers who, if they could be abolished miraculously, would not be missed; but bootleggers, panderers, fixers, and many racketeers have a social function and perform services for which there is some kind of public demand. In actual life the distinction is blurred; the same man may be a bootlegger and swindler, a thief and a procurer, a yegg and a racketeer. Nevertheless, the theoretical distinction is important, for the underworld presents a problem quite different from mere criminality.

The mere criminal who breaks the law solely for his own profit, or because he is provoked by passion, or because he is degenerate, does not raise the issues with which Americans living in places like Chicago or New York are so anxiously concerned. The issues that are most deeply perplexing and ominous are those presented by the underworld which defies the law, establishes a regime of terror and violence, and draws profits for services performed from conventionally respectable members of society. Against the mere criminal, whether he acts alone or as one of a gang, there are ranged the opinion and, except in instances of extreme political corruption, the whole force of organized government. The underworld has a different status. Its activities are in some degree countenanced by the respectable; from among them it draws its revenues; among them it finds many of its patrons; by them it is in various ways protected.

Because of the scale and character of its operation, the underworld is not comprehensible in the ordinary categories of crime. It is impossible, I think, to deal with it on the premise that it can be abolished by enforcing the law. It is integral to the policy which our laws have laid down, and to the assumptions upon which Americans have been taught to govern themselves. It is the creature of our laws and conventions, and it is entangled with our strongest appetites and our most cherished ideals. The fact that the underworld breaks the law which we all respect in principle, that it employs methods, such as bribery, terrorism, and murder, which we all deeply deplore, should not divert our attention from the main point, which is that the underworld performs a function based ultimately upon a public demand.

The underworld, as I am using the term, lives by performing the services which convention may condemn and the law prohibit, but which, nevertheless, human appetites crave. The most obvious example, and at the present time the most insistent, is of course, the supplying of liquor. Here we have a vast industry, engaging, it is said, the direct services of a million individuals, which by admission of the prohibition bureau in Washington does an annual business of a gross value at current prices approaching two billion dollars. This business is controlled by the underworld; its products are consumed by the flower of American manhood and womanhood. It is outlawed by our statutes. It is patronized by our citizens.

Being outlawed, the liquor business cannot be regulated by law. It cannot call upon the law for protection. Thus it is driven to improvise its own substitutes for law and order, and those substitutes involve more breaches of our recognized system of law and order. The liquor industry has not only to break down the prohibition law, but the tariff law and the revenue laws; it has to break down officers of the law by bribery; it ends by settling its own disputes, since it is outlawed from the courts, by coercion and murder. This whole fabric of systematic lawlessness rests on the fact that respectable society has driven outside the boundaries of its own law and order the merchant of liquor whom it continues to patronize.

The activities of the underworld are not confined to the supplying of liquor. In almost all American communities sexual gratification is limited by law or convention to married couples. This permitted sexuality does not begin to appease the lusts of men. To appease them there is extra-marital sexuality, in some measure under free relationships, but for the most part through prostitution in its many forms and disguises.

Many economic functions are involved in prostitution; they range from the procuring of women to the operation of dance halls, night clubs, bawdy houses, and places of assignation. As the whole business is illicit, is either contrary to law or is held to be disreputable, the services of prostitution, like the services of liquor, require lawbreaking, bribery, and coercion, and enlist men and women who have little or no stake in the social conventions, in honest government, or in the even-handed, effective administration of the law.

Another persistent and outlawed human appetite is the desire to gamble. In order to satisfy it, there are required expensive organization and paraphernalia. Many persons are needed to operate gambling houses, pool rooms, and bucket shops. They must resort to political corruption to prevent the enforcement of the prohibitions issued by legislatures, and to various forms of extra-legal coercion to protect themselves and extend their enterprises.

They interlock with bootlegging and prostitution, and since their trade is illegal and disreputable, it engages those who have little or no stake in the avowed standards of society.

There are other appetites to which the underworld ministers. It possesses the trade in drugs, but since drug addiction is abnormal in our society, the clientele of this trade is relatively small. Drink, sex, and gambling are the forbidden commodities for which there is the greatest demand; they serve desires which, however we may agree to regard them as vicious and damnable, are practically universal among men. There may be those who have never craved liquor or lusted for women or wanted to bet, but such men are too rare to be counted in considering social policy. Thus, while most men go through their lives without stealing or killing, or without any personal relation with a thief or murderer, it would be difficult to find an adult in a great city who is one hundred per cent blameless under the laws against sinful satisfaction.

The service of outlawed desires does not exhaust the functions of the underworld. It plays a part in the working of our economic system. No thorough study has, so far as I know, been made of this matter, and therefore I must speak tentatively.

My impression is that racketeering in many of its most important forms tends to develop where an industry is subject to excessively competitive conditions. Given an oversupply of labor and an industry in which no considerable amount of capital or skill is required to enter it, the conditions exist under which racketeering can flourish. The effort to unionize in the face of a surplus of labor incites to the use of violence and terrorism to maintain a monopoly of labor and thus to preserve and enhance the workers' standard of living. Labor unionism in such trades tends to fall into the control of dictators who are often corrupt and not often finical about enlisting gangsters to enforce the closed shop. The employers on the other hand, faced with the constant threat of cutthroat competition, are subject to easy temptation to pay gangsters for protection against competitors. The protection consists in driving the competitors from the field.

The fact that racketeering seems to infest the small, unstable, disorganized industries suggests rather strongly that we have here a perverse effort to overcome the insecurity of highly competitive capitalism, that the underworld through its very crude devices serves that need for social organization which reputable society has not yet learned how to satisfy. Indeed, one might go further and at least inquire whether certain forms of racketeering are not the result under adverse conditions of the devotion of legislatures, courts, and public opinion to the philosophy of laissez faire.

It would appear at least that rackets are in large degree perversions of the search for economic security, a diseased compensation in the lower reaches of capitalism for the instability of proletarian life, and the terrific struggle for existence which prevails in a population uprooted from the land, unprotected and undisciplined by its own guilds, and subjected to the daily hazards of the open market.

In the upper reaches of capitalism the rigors of laissez faire have been mitigated by superior organization, ampler resources, and greater knowledge; on the land the competitive principle is resisted by the stability of the earth itself; but in the cities among the unskilled workers and the little tradesmen, the capitalist theory of the textbooks has a terrible actuality. A very considerable part of racketeering must be looked upon as the exploitation of the need for security and the hunger for success among those who are always insecure and are haunted all their days by the dread of failure.

I do not mean to suggest that the functions of the underworld are honestly and rationally performed. By the very condition under which they are performed—subject to no law and to no recognized leadership, accountable to no social opinion, operating in the dark, branded as disreputable—they are inevitably pervaded by swindle and treachery. There is very little honor among thieves, there being none of the normal incentives of honor, and the romantic notion that the underworld has a code of its own which it obeys will be found, I think, to mean little more than that enough has to be given to keep the business and that the fear of reprisal regulates its dealings.

But if its functions are not performed honorably, they are at least performed. It is on this fact which we must, I think, fix our attention. It is necessary for us to realize that the principal occupations of the underworld, though they are illegal and disreputable in our society, have not generally been prohibited or even strongly reprobated in the greater civilization of which the American is only a province.

Not until very recently, and almost nowhere else in our Western world, have wine and beer or even strong drink been outlawed. On the contrary, they have been sanctioned for princes and peasants, celebrated in art and literature, and employed as symbols of man's communion with deity. In twentieth-century America the service of this whole human interest has been displaced from the region of social control to the underworld which lies beyond the frontiers of the law. However much we may dislike to recognize it, the same holds with respect to sexual gratification outside of monogamy. Prostitution is a very ancient institution; the effort to outlaw it completely is a rather new and peculiar social experiment. As for gambling, this is so constant a human passion that even some American communities attempt to give it legitimate and orderly satisfaction by licensing and supervising gambling halls.

Finally, the desire for freedom from the insecurity of destructive competition is not only not a vicious desire, but the essence of social order. That this desire is frustrated for large numbers of men, and thus perverted to dangerous devices, is due at last not to the wickedness of men but to laws and social policies which run counter to the invincible necessities.

We are, thus, forced to examine the very premises of our social morality if we are to determine intelligently our attitude toward the American underworld. It is today a great unmanageable, threatening fact in the life of our great cities. In face of it we cannot ask merely whether the machinery of law enforcement is as good as it might be. We shall have to go further, calling into question the wisdom of the laws themselves, asking ourselves what there is in the political consciousness of Americans which causes them to engage in experiments so noble in the motive, so impotent in the execution, so menacing in their effect. For the underworld is paved with the good intentions of our greatest idealists.

Europeans who read about the more spectacular aspects of the gang wars in Chicago, about the murder of Arnold Rothstein, the attack on Jack Diamond, and the fabulous immunity of Al Capone, naturally conclude, as the *Manchester Guardian* put it the other day, that "all the machinery of law exists in America, but the thing does not work properly." There is no disputing this conclusion. The thing does not work properly. That is why we have almost as many crime commissions as we have gangs collecting tribute and issuing death warrants. But though everybody thunders in the index about the increase of organized crime, nothing much is done about it. The general public is not really aroused, public opinion is not coherent and enlisted, officials are not effectively concerned.

Thus the voters in our large cities have as yet shown no disposition to get thoroughly rid of the politicians who submit to, profit by, and fumble with the activities of the underworld. Leaving out all the evidences of subterranean partnership, the indisputable fact is that the dominant political machines in cities like Chicago and New York have notoriously failed to suppress organized crime. Even on the assumption that they are manned by brave, incorruptible, and patriotic individuals from the mayor and the boss at the top to the patrolman and the precinct captain, the fact remains that they are demonstrably impotent against the powers of the underworld. Yet they continue to control the agencies of the law, and in spite of the fulminations of press, pulpit, and grand juries they are periodically confirmed in their control by large majorities of American citizens.

Somewhere or other there is a blockade of the civic will which paralyzes action; somehow or other, as the *Manchester Guardian* went on to say, "the public conscience does not function as it should." We find ourselves revolving in a circle of impotence in which we outlaw intolerantly the satisfaction of certain persistent human desires and then tolerate what we have prohibited. Thus we find ourselves accepting in their lawless forms the very things which in lawful form we repudiate, having in the end to deal not only with all the vices we intended to abolish but with the additional dangers which arise from having turned over their exploitation to the underworld.

There are obvious reasons why these paradoxes are not easily realized by the American voters. In spite of the magnitude of its operations, the ordinary householder has little personal contact with the grosser felonies of the underworld. Arnold Rothstein was murdered in a hotel which is a ten-minute walk from my home; Jack Diamond was shot in a hotel which is not much farther away. But for the fact that I am a newspaper man and know reporters who were at the scene shortly after the shootings, I should not, I think, have any greater conviction of their reality than I have about a murder in a novel by Edgar Wallace.

The detectives were a little less smart than they are in the books, and of course there was no solution. But I cannot recall that my primary emotion was one of indignation that defiant crimes had been committed in the city where I live. As far as I could observe my friends and myself, it seems that we enjoyed the Rothstein and Diamond affairs. For we city dwellers are connoisseurs of celebrated crimes, and here were two specimens which after examination turned out to be pretty good, but not quite up to the level of the Snyder, Elwell, and Hall-Mills cases.

I have little doubt that the shooting of Diamond amused New York for a few days and shocked it very little. This was due partially to the feeling that Diamond's life was not precious, but chiefly it was due to the fact that the shooting did not seem actually to have happened. Thus we must be acquitted of mere callous cruelty, however much we are damned for lack of imagination. It has never been accounted vicious to enjoy the murders in the Rue Morgue, and the same sort of innocence pervades New York's enjoyment of its big murder cases. For our civilization has become so extensive and complex that we are for the most part mere spectators of events in which by a hidden chain of causes we are implicated.

If the grosser crimes of the underworld are remote from our lives, its services are sufficiently close to inhibit our continuing indignation. The ordinary householder in American cities has considerable contact with the underworld, almost all of it of a kind which dulls his conscience. Unless he is the victim of a racket, has his house broken into, or is held up and slugged— all comparatively unusual experiences—he meets the underworld through the favors which it sells. From the underworld he, or at least many friends whom he respects, obtain their liquor. He knows this. But he does not allow himself to dwell too much on the knowledge that the cocktail comes from the bootlegger who operates under the jurisdiction of a criminal magnate, and that before the cocktail could be drunk, the Constitution and the laws had to be broken, public officials had to be deceived or corrupted, and some murders may have had to be committed.

With all of this complex of lawlessness the ordinary householder is dimly associated in a common defiance of the law and by the relationship of buyer and seller. There is no way of measuring the intangibles, but this must be a fact of prime importance in explaining why in the big cities one does not find the uncompromising hostility to the underworld which it is assumed should normally exist in a civilized society.

The bootlegging trade is not the only friendly and profitable bridge between respectability and the underworld. It is indubitably true that gangs have not infrequently been employed, and thus their existence encouraged, by business men. They have been used to break strikes. They have even been used in commercial warfare. It seems to me fairly certain that a history of gangs in Chicago and New York would show that the present development of racketeering, which is essentially the levying by gangsters of ransoms upon small businessmen, is rather closely connected with payments to gangsters to break strikes and to ruin commercial rivals. The extortion which gangs now practice has been and probably is now at times a voluntary payment to them for services rendered. Even today I should imagine that it would be a false and naive picture to suppose that racketeers prey entirely upon innocent victims. The relationship is more complex. The gangs do not merely prey; in some measure they also serve their victims. The business flourishes because there is a certain reciprocal profit in it.

Then there are the reciprocal relations between gangs and political machines. On this point we have not only the evidence of fairly extensive personal relations between certain politicians and the lords of the underworld, we have not only rather striking evidence in the careers of men like Capone, Rothstein, and Diamond that they exercised sufficient political influence to stay out of jail, but we know that the gangs play a considerable part in elections, particularly in primary elections. The suffrage in American cities is by no means pure: the tricks of colonizing districts, of repeating, of stuffing ballot boxes, and of terrorizing voters often require the assistance of gangs.

These relationships tend to blur the sharp distinction between civilized society and the underworld. The will to exterminate the underworld is necessarily blunted by the evident fact that the underworld performs many services which respectable members of society call for. Thus we have a code of laws which prohibit almost all the weaknesses of the flesh. This code of laws is effective up to a point. That point is the unwillingness of respectable people to engage in the prohibited services as sellers of prohibited commodities.

Respectable people are, however, willing to be consumers, patrons, and clients of these services. The underworld, having no respectability to lose, is the producer and seller of opportunities for gambling, fornication, drug-taking, and erotic amusement. The respectable world and the underworld interpenetrate at race tracks, bucket shops, poolrooms, prize fights, night clubs, speakeasies, backstage in the theaters, in bawdy houses and hotels of assignation.

There are, of course, millions of Americans who do not enter this twi-light zone in the whole course of their lives, but, on the other hand, there are numbers who do. That they deplore gang murders, the extortion of the racketeers, and even the grosser forms of bribery, we may take for granted. But they can hardly be very much interested in the abolition of the under-world's trade in goods which the law prohibits, the prevailing morality frowns upon, but their appetites desire.

In the larger cities the direct consumers of services that the underworld alone dares to provide are large in numbers; they are influential out of all proportion to their numbers. They shade out into the still larger class of reputable citizens who, though they have no contact at first or even second hand with the underworld, nevertheless have one thing in common with it. They are lawbreakers and they are glad to use pull to evade the conse-quences. It is difficult to speak accurately about this aspect of American social habit. One must rely on one's own observation. Mine is that scrupulous respect for all the laws and a refusal to accept favors is almost everywhere regarded as priggishness. The few men I have ever known who were really scrupulous have often wondered whether they were not suffering from some form of compulsion neuroses.

Certainly the general sentiment is to assume the right to beat the law. Different people have different points of resistance. I myself, for example, have no hesitation about breaking the prohibition law. I would not, how-ever, break the tariff law, much as I despise the existing law, except that I would break that section of it dealing with prohibited books. I would smug-gle any book I wanted to read. I would not violate the revenue laws. But I cannot develop much of a conscience about the archaic personal property tax in New York. I do not always obey the speed laws, but, if I were caught, I do not think I should care to bribe a policeman or to ask a politician to talk to the judge. I would bet at a race track if I felt like it.

The point of all this is that we are all so much addicted to lawbreaking that the existence of a great underworld which lives on lawbreaking is not wholly alien and antagonistic to the working assumptions of our lives. Because of their own strong addiction to lawlessness, Americans as a whole are by no means clear in their own minds as to the moral grounds on which they could challenge the underworld and go to war against it. Such warfare as they conduct is limited to the attempt to convict individuals of the more heinous crimes. These convictions are for many reasons difficult to obtain. Even when they are obtained they are of little account. For the heinous crimes are merely extremes of lawbreaking arising out of a high level of lawlessness.

The high level of lawlessness is maintained by the fact that Americans desire to do so many things which they also desire to prohibit.

We come here upon one of the fundamental patterns of our political consciousness. The dominant American tradition is that morality requires the absolute condemnation without compromise of the weaknesses of the flesh. This tradition is by no means universal in Christendom. It prevails, as I think Thomas Cuming Hall has shown convincingly, primarily among peoples schooled in the dissenting spirit. They feel that the carnal pleasures —drinking, fornicating, and gambling—cannot for one instant be tolerated as normal in human existence. This is not the view held by the more aristocratic tradition of Western Europe. That tradition is tolerant of human appetites, and far too worldly to seek to condemn absolutely what it seems impossible to abolish.

Due to a variety of causes operating within the last generation, the aristocratic tradition of compromise with human nature has been almost obliterated in American public life. In its place the dissenting democracy has become dominant almost everywhere, but most particularly in the legislative bodies. This dissenting democracy, being composed almost entirely of people without previous practice in the arts of government, has had very much more moral conviction than it has had human experience. It has legislated out of its convictions rather than out of the body of human knowledge, and it has been much more interested in affirming its ideals than in facing the problems of applying them.

Proceeding on the principle of no compromise with the devil, the first concern of the dissenting democracy has been to purge the statute books of anything which could be construed as countenancing sin. This passion for legislative purity is, I suppose, the ghost of that grandiose conception which the New Englanders found systematically set forth by Richard Baxter in his *Holy Commonwealth*, the idea that the civil state was to become the visible City of God. If this state was to express "that temporal dignity of the Saints, which undoubtedly would much bless the world," its statute books could make no concessions to the devil.

Whether or not this is the source of our American passion for a perfect idealism in the law, it is certain that this passion controls the mass-mind of America; and as direct democracy has advanced at the expense of representative government, the insistence on legislative declarations of perfection has been unchecked. Thus, to the amazement of the older nations of the earth, we have in the last thirty or forty years enacted new legal prohibitions against the oldest vices of man. We have achieved a body of statutory law which testifies unreservedly to our aspiration for an absolutely blameless and highly competitive life on earth.

The practical effect of this supreme moral achievement has been to lay upon the administrative branches of government the task of lifting the moral life of the American people above all temptation. Except in little utopian colonies here and there, no such stupendous thing has ever before been attempted by government. The people through their legislatures decreed that the American nation must be protected by officials against all opportunities to drink, to gamble, to fornicate, to see lascivious pictures, to read impure books, and also against attempting to protect their livelihood against the moral blessings of destructive competition.

This ambitious program of moral reform implied, of course, the establishment of the most despotic and efficient government ever seen on earth. The program called for thousands and thousands of resolute and incorruptible inspectors, policemen, prosecutors, and judges to enforce it. These could be had only by the expenditure of enormous sums of money. They could hope to carry out the program only by the suspension of most civil rights such as trial by jury, the sanctity of the domicile, freedom of speech and of publication.

But the very people who had enacted the program of moral reform which called for a tyranny, the dissenting democrats, happened also to be great lovers of liberty. They inherited another tradition along with that of the Holy Commonwealth, a tradition of profound distrust of executive and judicial authority, which they embodied in the Bill of Rights. Nothing has ever been able to induce them to set up a really strong executive government in America. Thus by their moral convictions they prohibited all sin, and by their liberal convictions they have kept the prohibitions from being enforced.

The enormous growth of activity in the underworld is the direct consequence of this contradiction in the American mind.

The underworld is what it is largely because Americans are too moral to tolerate human weakness, and because they are too great lovers of liberty to tolerate the tyranny which might make it possible to abolish what they prohibit. They have made laws which act like a protective tariff—to encourage the business of the underworld. Their prohibitions have turned over to the underworld the services from which it profits. Their prejudice in favor of weak governments has deprived them of the power to cope with the vast lawbreaking industries which their laws have called into being.

The dangers and inconveniences of this result are multiplying and have become ominous. The present deadlock between our legislative purposes and our administrative prejudices cannot continue forever. For while it lasts, lawlessness is growing, and in certain areas of the country the social structure is already badly shaken. Something will have to give way. Sooner or later the American people will have to make up their minds either to bring their legislative ideals down to the point where they square with prevailing human nature or they will have to establish an administrative despotism strong enough to begin enforcing their moral ideals. They cannot much longer defy the devil with a wooden sword.

Section 7   CRIME AS INDIVIDUALISM

From *Paths to the Present* by Arthur M. Schlesinger, 1949.

Geographic or horizontal mobility, however, was a less fundamental aspect of American life than social or vertical mobility, though the two were not unrelated. The European conception of a graded society, with each class everlastingly performing its allotted function, vanished quickly amidst primitive surroundings that invited the humblest to move upward as well as outward. Instead of everybody being nobody, they found that anybody might become somebody. In the language of James Russell Lowell, "Here on the edge of the forest, where civilized man was brought face to face again with nature and taught mainly to rely on himself, mere manhood became a fact of prime importance." This emancipation from hoary custom was "no bantling of theory, no fruit of forethought," but "a gift of the sky and of the forest."

Accordingly, there arose the ingrained belief in equality of opportunity, the right of all men to a free and fair start—a view which in one of its most significant ramifications led to the establishment of free tax-supported schools. This was far from being a dogma of enforced equality. To benefit from equality of opportunity a man must be equal to his opportunities, with the government serving principally as an umpire to supervise the game with a minimum of rules. The upshot was a conception of democracy rigorously qualified by individualism.

This individualistic bias sometimes assumed forms that defied government. The colonists in their relations with the mother country evaded unwelcome regulations and, prompted by their theologians and lawyers, insisted that acts of Parliament contrary to their "unalienable rights" were void. Within the colonies those who dwelt remote from centers of law and order adopted a like attitude toward the provincial authorities. The Scotch-Irish who illegally occupied Pennsylvania soil in the early eighteenth century contended "it was against the laws of God and nature, that so much land should be idle while so many Christians wanted it to labor on and to raise their bread." As a substitute for constituted authority the settlers sometimes created their own unofficial tribunals, which adjudicated property titles and punished offenders against the public peace. In other instances they resorted to the swifter retribution of individual gunplay, or of mob action and lynch law, for from taking the law into one's hands when it could not function it was but a step to taking the law into one's hands when it did not function as one wanted it to.

The tendency to violence so generated has continued to condition the national mentality to the present time. Thoreau, the great philosopher of individualism, knew of no reason why a citizen should "ever for a moment, or in the least degree, resign his conscience to the legislator," declaring that "we should be men first, and subjects afterward." A similar conviction undoubtedly inspired William H. Seward's flaming declaration to the proslavery Senators in 1850 that "there is a higher law than the Constitution," just as it actuated the thousands of churchgoing Northerners who secretly banded together to violate the Fugitive Slave Act. But generally it has been self-interest or convenience, rather than conscience, that has provided the incentive to lawbreaking.

Section 8   CRIME IN A COMPETITIVE SOCIETY

From "Crime in a Competitive Society" by M. Ploscowe, 1941.

Crime is not a fixed and definite concept. Every year brings a new crop of criminal laws. Every change in social philosophy, in methods of political and economic control, in attempts of government to bring our competitive system under closer supervision, brings with it marked changes in the content of the criminal law. Each of the New Deal laws, such as the Securities Act of 1933, the Agricultural Adjustment Act, the Investment Company Act, invokes the criminal law in aid of the socioeconomic measures provided by the statute.

This fluidity in the concept of crime makes it necessary to pose on the threshold of the inquiry into crime in a competitive society the question, "What kind of crime?" Clearly, the mechanics of causation, the threat to the community, the techniques of control, must be different in various types of criminality. Consider, for example, two types of delinquents who are products of the competitive system: (1) the offender who obtains relief money although he may be working for a low wage, and (2) the broker who persists in acting as an investment counselor without registering with the Securities Exchange Commission although he is required to do so by the Investment Company Act of 1940 (Chap. 686). It is difficult to make generalizations concerning crime which apply equally to offenders of such varying types.

Criminal Motivations

Unfortunately there are no limited or restricted categories of criminals that can be charged to the competitive system. There is hardly a crime in the Penal Law which in some way does not arise out of the vagaries of the socioeconomic system in which we live. The crimes which arise out of purely personal motives or because of individual peculiarities and abnormalities and which do not stem from the society in which the criminal lives are few and far between. They are more likely to be found in crimes against the person and in sex crimes than in crimes against property. But even in crimes against the person one runs across a considerable percentage which are an expression of the individual's desire to obtain as much of the world's goods as he can for himself without particular regard to the methods by which this is done. This is illustrated by the cold-blooded homicides carried out in Brooklyn by the combine known as Murder, Inc. A typical killing had one Puggy Feinstein for its victim. Its background has been described by Assistant District Attorney Burton B. Turkus of Kings County (Brooklyn) as follows:

> Pittsburgh Phil (Strauss) reported to Reles, in the presence of Martin "Buggsy" Goldstein, that he had been having dinner with the boss, who was Albert Anastasio. At the dinner table, the boss gave him a contract. Harry said, "The contract is to 'take' a fellow by the name of Puggy Feinstein. He's a little guy about five foot two. He comes from Borough Park. You can't miss him. He's got a puggy nose."
> The reason for the contract? "Well, he crossed Vince," was the testimony in the court. Vince referred to Vincent Mangano, once head of the Brooklyn waterfront. Reles said, "All right. If you need me, you know where to get me; I'm summering in the mountains. Send for me." Pittsburgh replied that he thought it would be easy, and that

he and Buggsy Goldstein could do the job themselves. This man, at the dinner table, secures a contract to kill a man whom he doesn't know for a reason that he is less concerned with!

Some time later, Strauss reported that he couldn't find Feinstein, and Reles warned him not to lose the contract. That may seem humorous, but the contract carried with it an annual retainer of $12,000 a year that came in from the garment district, via Anastasio to the East New York Brownsville mob, so that the latter would be on call for any assaults required in the garment district. So Reles was anxious that the contract be performed expeditiously.

In view of the fluidity of the concept of crime, and the wide variety of crimes that must be considered, we shall not attempt to formulate any universally applicable generalizations on crime in a competitive society. We shall content ourselves with presenting certain broad patterns of crime under competitive conditions.

Crime and Economic Change

First, there seems to be a definite relationship between the volume of crimes against property and the swings of the economic pendulum. When work is plentiful and wages are high, there tend to be fewer crimes against property than in times of depression. It might be taken as axiomatic that men will not starve, and if society will not provide for their needs and for the needs of their families in legitimate ways they will resort to illegitimate means of obtaining the basic essentials of food and shelter. The clearest proof of this axiom is the German and Austrian experience after the first World War when the entire economic organization of these countries was disrupted by the debasement of the currency. In both Germany and Austria there was a tremendous increase in crimes against property, which fell to normal levels as soon as the economic life of these countries was stabilized. Similarly, studies of the relation of unemployment to crime have shown that the volume of property crimes increases during periods of unemployment. One such study of unemployment and crime in Massachusetts causes Emma A. Winslow to conclude:

> Unemployment is revealed as an important causative factor in vagrancy and in crimes against property. Its influence upon other offenses, however, is comparatively slight and but occasionally seen. Other causes than the ebb and flow of the business tide must therefore be sought

for the explanation of these crimes. But the relative importance of offenses against property in the total of criminality
is such as to establish industrial stabilization as a significant element in any program of crime prevention. The
conclusion seems inescapable that the assurance of economic security might be expected to bring with it an appreciable reduction in the volume of crime.

Mere statistics on the volume of crime cannot tell the complete story of
crime during years of prosperity or depression. They provide no insight into
the character of individuals who commit these crimes. It would be desirable
to know, for example, how much of the increase in crime during periods of
depression should be chargeable to situational or occasional offenders who
are driven by poverty to their crimes and how much is due to the professional
and habitual criminals who must work harder during bad years because the
average haul from each crime is less than during periods of prosperity. Also
statistics on the volume of crime provide no insight into the relative social
damage resulting from crime. In terms of money or property stolen, embezzled or fraudulently obtained, it may well be that losses due to crime in
periods of prosperity may far exceed losses during periods of depression,
even though the number of crimes committed in the latter period may be
greater. The Insulls, Kruegers, Whitneys, Mitchells, Hopsons, and Musicas
functioned most effectively during the golden twenties when money was
plentiful. The losses which they inflicted upon investors make the average
crime of the ordinary thief in our criminal courts appear to be a mere pec-
cadillo by comparison.

White-Collar Criminals More Harmful

It is evident that different causative factors are at work in the crimes
of the run-of-the-mill thieves, burglars, and stick-up men and those of the
so-called white-collar criminals who do infinitely more damage to the community. This is clearly brought out in a recent report by the Citizens Committee on the Control of Crime. Writing of persons convicted of theft in New
York City in 1940, it stated:

> The defendants in these cases, with few exceptions, fol-
> lowed the usual pattern of evil doers in a great city.
> Forty-five per cent of them were under 25 years of
> age, and 28 per cent of them were under 21. Most of them
> were unmarried, were unemployed or at best were only
> casual, unskilled workers. Many of them never had had
> work of any kind. Dire need drove some of them to thiev-

ery, and there were few among them who did not live in at least comparative poverty.

Through the pattern ran the common threads of sub-normal mentalities (though there were not many of these); of poor health; of overcrowded or broken homes, and of life in neighborhoods where streets are the only play-grounds and conflict with the law is dominant sport.

Another picture lies behind this portrayal of a general situation. It is a picture of thievery by people who are not unemployed, who do not live in poverty, but in comfortable, even luxurious homes, who are of superior intelligence—of people who contradict almost every one of the standard theories of the "causes of crime."

The year ended June 30, last, was marked by an unusual sequence of such white-collar thefts . . .

Only a part of this great loss is included in the $3,000,000 estimated by the police to have been stolen during the year. Actually this loss is a sum apart from the other, since in only a few of these white-collar thefts was initial action taken by the police . . .

Here were people who, with few exceptions, suffered none of the compulsions, save opportunity, that customarily lead to theft. In many of them there would seem to have been only the "evil mind" that was, for so many generations, the accepted cause of wrongdoing, and that is still the cornerstone of the laws through which we seek to control crime.

These sixty-six cases by no means represent the total of the year's white-collar thefts. There were others that never reached the courts but were settled outside. There were many that were tried, not in the criminal but in the civil courts—misappropriations by fiduciaries threshed out in actions for accountings; actions for fraud and deceit that embraced all the essential allegations that spell out larceny. It is possible, indeed, that robbers and burglars and their like are small fry after all in the losses they cause.

About all that can be said about these two types of crimes is that they are both essentially products of the competitive system. The system creates the needs which must be met for both white-collar and professional criminals and the philosophy that justifies the technique used to satisfy these needs. Under any system a man must provide for the basic essentials of food and shelter for himself and for his family. Our competitive system, however, places a premium upon success. Success has been translated into monetary terms. It is not what a man is that matters, but what he has. The more he has, the greater his success. The more he has, the greater must be his effort to demonstrate to others how much he has. Hence the expensive car, the blonde and her expensive fittings, the frequentation at costly night clubs, the visitation at exclusive and expensive resorts, the placing of large bets, the indulgence in poker, bridge, or dice for high stakes, the taste for choice and expensive liquors, the desire for bigger and better parties, etc. Having acquired a taste for these symbols of success, any man would rather satisfy them legitimately. This is as true of the professional criminal as of the white-collar criminal. No man likes the threat of "the cops" hanging over his head. Unfortunately, the satisfaction of such desires is beyond the means of the "poor working sap," who stays within the limits of the law. Only a favored few in our competitive society have the wherewithal to indulge in these things, without the necessity of resorting to crime.

The professional criminal is not so fortunate. If he is to be a success, if he is to have and achieve the symbols of success, he must work at his specialty. He must be continually on the alert for new opportunities to commit crime and his activity must continue in periods of prosperity or in periods of depression. The risks may be great, but the rewards are also great, and the latter are a sufficient justification for this activity. As one criminal put it:

> The men of the underworld are the brainiest men in the world. They have to be, because they live by their wits. They are always planning something, a "stickup," a burglary, or some new "racket." They are constantly in danger. They have to think quicker and sharper than the other fellow. They have to "size up" every man they meet, and figure out what "line" to use on him. The leading men of the underworld can move in every circle of society. They are at home in Chinatown, along the "main stem," in gambling dives, or in the best hotels and the "Gold Coast." When they have a lucky "break" they can live like millionaires; when their money is spent they plan new schemes.

Our competitive economic system has provided not only the rewards and goals to be achieved by crime, but also patterns for criminal organization and multifarious opportunities for crime and the use of criminal methods. For many years the tendency in business has been toward the organization of larger and larger economic units and the elimination of competition through stifling of competitors, price controls, etc. In the activities of the anti-trust division headed by Thurman Arnold, we see a determined attempt to break up monopolies and monopolistic practices. Similarly, professional crime also tends to be organized on a monopolistic basis, on a national scale as well as locally. Under this organization, territories are assigned, activities are apportioned, and percentages of the "take" are set. Where law enforcement officials are amenable, they are tied into this organization by a percentage of the profits, thus negativing the possibility of the disruption of the organization of undue interference with its activities. As in business, groups of gangsters or individual gangsters may be dissatisfied with their place in the organization or with the profits that they are making out of its activities. The result is frequently war, which is settled by guns rather than by price cutting or other business methods. How much murder is part of this system of organized crime is illustrated by Assistant District Attorney Turkus:

> From the point of view of organized crime, the United States was classified into territories, headed by a gang chieftain. No racketeer, no "mug" or hoodlum in a territory could be executed without the approval of the boss of that district. There has not been an organized killing in the last ten years which was not approved by the gang chieftain of the sector in which the crime was committed. That may sound fantastic and incredible, but it is the truth.

Businessmen have been attempting to control the evils of competition, such as unfair business practices, price cutting, competition for sources of supply, etc., by organizing into trade associations. These associations offer excellent opportunities for racketeers to shake down businessmen; as a result the associations are frequently taken over by criminals lock, stock, and barrel. In one New York racket, a trade association was taken over with the simple threat, "If you fellows don't come along and put us on the pay roll, there will be busted heads and broken trucks." When the trade association is taken over, guns, bombs, assaults, acid, etc., often provide the means of carrying out its purposes. While the businessmen composing the association may continue to reap some incidental advantages from its activities, they usually must pay a high price for these advantages.

Labor unions have been playing a greater and greater role in our economic organization. The possibility of profit through the control of these unions has not been overlooked by criminals. This possibility is twofold. On the one hand, the threat of a strike or the promise of less onerous conditions in a labor contract can always be used to shake down employers. The recent indictment by a Federal grand jury of William Bioff and George E. Browne, leaders in the International Alliance of Theatrical Stage Employees (A.F. of L.) is an illustration of this type of activity. These gentry are accused of extorting $550,000 for their personal use from four of the major motion picture companies under a threat of tying up the industry by calling a strike of the 35,000 union members employed in the industry's mechanical crafts. When criminals secure control of labor unions, they also do not overlook the possibility of filching money directly from the union treasury. The most outstanding recent example of this type of unjust enrichment is the case of George Scalise, president of the International Building Service Employees Union, who was recently convicted of stealing $60,000 from his union.

Sometimes the racketeers obtain control of both the labor union and the trade association. This is what happened in the restaurant racket which was broken up in New York City some years ago:

> Dutch Schultz, Julie Martin, and some of their henchmen had the bright idea that the restaurant field was ready for them. They secured control of the officers of two local unions, and at the same time, took control of the trade association that was operating in that field. The extortion in this case was complicated by the fact that the racketeers could use the front of the association as well as the pressure of union officials to compel the payment of huge amounts of tribute.
>
> Not only did they control the local union, but they also controlled the employers. The squeeze of both the association and the labor union made it almost impossible for the businessmen to resist extortions of Schultz and his henchmen. But the workers in the unions as well as the businessmen suffered, for every extortion of this kind involves the selling out of men who pay dues to the union.

These are but a few of the niches and crannies of the competitive system into which the modern criminal fits and which he turns to his advantage.

It is a recognition by the criminal of the fact that while one may serve an apprenticeship in crime as a pickpocket, purse-snatcher, burglar, or stick-up man, the big money is in none of these rackets. One is not likely to achieve success by these out and out criminal techniques. It was an ex-burglar, Jack Blace, who coined the phrase, "You can't win." The big money —and success to the criminal is measured in terms of money—is to be made in activities which have a legitimate place in our competitive system but which can be perverted to criminal ends. There is nothing inherently criminal in the activities of a trade association or labor union. It is the possibility of using them for criminal purposes which makes them so popular with the professional criminal. In thus perverting legitimate organizations and legitimate activities, there is a similarity between the so-called white-collar criminal and the professional thug like Scalise. Scalise used his position as president of a labor union to steal from the labor union. Whitney used his position as president of the Stock Exchange and as a trusted fiduciary to steal funds entrusted to his care.

While on the subject of the rewards from criminality, one should note that the big money may also be made from crime in supplying demands for proscribed articles. The prosperity of the bootlegger of the 1920's has passed into history. But fortunes are still made in supplying demands for dope, prostitutes, opportunities to bet on horses, play numbers, etc. This simply means that the law of supply and demand operates in crime as elsewhere in our economic system. If certain things are desired intensely enough by people who are willing to pay for them, someone will come forth and supply that demand. This will be done despite all the law enforcement efforts to choke off the source of supply. Where the rewards are great enough there will always be criminals who will take the necessary chances to obtain these rewards. If they can buy immunity by sharing profits with corrupt law enforcement officials, so much the better. But with or without law enforcement, these rackets go on. Honest, energetic law enforcement merely serves to keep them in check.

By way of summary one comes back to the cliché of the French criminologist, "Societies have the criminals they deserve." This does not mean that the social and economic conditions of a competitive society are solely responsible for the crime with which we are familiar. All persons do not react in the same way to these conditions. The poverty which spurs one man to crime spurs another to become a business tycoon. Thus the personality factor in crime must never be overlooked. What the above cliché means is that a competitive society with its materialistic standards of success, its lack of security for the masses, its violent swings of the economic pendulum and violent economic struggles between classes, its tremendous urban populations and great contrasts between wealth and poverty, its corrupt law enforcement officials and its lack of a determined public opinion against crime, produces certain pressures which tend toward criminality. These pressures acting upon certain personalities give rise to the crimes with which we are familiar. The elimination of these pressures through the modification of the socioeconomic conditions which bring them about presents a fundamental problem in social engineering. Its complexity throws considerable doubt on the efficacy of many of the simple panaceas which have been advanced as a cure for crime. More play spaces for children, boy's clubs, visiting teachers, community councils, child guidance clinics, youth correction authorities, adolescent courts, Borstal institutions, increased probation staffs, and other measures advanced for the prevention of crime, are all worthy things in and of themselves. All of them may tend in some degree to curb delinquent careers and prevent crime. But none of them touches the fundamentals of crime in a competitive society.

The pessimist must note, however, that no change in our social organization or in our socioeconomic conditions can completely eliminate crime. No human society is perfect nor can any human society supply all the demands and desires of the human beings that compose it. The imperfections of society and the unsatisfied desires and demands will always lead certain types of personalities to overstep the bounds fixed by law and social mores and into the behavior that we call crime. Despite these facts, the social engineer must still take as a working hypothesis that a lessening of the rigors and pressures of the competitive system and the greater assurance to the individual of economic security are likely to lead to a diminution in the amount of crime.

Section 9   CRIME AS SOCIAL DISORDER

From *America as a Civilization* by Max Lerner, 1957.

The human harvest of the seeds of disorder may be found in the ominous "statistical profile" of crime in America. At mid-century there were about fifteen million arrests annually in those cities where the statistics are fairly regular—a figure which represents only a fraction of the total offenses committed. Most of the arrests are for larcenies, burglaries, auto thefts, and other offenses against property. In only one case out of twenty does the offense result in imprisonment. In the case of white-collar crimes, involving business cheating, embezzling, illegal stock market manipulation, tax evasion, defective merchandise, the proportion of offenses discovered to the total number committed is even smaller.

Despite a long history of prison reform and the relatively high standards of administration in Federal prisons, the condition of American prisons is still backward in most states, especially in the South, where the chain gangs are used to get cheap labor for public works and where race feeling is added to the usual inhumanity between captor and captive. In most prisons the inmates are still kept shut up in cell blocks, given largely meaningless labor, and cut off from the responsibility which alone can restore a man to a productive life. In a society which stresses sex they are also cut off from normal heterosexual relations, so that prisons fortify and even breed homosexual tendencies. A few voices are now asserting that "prisoners are people too," and experiments are being made in informal prison farms where the man can come closer to normal patterns of daily living and have their confidence in humanity restored.

But the individual criminal dwindles in importance before "rackets" and "syndicates." The racket is a pattern of extortion and tribute which urban brigands levy on night clubs, shopkeepers, bars, manufacturers, trade-unions, waterfront companies, and truckers, under threat of despoiling their goods or premises and even death. The syndicate is a business combine with a feudal structure of authority, organized to exploit activities beyond the law or on its margin-gambling, betting, slot machines, houses of prostitution, "call-girl" services, and narcotics.

These activities are not as marginal to American life as they are to American law. One trait on which the rackets and syndicates build is the belief in luck, which is deeply ingrained in a culture that underlines the big prizes. There is widespread betting on sports events—on horse racing, prize fighting, baseball, basketball, football. Slot machines are the center of rural and roadside taverns as well as of urban bars and luxury clubs. One of the purest forms of the belief in luck is the "numbers" or "policy" game, in which bets are placed on what numbers may turn up each day in officially published reports, such as Federal Reserve Bank statements. The crowds gathered around New York's newsstands for early editions of the morning tabloids are probably more interested in getting the racing results and the "numbers" pay-off than in the international news. The annual "take" from slot machines has been estimated at two billion dollars. The income from "policy" betting in Chicago alone, largely in the Negro areas, is estimated at fifty million dollars, most of it in nickels, dimes, and quarters. In such low-income Negro areas, "policy" may mean destitution for thousands of families—and wealth for the few men who organize and run it as a big business. For the gambling industry as a whole, including bookmaking, legalized or pari-mutuel betting, the "numbers" game, "policy," slot machines, and lotteries, the annual business has been calculated at fifteen billion dollars, involving an industry that ranks in gross sales with such major American industries as chemicals.

To protect these industries against the uneasy conscience of the community, an alliance is sometimes formed between the syndicates and rackets on the one hand, and on the other the political bosses, machine politicians, police-force officials, wire and phone services, trade unions, and seemingly respectable business concerns that operate as "fronts." It was this alliance which was the principal target of inquiry by the Kefauver Committee in

1951 and the McClellan Committee in 1957. The importance of these inquiries, as also earlier of the writings of Lincoln Steffens and the muckrakers, was that they made the American people aware of the tie-up between lawlessness, politics and the marginal aspects of business and trade-unionism. What they saw did violence to their cherished belief not only in law and order but in the healthy organization of their society. A few men went to jail, a few local administrators and labor leaders were thrust out of office, new Federal tax laws made the "bookie" profession a good deal more dangerous—but the basic pattern of the rackets and syndicates went on.

America today, as in the past, presents the picture both of a lawless society and an overlegislated one. In some of the earlier societies the reliance was less upon detailed legal norms and penalties than upon custom and the sanctions of community opinion. But America is the type-society of the West in which little is left to loose community action, and the characteristic way of dealing with crime is to set down definite statements of legal transgressions and punishments. Nevertheless, Americans consider crime a problem they cannot master, which will continue to grow because it is an outcropping of some inner disease of their society. Recognizing this, they also recoil from it, thus displacing on the criminal their own guilt and powerlessness—which may help explain why the treatment of crime has lagged. To feel mastery over the environment, over things and money, and yet to feel baffled by so elementary a fact as crime, has become a source of frustration.

Like the belief in luck, the habit of strong drink is something Americans worry about while many of them continue to practice it. The frontiersmen prided themselves on their drinking excesses: the isolation of life, along with its rigors, led to a plentiful consumption of homemade spirits. For the plantation leisure class of the Old South, heavy drinking was at once an antidote to boredom and the mark of hospitality for the landed gentry. Among the miners and cattle ranchers of the Far West, the frontier saloon was an outlet for the turbulence of new and lawless settlements. All these strands of social inheritance may still be found in American drinking, yet while the old reasons for heavy drinking no longer apply in the urbanized indoor society, the drinking remains. The new reasons for drinking are probably more closely connected with the driving tempo of life in America and the anxieties, frustrations, and aggressions it engenders. It should be added, however, that the practice of "local option" means that a large part of the nation is legally "dry," and what drinking there is must be done in private homes or by subterfuge. The heavy drinking is to be found in the Eastern centers, on the West Coast (California leads the nation in alcoholism), and in the centers of new wealth and social change, like Texas.

Not the least of American's mores are woven around the night club, the roadhouse, the public bar—and the private bar at home. Just as betting and gambling take on emotional overtones from the ritualized competitiveness of American sports, so liquor in the night hours and night spots takes on sexual overtones from the orgiastic arts of "hot music" and sexually revealing "revues" and "floor shows." The sexual revolution of the 1920's removed the restraints against drinking by women; except in the small towns, where the older mores prevail, women will be found drinking in public restaurants and bars, or at private parties at the "cocktail hour," which is as basic a national institution as afternoon tea for the British or the Continental *aperitif*. So crucial did the consumption of alcohol become in America that the Prohibition episode came closer to dividing the nation into two camps than anything since the Civil War, and the cleavage between "wets" and "drys" became a struggle between Guelphs and Ghibellines. Much of the network of rackets and syndicates goes back to these Prohibition days: so strong was the feeling against "law enforcement" that the American attitude toward the Prohibition agents in the 1920's was very like that of a Resistance movement toward an army of occupation.

Distinguishing between "social drinkers" and compulsive ones, there were some forty or fifty million of the former and about two and a half million of the latter, of whom at least a half million were confirmed alcoholics. While these figures seem large, the problem of alcoholism in America is not as serious as in European countries like Sweden and Germany. In their efforts to deal with alcoholism, Americans characteristically resorted to the device of a club, "Alcoholics Anonymous," whose members supported one another in their efforts to refrain from drinking. As for narcotics addiction, the narcotics traffic increased after World War II, and the vigilance against it tightened. About a fifth of the fifty or sixty thousand drug addicts were teen-agers, mainly from the metropolitan centers and especially the Negro areas. The smoking of "reefers" (marijuana) was more widespread among teen-agers than drug addiction; its danger lay in its leading so often to heroin or morphine.

To these items of social pathology we must add organized prostitution, illegal abortion, homosexuality in its more compulsive forms, and sexual offenses—especially against children—which were often in the headlines and roused intense popular anger.

These are all departures from the dominant norms of cultural health. Some of them, like crime, are deliberate attacks upon the norms; others, like delinquency, alcoholism, drug addiction, and prostitution, are forms of failure in living up to the norm. In some instances, as with homosexuals, or heavy drinkers who are not alcoholics, or those migrant and homeless men who are unemployed and who cluster in the flop-houses, it is a question of being on the margin of the norms. In the case of mental defectives (which

Americans tend to push away without much discussion except when there are drives to sterilize them by law) and in the case of sexual psychopaths, we are dealing with the clearly pathological. Some forms of disorganization fall under none of these categories, but—like many cases of suicide, for example—flow from normlessness, or the failure of any kind of values to take hold of the individual.

Americans are concerned and baffled about these phases of their society. Having found that many of their problems yield to technology and organization, they feel ordinarily that their way of life ought to move toward purpose and contain solutions. Yet in the norm-breaking and normless behavior we have discussed they find a spectacle to shake their belief in their own institutions. They see the social breakdowns as symptoms of the decadence and disintegration of American society as a whole. Things "fly apart at the center," reversing what Americans regard as the natural order: children grow up to become criminals, gangsters, gamblers, the face of innocence takes on the hideous mask of the narcotics addict, families are broken up by divorce, "nice girls" engage in promiscuous sex or even become professional prostitutes, the image of the clean-cut young businessman turns into that of the uncontrolled alcoholic or the compulsive homosexual, respectable citizens are revealed as white-collar criminals, and the basic activities of life are turned into rackets. Thus the Americans find the most cherished symbols of their society turned topsy-turvy.

Yet does disorganization always violate the essential spirit of the culture? Does it always mean the abnormal, pathological, anticultural? Actually the departure from norms may shed extraordinary light on the inner nature of the culture. In trying to explain why Americans are themselves deeply drawn to the gangster films which they know to be distortions of their urban life, one notes that a gangster is an American "cultural hero" in whom Americans recognize a symbol of the energy of their culture. Or take American criminologists, who stress the paradox of the "rationality" of the habitual criminal, in the sense that given his twisted antisocial premises, his acts flow logically from them. What they often ignore is a different kind of rationality: that the criminal takes seriously the barely concealed premises of the culture itself. He sees easy money being made and predacity practiced, knows that the rules are constantly broken, knows that there is an internal violence in the act of exploiting the market and ravishing the environment.

Thus the forms of American disorganization arise from the more naked drives within the culture itself, with the workaday masks stripped away that have hidden the sadism and ugliness which are part of the human condition and are to be found in every culture.

In every society forces are generated that are harmful to its functioning and in the end destroy it. It would be strange if this were not happening in America as well. But those who fix upon crime and rackets, divorce, prostitution, and alcoholism as proofs of American decadence and degeneration may be fixing upon the wrong symptoms of the wrong disease. Most of the phases of social pathology I have listed are the extreme applications of principles which, in lesser degree, may be healthy. The delinquent and the criminal, so greatly feared by Americans, are not so dangerous to the social fabric as they seem to be. The point about the gangster, the racketeer, and the syndicate operator—even the house-breaker and the burglar—is not that they scorn property but that they value it enough to be ruthless in seeking short cuts for making it their own. The adolescent delinquent, in turn, in the act of rebelling against family or school or community, may be seeking the cherishing love upon which the family and other primary groups must be based.

The principles by which American culture lives are those of freedom and acquisition, and—where the two meet—the freedom of acquisition. There are always a number of people who feel themselves left out of the operation of these principles, or who are too much in a hurry to wait, or who feel resentful because others seem to start with an unfair set of principles, and who therefore seek some equalizer. Since they feel at a strategic disadvantage in the competition of life, they feel justified in ignoring the usual inhibitions and in tearing down the accepted cement of social relations. Because they use a distorted version of the cultural energies to destroy social bonds and rip apart the cohesiveness of the society, they in effect pit the culture against the society.

One may deplore these dislocating energies, but they would seem to be an inherent part of a society in which the pace of life is set by freedom, competitiveness, and acquisitiveness, and they are part of the price the society pays for those informing principles. A society less free and less dynamic—one of tradition and status, or one of totally state-directed power—may escape some of these dislocations but be beset by others. The whole impulsion of American culture is to raise hopes and claims in the individual and spur him on to fulfill the hopes and nail down the claims. At the same time it is too young a society to have developed the kind of inner discipline which—let us say, in England—can serve to inhibit the full sway of the impulsion.

Take, for example, the extreme case of the narcotics "pusher," who is even willing to corrupt children and develop the narcotics habit in them in order to make customers for his product. He represents the principle of creating a market, inherent in the market economy. In the mid-1950's he was thriving in America mainly because the severely repressive Federal narcotics laws, with constant "crackdowns" by enforcement officials, kept increasing the danger of narcotics distribution and therefore the price and profits—without reaching at all the terrible sense of isolation which underlies the use of narcotics. But he is also an example of the desensitized man in whom the principle has run wild, like cells in a cancerous growth. Or consider the case of the racketeer, who on principle recoils from the notion of earning his bread by the sweat of his brow, but who invests great resourcefulness in applying *force majeure* at the most vulnerable points of business enterprise.

The racketeer is likely to come up from the slums, reaching for quick affluence by breaking the windows of the mansion of American success rather than by entering at the door. There are studies showing how the prominence of Jews, Irish, and Italians in urban crime has swung from one immigrant group to another as each has flooded into the United States, sought to orient itself in American society, and become assimilated to it. At the beginning they are dislocated from their old culture but have not absorbed anything of the new culture except its cruder aspects; they have demons within them to assert themselves in a challenging new environment, they have few inhibiting fences around them, and they are in a hurry. The violence with which intense slum youngsters imitate the values of the culture, even while distorting them, may be seen as their own form of flattery. What they do is legally and morally wrong, but instead of being a sign of the decay of American life it may be taken almost as a sign of its vitality.

One of the clues is the dynamism of rapid social change. Racketeering crops up mostly in the areas of new business enterprise which have not yet been reduced to order or become subject to tradition, and where economic change moves more rapidly. The most serious outcroppings of violence and crime come also at the times of greatest social change, involving a rapid migration of population, the shifting of industries, the contact and clash of subcultures, the improvement of living standards, and the opening of new perspectives for which people are not yet prepared.

As a case in point we may take the known fact, of the prevalence of reefer-and-dope addiction in Negro areas. This is usually explained in terms of poverty, slum living, and broken families, yet it would be easy to show the lack of drug addiction among other ethnic groups where the same conditions apply. One may guess that the rapid movement of Negroes from a depressed status to the improved status and partial freedoms of today, with new jobs and new living standards, has led also to the breaking down of old goals, while the new ones are still vague and seem inaccessible. I have noted in an earlier section that the passion for equality feeds on itself, setting the goals higher and making the distance from them more embittering. Drug addiction thus becomes one of the expressions of the isolation and normlessness that are the by-products of social advance, achieved under nerve-wracking stress, bitterly paid for. Where rigid status is being broken up and class lines shifting, and where a sense of social hope persists, social disorders are the tribute which the unbalanced individual pays to the naked premises of the culture.

Their real danger lies not in the pathology of cultural values but in their denial. The delinquencies and moral breakdowns which flow from the sense that only power counts and all American life is a racket are less dangerous than those which flow from the sense that nothing counts—not even the rackets. The breakdowns of family life or of sexual morality, and the crimes against property, by threatening the foundations of the American social structure, evoke counterforces in turn which solidify the social structure in its own defense. A frontal attack tends to be met by a defense in depth. Yet the disorganization which flows from the desensitizing of men, and from a lack of belief in any values, is a threat to the idea of social structure itself.

PART III

THE FORERUNNER OF THE SYNDICATE

ORGANIZED CRIME in mid-twentieth century America is the product of an evolutionary process, extending over more than a century. Contrary to popular belief, the cartelization of crime did not begin with Prohibition, although the Eighteenth Amendment provided a distinctive vigor and form to the syndicate. Nor did "crime incorporated" begin with the highly publicized Mafia, although individuals and groups commonly associated with it undoubtedly put their stamp on the underworld. The roots of organized crime can be found in New York, Chicago, and San Francisco, in Kansas, Texas, and Missouri, many decades before Volstead or Capone. The line of development from buccaneer to businessman, from fisticuffs to finance parallels the contour of the American economy. The binding tie from past to present is the very accurate word "gangster." The gang is an organized group, a culture within the culture, demanding of its members a loyalty above state, religion, and even family. In its primitive form it is juvenile, undirected, and violent; in its civilized form, it is adult, purposeful, and suave. This transfiguration from the primitive to the civilized is repetitive, recurring in one generation after another, in a kind of destructive creation wherein the brutes of yesterday become the criminal lords of tomorrow.

A lawless culture need not breed a class of professional criminals, organized gangs making a career of crime. But the chances are that such outlaw bands will arise.

Where there is disrespect for law, men will settle their quarrels directly, whether these disputes be personal or group. Shortly, the disputants will discover that a man with a gang is more powerful than a man without one. And so the gangs will arise.

In our early cities, they arose as street gangs among the poor, composed of young men carving out cobblestone kingdoms with some speakeasy (green grocery) castle. The constant clash among these gangs was far less business than fun. They did not fight for gain or profit but out of sheer animal and herd desire to mark off some "territory" against trespass.

Quickly, these young toughs discovered that there was money in their muscle. A gang leader could begin to levy tribute against the local houses of assignation and gambling, the opium dens, and even legitimate stores, especially retailers. The leader might cut in some of his boys. And thus, what began as juvenile roughhouse evolved into a business.

Intragang clashes took on the aspect of commercial competition as well as boyish high jinx. Cutting out and fencing off a "territory" became the base for establishing a little business empire run by a corporation ready to "chaw off" the ears of any interloping rival.

Once the gang was in existence, held together by the practice of violence both for fun and finance, society discovered many uses for this handy —and once quite inexpensive—instrument. If a man was personally wronged and felt that he lacked either the muscle or the mentality to revenge himself directly, he turned to the gangster to do the job for a consideration.

Gangs and gangsters were available not only to individuals who wanted to have an enemy's "ear chawed off," but also to social groups in conflict: economic or political. The gangs became mercenaries in class and party struggles, ready to serve as Hessians in our internal strife. For a contract they would be ready to crack a picket line or crack a scab, to terrorize a polling place or stuff the ballot box, to join a protest movement against the British, the Abolitionist, or the Civil War draft in New York City, to stage a kidnap scare against the owners of the Erie Railroad either to deliver the body of Daniel Drew to Commodore Vanderbilt or to make the Commodore look like the scoundrel he was.

Once in the social struggle, these mercenaries became almost indispensable to both sides. Their professional skill, their standing army, their ruthlessness, their disdain for police, courts, or even prison, their political pull, made these mercenaries highly effective troops. Against the amateurs of some cause, these "pros" had all the advantages of an organized cadre when dealing with a mob.

In a violent culture, the early gangs peddled a commodity that they produced by "doing it naturally"; namely, violence. Society demanded the item: the gangs provided a goodly supply, enough to keep the price quite low.

Jay Gould—business buccaneer—understood the role of the gangs when he boasted: "I can hire one half the working class to kill the other half."

Many years later, when the gangs had become the Syndicate, and they were able to render services not only with brass knuckles but with influence as well, Al Capone scorned the hypocrisy of the "good people" who assailed him. "Why," he spat, "the biggest bankers and businessmen and politicians and professional men are looking to me to keep the system going."

Our earliest gangs were juvenile herds, led by men just a few years older than their followers, spawned in the abject subcultures of our cities. Developing muscle in street struggles for control of their "territory," these gangs turned to local extortion and pillage. They hired out as mercenaries, individually or in group, to persons or "causes." With manpower and money, with the ability to push or pull a voting ward into line, these gangs developed political know-how at the grass-roots level and super know-how at the higher level of the "fix." These gangs were the ancestors of the modern underworld, with a lineage as traceable as a pedigreed pet.

The first gangs of Little Old New York were Irish. Indeed, so predominant was this ethnic element in the underworld from 1820 to 1890 that many students of the phenomenon concluded that crime was "hereditary" among the Irish.

"In the City of New York, where neither the juries nor the judges can be supposed to have a bias against the Irish, the proportion of convicts in Sing Sing prison who are Irish or of Irish parentage is almost 66 per cent, while the Irish population of the City is only 44 per cent, and that of the rural districts that send their convicts to that prison is not one-fifth of the number," noted an article on the "Origins of Crime in Society" in the *Atlantic Monthly* of 1881 (October, 1881, p. 458, by Richard L. Dugdale).

"This strikingly establishes," noted the scientifically minded author, "the force of *hereditary* tendencies in the formation of the criminal character."

In the excerpt from *Gangs of New York*, Herbert Asbury describes the first combines of street brawlers. In other volumes—*The Barbary Coast* and *Gem of the Prairies*—Asbury tells the stories of "Frisco" and "Chi."

In the excerpt entitled "The Hoodlums," Asbury describes the origin of a term that has passed into common usage. Taken from *The Barbary Coast*, these pages record the rise of a gang, juvenile in age, brutal in method, stylized in its manners, and mock heroic in its pretensions of defending the true American.

The hoodlums were a caricature, an ironic cartoon, of Frisco society. The "uniform" was a mockery of upper crust fashion; the war against the Chinese a travesty of upper crust distaste for the Asiatic; the total disrespect for law merely an ugly, logical conclusion to the decades of gangsterism, political corruption, and vigilantism that had preceded. The hoodlums were San Francisco—gold town in the Gilded Age—presented as a *reductio ad absurdum.*

The hoodlums preyed on the Chinese, feeding their juvenile pockets and passions: robbery, rape, and arson in the oriental quarters. But through it all stormed a senseless sadism: beatings, brandings, slitting of ears and tongues with no other "motive for atrocity than the brutal instincts of the young ruffians who perpetrated it" (*San Francisco Times,* July 30, 1868).

In a later age, these sadists might have been termed shock troopers for some virulent racist movement. In San Francisco of the 1870's and '80's, they appeared to the community simply to be vicious youth preying on a helpless people. To themselves the hoodlums appeared as men of distinction, using their infamy and repute to scare off punishment. "I'm a Hoodlum. You can't arrest me," one hoodlum told the police.

Today, the word has taken on dictionary meaning as a "young rowdy." It has a more delineated meaning in the underworld, where the "hoodlum" is a lowly figure, just above the "punk." The "punk" runs minor errands of mischief, while the "hoodlum" is assigned to violence. In both cases, however, these low men on the criminal totem pole take orders but don't give them.

While the word "hoodlum" has changed meaning, the original phenomenon continues to repeat itself through our history, as new generations of youth arise, making virtues of their elder's vices, to fly a crusader's flag over their immature violence.

The Hoodlums were not the only great gangs of San Francisco. The Hounds were a collection of New York ruffians who arrived in California via service in the Mexican War to prey on the Mexican Chilenos.

At a later time, there were the Sydney Ducks, expatriates from "down under." In San Francisco, they enjoyed the evil reputation of the early Irish and the latter-day Sicilian of New York. The Ducks were credited with every major crime, including many of which they might well have been innocent. If trouble brewed in the coastal city, it was common to say that the "ducks are cackling in their pond."

All three of these combines were broken up by vigilantes. The law itself appeared to be helpless, for the same reason that law has often found itself futile when confronting the organized underworld: alliance with politicians, bribing and intimidation of police, terrorization and corruption of witnesses.

Like the earliest gangs of New York, these organaized mobs were primarily free-floating chunks of violence. Purpose was secondary, a rationale for brutality, located in a deep-seated prejudice—whether it be against the Mexican Chilenos, against the Chinese, or, as in the case of the Ducks, against the prevailing dominant culture. In all cases, however, these gangs composed the raw stuff for organized crime.

The story of the early gangs—whether New York, San Francisco, or the frontier—is told against a background of conflict: ethnic, economic, and political. It is the tale of men making their own law, legislating with their fists, striking out against real or imagined enemies. While the early gangs of New York were Irish, the early mobs of the West Coast were immigrants from Australia, New York, and—if one includes the tongs—from China.

Over the years, different ethnic groups were charged with being criminal in nature. At the turn of the century and into the mid-twenties, Jewish gangsters played a major and almost a dominant role in New York. As today with the Italians and a century ago with the Irish, the onus fell on the Jews at one time. Indeed, certain writers on Jewish affairs even felt called upon to protect the good name of the Jews.

Similar apologias have been written for the Irish, Italians, Chinese, Australians, and others. Taken collectively, they prove that no people is immune from evil expressed in organized crime. Indeed, not even the oldest native stock is exempt, as evidenced by the history of our frontier, running from the Doanes and Harpes of Revolutionary days to the Wild Ones of more recent times. Breakdown of law, such as was noted in New York and San Francisco, was a perennial state on the frontier. Even an efficient government would have had great difficulty in policing the vast land mass of the frontier. Against such a background, it was inevitable that individual men and gangs of men—for virtue or vice—should take the law in their own hands.

Out of this disorder came great men, heroic in their own right and made more heroic by legend. Some were on the "wrong" side like the Jameses, Belle Starr, the Daltons, the Youngers; others were on the "right" side like Wyatt Earp, Billy Tilghman, Bat Masterson. Somewhere in between is Billy the Kid, pictured alternately as a golden-haired Galahad of the Southwest or a simpering juvenile killer from Brooklyn. But no matter where they stood with the angels or the demons, these "great" ones are admired by America, an admiration enhanced by America's own inventions about these heroes.

The cumulative tales of these men are America's *Aeneid* and *Odyssey*. These are the tales of the swift wanderers traveling over wide lands, experiencing the unexperienced. Of men who knew not fear and who showed no mercy to men who did know fear. Of warriors who knew how to kill and to die: you kill head-on and you die with your boots on. Of heroes whose motives, properly probed, could justify their seemingly murderous ways: driven by revenge, sympathy for the poor, hatred for the rich. Because this great epic, composed by the people out of recollections, exaggerations, and fabrications, has never been edited down to one great volume, versions of the same events vary and continue to vary with the retelling by word of mouth, in writing, movies, stage, ballet, music, television. Should some imaginative author a thousand years hence gather together this vast body of tales to compose one panoramic portrait of frontier America, written with an eye to essence rather than ingredients, to the poetic truth rather than the prosaic details, the end product would be a volume in which Wyatt Earp might seem an Odysseus, Billy the Kid a Galahad, Jesse James a Robin Hood, and Belle Starr a Joan of Arc.

The imaginative appeal of the frontier is epic in character because many of its values are the values of America: the code of rapacious men descending on a virgin land. "Grab what you can. Hold what you can. Do it yourself. When you need aid, turn to your clan, to your blood brothers. Ignore the law, until it can no longer be ignored, and then try to become the law or live the outlaw."

In miniature, this may be the pattern of any *new* culture, where authority is personal and not social. On the frontier this pattern stood out in high relief because the land, the fur, the buffalo, the waters, the gold and silver, the timber and ore were there to be *had* by those who could *hold*. To the extent that America as a whole is a *new* culture with minimal traditional authority and maximum natural resources, the pattern of rapacious men in a virgin land may apply to the whole nation, making the story of our frontier the story of America.

The gangs of the West were something more than aggregations of individual outlaws. They reflected social conflict: cattleman versus homesteader, sheep man versus cattleman, rebel versus Yankee, white versus Indian, settlers versus Mexicans, politicians versus land owners. In some cases, the interested parties themselves composed gangs to protect their income and status. Almost invariably, however, they turned to hired guns, cold killers engaged under contract.

In the great war of Johnson County, Wyoming, for instance, the great cattleman's association hired a private army to war against the small cowmen who were charged with rustling. In describing this war, William H. Kittrell, in his introduction to A. S. Mercer's *The Banditti of the Plains,* wrote: "The invaders of Johnson County were executioners, cold, determined, and implacable. They were numerous, well fed, well paid, fully armed, and splendidly mounted. Such men . . . were not . . . bandits in the way the West knew and recognized them. They were killers out to fulfill the terms and provisions of a contract between parties of the first part and parties of the second part." (pg. xxv.)

The single greatest source of gang conflict along the frontier revolved around the Civil War, with its prelude in bleeding Kansas and its postlude all over the widespread West. The Civil War liberated the slaves. It created a new ruling class in the North. It created a new class of conquered in the South. Out of the rebel army issued new gangs, outlawed by sentiment and edict from the America of the Yankee.

The most famous of these carried the banners of James, Younger, Dalton, and Starr. And while each of these carried its separate name and each gained enough prominence to earn separate chapters, magazine articles, books, and movies, these distinct bands were closely related by method, purpose, time, region—and blood!

This breed, related by blood and bloodshed, galloped across Missouri, Oklahoma, Arkansas, and Texas at a time when these regions were the battlefields for multiple wars, of which the Civil War was merely the major conflict. This clan was southern, antifederal, and felt itself bound by no laws. Its point of origin was the bitter war between the Missouri Bushwhackers and the Kansas Jayhawks, a border conflict that was not only part of the Civil War but prelude and postlude as well. In the struggle over bleeding Kansas, the Southern sympathizers out of Missouri and the Northern sympathizers out of Kansas fought a mean, back-stabbing, ambushing guerrilla war with no quarter for anyone, including women and children. The bitterness lingered for generations. It expressed itself in hatred of the federals. So long and deep did this scar run that President Harry S. Truman was able to relate that when he returned as a soldier from World War I, his grandmother would not let him come into her household wearing the hated uniform of the U. S. government.

While horse and cow thievery were among the earliest activities of the James-Younger band, its members soon learned to hit the jackpots of wealth in their region by staging the first bank robbery and then moving on to stage coach and train holdups. In this work, the Western outlaws established a pattern of banditry: moving gangs hitting a moving target. This development was both a continuation of an earlier practice (by the highwayman) and a forerunner of a later practice; namely, the control of transportation as the key to establishing a racket.

The highway has for centuries been the preserve of the bandit who wished to gather in great goods and gold in a hurry. On the highway, the traveler conveying his personal wealth or his commodities was exposed, moving outside the normal defenses and protections of the walled city and its buildings and its police. The bandit could appear out of nowhere on his swift mount, strike quickly, and disappear among the rocks and trees. The outlaw had all the advantages of the speedy aggressor moving against an unpoliceable line stretching over hundreds or thousands of miles. So common was the practice of pillage on the thoroughfare that it became institutionalized in the person of the "highwayman."

In the simple economy of the 1860's, the highway was the avenue over which were transported gold, valuables, and persons worth looting. In the complex economy of a later century, the highway became the artery of business and commerce, whose control made it possible to dominate both producers and merchandisers. In the days of Jesse James the assault on the highway was a threat to individuals; in the days of Dave Beck the assault on the highway was a threat to the society. In the middle of the nineteenth century, the highwayman operated like an outlaw; in the middle of the twentieth century, the "highwayman" operated like a businessman. The former operated by sporadic raids, like a pirate; the latter operated by levying fines, etc., like a tax collector.

Among the bad men of the West there stalked an honest cop, Wyatt Earp of current TV fame. The excerpt "The Frontier" is the story of the "honest cop and the system," the brave and clean soul trying to clean out the Augean stable of lawlessness.

The excerpt on Denver, entitled "The Gang Runs Denver," provides another locale with still another ethnic background.

As the nineteenth century drew to an end, the pure brute began to lose status in gangdom. "The Passing of the Brute" describes the rise of a new type: the gangster with a businesslike veneer. The dramatic struggle between Monk Eastman and Paul Kelly marks the Götterdämmerung of the street brawler.

Johnny Torrio, one of the young hoods of this era, was sent to Chicago to serve as bodyguard for Big Jim Colisimo. In a time-honored fashion, the bodyguard became his master's assassin. And by that act, Torrio united the gangs of New York and the gangs of Chicago.

Up to the time of Torrio, the line of succession in the Windy City ran from Mike MacDonald (politician with underworld machine) to Mont Tennes (gambler in control of the wire service) to Colisimo (bootlegging muscle-man). Then came Torrio, whose New York bodyguard, Al Capone, did to Torrio what Torrio did to Colisimo.

The excerpt entitled "The Early Chicago Story," records the colorful period from Mike to Mont. This piece sets the stage for the bloody era to follow, the great beer battles of the Prohibition era, out of which arose the national syndicate.

Section 10 **THE EARLY GANGS OF NEW YORK**

From *The Gangs of New York* by Herbert Asbury, 1927, 1928.

The most important gangs of the early days of the Bowery district were the Bowery Boys, the True Blue Americans, the American Guards, the O'Connell Guards, and the Atlantic Guards. Their membership was principally Irish, but they do not appear to have been as criminal or as ferocious as their brethren of the Five Points, although among them were many gifted brawlers. The True Blue Americans were amusing, but harmless. They wore stove-pipe hats and long black frock coats which reached flappingly to their ankles and buttoned close under the chin; their chief mission in life was to stand on street corners and denounce England, and gloomily predict the immediate destruction of the British Empire by fire and sword. Like most of the sons of Erin who have come to this country, they never became so thoroughly Americanized that Ireland did not remain their principal vocal interest. The other gangs were probably off-shoots of the Bowery Boys, and commonly joined the latter in their fights with the roaring denizens of Paradise Square. Their exploits earned them no place of importance in gang history.

For many years the Bowery Boys and the Dead Rabbits waged a bitter feud, and a week seldom passed in which they did not come to blows, either along the Bowery, in the Five Points section, or on the ancient battleground of Bunker Hill, north of Grand street. The greatest gang conflicts of the early nineteenth century were fought by these groups, and they continued their feud until the Draft Riots of 1863, when they combined with other gangs and criminals in an effort to sack and burn the city. In these early struggles the Bowery Boys were supported by the other gangs of the Bowery, while the Plug Uglies, the Shirt Tails, and the Chichesters rallied under the fragrant emblem of the Dead Rabbits. Sometimes the battles raged for two or three days without cessation, while the streets of the gang area were barricaded with carts and paving stones, and the gangsters blazed away at each other with musket and pistol, or engaged in close work with knives, brickbats, bludgeons, teeth, and fists. On the outskirts of the struggling mob of thugs ranged the women, their arms filled with reserve ammunition, their keen eyes watching for a break in the enemy's defense, and always ready to lend a hand or a tooth in the fray.

Often these Amazons fought in the ranks, and many of them achieved great renown as ferocious battlers. They were particularly gifted in the art of mayhem, and during the Draft Riots it was the women who inflicted the most fiendish tortures upon Negroes, soldiers, and policemen captured by the mob, slicing their flesh with butcher knives, ripping out eyes and tongues, and applying the torch after the victims had been sprayed with oil and hanged to trees. The Dead Rabbits, during the early forties, commanded the allegiance of the most noted of the female battlers, an angular vixen known as Hell-Cat Maggie, who fought alongside the gang chieftains in many of the great battles with the Bowery gangs. She is said to have filed her front teeth to points, while on her fingers she wore long artificial nails, constructed of brass. When Hell-Cat Maggie screeched her battle cry and rushed biting and clawing into the midst of a mass of opposing gangsters, even the most stout-hearted blanched and fled. No quarter was asked or given by the early gangsters; when a man fell wounded his enemies leaped joyfully upon him and kicked cr stamped him to death. Frequently the police were unable to disperse the mob, and were compelled to ask the National Guard and the Regular Army for aid. The city soon became accustomed to regiments of soldiers marching in battle array through the streets to quell a gang riot. Occasionally the artillery was called out also, but generally the gangsters fled before the muskets of the infantrymen. Much of this work was done by the Twenty-seventh, later the Seventh, Regiment.

Little knowledge of the activities of most of the early Bowery gangs has survived, but the lore of the street is rich in tales of the Bowery Boys and the prowess of their mighty leaders. Sometimes this gang was called Bowery B'hoys, which is sufficient indication of its racial origin. It was probably the most celebrated gang in the history of the United States, but before the eminent Chuck Conners appeared in the late eighties and transformed the type into a bar fly and a tramp, the Bowery Boy was not a loafer except on Sundays and holidays. Nor was he a criminal, except on occasion, until the period of the Civil War. He was apt to earn his living as a butcher or apprentice mechanic, or as a bouncer in a Bowery saloon or dance cellar. But he was almost always a volunteer fireman, and therein lay much of the strength of the gang, for in the early days before the Civil War the firemen, most of them strong adherents of Tammany Hall, had much to say about the conduct of the city's government. Many of the most eminent politicians belonged to the fire brigade, and there was much rivalry between the companies, which gave their engines such names as White Ghost, Black Joke, Shad Belly, Dry Bones, Red Rover, Hay Wagon, Big Six, Yaller Gal, Bean Soup, Old Junk, and Old Maid. Such famous New York political leaders as Cornelius W. Lawrence, Zophar Mills, Samuel Willetts, William M. Wood, John J. Gorman and William M. Tweed were volunteer firemen. In still earlier days even George Washington was an ardent chaser after the fire engines, and for a short time during his residence in the metropolis was head of the New York department. Before the formation of a paid fire fighting force one of the great events of the year was the Fireman's Parade, and great crowds lined the sidewalks and cheered the red-shirted, beaver-hatted brawlers as they pulled their engines over the cobble-stones, while before them marched a brass band blaring away at *Solid Men to the Front,* a rousing tune which was a favorite for many years.

But the rivalry between the fire companies whose membership included men of substance was friendly if strenuous, while the Bowery Boy loved his fire engine almost as much as he did his girl, and considered both himself and his company disgraced if his apparatus was beaten to a conflagration. And the acme of humiliation was to roll to a fire and find that all of the fire plugs had been captured by other companies. To prevent this the Bowery Boy resorted to typically direct methods. When the fire alarm sounded he simply grabbed an empty barrel from a grocery store and hurried with it to the fire plug nearest the burning building. There he turned the barrel over the plug and sat on it, and defended it valorously against the assaults of rival firemen until his own engine arrived. If he succeeded he was a hero and his company had won a notable victory. Frequently the fight for fire plugs was so fierce that the Bowery Boys had no time to extinguish the flames.

The original Bowery Boy, who followed his chieftain in so many forays against the hated Dead Rabbits and other Five Point gangs, was a burly ruffian with his chin adorned by an Uncle Sam whisker—the type of American which is still portrayed by the English comic weeklies. On his head was a stovepipe hat, generally battered, and his trousers were tucked inside his boots, while his jaws moved constantly on a chew of tobacco as he whittled on a shingle with the huge knife which never left his possession. In later years, a little before the time of Chuck Conners, the type changed as new fashions in men's clothing appeared, and the Bowery Boy promenaded his favorite thoroughfare with his head crowned by a high beaver hat with the nap divided and brushed different ways, while his stalwart figure was encased in an elegant frock coat, and about his throat was knotted a gaudy kerchief. His pantaloons, out almost as full as the modern Oxford bags, were turned up over his heavy boots. The hair on the back of his head was clipped close and his neck and chin were shaven, while his temple locks were daintily curled and heavily anointed with bear's grease or some other powerful, evil-smelling unguent. His downfall had begun in those days, but he was still an unruly and belligerent citizen, and it was unwise to give him cause for offense.

Some of the most ferocious rough-and-tumble fighters that ever cracked a skull or gouged out an eyeball fought in the ranks of the Bowery Boys, and from their rough school emerged many celebrated brawlers and political leaders. Butcher Bill Poole, a famous gangster and ward heeler, owed allegiance to the Bowery Boys, and so did his murderer, Lew Baker, who shot him to death in Stanwix Hall in 1855.

But the greatest of the Bowery Boys, and the most imposing figure in all the history of the New York gangs, was a leader who flourished in the forties, and captained the gangsters in the most important of their punitive and marauding expeditions into the Five Points. His identity remains unknown, and there is excellent reason to believe that he may be a myth, but vasty tales of his prowess and of his valor in the fights against the Dead Rabbits and the Plug Uglies have come down through the years, gaining incident and momentum as they came. Under the simple sobriquet of Mose he has become a legendary figure of truly heroic proportions, at once the Samson, the Achilles, and the Paul Bunyan of the Bowery. And beside him, in the lore of the street, marches the diminutive figure of his faithful friend and counsellor, by name Syksey, who is said to have coined the phrase "hold de butt," an impressive plea for the remains of a dead cigar.

The present generation of Bowery riffraff knows little or nothing of the mighty Mose, and only the older men who plod that now dreary and dismal relic of a great street have heard the name. But in the days before the Civil War, when the Bowery was in its heyday and the Bowery Boy was the strutting peacock of gangland, songs were sung in honor of his great deeds, and the gangsters surged into battle shouting his name and imploring his spirit to join them and lend power to their arms. He was scarcely cold in his grave before Chanfrau had immortalized him by writing *Mose, the Bowery B'hoy*, which was first performed before a clamorous audience at the old Olympic Theater in 1849, the year of the Astor Place riot.

Mose was at least eight feet tall and broad in proportion, and his colossal bulk was crowned by a great shock of flaming ginger-colored hair, on which he wore a beaver hat measuring more than two feet from crown to brim. His hands were as large as the hams of a Virginia hog, and on those rare moments when he was in repose they dangled below his knees; it was Syksey's habit to boast pridefully that his chieftain could stand erect and scratch his knee-cap. The feet of the great captain were so large that the ordinary boot of commerce would not fit his big toe; he wore especially con- structed footgear, the soles of which were copper plates studded with nails an inch long. Woe and desolation came upon the gangs of the Five Points when the great Mose leaped into their midst and began to kick and stamp; they fled in despair and hid themselves in the innermost depths of the rook- eries of Paradise Square.

The strength of the gigantic Mose was as the strength of ten men. Other Bowery Boys went into battle carrying brickbats and the ordinary stave of the time, but Mose, when accoutered for the fray, bore in one hand a great paving stone and in the other a hickory or oak wagon tongue. This was his bludgeon, and when it was lost in the heat of battle he simply up- rooted an iron lamp-post and laid about him with great zeal. Instead of the knife affected by his followers, he pinned his faith on a butcher's cleaver. Once when the Dead Rabbits overwhelmed his gang and rushed ferociously up the Bowery to wreck the Boy's headquarters, the great Mose wrenched an oak tree out of the earth, and holding it by the upper branches, em- ployed it as a flail, smiting the Dead Rabbits even as Samson smote the Philistines. The Five Points thugs broke and fled before him, but he pur- sued them into their lairs around Paradise Square and wrecked two tene- ments before his rage cooled. Again, he stood his ground before a hundred of the best brawlers of the Points, ripping huge paving blocks from the street and sidewalk and hurling them into the midst of his enemies, inflict- ing frightful losses.

In his lighter moments it was the custom of this great god of the gangs to lift a horse car off the tracks and carry it a few blocks on his shoulders, laughing uproariously at the bumping the passengers received when he set it down. And so gusty was his laugh that the car trembled on its wheels, the trees swayed as though in a storm and the Bowery was filled with a rushing roar like the thunder of Niagara. Sometimes Mose unhitched the horses and himself pulled the street car the length of the Bowery at a bewildering speed; once, if the legend is to be credited, he lifted a car above his head at Chatham Square and carried it, with the horses dangling from their traces, on the palm of his hand as far as Astor Place. Again, when a sailing ship was becalmed in the East River and drifting dangerously near the treacherous rocks of Hell Gate, Mose pulled out in a rowboat, lighted his cigar, which was more than two feet long, and sent such mighty billows of smoke against the sails that the ship was saved, and plunged down the river as though driven by a hurricane. So terrific was the force of Mose's puffs, indeed, that the vessel was into the Harbor and beyond Staten Island before it would respond to the helm. Occasionally Mose amused himself by taking up a position in the center of the river and permitting no ship to pass; as fast as they appeared he blew them back. But Mose was always very much at home in the water; he often dived off at the Battery and came up on the Staten Island beach, a distance which is now traversed by ferry boats in twenty-five minutes. He could swim the Hudson River with two mighty strokes, and required but six for a complete circuit of Manhattan Island. But when he wanted to cross the East River to Brooklyn he scorned to swim the half mile or so; he simply jumped.

When Mose quenched his thirst a drayload of beer was ordered from the brewery, and during the hot summer months he went about with a great fifty gallon keg of ale dangling from his belt in lieu of a canteen. When he dined in state the butchers of the Center and Fly markets were busy for days in advance of the great event, slicing hogs and cattle and preparing the enormous roasts which the giant needs must consume to regain his strength; and his consumption of bread was so great that a report that Mose was hungry caused a flurry in the flour market. Four quarts of oysters were but an appetizer, and soup and coffee were served to him by the barrel. For dessert and light snacks he was very fond of fruit. Historians affirm that the cherry trees of Cherry Hill and the mulberry trees of Mulberry Bend vanished because of the building up of the city, but the legend of the Bowery has it that Mose tore them up by the roots and ate the fruit; he was hungry and in no mood to wait until the cherries and mulberries could be picked.

The political geniuses of Tammany Hall were quick to see the practical value of the gangsters, and to realize the advisability of providing them with meeting and hiding places, that their favor might be curried and their peculiar talents employed on election day to assure government of, by, and for Tammany. Many ward and district leaders acquired title to the green-grocery speak-easies in which the first of the Five Points gangs had been organized, while others operated saloons and dance houses along the Bowery, or took gambling houses and places of prostitution under their protection. The underworld thus became an important factor in politics, and under the manipulation of the worthy statesmen the gangs of the Bowery and Five Points participated in the great series of riots which began with the spring election disturbances of 1834 and continued, with frequent outbreaks, for half a score of years. In this period occurred the Flour and Five Points riots, and the most important of the Abolition troubles, while there were at least two hundred battles between the gangs, and innumerable conflicts between volunteer fire companies.

During the summer of 1834 the opportunities for the gangs to engage in their natural employment were greatly increased by the appearance of two new political groups, the Native Americans and the Equal Rights Party. The latter was a disgruntled faction within Tammany Hall, and was vociferously in favor of equal rights for all citizens, and opposed to bank notes and the establishment of monopolies by legislation. The Native Americans deplored the election of foreigners to office, and vigorously demanded the repeal of the naturalization laws by which Tammany Hall had gained such an enormous following of Irish voters. The Native Americans took the place of the Whigs in some of the municipal elections, and both followed the example of Tammany and hired gangsters to blackjack their opponents and act as repeaters at the polls.

The Bowery gang known as the American Guards, the members of which prided themselves on their native ancestry, was soon devotedly attached to the Native Americans party, and responded joyfully to the appeals of its ward heelers and district leaders. During the summer of 1835, about a year after the election riots, bitter enmity developed between this gang and the O'Connell Guards, which had been organized under the aegis of a Bowery liquor seller, and was the particular champion of the Irish element of Tammany Hall. These gangs came to blows on June 21, 1835, at Grand and Crosby streets on the lower East Side. The fighting spread as far as the Five Points, where the gangsters of Paradise Square took a hand and the rioting became general throughout that part of the city. The Mayor and the Sheriff called out every watchman in the city, and the force managed to stop the fighting without the aid of soldiers, although several companies were mustered and remained in their armories overnight. Dr. W. M. Caffrey, a noted surgeon, was killed by a brickbat while trying to make his way through the mob to attend a patient, and Justice Olin M. Lowndes was seriously wounded when he entered the riot area with the police.

Several minor conflicts over the Abolition movement occurred late in 1833, and the homes of many prominent Abolitionists were bombarded with stones and bricks, but for the most part the anti-slavery agitation was obscured by the excitements of the spring election, for it was the first time that a mayor had been elected by direct vote and there was fierce fighting for three days between Tammany and the Whigs before the former was finally victorious. About the middle of 1834 the feeling against the Abolitionists, which was always very strong in the metropolis, once more flared into open violence, and on July 7 mobs attacked the Chatham street Chapel and the Bowery Theater, where Edwin Forrest was playing in *Metamora* for the benefit of the manager, an Englishman named Farren. When the police drove the rioters from the playhouse they roared down to Rose street, now a dingy thoroughfare in the residential street lined with pretentious mansions. There they launched an assault against the home of Lewis Tappan, a prominent Abolitionist, and smashed the doors and windows with stones. Swarming into the building, they wrecked the interior and pitched the furniture into the street, where it was arranged in huge piles and oil poured over it. In throwing out the pictures which had adorned the walls one of the gangsters came across a portrait of George Washington, and another thug tried to snatch it from his arms. But the discoverer hugged it to his breast and shouted dramatically:

"It's Washington! For God's sake don't burn Washington!"

His cry was taken up in the street, and the mob began to shout in unison: "For God's sake don't burn Washington!"

A line was formed, and the painting of the first President was passed tenderly down the stairs and into the street, where a group of huge bullies bore it aloft to a neighboring house. There it was installed upon the verandah and carefully guarded until the end of the riot. Sporadic outbreaks occurred during the next few days, and on July 10 a mob did great damage to residences and business houses in Spring, Catherine, Thompson, and Reade streets, while another great throng, composed almost entirely of Five Points gangsters, terrorized the area around Paradise Square. The rioters there appeared to be well organized, for runners were kept passing between the different gangs, and scouts patrolled the streets to give warning of the approach of the police and soldiers. The word spread that the gang chieftains had resolved to burn and loot every house around the Five Points that did not have a candle in a window, and soon the entire Paradise Square district blazed into illumination.

Nevertheless, a dozen buildings were sacked and set on fire, and by midnight the heavens glowed with the glare of the conflagration, while a dense pall of smoke hung low over that part of the city. Five houses of prostitution were burned, and the inmates, stripped and parcelled out among the gangsters, were shamefully mistreated. St. Philip's Negro Church in Center street was destroyed, as were three houses on the opposite side of the street, and one adjoining the church. Throughout the night the screams of tortured Negroes could be heard, and an Englishman who was captured by the thugs had both eyes gouged out and his ears torn off by the frenzied rioters. But at one o'clock in the morning, when the blare of bugles told of the coming of the military, the gang chieftains dispersed their thugs, and half an hour later the Five Points was quiet except for the tramping of the troops and the wailing of the unhappy victims who mourned beside the ruins of their homes. The next night the rioters wrecked a church in Spring street and barricaded the thoroughfare with furniture, but were routed by the Twenty-Seventh Regiment of Infantry, which destroyed the fortifications and chased the mob away without firing a shot.

The worries of the city authorities were enormously increased by the great fire of December 16–17, 1835, which raged for a day and a half with the thermometer at seventeen degrees below zero, and devastated thirteen acres in the heart of the financial district. The loss was more than $20,000,000. The conflagration started at No. 25 Merchant street and swept into Pearl street and Exchange Place, burned southward almost to Broad street, eastward to the East River, and from Wall street to Coenties Slip. Every building on the south side of Wall street from William street to the East River was destroyed, and the flames were not checked until Marines from the Navy Yard dynamited the Dutch Church, the Merchants' Exchange and other buildings, and created a gap which the fire could not cross. Several hundred houses were burned, and at least fifty others were wrecked and looted by criminals, who also raided the great heaps of furniture, jewelry and clothing which were piled in the streets without adequate guard. Much valuable property was recovered by the police a week later in the hovels of the Bowery and Five Points. Many houses and stores were set on fire by the thugs, and one man who was caught applying the torch to a building at Broad and Stone streets was seized by a group of irate citizens and hanged to a tree. His body, frozen stiff, dangled for three days before the police found time to cut it down.

Section 11   **THE HOODLUMS**

From *The Barbary Coast* by Herbert Asbury, 1933.

The most industrious persecutors of the Chinese in San Francisco were the hoodlums, young thieves and brawlers who were a veritable thorn in the flesh of the police for more than a quarter of a century. They ranged in age from twelve to thirty years and operated in organized groups which, with the exception of the Sydney Ducks and the Hounds of gold-rush days, were the only criminal gangs that the San Francisco underworld has ever produced. In general characteristics, and especially in deportment and dislike of honest labor, the hoodlums were identical with the larrikins of Australia, the hooligans of London, and the roughs and bullies of the Bowery and Five Points districts of New York. But the name by which they were designated was of San Francisco coinage. It was first used by newspaper men there during the latter part of 1868, and for at least two years always appeared in print spelled with a capital H and enclosed within quotation marks. Its first appearance as a common noun was probably in 1872, when the Sacramento *Weekly Union* of February 24 asked editorially if the boys of that city were to be "trained as polite loafers, street hounds, hoodlums, or bummers?" Within five years the word was in general use throughout the United States and had taken its proper place in the American language as the peculiarly apt designation of a young rowdy of criminal tendencies. The exact derivation of "hoodlum" is unknown, and probably always will be, in common with many other words and phrases of journalistic parentage. During the autumn of 1877 various newspapers and magazines attempted to trace its origin, but none succeeded in obtaining any definite information. In its issue of September 26, 1877 the *Congregationalist* published this account:

> "A newspaper man in San Francisco, in attempting to coin a word to designate a gang of young street Arabs under the beck of one Muldoon, hit upon the idea of dubbing them 'noodlums,' that is, simply reversing the leader's name. In writing the word, the strokes of the 'n' did not correspond in height, and the compositor taking the 'n' for an 'h' printed it hoodlums."

On October 27, 1877 the San Francisco *Call* contributed this bit of philological lore:

> "Before the late war there appeared in San Francisco a man whose dress was very peculiar. The boys took a fancy to it, and organizing themselves into a military company adopted in part the dress of this man. The head-dress resembled a fez, from which was suspended a long tail. The gamins called it a 'hood,' and the company became known as the 'hoods.' The rowdy element of the city adopted much of the dress of the company referred to, and were soon designated as hoodlums."

A third theory, favored by the present Chief of the San Francisco Police Department, William Quinn, describes the word as a corruption of Hoodler, the family name of several boisterous brothers who were frequently the objects of police attention. Another has it that the term was first applied to girls who wore a hood-like bonnet and were called "hoodlum girlums" by the street boys, who had invented a sort of pig-Latin by adding the syllable "lum" to every word. Still another, and the most plausible of all, was thus given in the Los Angeles *Express* of August 25, 1877:

> "A gang of bad boys from fourteen to nineteen years of age were associated for the purpose of stealing. These boys had a rendezvous, and when danger threatened them their words of warning were 'Huddle 'em! Huddle 'em!' An article headed 'Huddle 'Em,' describing the gang and their plans of operation, was published in the San Francisco *Times*. The name applied to them was soon contracted to hoodlum."

The man who gave this information to the *Express* had been a reporter on the staff of the *Times*, and the article referred to appeared in the latter newspaper about the middle of 1868, after the police had obtained evidence implicating the gang in more than forty robberies and had arrested several of the youngsters. The juvenile miscreants were regularly organized, and operated under the leadership of an elected captain, who planned the crimes and assigned members of the band to commit them. Their rendezvous was an abandoned shack on an old wharf, with an entrance underneath. They stole whatever they could lay their hands on and sold their loot to fences and dealers on the Barbary Coast, in the dives of which they spent their gains. The doings of the gang occupied considerable space in the newspapers for a brief period, and the boys were called, and likewise called themselves, the "Huddle 'ems." Journalists soon began referring to other youthful scoundrels as "huddle 'ems," then as huddlems and hudlems, and finally as hoodlums. The transition to hoodlum was a perfectly logical development, the more so since a majority of unlettered men are prone to lengthen their vowels, and, in particular, to pronounce the short "u" as "oo." A striking example of this tendency is the fact that the name of the former heavy-weight champion of the world is pronounced Tooney quite as often as Tunney, especially among his former associates. Another is the widespread pronounciation of "gums" as "gooms." A California writer whose memory goes back to the early days of the hoodlums and who has delved deep into the little-known phases of San Francisco life, says that he distinctly remembers the pronunciation of the word by his parents and others as "hudlem." "To my knowledge," he wrote, "it was never a police call or cry of warning, but was a password or cue for gang action—to surround, push and force the victim or victims of rowdyism into an advantageous position for mauling. I never saw a hood worn by anyone but girls and women. The appearance of a boy or man with his coat-tails turned back and up, inside out, over his head—a rough custom of the time—may account for the hood theory."

The memberships of many of the early hoodlum gangs included girls, and several were captained by maladjusted representatives of the so-called gentler sex. Curiously enough, or perhaps not so curiously, these girls were almost invariably more ferocious than their male companions, and their fertile minds devised most of the unpleasant methods of torture which the hoodlums employed upon their victims. One feminine rowdy who flourished during the latter part of 1878 was a thirteen-year-old girl known as Little Dick, who led a gang of more than twenty boys of about the same age. She was finally sent to a corrective institution, after she had stolen a hundred revolvers from a gun-shop, distributed some among her followers, and sold the remainder on the Barbary Coast. She said frankly that she found her greatest delight in throwing red pepper into a Chinaman's eyes or in hanging him up by his queue.

All of these hoodlums, of whatever age, possessed a violent antipathy to the Chinese and tormented them at every opportunity and in every conceivable way. A favorite pastime of the younger hoodlums was to board street cars on which Chinese were riding, tie the yellow men's queues together, and, if possible, cut off the ends. They were as proud of these bits of Oriental hair as a savage Indian was of an enemy's scalp. There was great rivalry among the gangs as to which could accumulate the greatest number of queue ends, which the hoodlums made into belts or cap tassels or used to decorate the walls of the shacks or rooms where they made their headquarters. The more mature hoodlums sometimes indulged also in these mischievous practices, but in the main their activities were much more criminal and vicious. They set fire to the laundries and wash-houses; invaded these and other Chinese business establishments and robbed and beat the proprietors; stole the earnings of the slave girls, and stormed the houses wherein the latter were on display and compelled them to submit to frightful abuses. Without provocation, they attacked every Chinese who ventured into parts of the city where the hoodlums were especially numerous and powerful, notably the waterfront, the Telegraph Hill district and the northern purlieus of the Barbary Coast, and the section known as Tar Flat, near the gas-works south of Market Street. A typical exploit of the hoodlums occurred during the summer of 1868, when a score of youthful rowdies captured a Chinese crab-catcher and dragged him beneath a wharf. There they robbed him, beat him with a hickory club, branded him in a dozen places with hot irons, and then slit his ears and tongue. "There was apparently no other motive for this atrocity," said the San Francisco *Times* of July 30, 1868, "than the brutal instincts of the young ruffians who perpetrated it. Such boys are constantly hanging about our wharves eager to glut their cruelty upon any Chinaman who may pass."

Hundreds of more or less similar attacks were reported to the police during the next twenty or thirty years, but the most serious of all the hoodlum outbreaks against the Chinese took place some nine years after the capture and torturing of the crab-catcher. Throughout the summer of 1877 San Francisco labored in the throes of a business depression that began with the closing down of several of the mines in the Comstock Lode, with resultant heavy losses to San Francisco investors and business men; and which was intensified by crop failures and the railroad strikes that were bringing riots and bloodshed to the Eastern states. Throughout the Bay district scores of factories and retail establishments closed their doors, and the streets of San Francisco were soon thronged by unemployed men, many of whom joined the ranks of the hoodlums. Although several factors had combined to cause the lull in business activity, political demagogues preached the gospel that it was due entirely to the presence of the Chinese in California, declaring that the pestiferous Orientals were filling thousands of jobs which should have gone to white men. For weeks almost every vacant lot in San Francisco was the scene of daily meetings at which irresponsible, crack-brained spellbinders denounced the Chinese and demanded that they be ejected from the sacred soil of California by fair means or foul.

Such violent harangues, delivered to audiences which were largely composed of hoodlums and restless discontented men without work, soon bore their natural fruit. On the night of July 24, 1877 a gang of several hundred hoodlums attacked Chinese laundries and wash-houses in various parts of the city, wrecking several and setting fire to a wash-house at Turk and Leavenworth streets. The police were not numerous enough to disperse the rioters, and throughout the night the hoodlums surged howling through the streets, attacking every Chinaman who hadn't barricaded himself within doors. Half a dozen were badly beaten before they could find shelter, and several Chinese prostitutes were dragged from their houses and horribly abused by large gangs of men. Next morning San Francisco awoke to face a situation very similar to those which in former years had caused the formation of the Vigilance committees, with the machinery of law-enforcement practically helpless and the city in danger of domination by the criminal element.

Section 12 **THE FRONTIER**

From *King Crime* by H. C. Owen, 1932.

America is rather fond of putting forward "the frontier" as an explanation of crime conditions. There is a good deal in it, of course, but not so much as is claimed. It is somewhat too easy; rather like that exculpatory, "Well, if these gangsters kill each other, who cares? The more there are dead the better." That is a view which is becoming slightly démodé.

In his book *Our Business Civilisation*, Mr. James Truslow Adams, whose family was in America a hundred years and more before the Revolution, and who knows London as well as New York, has this to say of the frontier:

> One other element may be taken into consideration, the effect of the frontier. Until thirty years ago America has always had a frontier, and that fact has been of prime importance in many respects for the national outlook. For our purpose we may merely note that in the rough life of the border there is scant recognition of law as law. Frequently remote from the courts and authority of the established communities left behind, the frontiersman not only has to enforce his own law, but he elects what laws he shall enforce and what he shall cease to observe. Payment of debt, especially to the older settlements, may come to be looked on lightly, whereas horse stealing may be punishable with shooting at sight.

Mr. Adams does not attach undue importance to the frontier. The chapter of his book from which this quotation is taken is called "Our Lawless Heritage," and in it he traces the American attitude to law, and disrespect for it, back to the earliest colonial times. He shows that the colonials always obeyed exactly what laws suited them and disregarded those that didn't. It helps to explain the Revolution. Quite irrespective of what the laws were about, why should men living in the semi-wilderness of newly settled America obey laws made by bewigged old gentlemen living in an utterly remote city called London? Perhaps it was too much to expect of human nature, especially pioneer human nature. One may go further and say, that the mere fact that laws were promulgated under kingly authority in London was sufficient to ensure that the colonists would take the keenest pleasure in flouting them, whether they were good laws or bad.

> As the Revolution drew nearer, the radicals made it a point of patriotic duty to break the English laws, and force and mob violence became more and more common. The Boston Tea Party is a case in point. That wanton destruction of fifty thousand dollars' worth of property was in no way essential to the patriotic cause, and was condemned by many of the patriotic party.

That, of course, is not the view that is imbibed by the American schoolboy. Mr. Adams shows how common this mob violence was, both before the Revolution and long after it. So it is up to our own day. It was introduced into practically all political and social disputes, and was employed impartially against Catholics, Mormons (even before they had discovered that a plurality of wives was desirable), against those who wished to abolish slavery, in racial riots and in many other ways. There was a death-roll in Kansas of two hundred in the disputes concerning whether she should enter the Union as a slave or a free State. Lynching, tarring and feathering and riding on a rail were some of the minor details of these mob movements.

In answering the questions so often asked as to whether Prohibition has made of America a nation of law-breakers, Mr. Adams says:

> Lawlessness has been and is one of the most distinctive American traits. It is obvious that a nation does not become lawless or law-abiding overnight. The United States is English in origin, and, even making allowance for the hordes of "foreigners" who have come here, there must be some reason why today England is the most law-abiding of nations and ourselves the least so. It is impossible to blame the situation on the "foreigners." The overwhelming mass of them were lawabiding in their own lands. If they become lawless here it must be largely due to the American atmosphere and conditions. There seems to me to be plenty of evidence to prove that the immigrants are made lawless by America rather than that America is made lawless by them. If the general attitude towards law, if the laws themselves and their administration, were all as sound here as in the native lands of the immigrants, those newcomers would give no more trouble here than they did at home. This is not the case, and Americans themselves are, and almost always have been, less law-abiding than the more civilised European nations.

This is a very important passage. It utters a thought which is inevitably always more or less present in the mind of one who gives any attention to this subject, but perhaps it comes much better from an American than an English writer. Imagine what Mussolini would do to an Al Capone in Italy, and how soon he would do it! And how amazing it is that with the Mafia stamped out in Sicily, this appalling organisation of extortion, kidnapping and assassination should flourish in great American cities, and terrorise the better-class Italian citizens into paying tribute! It may be true that a great portion of crime comes from "foreign" residents. But everything is done to make it easy for them.

In *The American Illusion* I wrote:

> Side by side with the inevitable lawlessness of a pio-
> neer country the cities have grown up from nothing, have
> copied from the wilderness the law of the jungle, and
> made a dingy side street in a new city more dangerous
> than ever was an Indian trail. We used to think that the
> "Wild and Woolly West" was not too safe a place, with its
> notorious "bad men." But the modern gunman of the cities
> has made the species flourish like rats in a sewer.

But although many of us have read, at one time and another, a consider-able amount of Western literature, few of us have any idea of what conditions were really like in those days. Certainly to visit Kansas City today will not give any idea of what a typical lawless "cow-town" of the 1870's was like. Kansas City has now, or had in 1928, 13,169 hotel rooms, 8,922 of which are provided with a bath, and though it has its fair share of modern crime, it does not help one to recapture the atmosphere of the old days of shacks and six-shooters.

Most of our impressions of old Western days are derived from fiction, and that is not too reliable a guide. But fortunately American writers have been reconstructing frontier history before it is too late to know the facts of it, and in the remainder of this chapter we are able to take a social peep into the life of a typical—indeed a notorious—cow-town, almost as though the events described were taking place before our wondering eyes.

The Kansas "cow-towns" of the 1870's included Abilene, Newton, Cald-well, Ellsworth, Hunnewell, Hays, Wichita, and Dodge. One town was like another in the heydey of their untrammelled iniquity, blatantly lawless, up-roariously sinful and boastfully bad. "Too wild to be curried, too tough to be tamed," as the local braggarts put it. Each town had an unconsecrated grave-yard known as Boot Hill, in which were buried all those who died with their boots on.

These various towns—they were really villages—were terminals of the long trail from Texas, up which during a short period of years 100,000,000 beef cattle and 10,000,000 horses were brought, mostly for transport by rail to the eastern areas of the United States. The cowboys who brought them up were all Texans, although they were not all born in that wide state, hailing also from New Mexico, Colorado and Arizona. But they were all Texans to the cattle trade. They were the trouble makers of the frontier, and in times of trouble the Texans all stood together. Many of them were veterans, or sons of veterans, of the Southern forces in the Civil War, and still cherished a lively hate of the Northerners. Mr. Stuart N. Lake writes in his book *Wyatt Earp—Frontier Marshal:*

> To them, the Lost Cause was still a living issue; one to justify particularly any subterfuge by which a Northern man might be discomfited in any degree, or, if fate was kind, goaded into a fight. To a trail outfit of this character, the completeness of success on a season's drive to Kansas was measured in the names of Northern settlements they had "treed" or of Northern men—peace officers preferably —they had killed, which could be chalked on the sides of the homeward-bound chuck-wagon as a record for Texas to read and envy.

These cow-towns, with only a few hundred actual inhabitants, would have a score or more of saloons and gambling-houses, and half a score of dance-halls, in which the girls were hostesses in the most generous sense. Honky-tonks and hurdie-gurdies these prairie houses of assignation were called, and they were open all the twenty-four hours. In such a town there might be 2,500 cowboys from Texas populating the main street, wandering from one resort to another with their tens of thousands of head of cattle grazing the local prairies, easily available for rounding up at any moment, to be transported to the Eastern States. Every man wore two six-shooters at his belt. Even in those days also (as was noted with the gangs of New York), the custom was known of carrying a pistol under the armpit. Apart from the throngs of cowboys, all of them likely to "break loose" at any moment, there were famous gun-fighters and notorious gunmen. The gun-fighter was not a bad man. The gunman was. Cold-blooded assassination was frowned on. All shooting had to be done face to face. Many men could shoot from the draw with amazing dexterity. It can be imagined that among such a community the official who was upholding the law, even in the most rough-and-ready fashion, had to be a man of exceptional qualities.

> Against the hordes of wild and lawless gun-toters, as well as against the throngs of rustlers, murderers, thugs and highwaymen who flocked to fatten upon the untold

riches in cattle and coin which the gunmen themselves
commanded, the gun-fighter came upon the Western stage,
as fearless, as reckless of his life, and as skilled with
weapons as the outlaws he was to subdue. . . . As a rule,
this gun-fighting peace officer bore the title of marshal,
and he was far more than a policeman; often he was, perforce, not only the arresting officer but witness, prosecuting attorney, jury and executioner all in one.

In the summer of 1873, Ellsworth, by a combination of circumstances,
found itself exalted into being the wildest cow-town of the West. In this
little place of 300 settled inhabitants there were at least 1,500 Texan cowboys,
all with long months of hard work in a featureless wilderness behind them,
and with plenty of money to spend. To them the sun-baked plaza of Ellsworth, ankle deep in dust, with the saloons, dance-halls and "hotels" surrounding it, was Broadway. Owing to a great financial slump throughout the
country, there were 150,000 cattle grazing on the vast prairies surrounding
the little town, waiting for better prices before being shipped East, and the
Texans had to stay near them. Thus for a few short months Ellsworth was a
miniature metropolis of toughness, with cowboys sleeping six and seven in
a room.

The elders of the city had done very handsomely, as they thought, in
providing a counterpoise to all this lawlessness. They engaged a marshal,
Brocky Jack Norton, and three deputy-marshals, Happy Jack Morco, Charlie
Brown and Ed Crawford. The county sheriff C. B. Whitney, had also come
into town with a deputy sheriff, John Hogue. All were very noted men with
the .45, and several had long records of legitimate killings behind them.

But there were also in town two brothers with as tough reputations as
any of the wide Wild West, Ben and Bill Thompson, hailing from England.
They had emigrated to Texas with their father as youths or boys, and Ben,
the elder, had fought with a Texas regiment in the Civil War, became—so it
was said—a captain, and afterwards fought in Mexico for the Emperor
Maximilian, returning to Texas with the collapse of the empire. By the early
1870's, he and his brother had gambled and shot their way "through almost
every frontier town between the Rio Grande and the Canadian line."

Gambling was their trade now, and for some two months Ben had been
operating his faro bank at the modest Grand Central Hotel of Ellsworth,
and doing just what he pleased with the town. He was the acknowledged
leader of his tough younger brother, Bill, and of all the other Texans. Ben's
record as Wild West killer was very long. Reports gave him fifty victims,
but it has been definitely established that by the time they arrived in Ellsworth the two brothers had killed at least twenty-seven men in their various
gun-fights.

There was another famous visitor in town. This was Wyatt Earp, a young man, but already famous as a buffalo hunter, famous also as a marvellously quick and sure revolver shot, and destined to be known as one of the greatest marshals in all the West. A quiet young man, he had come to see what the cattle business was doing as a change from buffalo hunting. But the slump was on; there was nothing to do in Ellsworth but hang around. Wyatt Earp, being no drinker, was passing his time with a little desultory gambling.

The word is now with Mr. Stuart N. Lake:

> Early in the afternoon of August 18, 1873, Wyatt Earp had the sun-scorched Ellsworth plaza almost to himself as he lounged in the shade of a wooden awning which sheltered jointly the front of Beebe's General Store and Brennan's Saloon, next door. At intervals someone passed on the walk, a group of cowboys came out of one saloon to enter another, or a sweating horseman rode in from the prairie, hitched his cayuse and sought relief from the blazing heat at a favourable bar. For the most part, the dusty cow-town square was devoid of all life except the drooping horses tethered to the rails at either side of the roadway and the attendant swarms of flies. Sweltering, wild and woolly Ellsworth appeared as peaceful as some cool green-and-white New England village.

> In a saloon three or four doors beyond Brennan's Wyatt knew, an open poker game was in progress, with stakes of unusual size and with several herd owners and cattle buyers at the table. Play had been under way for some hours and had become so high that when word of it reached the Grand Central, the Thompsons placed their faro bank in charge of an assistant and hastened over to sit in. When informed of a table rule forbidding players to wear guns, Ben and Bill were still sufficiently intrigued by the size of the pots to send their weapons back to the Grand Central and draw cards. Wyatt had heard that after the Thompsons joined the game they took to forcing the play, that Bill was drinking steadily and getting mean. Whereupon he was well satisfied that he had declined an earlier invitation to sit in. Wyatt had small fancy for the Thompsons in any case, least of all for Bill in a poker game for high stakes, and drunk.

> From the saloon in which the Thompsons were gambling the sudden uproar of a violent quarrel was followed by the appearance of the brothers on the plaza. They came out of the door on the run, Bill cursing loudly and shouting threats over his shoulder as the pair made for the Grand

Central. A moment later they came out of the hotel and headed back toward the saloon, Ben carrying a double-barreled shot-gun and Bill a rifle. At the rail in front of the saloon stood a pair of horses hitched to a hay-wagon, and behind this rack the Thompsons took their stand; Bill still shouting threats and imprecations and Ben now adding his profanely insulting invitations to those inside the saloon to "Come out and make your fight."

Wyatt stepped from the walk into Beebe's doorway, where he would have cover from stray lead while he kept an eye on proceedings. By this time the racket made by the belligerent brothers had drawn several hundred persons from the various establishments bordering the plaza, as hopefully interested spectators of the impending fight. From his store, Sheriff Whitney hurried to the scene, stopping at Beebe's doorway to ask Wyatt if he knew what had started the row. The question was answered by another onlooker, who had been a bystander at the poker game.

"John Sterling (a wealthy herd owner) slapped Bill Thompson's face," this person volunteered. "Bill got nasty and John gave him the flat of his hand across the mouth. Then Bill invited John to get a gun and meet him outside. John hit him again, and knocked him out of his seat. Then Bill and Ben ran after their guns."

Sheriff Whitney was in his shirt-sleeves and palpably unarmed, yet without further hesitation he walked over to the hay-wagon where the Thompsons stood with cocked weapons, waiting for someone to come out of the saloon.

"You keep out of this, sheriff," Ben warned. "We don't want to hurt you."

"Don't be foolish, Ben," Whitney replied.

Thompson's rejoinder was a torrent of profanity directed at Sterling and his friends, whereupon the sheriff went into the saloon. He returned to the walk a few minutes later with word that Sterling had been forcibly prevented from coming out to fight, and had been taken by friends to his camp outside of the town by way of the saloon's rear door.

Whitney knew that the Thompsons would not attack the Sterling camp, where the cattleman would have the support of a score of cowboys, but he did fear that Sterling might be shot on sight by one of the Thompsons when he again came into Ellsworth. As this was to be avoided if possible, the sheriff tried to smooth over the quarrel. He invited the Thompsons into Brennan's saloon for a drink and a talk. The cow-punchers and merchants who had flocked out to see a fight returned to their pursuits indoors, and as Wyatt moved back to his lounging place between Brennan's doorway and Beebe's entrance, he again had the plaza to himself. Fifteen minutes later Whitney came out of the saloon alone and stopped to talk.

"They've calmed down a bit," the sheriff reported, "and they've promised they won't go gunning for Sterling. They're inside with a bunch of Texas men."

"Did you take their guns away from them?" Wyatt asked.

"No," Whitney replied; "they wouldn't have stood for that."

Before Wyatt had time to comment on this matter, Bill Thompson appeared in Brennan's doorway with Ben's shotgun.

"I'll get a sheriff if I don't get anybody else," he declared. As Wyatt and Whitney turned to face him, Bill fired both barrels of the gun—eighteen buckshot—point-blank into the sheriff's breast and ran back into the saloon.

Wyatt caught Whitney in his arms as he reeled under the impact of the shotgun charge.

"I'm done," the sheriff gasped. "Get me home."

At the roar of gunfire, saloon, hotels and stores spouted 500 men into the plaza, nine-tenths of them Texas gun-toters, the unarmed minority Ellsworth citizens. As Wyatt carried Whitney to a wagon standing in the roadway, Ben and Bill Thompson walked out of Brennan's to the string of saddled cow ponies hitched at the nearest rail, Ben covering the flank of their course with the rifle, Bill the other with the shotgun. In front of the Grand Central the Thompson following was collecting under the leadership of George Peshaur, Cad Pierce, Neil Kane and John Good. The brothers were protected from attack in that quarter. Ben and Bill swung their gun muzzles back and forth to hold in check any move against them as they argued over ensuing procedure. The account of what followed as given in that week's issue of *The Ellsworth Reporter* confirms Wyatt Earp's recollection.

Friends of Sheriff Whitney volunteered to take the dying man home, and Wyatt turned his attention to the Thompsons, still arguing at the horse rail. In anticipation of shooting that might become promiscuous, he stepped again into the protection of Beebe's entrance and peered from the cover of the door casing around the plaza for a sight of the Ellsworth peace officers. None were within view. Wyatt turned as Beebe's door opened at his shoulder, and there was Happy Jack Morco, Indian fighter and six-gun expert, with two belts of ammunition around his waist and a .45 at either hip. Happy Jack had approached by way of Beebe's rear entrance. Wyatt gave way to let Morco reconnoiter.

Happy Jack peeped cautiously around the door casing. Without pausing in his argument with his brother or troubling to sight his rifle, Ben took a pot-shot. The bullet splintered the woodwork half an inch above the deputy marshal's head, and he ducked for cover.

"Too high," Ben informed Bill with an oath of regret. "Get on that horse and get out of here before Whitney's friends get organised. Take this rifle and give me my shotgun. I'll cover your get-away."

As Bill Thompson rode out of shooting range, Ben, still covering the assembled citizens with his shotgun, backed over to the Grand Central. A Texas man brought out his six-guns and their ammunition belts, which he buckled into place. With his favourites at his hips and the shotgun in the crook of his arm, he paraded up and down in front of the hotel, shouting taunts and threats at the town of Ellsworth in general and its peace officers in profane particular. At his back were 100 Texas men, at least half of them man-killers of record and the rest more than willing to be. Peshaur, Pierce, Good and Kane were in line, slightly in advance of the crowd. In groups, at other points around the plaza, possibly 300 or 400 more of the Texas element were distributed. Every manjack of them had six-guns at his hips and a gun hand itching for play. As Ben Thompson halted his tirade for a moment, Cad Pierce stepped into the limelight.

"I'll give $1,000 to anybody who'll knock off another marshal!" he shouted.

As the cowboys yelled their appreciation of this offer, Deputy Marshal Brown appeared for an instant at the far end of one of the railroad buildings. A hundred .45 slugs whined across the plaza, and Brown took cover.

Wyatt and Happy Jack Morco were still in Beebe's doorway, and Ben Thompson was still strutting up and down before his six-gun satellites, when Mayor Miller edged around the corner and joined the two in the store entrance. Brocky Jack Norton, the marshal, came through Beebe's from the rear; he, too, wore a pair of .45-caliber guns. Deputy Marshal Brown, armed with a rifle and revolvers, was somewhere behind the railroad shacks. Deputy Marshal Crawford had not made the gesture of plaza appearance. While Wyatt and several others who were in the store behind him listened, the mayor wasted ten minutes of time and breath in issuing orders to his marshal and deputy for Ben Thompson's capture. Neither Brocky Jack nor Happy Jack relished the risk involved by obedience, and said so.

Mayor Miller tried another tack. He called across the plaza to Thompson, ordering the gunman to lay down his arms and submit to arrest. Ben answered with raucous profanity, at which his followers whooped their glee. Ellsworth was treed at the tip of the topmost limb.

"Nice police force you've got," Wyatt said to Miller. The mayor apparently noticed him for the first time.

"Who are you?" Miller demanded.

"Just a looker-on," Wyatt replied.

"Well, don't talk so much," Miller snapped. "You haven't even got a gun."

As Wyatt was in shirt-sleeves, it was evident that he was unarmed. He seldom carried weapons in the settlements, and those he owned were in his hotel room.

"It's none of my business," Wyatt admitted, "but if it was, I'd soon get me a gun, and I'd either arrest Ben Thompson or kill him."

Brocky Jack erred, as far as his job was concerned.

"Don't pay any attention to that kid, Jim," he advised.

But Miller was desperate. "You're fired, Norton," he said. "You too, Morco." As he spoke, the mayor snatched the marshal's star from Brocky Jack's shirt front. "As soon as I can find Brown and Crawford, I'll fire them." He turned to Wyatt Earp. "I'll make this your business. You're marshal of Ellsworth. Here's your star. Go into Beebe's and get yourself some guns. I order you to arrest Ben Thompson."

To the best of Wyatt Earp's recollection, he voiced no formal acceptance of his impromptu appointment as an Ellsworth peace officer. Without a word to the mayor or the chagrined marshals, he turned and walked to Beebe's firearms counter and asked for a pair of second-hand .45's, with holsters, cartridge belts and ammunition.

"New guns," he explained in after years, "would have been stiff and might have slowed me down. The same would have held true with new holsters. So I asked for equipment that had been used."

Selecting two six-shooters with trigger dogs that some former gunwise owner had filed to split-second smoothness, and a pair of well-worn holsters, Wyatt tested the weapons thoroughly, loaded five cylinders in each, spun them, filled the cartridge loops of the belts, settled his weapons to the preferred positions at his hips and walked out to the plaza. He said nothing to Mayor Miller or the two Jacks as he passed them. Not one of the three offered him either company or advice. Beebe's clerk was but one of several Ellsworth citizens who always asserted that the trio remained huddled in the doorway while the youthful marshal *pro tem* walked out to face the deadliest gunman then living.

Wyatt Earp's short journey across the Ellsworth plaza under the muzzle of Ben Thompson's shotgun has been described a thousand times in all its detail in the reminiscent yarns of old-timers, with whom, as the most competent judges of its significance, it established for all time his preeminence among gunfighters of the West, but for some reason the episode has been ignored in written tales of later years. The fact that Ellsworth never attained in the popular mind the fame of Wichita and Dodge as a top-notch cow-town, that its glory was but a season long, may have been responsible for this oversight; at any rate, not more than a handful of the narrators of Earp history seem to have been aware that Wyatt was marshal of Ellsworth for one illustrious hour.

His appointment, it is true, was not entered in the municipal records, and he was never paid for the time he served, yet the amazing single exploit of his brief incumbency was the word-of-mouth sensation of '73 from the Platte to the Rio Grande.

As the young man stepped from the shelter of Beebe's door he pulled once at the brim of his black sombrero as if to set it more firmly in place, and started diagonally across the plaza toward the Grand Central. Thompson and his Texas men, of course, saw him coming, and Ben squared around, shifting his shotgun before him to hold the weapon across his stomach, with his left hand under the barrels and his right on the grip and triggers. From that position a single motion would bring it into play.

Ben Thompson was a squarely built, stocky fellow, about five feet eight inches in height and weighing probably 170 pounds. The pudginess of his face was emphasized by bushy brows above his wide blue eyes and a sweeping mustache which drooped underneath his fat cheeks. Although only thirty years old, he had the appearance of greater maturity, and this, as well as his bulkiness, was accentuated as he squatted slightly in readiness for the most effective handling of his gun.

Wyatt Earp, as he walked across the plaza, looked like a mere boy, the onlookers always said. Despite his six feet of height and his exceptional strength, he gave the impression of youth and slenderness. As he walked, his hands swung easily at his sides, conveniently close to his holsters, but making no overt moves.

As Earp reached a point possibly fifty yards from Thompson, Cad Pierce said something, to which Ben snarled over his shoulder a reply. Pierce subsided and, with the rest of the Texas men, waited for his leader to call the turn.

Wyatt Earp had a definite course of action firmly fixed in his mind as he advanced toward the 100 or more half-drunken cowboys, any and all of whom were keyed to cutting loose at him with twice that many guns for the mere satisfaction of seeing him die. He knew that to half the men in the crowd he was probably an utter stranger, and that the rest knew him only casually by sight or by name; that he had no fear-inspiring record as a killer, and, so far as anyone in Ellsworth might know, he had never gone for his guns against a human adversary in all his life. He realised that he was a target that not one man in the 100 could miss at fifty yards. That he was heeled with a pair of guns was evident to all; one false or hesitant gesture with either of his hands and he was fair game for the first man to draw.

"I knew what I would do before the mayor pinned Brocky Jack's badge on my shirt," Wyatt said in recounting the affair.

"I based my action on my certain knowledge of Ben Thompson's vanity and of the Texas men in his crowd. In the first place, I knew better than to walk out of Beebe's with a gun in my hand. If I had, I would have been filled with lead before I reached the road. But I also knew that as long as I did not draw, the Texas men would leave it to Ben to make the play; he would have turned and shot any one of them who dared to cut loose before he opened the ball. Whatever happened would first be between him and me.

"So all I had to do was keep my eye on Ben's shotgun—not on the muzzle, but on the point where his right hand grasped the grip and trigger guard. That, at the same time, held my eye on the target I had selected—his stomach just back of his hand. I figured that he'd wait for me to get within thirty or forty yards of him to make his weapon most effective, and that he could not get his shotgun into action without telegraphing the move, as a boxer might put it, through his wrist. When I saw his wrist move to put his arm muscles into play, I'd go for my guns, and I had enough confidence in myself to be certain that I could put at least one slug into his belly before he could pull a trigger.

"I realised that after I'd plugged Ben some of his crowd might get me, and I had some idea, I suppose of taking as many of them with me as I could. Beyond having figured to get Cad Pierce after I got Ben, if that was possible, and I don't recall thinking much about that. The Whitney shooting had incensed me to a point, I imagine, where all I really cared about was heading Ben Thompson into his hole. The mayor had told me to arrest him, and I intended to do that if I could. But it was a moral certainty that he'd try to shoot. If he did, I knew that I'd kill him. I could hit a target the size of his stomach ten times out of ten shots with a .45 at any range up to 100 yards, and I had perfect confidence in my speed."

When Wyatt Earp was about forty yards distant, Ben Thompson called to him.

"What do you want, Wyatt?"

"I want you, Ben," Wyatt replied, walking steadily forward.

Neither Ben Thompson nor any onlooker, and least of all Wyatt Earp, has offered a completely satisfactory explanation for what followed. Thompson made no move with his gun, and did not speak again until Wyatt was less than thirty yards away.

"I'd rather talk than fight," the killer suggested.

"I'll get you either way, Ben," Wyatt assured him, without halting in his stride.

"Wait a minute," said Thompson. "What do you want me to do?"

"Throw your shotgun into the road, put up your hands and tell your friends to stay out of this play," Wyatt answered. Less than fifteen yards now separated the men.

"Will you stop where you are and let me talk to you?" Ben asked.

Wyatt halted for the first time since leaving Beebe's.

He now knew positively that he could take Thompson, alive or dead, whichever way the gunman chose to turn events. He had Ben talking, which is the gravest error possible to a gun-thrower who has serious business at hand.

"What are you going to do with me?" Thompson asked.

"Kill you or take you to jail," Wyatt informed him.

"Brown's over there by the depot with a rifle," Ben objected. "The minute I give up my guns he'll cut loose at me."

"If he does," Wyatt promised, "I'll give you back your guns and we'll shoot it out with him. You'll be my prisoner, and as long as you're in my custody, the man that gets you will have to get me."

Thompson hesitated.

"Come on," Wyatt ordered; "throw down your gun or go to fighting. Which is it?"

Ben Thompson grinned. "You win," he said, tossed his shotgun into the road and shoved both hands above his head.

Wyatt Earp's guns were still in their holsters. Now, for the first time, he moved his hand to the butt at his hip.

"You fellows get back," he ordered the Texas men. "Move."

As they obeyed, Wyatt stepped up to Thompson and unbuckled his prisoner's gun belts.

"Come on, Ben," he said. "We'll go down to the calaboose."

With the famous Thompson six-guns dangling from the belts which he carried looped in his left hand, Wyatt marched his prisoner across the plaza to the court of Judge V. B. Osborne. Until he reached the entrance to the judge's office, no one of the onlookers spoke to him or moved to follow. Once Wyatt and Ben were inside, the mayor and his erstwhile officers hurried after them. A moment later 500 milling men stormed at the narrow doorway, with Thompson's friends in the forefront of the mob.

Deputy Sheriff Hogue, who had just ridden into town, forced a way through the crowd, and as Wyatt was explaining the situation to him, a messenger from the Whitney home arrived outside with the shouted news that the sheriff was dead. The announcement was premature—Whitney actually lived for several hours after the Thompson hearing—but to the mob it was final, and they disposed themselves accordingly.

There was some talk of lynching, but Wyatt anticipated no trouble of that nature which he could not handle; real danger, he knew, would come with any attempt on the part of the Texas men to rescue Ben from the toils of the law. The Thompson element in the crowd dictated his next move. Peshaur, Pierce, Kane and Good shouldered into the front rank of spectators, each of the quartet with his .45's belted to his waist, and Pierce carrying the shotgun with which Whitney had been assassinated and which Ben had thrown into the road. Wyatt spoke to Hogue in an undertone, then turned on the gunmen.

"Get out of here," he ordered. "Pierce, take your crowd outside and keep 'em there. There'll be no lynching and no rescue."

Pierce looked to Thompson for some signal.

"Better go, Cad," Ben suggested. "Wyatt means what he says."

With the court-room cleared, Hogue was stationed at the door to hold back the crowd, and Thompson's arraignment proceeded.

"What's the charge?" asked Judge Osborne.

As no one else volunteered a reply, Wyatt suggested that Ben was probably an accessory to murder. The judge turned to Mayor Miller as the proper person to indicate the enormity of Thompson's offence against the Ellsworth citizenry. The mayor hesitated, possibly in embarrassment under the keen blue eye of his hastily selected peace officer, considered the economic importance of the Texas men to the community, then offered as an amendment his opinion that maybe Ben had disturbed the peace.

"Guilty," said the judge. "Twenty-five dollars fine."

Thompson grinned, as he peeled the assessment from a roll of greenbacks.

"Do I get my guns?" he inquired.

"Certainly," said the Judge. "You have paid your fine and the marshal will restore any property he may have taken from you."

As Thompson reached for his gun belts, Wyatt issued his last order as an Ellsworth peace officer.

"Ben," he said, "court or no court, don't you put those on here. You carry them straight to the Grand Central. Don't stop to talk with anyone on the way. Don't so much as hesitate. I'll be watching you from the doorway. Keep moving until you're out of my sight. After that, what you do will be none of my business."

Wyatt stood at the entrance to the judge's office with

his eye on Thompson until the gunman disappeared through the doors of the Grand Central. Then he turned to Mayor Miller who stood beside him.

"Here," he said, "is your badge and here are the guns I got at Beebe's. I don't need 'em any longer."

"Don't you want to be marshal of Ellsworth?" Miller asked.

"I do not," Wyatt replied.

"We'll pay you $125 a month if you'll keep the job," the mayor offered.

"Ellsworth," Wyatt answered sententiously, "figures sheriffs at twenty-five dollars a head. I don't figure the town's my size."

After reading that it is unnecessary, even an anticlimax, to write anything more about the frontier. It is all there, and the types represented by Wyatt Earp, Ben Thompson and the ladies of the dance-halls are all playing their parts in the American situation today. And the "honest cop" in Chicago and elsewhere has perhaps even a more difficult role to play in 1932 than Wyatt Earp had in 1873.

Section 13   THE GANG RUNS DENVER

From *Fighting the Underworld* by Philip S. VanCise, 1936.

Crime is of two kinds—organized and unorganized. The ordinary murderer, highwayman, thief, or embezzler is an unorganized criminal who operates by himself. When he commits a crime the hand of everyone in society is raised against him. He is easily apprehended, speedily convicted, and lands in the penitentiary with very little difficulty.

The other class of criminals, however, the organized groups, work in gangs running from two or three to almost any number. They may devote their energies to one community, or spread across the country from coast to coast, or become international in their scope. Among these are racketeers of all kinds—kidnapers, bank-robbers, bootleggers, dope-peddlers, and confidence-men.

All of them secure some measure of protection either from the police departments, Federal agents, or elected officials. In some towns only a limited assistance is given; in others the system is almost airtight—so much so that criminals belonging to the organization may ply their trade with impunity, while those outside the pale are arrested and run out of town, or suffer the extreme penalty of the law.

In 1922, Denver was in the ironclad class and had been for many years. The evil genius and dominating power in its underworld was Lou Blonger, a short, heavy-set, affable fellow of French-Canadian descent, who came to this country from Canada in his early boyhood, and settled in the Western mining camps. He first appeared in Denver in 1880 with his brother Sam as a bartender, then became the proprietor of a saloon with all the early-day accessories of a dance-hall and the necessary girl attendants, roulette wheels and all kinds of gambling. As society became more respectable in the West, the girls were first eliminated, then the gambling, until only the saloon was left.

Accustomed from the early days to paying the police for protection and special privileges for his own place, and owing to his native shrewdness and innate knowledge of police conditions, Blonger gradually attained a position of affluence in the community. In the late eighties he became a 'fixer' and the friend of the Chief of Police, and in large measure determined what protected crooks should operate in the town. This power once attained was pushed to the utmost, so that, as time passed, he gradually 'got something on' various aspirants for, or those holding, public office, until his will and money were powerful factors in the political field in the Rocky Mountain metropolis.

At one time, while Blonger was operating a saloon, a private telephone line ran directly from his office to that of the Chief of Police, and upon his orders men were arrested or turned loose. He was the king of the Denver underworld.

In the early nineties Soapy Smith came to town. Soapy was then known throughout the West as a slicker, or con-man, and his method of operation was rather open and aboveboard, simply setting up a wagon with flaring gasoline torches and a large number of packages of soap wrapped up in paper, standing by a little table giving the 'ballyhoo' talk to get a crowd together, and then offering to sell soap with five or ten dollar bills in it for one dollar a cake.

He would pick up several bars and apparently wrap a five or ten dollar bill with each, then carelessly throw the cakes on the table with the others, mix them up, and sell them at one dollar apiece, or bet any amount with any of the spectators that they could not pick a package with the cash in it. The money, of course, he would always palm, although once in a while a sucker, as victims are called, would get a cake to stimulate trade. Soapy would harvest from fifty to a hundred dollars a night. Blonger got half as his share for keeping the police away.

In those days the gold-brick artist flourished and every circus carried its quota of pickpockets, shell-game experts, and other grafters. When they came to town, all called at Blonger's office to get permission to operate, and one of his men would be on the job to get his fair share of the cut.

By 1898, so notorious had Blonger become that in that year the *Rocky Mountain News* carried a front-page article about his having been trimmed by an even cleverer rascal. Its headlines read: 'Got caught—Lou Blonger complains that he has been buncoed. Strange news for the police.'

And then it went on to state:

Lou Blonger has been buncoed. This is about the most startling piece of news the police department has received in a long time. It is not hard work to find it, either, as Blonger 'yelled' louder than the backwoodsman from Indiana who bought the gold brick. It was a long time before Blonger could induce the detectives to take the 'yell' seriously.

Yesterday evening Blonger appeared at the police station much excited and exclaimed that he had been buncoed. All the detectives were taken with a fit of laughter. Their mouths stretched and their sides shook. Tears rolled down their cheeks and it was fifteen minutes before they could compose themselves. They were listening to Blonger's tale of woe.

Blonger has the reputation of being a bunco-man himself and for years had everything his own way on lower Seventeenth Street, where he successfully managed a gang of the shrewdest confidence-men in the country. This was the reason the detectives laughed so heartily when Blonger said he was buncoed.

Two years later Dick Turner, a deputy sheriff from Weld County, came to Denver and stopped at the Albany Hotel. Shortly afterwards, while in the lobby, he was 'picked up' by a con-man who tried to swindle him, but Turner was too shrewd, and got away. He then went to the police, secured a detective and went back for his man. The fellow was still there, looking for another victim, and as he was being arrested Lou Blonger came in.

'What's all this fuss about?' demanded Lou.

'Nothing much, except one of your boys is running a little wild,' responded the detective.

Quickly getting the details, Blonger turned on the man and said: 'You were recommended to me as a first-class bunco artist, and the first thing you do, you damn——, is to pick up a deputy sheriff. What the hell are you tackling the Law for, anyway? Don't you have sense enough to let Colorado people alone in Denver? I paid your transportation to Denver and put you to work. Now you walk back, and start now.'

And getting a hack, Blonger, the deputy sheriff, and the city dick accompanied the disconsolate crook to the city limits, where, under Lou's caustic tongue, he started the hike east over the railroad ties.

Lou also liked the ladies. In his early days he had married a successful variety actress, who was a high-class woman, but as he grew older they drifted apart. They were never divorced, and he spent some of his time with her. But his real romance arose out of an arrest. Two of the city detectives were not in the good graces of Mike Delaney, Chief of Police in 1904. So, one evening, when they were having dinner with two girls, the patrol wagon backed up to the door, and under Delaney's orders all four were arrested and thrown into jail. The officers made bond and got out at once, but Mike refused to release the women.

One of the men then went to Blonger and told him about the girls, and Lou at once telephoned Delaney and ordered him to let them go. He did, and the next day they called on Blonger to thank him for his help. Immediately he was attracted to the younger one. She was only about nineteen. He gave her a musical education and lavished money on her until her marriage a few years later.

Shortly afterwards, however, she divorced her husband, and from then on was Blonger's mistress. She called for him in the evening, drove him out to his farm, and was constantly subject to his beck and call. Her name in this book is Berna Rames.

In 1921, Blonger built a beautiful bungalow for Berna on Capitol Hill, at 601 Williams Street, right across the alley from fashionable Ascension Episcopal Church. It cost thirty thousand dollars. Nothing was spared in its construction, and only the best material was used.

A large garage was in the high-ceilinged basement, with a covered roof over a walled-in entrance-way. Small windows enabled the occupants of the house to see what visitor was calling before opening the door for his car. And at night prominent politicians, with side curtains drawn to hide the occupants, drove to the garage entrance, there to be identified and admitted for their private business. An adjacent large billiard room, with cozy fireplace and comfortable chairs, was the setting for the conferences.

The town became more and more protected as the police and various officials came under the sway of the underworld, and many kinds of confidence-games began to be evolved. At first there would be only three or four men in each group and they would use a 'salted' mine, or a swindle of any sort to separate the victim from his money. Then came the era of fake-horse-and-foot-races, and wire-tapping, which allowed much larger gangs to operate.

In them the victim always engaged in a crooked deal, and this narrowed the field of suckers to the inherently shady classes of the community. This weakness made it impossible for gangsters to reach out for honest but careless men who might be willing to go into a good investment if it looked as if they had a sure thing for their money. But for fifteen years these fake-race swindlers flourished all over the country.

In the foot-race the victim would usually have a secret meeting with the man whom he was betting against in which that fellow would agree to throw the race.

In the horse-race he would be led stealthily to the stall where dope was apparently shot into the opposing animal.

In the fake wire-tapping he was taken to a room fixed up as a pool-hall with telegraph instruments ticking merrily, with huge blackboards on which the names of the horses appeared with the betting odds, and the results of the races. A good-sized crowd of boosters would be present making bets and winning and losing money in large amounts. He was then taken to another room which had only a single telegraph company, that the operator was bribed so as to relay the races slowly to the poolhall, and that they therefore got the information and final outcome of the race in advance of the time when the pool-hall downstairs closed its bets. So he was told that in this way they could go down and make a great cleaning playing any horse.

In these dealings, of course, the victim was trying to win by a dishonest transaction, but was dealing with rogues smarter than himself. When he lost his money and started to fight, they laughed at him and told him that he was a crook himself—that if he wanted to prosecute he could go as far as he wished, but that he couldn't get anywhere, and might land in the penitentiary himself.

While this was an incorrect statement of the law, and a vigorous prosecution would have convicted the gang, the sucker was so guilty and they were so adroit that only a small percentage ever complained to the authorities. When they did, the police departments in turn also called them crooks and refused to help them, so that a prosecution was almost unheard of. The Federal Government finally stepped in with its famous Maybray gang prosecution at Council Bluffs in 1910, in which all the defendants were convicted and this class of criminality effectually stopped. But the Denver chieftain, though involved, escaped.

As soon as prosecution was rumored, powerful political influences were set in motion to prevent any exposure of Blonger's connection with the gang. To insure success, the partner of the United States District Attorney, accompanied by a deputy United States Marshal, went to Council Bluffs. They persuaded the Federal authorities to omit Lou Blonger from the list of those indicted. But to make sure that no possible whisper of that name should occur, all during the trial, which lasted several weeks, the lawyer and the Deputy Marshal were in daily attendance. Their efforts were successful, because not a witness testified about Denver or its squat overlord.

Meanwhile, to Blonger's charmed circle had been added an assistant who relieved Blonger of details and left him free for larger operations. About 1896 this man—a little fellow, only twenty-two years old, agile, wiry and active, about five-feet-five in height, with a heavy head of wavy black hair, named Adolph W. Duff, alias 'Kid Duffy'—appeared in the underworld in Colorado Springs. He was a pickpocket, opium-smoker or hop-head, and gambler. He was befriended by a man named Byron Hames, who lent him enough money to get on his feet. Duff established friendly relations with the police department, ran out the other grafters, and became an underworld leader, ending by chasing his friend Hames out of the place without repaying him anything.

Duff soon became one of the members of the old Webb City gang, later the Maybray, already referred to, and helped to trim suckers in fake foot-races in the Garden of the Gods. He never served time, though he was frequently arrested and had many felony cases filed against him in the District Court. On at least four occasions these cases were dismissed by request of the District Attorney of El Paso County.

Then, in 1902, it was charged that the Colorado Springs Captain of Detectives, gangster Adolph W. Duff, and six others unlawfully hired, persuaded, and induced Pat McNellis the prosecuting witness against Duff on a con-game charge, to leave the State of Colorado. The case was never tried, but the Chief of Police and Captain of Detectives lost their jobs.

Duff had made two early attempts to extend his operations to the richer Denver field, but failed to contact Blonger, and so was unsuccessful. The Denver police blotter shows arrests of Duff in 1897 and 1903 on the charge of 'bunco'; both times a conviction in police court, with sentences suspended on condition that he leave town! So he returned to the city at the foot of Pike's Peak.

Finally Duff's power in Colorado Springs completely collapsed when in 1904 he was charged with keeping a policy wheel. Later the same year he pleaded guilty to gambling and was sentenced to thirty days in the county jail and fined seven hundred dollars, his first conviction of any kind! All punishment was canceled, however, when his attorneys filed a plea that he had no money and his family was suffering.

His power in Colorado Springs broken, Duff went to Denver and joined Blonger. The latter had now reached the point where he craved respectability, and wanted to work from behind the scenes, where he would never come in actual contact with the victims. Lou had always shunned the spotlight, so much so that except for a few occasions in the early days when the city directory gave his occupation as 'saloon' and 'club-rooms,' he was listed as a business man under the head of 'mining.' So in a short time Duff became the active manager of the Denver gang, and Lou's first lieutenant.

Duff spent his summers in Denver with Blonger. During the fall he operated with con-men in other States. In those places he was usually only one of the players, though occasionally he was a partner of the local fixer. He was arrested in San Francisco and Kansas City, and his picture placed in their galleries, but his pull enabled him to escape trial. In fact he had such good connections in Kansas City that he first had his picture sequestered and then removed from its police records. Then after Duff joined Blonger, his old Denver police record was 'lost' and could not be found; and was not located until 1923.

Duff was married to his own niece, a very handsome woman. She had two small brothers who passed as his boys. When they reached college age, they entered the University of Colorado, where their money was of material assistance in their induction into the exclusive ranks of an Eastern fraternity which catered to the socially elite.

As Blonger's and Duff's activities spread, both acquired wealth and large real estate holdings followed. They opened offices on the third floor of the American National Bank Building, where the name of each appeared on the door, Blonger as in mining, and Duff in the insurance business.

Blonger also blossomed out as a farmer, and bought a cherry orchard at Beehive, five miles west of Denver. Here he grew the finest dark red cherries which could be produced in Colorado. The main purpose of the orchard, however, was not to make money, but to furnish presents of the fruit for his political friends. Each July drays were busy carrying full crates of Blonger's best to judges and other office-holders, policemen, party committees, and favored underworld friends. This annual event was eagerly looked forward to, and became a sure index as to whether or not one was still in the good graces of the boss.

Yet behind the scenes the gang was in full operation. In June, 1916, a number of their men went up the South Platte to Gill's Resort for a few days of fishing and poker. There they got into a fight, as a result of which one Frank Hughes Turner was shot and killed by Christopher Wilson, alias Brown, and the rest of the mob helped him escape. None of the witnesses were put under bond, and a few days later all of them quietly left the State.

During the next four years, Blonger saw that these members of his gang were well scattered and remained outside of Colorado. Wilson then came back in January, 1920, and gave himself up. He was promptly released on a $5000 bond, furnished by his Denver leader. Three months later he pleaded guilty to involuntary manslaughter and was sentenced to one day in jail, which he cheerfully served. Wilson, however, was now a well-known character in Denver, so Lou never allowed him to return. But his hide was saved!

After Blonger and Duff got together, they and other confidence-game artists developed the 'pay-off' game, a big money deal which numbers its victims by the tens of thousands, which drags in millionaires, play-boys, ministers, bankers, business men, lawyers, and others, and which furnishes steady employment—except when interrupted by short visits in the penitentiary—to over five hundred of the cleverest crooks in America. They fight for big stakes, from $5000 up, and they rely on crooked bankers, politicians, and police for protection. For the pay-off game organizes the underworld vertically. Built on deception, manned by rogues, and covered up by respectable veneer, it is a national problem. In 1934 the United States District Court in New York City tried a $1,500,000 case involving transactions in Reno, Nevada, and daily for twenty-five years the press has carried stories of the depredations of these pay-off mobs.

And so the gang throve, getting more and more bold and powerful. Entrenched locally, they had their allies in similar gangs all over the country. The Wolves of Seventeenth Street roved Denver, arrogant, powerful, and wealthy. They feared neither law nor man, as all apparently had their price.

Section 14 **PASSING OF THE BRUTE**

From *The Gangs of New York* by Herbert Asbury, 1927, 1928.

The moving pictures and the stage have always portrayed the gangster as a low, coarse person with an evilly glinting eye, a chin adorned with a rank stubble of unkempt beard, a plaid cap drawn down over beetling brows, and a swagger which in itself was sufficient to inform the world that here was a man bent on devilment. It is true that there were many such, and in the lore of the gangs there are numerous tales of their mighty exploits, but in the main the really dangerous gangster, the killer, was more apt to be something of a dandy. He dressed well, he shaved daily, he kept his nails manicured and his hair oiled and plastered to his skull, and when his gang gave a racket he generally contrived to grace the festivities in all the glory of a dress suit. In the days of the Dead Rabbits and the Bowery Boys, and later when Dandy Johnny Dolan of the Whyos was the fashion plate of gangland, the gangster was a bit man; but in the course of years the misery and congestion of tenement life took their toll, and police and prison records show that the average gang member of the time of the Gophers, the Eastmans and the Five Pointers was not more than five feet and three inches tall, and weighed between 120 and 135 pounds.

Such noted followers of Paul Kelly as Eat 'Em Up Jack McManus and Louis Pioggi, better known as Louie the Lump, who was but a slim and beardless boy when he acquired a reputation as a murderer, followed the fashions with great care; and even Biff Ellison, for all his hugeness and great strength, was a fop in matters of dress. Ellison dearly loved to sprinkle himself with scent, of which he had his own private blend especially compounded by a druggist sworn to secrecy. Johnny Spanish was always arrayed like a lily of the field, as were Kid Twist and Richie Fitzpatrick, the most famous of Eastman's lieutenants; and Razor Riley, a noted Gopher who weighed less than a hundred pounds, but made up for his lack of heft by an amazing proficiency in the use of revolver, blackjack, and a huge razor which gave him his nickname. And Paul Kelly, who is now reformed and honorably occupied as a real estate broker and business agent for labor unions, was a perfect example of this type of gangster. Throughout his long career as chief of the Five Pointers, Kelly exercised power second only to that of Monk Eastman, yet he was a dapper, soft-spoken chap who seldom engaged in rough-and-tumble fighting, although in his early youth he had been a bantam-weight pugilist of more than local renown. He resembled a bank clerk or a theological student more than a gang chieftain, and his dive, the New Brighton, was one of the flashiest palaces of sin in the city. Unlike most of his fellows, Kelly was fairly well educated. He spoke French, Spanish, and Italian, and with his well-bred manner could have moved at ease in relatively cultured society.

The story is told of a woman who went to New Brighton in Great Jones street, under the protection of a Headquarters detective, for the express purpose of seeing Paul Kelly, who had been mentioned in the newspapers in connection with some particularly sensational gang affray. For some time they sat in the midst of thieves and gangsters, literally surrounded by the current of miserable humanity which boiled up in the Bowery and Chatham Square and swirled through Chinatown and the East Side. Meanwhile they chatted with a dark, quiet little man who had been sitting at a table when they entered. He entertained them for half an hour with a dissertation on art, and then the woman and her escort departed. As they stepped out of the place the woman said:

"I am sorry we did not get to see Paul Kelly."

"Why," said the detective, "that was Paul Kelly you were talking to."

"Good gracious!" she exclaimed. "I thought he was slumming, too!"

But no one would ever have mistaken Monk Eastman, a worthy successor to Mose the Bowery Boy and as brave a thug as ever shot an enemy in the back or blackjacked a voter at the polls, for a bank clerk or a theological student. So far as looks were concerned, and actions, too, for that matter, Eastman was a true moving picture gangster. He began life with a bullet-shaped head, and during his turbulent career acquired a broken nose and a pair of cauliflower ears, which were not calculated to increase his beauty. He had heavily veined, sagging jowls, and a short, bull neck, plentifully scarred with battle marks, as were his cheeks. He seemed always to need a hair cut, and he accentuated his ferocious and unusual appearance by affecting a derby hat several sizes too small, which perched precariously atop his shock of bristly, unruly hair. He could generally be found strutting about his kingdom very indifferently dressed, or lounging at his ease in the Chrystie street rendezvous without shirt, collar, or coat. His hobby was cats and pigeons—animals have always seemed to possess a fascination for gangsters; many of them, after they reformed, or had been compelled by the police to abandon the active practice of thuggery, opened bird and animal stores and prospered. Monk Eastman is said to have owned, at one time, more than a hundred cats and five hundred pigeons, and although they were offered for sale in his bird and animal store in Broome street, it was seldom that he could be induced to part with any of them. He sometimes went abroad, on peaceful missions, with a cat under each arm, while several others trailed along in his wake. He also had a great blue pigeon which he had tamed, and which perched on his shoulder as he walked.

"I like de kits and boids," Eastman used to say. "I'll beat up any guy dat gets gay wit' a kit or a boid in my neck of de woods."

When a reporter once asked Eastman, a few months before his death, how many times he had been arrested, the gang leader replied that he would be damned if he knew; and at Headquarters the police said that they had lost count of the number. "What difference does it make?" asked a detective who had often performed the thankless task. "The politicians always sprung him. He was the best man they ever had at the polls." Nor could Eastman number his marks of battle. He had at least a dozen scars from knife wounds on his neck and face, and as many more on other parts of his body. He boasted that he had been shot so often that when he climbed on the scales he had to make allowance for the bullets imbedded in his body. When he enlisted in the New York National Guard at the outbreak of the World War and stripped for examination, the physicians thought they had to do with a veteran of every battle since Gettysburg. They asked him what wars he had been in.

"Oh!" replied Eastman, grinning, "a lot of little wars around New York!"

The merciless warfare between the great captains kept the Chatham Square, Bowery and Chinatown districts in an uproar of excitement and terror, for not all of the gangsters were good shots, and their wild bullets frequently injured non-combatants and smashed windows. Occasionally the police appeared in force and made spectacular pretence of clubbing both sides, but in general these were meaningless gestures, for both Eastman and Kelly had strong political connections and were in high favor with the Tammany Hall statesmen. Eastman, in particular, became an especial pet of the Wigwam; for years he served the Tammany organization in many ways, and was especially useful around election times, when he voted his gangsters in droves and employed them to blackjack honest citizens who thought to cast their ballots according to their convictions. Whenever Eastman got into trouble Tammany Hall lawyers appeared in court for him and Tammany bondsmen furnished his bail, which was promptly forfeited and the case expunged from the records. In the intervals between his political engagements Eastman did what may best be described as a general gang business. He became interested in houses of prostitution and stuss games, he shared in the earnings of prostitutes who walked the streets under his protection, he directed the operations of his pickpockets, loft burglars and footpads, and provided thugs for men who wished to rid themselves of enemies, graduating his fees according to the degree of disability desired. Eastman himself sometimes led selected members of his gang in raids upon the stuss games which flourished throughout the East Side, and also, on occasion, personally accepted a blackjacking commission.

"I like to beat up a guy once in a while," he used to say. "It keeps me hand in."

Eastman had frequently felt the thud of a fist against his flesh while officiating as Sheriff of the New Irving, but it was not until the summer of 1901 that he experienced his first contact with a bullet. Then, having ventured abroad without his body guard, he was assailed in the Bowery, near Chatham Square, by half a dozen Five Pointers who fell upon him with blackjack and revolver. Unarmed except for his brass knuckles and his slung-shot, Eastman defended himself valiantly, and had knocked down three of the attacking force when a fourth shot him twice in the stomach. They fled, leaving him for dead upon the sidewalk, but he scrambled to his feet and staggered to Gouverneur Hospital, closing a gaping wound with his fingers. For several weeks the gang leader lay at the point of death, but in conformity with the code of the underworld he refused to divulge to the police the name of the man who had shot him. Meanwhile the war with the Five Pointers proceeded with redoubled ferocity, and a week after Eastman had been discharged from the hospital the police found a dead Five Pointer lying in the gutter at Grand and Chrystie streets; he had been decoyed from his accustomed haunt by a woman and shot to death.

For more than two years the conflict between the Eastmans and the Five Pointers raged almost without cessation, and the darkened streets of the East Side and the old Paradise Square section were filled night after night with scurrying figures who shot at each other from carriages, or from that strange new invention, the automobile, or pounced one upon the other from the shelter of doorways, with no warning save the vicious swish of a black-jack or section of lead pipe. Stuss games owned by members of the Eastman clan were held up and robbed by the Five Pointers, and Kelly's sources of revenue were similarly interfered with by the redoubtable Monk and his henchmen. Balls and other social functions in New Irving and Walhalla Halls were frequently interrupted while the gangsters shot out their mutual hatred without regard for the safety and convenience of the merry-makers; and the owners of dives and dance halls lived in constant fear that their resorts would be the scene of bloody combat, and so subject them to unwel-come notoriety. But it was not until the middle of August, 1903, that the crisis of the war was reached and the gangs met in the battle which marked the end of the feud, for it aroused the politicians to a realization of the needless slaughter of their most valuable assets, and awakened the general public to a knowledge of the power of the gangs.

There had been desultory fighting throughout the hot days of summer, and at eleven o'clock on a sultry August night half a dozen prowling East-mans came upon a like number of Five Pointers preparing to raid a stuss game in Rivington street, under the Allen street arch of the Second avenue elevated railroad. The game was in Eastman territory and was known to be under Monk's personal protection, for it was operated by one of his friends who faithfully gave him a large percentage of the take. The indignant East-mans promptly killed one of the invading Five Pointers, and after a flurry of shots the adherents of Paul Kelly sought refuge behind the pillars of the elevated structure, whence they emerged cautiously from time to time to take pot shots at the Eastmans, who had availed themselves of similar protection. After half an hour of ineffectual firing, during which two policemen who attempted to interfere fled down Rivington street with their uniforms full of bullet holes, messengers were dispatched to the headquarters of both gangs, and within a short time reinforcements began to arrive.

The politicians suffered excruciating pain when they opened their news-papers and read the accounts of the fighting under the elevated structure. Having provided burial for the dead and proper hospital care for the wounded, they called upon Eastman and Paul Kelly and impressed upon them the obvi-ous fact that such wholesale combat jeopardized their usefulness. The gang chieftains were told that no one objected to an occasional murder or black-jacking if they were strictly in line of business, and then even a little fancy sniping now and then might be overlooked, for everyone knew that gangsters would be gangsters; but that engagements in force terrorized the East Side and must stop. A meeting between Eastman and Kelly was arranged, and a few days later the gang leaders came face to face in the Palm, an unsavory dive in Chrystie street near Grand, Kelly having been guaranteed safe conduct at the request of the Tammany politicians. Tom Foley, a notable figure in the councils of the Wigwam, who had employed Eastman to good advantage during a hot campaign in the Second Assembly district, acted as mediator, and after he had presented the case for peace, with covert threats that both gangs would be smashed if they continued their private feud, Kelly and Eastman agreed to stop the shooting and stabbing. It was further agreed that the disputed strip between the Bowery and Nigger Mike's should be neutral territory, subject to the operations of either gang. Foley then gave a ball to celebrate the truce, and just before the grand march Eastman and Kelly met in the center of the dance floor and ceremoniously shook hands. Thereafter they viewed the revels of their followers from a box, while the Eastmans and the Five Pointers danced with each other's girls under the benign eye of Tom Foley; and there was peace on earth and good will toward men.

The truce between the Eastmans and the Five Pointers was scrupulously observed by both sides for several months, but in the winter of 1903 an Eastman named Hurst wandered into a Bowery dive and became involved in a weighty argument with a disciple of Paul Kelly, one Ford, the issue being the bravery of their respective chieftains. The dispute ended in a fight, and Hurst was badly mauled; it is related that his nose was broken in two places and one of his ears twisted off. Monk Eastman immediately sent word to Kelly that Ford's life was forfeit, and that if Kelly did not care to attend to the matter of putting him out of the way, the Eastmans would invade the domain of the Five Pointers and take summary vengeance. As Monk expressed it, "He'll wipe up de earth wit' youse guys." Kelly replied tartly that the Eastmans were welcome to Ford if they could take him, and both sides prepared for war. But again the anxious politicians interfered, and once more a meeting was arranged between Eastman and Kelly, who made no promises but agreed to talk the matter over in the presence of neutral persons. Accompanied by armed body-guards, the gang leaders again met in the Palm. They shook hands with great formality and then, each with a huge cigar between his teeth and a hand on his revolver, sat at a table and proceeded to discuss ways and means to retain their honor and at the same time keep their thugs from each other's throats. They recognized that something must be done, for the politicians had informed them that if another outbreak occurred protection would be withdrawn and the police permitted to wreak their will upon them. And there were many policemen who yearned for just such an opportunity, for the honest members of the force had long suffered at the hands of the gangsters.

After much discussion it was agreed that the issue of supremacy should be decided by a prize fight between Kelly and Eastman, the loser to accept the overlordship of the victor and be content to remain strictly within his own domain. On the appointed night the gang chieftains, each accompanied by fifty of his best fighters, repaired to an old barn in the farthest reaches of The Bronx. Because of his early experience in the professional prize ring, Kelly possessed superior science, but it was offset by Eastman's weight and greater ferocity. They fought for two hours without either gaining an advantage, and at length, after they had collapsed and lay one across the other still trying feebly to strike, their followers loaded them into carriages and hauled them to the East Side and the Five Points. The bout was pronounced a draw, and as soon as they had recovered from their wounds the gang chieftains marshalled their resources and prepared for war to the finish, despite the protests of the politicians.

There were a few unimportant skirmishes, but the end of Monk Eastman's rule was in sight, and great trouble was also brewing in the pot for Paul Kelly. Eastman's downfall came first. At three o'clock in the morning of February 2, 1904, he and Chris Wallace, having gone far afield to Sixth avenue and Forty-Second street, to blackjack a man who had annoyed one of the gang leader's clients, saw a well-dressed young man staggering uncertainly down the street. Behind him, at a distance of some few yards, was a roughly dressed man who the gangsters thought was a lush worker waiting for his victim to fall. Eastman and Wallace promptly held up the young man, but it developed that he was a member of a rich family, and that the rough-looking man was a Pinkerton detective hired to protect him while he sowed his wild oats. The Pinkerton method has always been to shoot first and then ask questions of criminals, and as soon as Eastman and Wallace had poked their revolvers under the young man's nose and begun to slip their nimble fingers into his pockets, the detective promptly shot at them. The surprised gangsters returned the fire, and then fled down Forty-second street, turning occasionally to send a warning bullet in the direction of the pursuing Pinkerton. But at Broadway and Forty-second street, in front of the Hotel Knickerbocker, they ran into the arms of a policeman. Wallace escaped, but the patrolman knocked Eastman down with his nightstick, and when the gang leader regained consciousness he was in a cell in the West Thirtieth street station, and had been booked on charges of highway robbery and felonious assault. Indictments were promptly procured, and although at first Eastman laughed at the efforts of the District Attorney to bring him to trial, he became frantic when Tammany Hall ignored his appeals for aid. He was abandoned by his erstwhile friends, and almost before he knew what had happened to him he had been tried, convicted and was on his way to Sing Sing Prison under a ten-year sentence. Paul Kelly professed profound grief when he heard of his rival's misfortune. "Monk was a soft, easy-going fellow," said Kelly. "He had a gang of cowards behind him, second story men, yeggs, flat robbers and moll-buzzers. But he was a game fellow. He fought everyone's battles. I'd give ten thousand dollars to see him out of prison." The politicians, however, would not give ten cents, and so Eastman donned the stripes, and was never more a power in the underworld.

Section 15 **THE EARLY CHICAGO STORY**

From *Syndicate City* by Alson J. Smith, 1954.

When the police, politicians, and other chronic defenders of the status quo in Chicago decry mention of the city's crime on the grounds that it's "old stuff," they are so right. Crime and politics were wedded in unholy matrimony on the spit of sand where the Chicago river empties into Lake Michigan as early as 1670, when an unregenerate French trader and trapper known to the Indians as "The Mole" built a shelter on the site and promptly began the illegal sale of rum to the benighted Potawatamies. His real name was Pierre Moreau and he got away with his bootlegging because Count Frontenac, the Governor of New France, was a friend of his. The efforts of Father Jacques Marquette and his Jesuit colleagues to save the souls of the Potawatamies were not rendered any easier by Moreau's activities, but their protests to the Count got them nowhere. Thus was established a pattern that has dominated the city for almost three hundred years.

The motley collection of shacks and huts that clustered about old Fort Dearborn got itself incorporated as a town in 1833. In 1835 a wave of reform swept over the Mississippi Valley and resulted in the ejection of hundreds of gamblers from Vicksburg, Natchez, New Orleans, and St. Louis, and the blacklegs, casting about for new locations, were delighted to find that the mudhole called Chicago had neither law nor any civic virtue to be outraged. Not until August of 1835 was there so much as a constable in the town, and most of the inhabitants were engaging in wild real estate speculation, swindling the Indians and each other with the greatest abandon. Here, indeed, was a field white unto the harvest. The gamblers arrived in droves, followed by prostitutes and pimps, and then by all manner of riff-raff—hoodlums, rowdies, con men, pickpockets, footpads, gunmen, garroters, horse thieves and counterfeiters. The so-called, "better element" was too busy gambling in real estate to pay much attention to the newcomers, and by the early 1840's— less than ten years after its incorporation as a town—Chicago had more gambling houses than either Cincinnati or St. Louis and was the most important gambling center north of New Orleans and west of the Alleghenies. The real estate boom collapsed, but the professional gamblers kept on doing business as usual and Chicago's reputation as the wickedest community this side of Sodom and Gomorrah was firmly established. Many of the emigrants bound west by wagon-train were so intrigued by the city's open debauchery that they stayed on, and these additions to the rapidly growing population were, *ipso facto*, not of the type to institute any far-reaching reforms. Chicago's reputation attracted to the city citizens who came because they liked the town the way it was.

The Civil War years cemented Chicago's unsavory reputation. The booming, still-muddy metropolis of the plains teemed with suckers—soldiers on leave, laborers with their jeans stuffed with easy war-work currency, swindling contractors, emigrants heading west, river and lake roustabouts. The gamblers rode high; Randolph Street between Clark and State was known as "Hair-trigger Block," while Clark from Randolph to Monroe was called "Gambler's Row." The *Tribune* nicknamed the intersection of Randolph and Dearborn "Thieves Corner." On "Hair-trigger Block" were elegant gambling houses like Frank Connelly's "Senate" and the picturesque establishments of colorful blacklegs like George Trussell, Cap Hyman, Johnny Brown, Col. Wat Cameron, Jere Dunn, White Pine Russell, and Theodore Cameron, who had two houses and provided free bird-and-wine suppers for the frequenters of his resorts.

Through the 60's, 70's, and 80's Chicago increased mightily in population, wealth, and deviltry. The gamblers kept pace with the city's growth; all through the 1870's thirty first-class gambling houses ran wide-open on Clark, Dearborn, State, Randolph, Madison and Halsted Streets. From Mike McDonald's "Store" at the northwest corner of Clark and Monroe a coterie of big gamblers, headed by Mike himself, controlled the city. Among the important gamblers were the Hankins brothers, George and Al, Billy Fagan, and Harry "Prince Hal" Varnell. They operated in the grand manner. Billy Fagan's joint was known as the "House of David" and was decorated with paintings of voluptuous nudes, but one room of the house was "reserved for prayer meetings and gospel services." Prince Hal Varnell kept his place open twenty-four hours a day and employed fifteen croupiers, twenty-five faro dealers, and between forty and fifty cappers and ropers. The Hankins boys cleared an average of $1,400 a day; Mike McDonald turned an $800,000 profit in one year.

Some of these rascals had color and some were out-and-out crazy. The Hankins brothers were very superstitious; they burned an old shoe each morning to bring them luck, and went around putting pinches of salt and pepper on the chairs of their establishment to hoodoo the players. (Both died broke; Al was smothered in a folding bed; and George was a pauper when he passed away in Gary in 1912. Ran out of salt and pepper, maybe.) Still another "character" was Johnny Lawlor, who when he lost, would scream, butt his head against the wall, and try to pull off his ears.

The gamblers had been followed in their hegira to Chicago by their usual camp-followers, the prostitutes, with their retinue of pimps and "solid men." During the Civil War, Wells Street had so many brothels that the city fathers changed its name to Fifth Avenue, on the grounds that it was a disgrace to the fair name of Captain Billy Wells. Conley's Patch, Shinbone Alley, and the Chicago Patch were the names given to some of the larger agglomerations of *maisons de plaisir*. Most of the houses were mere shacks and shanties, but one—Lou Harper's place at 219 Monroe—was an elegant parlor-house, the first of many ornate palaces of bawdry to decorate the Chicago scene. The houses were supplemented by an army of streetwalkers; in 1860 the *Tribune* estimated that there were more than 2,000 of the latter in the business district alone.

It was the custom in those days for the big gamblers to pair up with the big brothel-madames; the former would load the latter down with pounds of diamonds and parade them openly as their mistresses. Cap Hyman was the consort of an enormous muscular madame known as Gentle Annie Stafford, and George Trussell kept company with an amazon named Mary Cosgriff, but better known as Irish Mollie. Neither Cap nor George entertained any idea of eventually marrying these well-endowed ladies, but Annie and Mollie, with a whore's secret yearning for respectability, had other plans. Cap just laughed when Annie mentioned the subject, but he stopped laughing when she invaded his establishment on Hair-trigger Block, routed him from rest on a couch with a horsewhip, and flogged him out the door and up Randolph Street into the waiting arms of a Justice of the Peace. George Trussell never did recover from the shock of learning Irish Mollie's plans for him because she shot him at the bar of Seneca Wright's saloon as soon as he said "no." Chicago justice was immediate and characteristic; Irish Mollie was convicted and sentenced to a year in prison, but before she served a day she was pardoned by the governor and went back to brothel-keeping.

Some of the most picturesque of the old-time madames were strapping Negresses who drifted up from the South in the wake of the gamblers. Among them were the "Bengal Tigress," "Big Maud," and "Black Susan." They were tough customers in a brawl. Black Susan took the prize for size; she tipped the scales at an even 449 and the police never could figure out how she had gained entrance to her establishment in the first place, since her beam was too broad for the doors and windows. A series of raids on her rambling shack-like joy-emporium brought nothing but discomfiture to the policemen, because they could not get Black Susan through the doors or windows to ride her down to headquarters and book her. She finally fell victim to one of the most tireless and ingenious police officers in all Chicago history, a man whose energy puts to shame all more recent practitioners of the Pinkerton art in the Windy City—Detective Clifton R. Wooldridge. Wooldridge was a little man, weighing only 155 pounds, but he had 100-proof courage in every pound and an agile mind packed with useful information. He employed scores of disguises and was the one police officer the underworld hated, being known throughout the "patches" as "that damned fly-cop."

After a patient study of the Black Susan situation, Wooldridge went into action. He had a paddy wagon drive up to the back door of Susan's seraglio, whereupon he alighted and read the warrant for her arrest in a fine, sonorous voice. Fancying herself impregnable behind the narrow frames of her doors and windows, Black Susan cackled derisively. Wooldridge then had his underlings remove the back door and saw out the frame and two feet of the wall. He placed two rough oak planks, each sixteen feet long and a foot wide, between the doorsill and the rear end of the patrol wagon. A horse was unhitched and a rope made fast around Black Susan's ample waist; the other end was attached to the horse's collar. At Detective Wooldridge's stentorian "Giddap!" the horse headed in the general direction of Milwaukee, keelhauling Black Susan along the unplaned planks on her stern. The result was an amazed, discomfited, and pained madame with her awe-inspiring posterior full of splinters. Wooldridge generously allowed one of Black Susan's coryphees to accompany her to the police station and extract the splinters en route.

From the time of the Civil War almost until the turn of the century the city of Chicago, its underworld, its police, and its politicians were dominated by one man. A crack reporter, Richard Henry Little, says of him: "He never held office, but he ruled the city with an iron hand. He named the men who were to be candidates for election, he elected them, and after they were in office they were merely his puppets." The man's name was Michael Cassius McDonald, and he was a gambler. Mike had first come to Chicago in 1854 as a boy of fifteen; by that age he was already an accomplished swindler, being a candy butcher on railroad trains entering the city and specializing in half-filled boxes. He first appears in the annals of the city in 1861, when he was listed as a sponsor of the so-called "Irish Rally," which was called to enlist the support of Irish-Americans for the Union cause in the Civil War. Mike lent his name to the Union but not his person; he had other fish to fry and although he was a ripe twenty-two years of age had no difficulty in outwitting the draft. He was a prominent gambler and denizen of Hair-trigger Block up until after the Fire, when he branched out into politics as the mortal foe of Joseph Medill, who had been elected mayor on a let's-rebuild-Chicago platform, and who cracked down hard on gamblers and other underworldlings and closed the town about as tightly as it has ever been closed. Mc-Donald gathered the town's gamblers together at "The Store" in 1873 and for the first time in the city's history organized the underworld for political action. The riffraff called themselves "Mike McDonald's Democrats," and they elected Harvey Colvin mayor. Colvin was Mike's man; during his two-year term in office Mike ran Chicago, and the town was so wide-open that a popular revulsion set in and another "reform" mayor, Monroe Heath, Re-publican, was elected to office in 1876.

Mike used this period of comparative calm to build up his political machine and in 1879 the Mike McDonald Democrats surged back into power, carrying Carter Harrison (the first "Our Carter") to a glorious victory on the wings of the ballots of gamblers, prostitutes, the liquor interests, and the politically-organized underworld. For the next twenty years "The Store" was not only the sporting center of Chicago but also its unofficial City Hall, where city officials, politicians and police officers mingled with the dregs of the underworld and took their orders from Mike McDonald. "The Store" submitted to two regular raids a year just for appearances' sake; on each occasion some packs of cards were torn up by the raiding officers while the expensive roulette wheels, chuck-a-luck cages, faro layouts, etc. remained discreetly covered. One or two minor employees were arrested as "keepers" on these occasions and let off with small fines; Mike himself, of course, was never bothered.

Having built up an unbeatable political combination, Mike turned his organizational talents back to business. With the Hankins brothers and "Prince Hal" Varnell he set up the city's first "Syndicate" and the one which was to bequeath its name to the present agglomeration of underworld power. Mike's "syndicate" cornered bookmaking privileges at all Chicago and Indiana tracks; in one season it turned a neat $800,000 profit. Mike's partner, "Prince Hal" Varnell, branched out into politics and got himself an appointment as warden of the Cook County Insane Asylum, which he speedily transformed into a pleasure spa and health resort for his political cronies. Many politicians actually lived at the Insane Asylum during Varnell's regime as warden. There were tart suggestions from some citizens that the city would be more adequately governed if the bona fide inmates of the looney bin were permitted to run things from City Hall while the politicians took their ease at the asylum. Varnell eventually overplayed his hand, stealing so much from the asylum's funds that even Mike McDonald couldn't save him. He served a year at the Illinois State Penitentiary at Joliet.

McDonald was a complete cynic. There are some who claim that he and not P. T. Barnum originated the phrase "there's a sucker born every minute." They say that when Mike opened "The Store" an employee expressed the fear that the setup was too big and there wouldn't be enough customers, to which Mike replied, "Ah, don't worry—there's a new sucker born every minute." He was right, at least in so far as his own business was concerned. With his gambling profits he branched out into legitimate business, buying the Chicago *Globe* and making it the official organ of the Mike McDonald Democrats, and getting himself elected treasurer of the Lake Street Elevated Railway, which promptly became known as "Mike's Upstairs Railroad." In his spare time he suckered the city and county, offering to paint the City-County building at Clark and Randolph with a special waterproof protective fluid. The offer was duly accepted and Mike and his gang presented the county with a bill for $128,250. But before it could be paid some busybody discovered that the "waterproof protective fluid" was nothing but colored water. A few underlings went to jail for that, but Mike wasn't touched.

Mike also hated policemen, his attitude dating back to the days when they had harassed him on the trains for shortchanging his candy customers. He never had any trouble with them after he reached his majority, and took a vengeful delight in humiliating them in various ways, moving them about and demoting them. It is probably apocryphal, but there is a story that two politicians approached Mike for a contribution of $2. "We're burying a policeman," they explained. "Here's ten dollars," said Mike; "bury five of 'em."

Mike's long reign as gambling czar of Chicago was brought to an untimely end by wife trouble. He had been married for years to one Mary Noonan, and Mary had once discomfited him by running away to San Francisco with an actor. Mike had brought her back and she thereupon became very devout, so much so that she had to have a priest to the house to recite daily prayers. Finally she and the priest eloped to Paris, whereupon Mike gave up the Catholic faith, got a divorce, and married Dora Feldman, the divorced wife of a professional ball player named Sam Barclay. To please Dora, Mike became a Jew, even going so far as to get himself circumcised. His luck with wives was still no good, however; the new Mrs. McDonald had a young lover named Webster Guerin, and when Webster was shot and killed she was arrested and charged with the crime, which did not seem too strange in view of the fact that she had been found standing over the body with a still smoking revolver in her hand. That broke Mike; he died in 1907, after throwing away his black skullcap and re-embracing Catholicism. A year later Mrs. McDonald II was acquitted of the murder of Webster Guerin by a jury of her peers in another characteristic performance of Chicago justice.

The power which fell from the faltering hands of Mike McDonald was seized not by one but by several heirs apparent. Prince Hal Varnell had brought a comical massage artist by the name of John Coughlin into politics, and John, better known as "Bathhouse" or simply "The Bath," had been elected alderman in the First Ward. John, in turn, had tapped little Michael

Kenna, "Hinky-Dink," for fame and fortune, and The Hink, a shrewd and unscrupulous boodler, had been elected as the junior First Ward alderman. The Hink, with some assistance from The Bath, had organized the brothel-keepers, madames, prostitutes, and saloon-keepers of the ward into an efficient political organization, one that was able to throw a lot of votes to the Mike McDonald Democrats. When Mike's power began to decline, the Hink and The Bath inherited much of his political clout in the First Ward; the gamblers and brothel-keepers began paying protection money directly to the alderman. Downtown, they took over from Mike.

On the southwest side, down around the stockyards, a gambler with a gilt-edged reputation and a history-making name picked up such pieces of the McDonald empire as happened to be lying within reach. This was Big Jim O'Leary, scion of the family whose cow kicked over the lantern back in '71 and thereby ruined several fire insurance companies. O'Leary was a colorful character, but in retrospect he appears as a mere custodian of power. When another Big Jim, Colisimo, was shot to death in his restaurant on Wabash Avenue in 1920, the shooting took place shortly after Colisimo had placed an order for some bootleg hootch with Big Jim O'Leary and while he was impatiently awaiting its arrival. But the connection, if any, has remained an underworld secret.

The man who inherited most of Mike McDonald's clout was the renowned Mont Tennes, who, as early as 1901, was dominating gambling on the North Side from his saloon at Sheffield Avenue and Center Street. Of Mont, the Illinois Crime Survey said: "If the complete life history of Mont Tennes were known in every detail, it would disclose practically all there is to know about syndicated gambling as a phase of organized crime in Chicago in the last quarter century. He was avowedly a real estate man, for a period the owner of a cash register company, and for more than a score of years the proprietor of the General News Bureau, controlling the wires. . . . repeated exposés have always found him in control of strings of hand-books and gambling houses in Chicago and other urban centers."

Tennes, although well-known on the North Side, did not come into city-wide prominence until 1904, when he suddenly blossomed out as the backer of several hundred hand-books, and formed an alliance with Alderman Johnny Rogers, who controlled gambling on the West Side. Tennes had his own pet alderman in the person of James "Hot Stove Jimmy" Quinn, whose nickname derived from his favorite characterization of his friends: "He's so crooked he'd steal a hot stove."

After lining up Rogers and the West Side, Mont Tennes pulled the coup that was to make him rich. A man named Payne in Cincinnati had worked out a system of transmitting race results by wire, and Mont purchased a Chicago monopoly on this service for $300 a day. This meant that every handbook in the city that wanted quick race results had to pay Mont. Mont's fee was an even split on the book's profits. The handbook operators howled with pain. The Loop, in the persons of The Hink and The Bath, and the South Side, under the leadership of Big Jim O'Leary, fought back with bombs and guns. Tennes was slugged while out walking with his wife. Eight bombs were exploded between June and October 1907. The air resounded with the detonations of dynamite, the boom of shotgun shells, the thud of rubber hose on derby hat, and the steady crashing of broken glass. While the casualties mounted, Police Chief George Shippey remarked: "Looks as if there's a big gamblers' war on in Chicago. I still maintain, however, that there is no gambling worthy of the name in existence at present."

In 1908 the opposition gave in and was permitted to join up with the Tennes syndicate, Mont having compromised to the extent of offering to assume half of the loss of any book affiliating with him. By 1911, he was in complete and undisputed control of all Chicago gambling, and ready to go on to new fields.

In 1910 Mont set up his own race-wire service, the General News Bureau, and after a short struggle drove the Payne Service out of business. This made Mont the boss of race-track gambling all over the United States and Canada. He ruled with an iron hand, enforcing his decrees with guns and bombs. In Chicago alone ninety poolrooms paid $3,600 a week for General News Service. The North Side saloon-keeper was now many times a millionaire, politically impregnable. In his two brushes with the law, he came off an easy winner.

The first of these came in 1916, when the Chicago *Daily News*, running one of its periodic exposés of political corruption, published a long list of hand-books and demanded an answer to the question "Does Tennes control the Police Department?" An investigation followed and ended up in the United States District Court presided over by Judge Kenesaw Mountain Landis, the fiery jurist who was later to become czar of baseball. Tennes was subpoenaed, but he refused to answer any questions "on the grounds that I might incriminate myself." Clarence Darrow was Mont's lawyer. Judge Landis castigated Mont as a corrupter of youth and told the gambler that his profits were "covered with dirt and slime because young men are being made criminals." This sermon had about as much effect on Mont as a Bull of Excommunication might have had on Satan. The investigation finally came to nothing when the Illinois Bell Telephone Company refused to cooperate on the grounds that interstate transmission of sporting news was not a crime and that local gambling was not within the jurisdiction of the Federal court. State and city authorities refused to pursue the matter further, and Mont was home free.

Mont licked the law again in 1920 when Chief of Detectives Michael

Hughes unexpectedly raided one of the Tennes books at 17 South Clark. State's Attorney Robert E. Crowe went to the Grand Jury and got Tennes indicted, an excusable error since Crowe was new on the job, but Mont signed up Crowe's predecessor as State's Attorney, Maclay Hoyne, as his lawyer, and Hoyne got the case nol-prossed because the prosecution could not show a conspiracy.

By this time Tennes was getting old and his retirement was announced periodically. But as late as 1925 he was still very much in evidence; on August 21 of that year bandits raided his book at 120 South Clark, lined thirty employees up against the wall, and escaped with money and jewelry valued at $20,000. Police pursued the bandits through the Loop; hundreds of citizens joined the chase and thousands witnessed it. But fifteen minutes later the police threw a blanket of secrecy over the whole thing. No report was ever made on it. A traffic cop who had the temerity to talk to a reporter was censured by Police Department bigwigs. Tennes was untouchable.

In 1927, old Mont finally did retire. He sold half of the General News Bureau to Moe Annenberg, who published newspapers in Philadelphia and New York, as well as the *Racing Form,* and Moe named James M. Ragen as his general manager. Annenberg and Ragen then bought up all the racing information services in the country that they didn't already control, and Ragen was killed in 1946 when he had a falling out with the Capone Syndicate over control of the Continental Press. This latter was the service that arose phoenixlike from the ashes of the General News Bureau, brought low by the indictment and subsequent imprisonment of Annenberg on charges of income tax fraud. So Ragen was gathered to his fathers, Annenberg went to jail, and The Outfit picked up the pieces of the racing information empire.

Long before Mont Tennes retired, a genius of the first order had arrived on the Chicago scene, an underworld businessman who was to create a bootlegging empire, superimpose it on the vice structure created by The Hink and The Bath and the gambling dynasty that Mont Tennes had inherited from Mike McDonald, and forge the whole thing into an evil oligarchy that would be, as Jim Ragen said, "as strong as the United States Army."

This man's name was John Torrio.

PART IV

THE EVOLUTION OF THE SYNDICATE

IN THE BEGINNING, there were the gangs playing roughhouse. They peddled violence. In the cities, they were useful adjuncts to the business of prostitution and politics. On the frontier, they became hired guns to social groups in conflict and, in between, turned to train holdups, bank robbery, and gambling.

By the turn of the century the gangs began to subordinate violence to business. The struggle between Monk Eastman and Paul Kelly—a pitched battle on the streets of New York—was far more than a battle between two individuals. The fall of Monk was the Götterdämmerung of the old-fashioned gangster: all fist and no finance. The rise of Kelly was the beginning of the racket: the financier with the fist.

The new idea was to "muscle in" on going concerns to establish a firm and steady base for a regular income. In the past, when a Big Josh Hines, in the 1880's, "muscled in," the operation was a sort of retail personalized act. Big Josh would threaten to "wreck the joint" unless there was a payoff to him. The extortion produced results, and Hines enjoyed the luxuries and comforts of the pirate entrepreneur. But the new scheme of things was to muscle in on a whole field of endeavor rather than on an occasional enterprise. The new approach was to organize an industry.

One of the first industries over which the underworld established its control was prostitution. Another was gambling. In both these cases, "extortion" was easy. The owners of the houses of pleasure had no recourse to the law, since they operated outside the pale of the law. They were always prey to the shakedown. Their real protection was to bring in a "protector" as partner.

True ownership of brothels and gambling parlors was difficult to establish. Were they owned by their seeming managers who were merely paying off police and underworld for protection? Or were they owned by gangsters who installed soft-spoken managers? Or—alas—were they really owned by the police?

In the first decade of this century, the "system" was for the police to organize the setup, allowing nominal ownership to reside where it pleased, so long as the organizers of the system took the lion's share. As New York entered its second decade, a struggle developed over control of Gotham's brothels. The contenders were Charles Becker, a police lieutenant, and Tom Foley, close associate of Tammany boss Murphy.

In the course of a scandal arising from this rivalry it became clear that the police were in direct control of vice and gambling. It was further evident that, for the moment, this well-publicized indecency had to halt. And now a new type of "controller" was needed: not a brute like Monk Eastman nor a man in uniform like Charles Becker, but a respectable sort of citizen, like Arnold Rothstein!

Rothstein was the go-between par excellence. Rothstein was the fixer, the matchmaker, and later the financier. He moved freely in all circles: politicians and statesmen, bankers and bums, high society and low hoods, beautiful women and spendthrift sports.

The age of A. R. was also the period of Prohibition. The Eighteenth Amendment gave the underworld a new commodity to peddle: alcohol. Like violence, sex, and gambling, alcoholic beverages were now illegal. The market was strong for the commodity; the product was easy to come by; the entrepreneurs were plentiful.

If one were to total the number of Americans who violated the Eighteenth Amendment, whether it be as producers of alky, or conveyors, or peddlers, or "protectors" of the trade, or as consumers, the grand total would probably place an overwhelming majority of Americans in violation. This kind of a situation—public acceptance of legal violation—is a perfect environment for the criminal. His hiding place is the entire nation!

When the whole nation becomes a hiding place for the criminal, he can move out of his limited environment, out of the casbah in which he normally retires for protection. The early street gangs of New York, Chicago, and San Francisco came out of subcultures, very often pockets of immigrant settlements. Within this subculture, the gang leader could find a safe place. He could retire, in moments of need, to his people to protect him against—at least, not to squeal on him to—the "outsiders."

When the underworld moved into vice and gambling, the "outlaw" elements had access to a select few of the higher classes. And while these connections might be useful on some occasions for a "fix," they were not too valuable if the "gentleman" involved wanted both his pleasures and his privacy.

The Prohibition Era turned a large part of America into a kind of "subculture," a huge group living like the outlaw—distilling by moonlight, tucking booze away in the hip pocket, sneaking into speakeasies, conspiring against the government. By identifying himself with this vast subculture, the bootlegger was able to move around with greater acceptance and freedom than did his colleagues of the brothel and the gaming board.

Prohibition did more to give the organized criminal respectability than any other single force in our national history. Prohibition also made the underworld's cup run over. The over-all "take" from the liquor sale to a thirsty and war-bloated consuming public was gargantuan. The underworld reached for the lion's share of this "take," through a series of beer battles, in the attempt to establish regional and then national monopolies.

Not all bootleggers were criminals. Certainly, by the mores of their times, most of them were not. But the organized criminal element was in a position to do in the bootlegging business what it had done in vice and gambling. The organized gang could establish a monopoly.

The big profits in bootlegging did not come from a still in the cellar turning out a few gallons for sale to the neighbors. The great income came from giant breweries servicing a whole city, several cities, or states. The "big buck" came from the "imports," the rum-running from the French islands off the coast of Canada, across the border, from beyond the three-mile limit.

To conduct this kind of business required "organization," contracting for the stuff in many lands, getting it past the coastal patrol, landing it on the docks, loading it onto trucks, carting it to warehouses, delivering it to the retail outlets. This was big business, necessitating big money. This also meant establishing the right connection with government agents. To protect the basic investment involved in such a complex and costly undertaking, the entrepreneurs had to guarantee themselves an extensive market.

In all of these undertakings, the experiences of the underworld made them peculiarly apt for the job. They had the cash, accumulated with minimal accounting to the Bureau of Internal Revenue. They had the right contacts with police and politicians. They had the strong arm to collapse or kill a competitor. They were also at home on the highways—an old tradition in the West, a more recent technique in the East (built up around a number of petty rackets from artichokes to onions).

In the struggle for control of alcohol, there developed tight interstate and international alliances. The bigwigs of the underworld developed a national purpose, beginning to weave together the various ethnic gangs into a coast-to-coast network.

As this great corporation developed, there ensued the inevitable internal struggle for positions on the board of directors, for president of the company. The great killings of the Capone Era were the result of these struggles: to wipe out giant competitors and to establish internal control.

In two excerpts, the evolution of the underworld in the Prohibition Era is described.

The first of these, by Virgil W. Peterson, describing the dynastic succession from Colisimo to Torrio to Capone, is set against the double background of the Irish versus Italian struggle and the palace revolutions within the latter group. The book from which this chapter is excerpted, *Barbarians in Our Midst,* is not only a classic volume on the underworld but is also a rare political history of an American city—showing the tie between the upper and nether worlds in Chicago.

The brief excerpt entitled "The Capone Era" is the simple, prosaic recital of a mass murder, not as dramatic as the celebrated St. Valentine's Day Massacre, but a reminder that the "massacre" was just one of many wholesale slaughters to establish a business empire.

The Prohibition Era also coincided with the rise of the Italians in the underworld. Prior to the 1920's, organized crime in the United States, especially in the big cities, was dominated by names of Irish and Jewish origin. Paul Kelly (born Paolo Vaccarrelli) was one of the first prominent gang figures of Italian extraction. In New Orleans, before the turn of the century, Italians were prominent in a major criminal scandal. But, as a whole, the Italians did not come to the fore nationally until the 1920's, when the name of Capone became identified with gangdom.

In the excerpt entitled "The Ethnic Succession," Daniel Bell—a sociologist—provides an interesting theory on the rise of the Italians in the underworld.

When the Eighteenth Amendment appeared to be due for repeal, the underworld faced a crisis. It was losing its biggest business. Without illegal alcohol, organized crime would have to fall back on prostitution and gambling. Not only would this mean a major loss of income, but it would also mean retrenchment in personnel, with the accompanying danger that some of those who would have to be let out would form their own mobs, would turn state's evidence, would wreck the entire corporate setup. The great national network that had been established had to find new sources of revenue.

The underworld turned to industry, labor, and real estate. All three were "naturals" because the underworld was already in these fields. Early in the century, organized crime had begun to establish its "rackets." By moving in at the point of transportation—waterfront, market, or trucking—the underworld could levy tribute on manufacturer and retailer. It was generally easier to start with the retailer because he was small, without influence, easily scared, and easily bankrupted. Once the selling end of a business was organized, pressure could be put on the manufacturing end. Then it became possible to play both ends against the reluctant and recalcitrant. This technique was highly perfected, albeit only in corners of the American economy, before the 1930's. With the passing of Prohibition, the industrial rackets moved into high gear.

Gangland's involvement with labor—in particular at the point of industrial strife—was also not without early precedent. Struggle between labor and capital—like struggle between Democrats and Republicans—often involved violence. Originally and normally the violence was amateurish, pitting hungry scab against hungry striker. But as organization and technique moved on to the labor-management front, the disrupting parties reached out for "pro's," in the same way that business and government have done. And once the professional guerrilla appeared on the labor front, his high skill made him almost indispensable to both sides.

In his early relations with labor, the hood was a servant. But as Prohibition began to run out, the gangs turned to the unions to master them, to take over—*behind* a front or *out in* front. Some of these unions had treasuries. Other unions were poor, but—in the hands of hoods—could be used for extortion. In either case it was a business worth looking into.

The third "natural" for the post-Prohibition underworld was real estate. Organized crime was not unaccustomed to holding property: clubs, bars, hotels, disorderly houses. Through their political ties, they had learned the ABC of "honest graft," the process of buying land or property cheaply and selling it to the city or county for a handsome price. The huge fortunes of rum-running gravitated easily toward real estate, more easily than into manufacture—a field with which the underworld was unacquainted, involving skills that were somewhat strange. With money in real estate the beer barons could see their fortunes multiply with a clarity spelled out many years before by Henry George.

In the period of the 1930's, the common noun used to describe the various penetrations of the underworld into legitimate business was "racketeering." In a Senate investigation of the "rackets" in the early 1930's, the committee spent its opening days on the matter of definition, almost as if finding the right words to describe the evil might exorcise the devil right out of our fair and virgin land.

One of the witnesses before this committee was the eminent historian and criminologist, Harry Elmer Barnes. Part of his testimony is included in the excerpt entitled "The Racket as Ideal."

Many years later a DA with a flare for the historical and sociological wrote a brilliant piece on "Racketeering," included here under the title "The Racket Defined."

In the Senate investigation of racketeering, testimony gathered at Detroit from Clayton Ettinger concluded that "practically 1 dollar out of 4 spent by our people in the United States per year is spent because of crime." The witness argued, from his examination of criminal grip on business, that "society, in a sense, has formed a partnership with crime."

At these same hearings the investigators invited testimony on labor, primarily from unionists who told tales of unions that had been taken over by gangsters and of other unions where gangsters were trying to move in. Probably, the most colorful, yet revealing, testimony came from Steve Sumner, an officer of the Milk Wagon Drivers' Union. This union, part of the

teamster trade, was then under assault from the Chicago underworld. Sumner's testimony is entitled "Into the Trade Unions." The labor people were
preparing for bloody war—literally. A full generation later, the unions in
the teamster trade were at the very center of an investigation that once more
"shocked" America.

The excerpt entitled "The Labor Skates and I" is Roger Touhy's version
of how the Capone mob planned to move in on labor. The excerpt, like the
book, was written by Touhy after twenty-five years in jail, on what he claimed
were faked charges concerning the alleged kidnaping of Jake ("The Barber")
Factor. The "frame-up," according to Touhy, was Capone's way of using
the Chicago machinery of law to get rid of a business competitor. While
Touhy's testimony should probably be taken *cum grano salis,* there is enough
that Touhy knew and was ready to discuss publicly, it seems, for somebody
to have "mowed him down," after his prison release, on the ever-bloody
streets of the Windy City.

The essay entitled "Into Hollywood" describes the use of a union to
shake down an industry.

While the first sallies of the underworld into business and labor were
acts of prey against weak victims, the money men of gangdom soon gathered
the know-how to "create": namely, to set up their own businesses and get
their own union charters. By the end of the 1930's, the underworld was involved in a many-sided operation. At the lowest level was the old street
gang, the mailed fist ready to extort from business, beat up labor, deliver
power to politicians, discipline a dissenter within the rising structure of the
Syndicate. At the next level were the many illegitimate businesses: with
dope, gambling, and prostitution at the top of the list. At the next highest
level, the underworld was beginning to manage trade associations and unions.
At the highest level, it was setting up businesses, investing in legitimate
concerns, and putting politicians into business.

The period in the 1930's between the repeal of the Eighteenth Amendment and the Great Depression, when the Syndicate was being structured, is
described in the person of its central figure in "The Lepke Era" by Andrew
Tully.

The making of the modern underworld, like the formation of modern
nations, necessitated the unification of many forces. The feudal barons of
crime had to be subdued. Authority had to be defined. Law had to be established. Talents had to be harnessed. Ideas had to be created. An *entente
cordiale* with the surrounding society had to be worked out. And all this
had to be done on a leviathan scale, yet hidden from the public eye.

While many investigators, newspaper men, and students suspected what
was happening, spoke about what was happening, and denounced what was
happening, virtually no one had the evidence—the kind of evidence that

would stand up in court—to prove the charge. Testimony was hard to get from within the underworld, with its mores of group loyalty and death to the traitor. The "state within a state" was rising, but there were no voices within that "society within a society" to tell the tale.

The one great document on the underworld as seen by an insider, never published and probably never to be published, is "The Confession of Kid Twist." The Kid—Abe Reles—was one of that Brooklyn gang known as Murder Inc. He was one of the enforcers of the law, the combined police and military of the underworld social order. He was high enough up to "know." He was low enough down to fear liquidation as a result of internal mob politics. He was defiant enough to "rat." And he was smart enough to have stored up a mass of evidence, backed by a capacity for total recall. For days on end, he spoke to the DA's people. He sent some of America's top men of crime to the chair with his infallible memory and biting tongue. He was America's prime weapon against Crime Inc., and he was guarded like a ton of uranium. His total outpourings must be the best eyewitness account of the underworld ever produced.

The nearest the public will ever come to knowing what he said, however, is contained in the epic book *Murder Inc.* by the Assistant DA who handled Reles, Burton B. Turkus. The excerpt entitled "Murder Inc." is more than an account of that outfit. It is a summary, chronology, and commentary on the evolution of the modern underworld—from feudalism to statism, from the underworld's articles of confederation to its constitution!

Section 16   **FROM TORRIO TO CAPONE**

From *The Barbarians in Our Midst* by Virgil Peterson, 1952.

It is questionable whether the change in the city administration placed much fear in the heart of John Torrio. The members of his organization were too firmly fixed in the political structure of the city to become very much concerned over who occupied the mayor's chair. Almost simultaneously with the election of Mayor Dever, however, Torrio began giving more attention to the development of his illicit operations beyond the city limits. His gambling and vice resorts in Burnham, Illinois, were still flourishing. He was well established in Stickney, Illinois. He now conceived the plan of establishing the headquarters for his gambling and beer distribution activities in Cicero. The principal obstacle to this move was Eddie Tancl, a Bohemian prize fighter and cafe proprietor who was strongly rooted in Cicero. And Tancl had no intentions of moving aside for John Torrio or anyone else. In overcoming the opposition of Tancl, Torrio resorted to a carefully planned stratagem. Without seeking any official protection, he opened a bawdyhouse in Cicero. Naturally the police raided it with dispatch. He moved it to a second location and again the Cicero police raided the brothel and forced it to close. Now Torrio was ready for his master stroke. At the gangster's instigation, Sheriff Peter Hoffman moved into Cicero with raiding parties and put its flourishing slot machines out of business. The blow was fatal. An immediate truce followed between Torrio and Tancl without a shot having been fired. Torrio and his first lieutenant, Al Capone, started gambling and beer operations in Cicero. The slot machines began clicking again. Peace reigned temporarily, but Cicero still remained disputed territory.

John Torrio was rapidly becoming one of the most powerful gangsters in the nation. From gambling and illicit beer operations he had become tremendously wealthy. He owned the West Hammond and Manhattan breweries and was interested in others. With his family he toured Europe. In Italy he purchased a villa for his mother. He was held in high esteem by the William Hale Thompson Republican organization. His political power even extended to the state capital in Springfield. When Harry Guzik and his wife, Alma, were convicted as panders, Torrio had sufficient influence to secure their pardons from Governor Len Small before they had served any part of the sentences imposed on them.

It is not surprising that as the Cicero elections approached in the spring of 1924 that the political support of the Torrio gang was sought by opportunistic politicians. For many years the organization headed by Joseph Z. Klenha, president of the village board, had controlled Cicero as a result of clever political deals. But in 1924 the Democrats decided to enter a separate list of candidates on the ballot. This maneuver presented a threat to the political fortunes of Klenha, who was running on the Republican ticket. To prevent a possible Democratic victory, Republican committeemen conceived a brilliant plan of action. Edward Vogel, a slot-machine boss, was designated as an emissary to approach the Torrio gang for support for the Republican candidate. Vogel consulted with Louis La Cava, a Torrio lieutenant, and an alliance between the Cicero Republicans and the Torrio criminal organization became a reality.

Election day in Cicero arrived on April 1, 1924. The Torrio stalwarts had no intention of permitting any element of chance to enter into the contest. They were professional gamblers—and gamblers never gamble! In one of the most disgraceful episodes in American municipal history, Torrio gangsters conducted an armed invasion of the thriving suburb of Cicero. Armed with machine guns, they manned the polls. Automobiles filled with gunmen patrolled the streets. Polling places were raided and ballots stolen at gunpoint. Voters were kidnapped and transported to Chicago where they were held captive until after the polls closed. Others were slugged and shot. A reign of terror prevailed. The county judge in charge of elections dispatched seventy patrolmen, five detective bureau squads and nine automobile squads from Chicago to Cicero to restore order. When Chicago police approached a polling place manned by Torrio gunmen a pitched battle took place. In the fusillade, Al Capone's brother, Frank, fell mortally wounded and another man was seriously injured. It is needless to mention that the Torrio-Capone candidate for village president was elected. And Cicero became known throughout the nation as one of the toughest places in America, a reputation it was to retain for many years. Its main streets were filled with gambling establishments and houses of prostitution. It remained the Torrio headquarters for illicit beer distribution. The only law observed in the place was the law decreed by the Torrio-Capone gangsters. They owned Cicero—lock, stock and barrel.

Following the election day gun battle, Frank Capone was given an elaborate funeral. Floral pieces costing over twenty thousand dollars were supplied by Dion O'Banion's florist shop, which was across the street from the Holy Name Cathedral, only a few blocks north of Chicago's busy Loop.

Dion O'Banion, incidentally, was a most unusual florist; he not only furnished flowers for funerals but also provided the corpses. Mayor Dever's chief of police, Morgan Collins, once attributed at least twenty-five murders to this tough gunman who had been reared on the city's "near North Side." While still a mere youth he had served sentences in the House of Correction for robbery and for carrying concealed weapons. During a fierce newspaper circulation war he was employed as a terrorist. He also tried his hand at safe-cracking. In the midst of blowing open the safe of a labor union in the Postal Telegraph Building he was caught red-handed by the police, but after the payment of bribes, the police became forgetful and it was decided the case against him was weak. On another occasion O'Banion shot two men in the entrance of the La Salle theatre. This time he was not even prosecuted. He had developed into a powerful underworld leader in his own right, and his prestige was further enhanced when he became aligned with John Torrio, who placed him in charge of gambling and bootlegging activities on the North Side. Although it was outside his territory, the Torrio gang also promised O'Banion a percentage of the profits of the Ship, one of the most notorious gambling houses in Cicero.

On November 3, 1924, O'Banion attended a conference held in the Ship for the purpose of dividing the previous week's profits. Also present at the meeting called by Al Capone in the absence of Torrio were Frank Nitti, Frank Maritote (alias Frank Diamond), Earl "Hymie" Weiss, Frankie Rio and Vince Drucci. Capone explained to his confederates that Angelo Genna had lost $30,000 at the Ship's gambling tables the week before and had left his I.O.U.'s covering that amount. Capone suggested that the debt be cancelled. Dion O'Banion strenuously objected and issued an ultimatum to Angelo Genna by telephone giving him one week to pay. Angelo Genna was a powerful leader in the Unione Siciliana. He was a vicious killer and was not easily intimidated. It so happened, therefore, that on November 10, 1924, three men entered O'Banion's flower shop at 738 North State Street in Chicago. One of them grasped the outstretched hand of O'Banion in a friendly greeting. The other two emptied their revolvers into his head at close range. A silver-bronze casket valued at $10,000 was brought from Pennsylvania in a special car for O'Banion's corpse. His wake was attended by prominent politicians including five judges of the Municipal Court. Also present to pay his respects was Alderman Dorsey Crowe. Only a short time before his death O'Banion had worked diligently in behalf of Crowe's election. As the hearse carried the tough gangster to his last resting place, it was followed by a huge funeral procession made up in part of judges, legislators and aldermen.

By 1924, John Torrio had reached the height of his power. Politicians vied with one another for his support. Rival gangsters feared him. His allies included Louis Alterie, Frank McErlane, Hymie Weiss, Dapper Dan McCarthy, Dan McFall, and scores of others. Some of the nation's most vicious killers were at his beck and call. Nevertheless Torrio's position was still far from impregnable. His power stemmed from corrupt political alliances and was enforced by the guns of gangsters, but it was a power that lacked stability. Politicians could usually be kept in line. Gangsters, however, had a habit of changing sides. The lines of battle were constantly shifting. Guns spitting forth bullets and death in behalf of Torrio and his gang one day were frequently employed by the same killers the next, in the interest of opposing forces. The murder of Dion O'Banion touched off a series of gang slayings. Angelo Genna was murdered on May 26, 1925, his brother Michael was killed on June 13, and a third brother, Anthony, was ambushed and slain on July 8.

Several months before the O'Banion murder an incident occurred which was to serve as the beginning of Torrio's downfall. On May 19, 1924, Chief of Police Morgan Collins directed a raid on the Sieben Brewery where thirteen truckloads of beer were waiting to be convoyed through the streets of Chicago by Torrio gunmen. Among the numerous men arrested were John Torrio, Louis Alterie and Hymie Weiss. The defendants were turned over to the Federal government for prosecution. Rushing to the aid of the gunmen in custody, William Skidmore, professional bondsman and gambler-politician, secured the release of several on bail. A total of thirty-eight defendants were indicted by a Federal grand jury. John Torrio received a sentence of nine months in the Lake County Jail. The gang leader's ironclad immunity had been broken, and the Chicago police had given the Federal authorities a helping hand. This was not only perplexing—it was utterly humiliating.

On January 24, 1925, just before Torrio began serving his sentence, an attempt was made to assassinate him. Three men, believed to have been George "Bugs" Moran, Hymie Weiss and Vince Drucci, were the assailants. One witness positively identified Bugs Moran as the man who jumped from a car and fired upon Torrio, but Moran was not even indicted. Torrio was rushed to the Jackson Park Hospital where he was brought back to health, but not happiness. His escape from death had been only by the narrowest of margins. With one gangster after another meeting violent death, Torrio decided to abdicate his throne to Al Capone and leave the turmoil of Chicago gangland battles forever. After serving his nine-month jail sentence he therefore returned to New York City where he eventually became affiliated with an underworld group which included such well-known gangsters as Frank Costello, Charles "Lucky" Luciano, Meyer Lansky, Benjamin "Bugsy" Siegel and many others. About ten years later he was sentenced to two and one-half years in jail for evasion of the Federal income tax.

The illicit empire which Torrio was abandoning was worth millions. This fact was definitely established by records seized by the police on April 6, 1925, during a raid on lavishly furnished offices at 2146 South Michigan Avenue in Chicago. The South Michigan Avenue address had served as the gang headquarters since the syndicate had been ousted from the Four Deuces several months earlier. Arrested by police in the raid were John Patton, who had won fame as the "Boy Mayor of Burnham," Robert Larry McCullough, once convicted for burglary, Frank Nitti, Leo Clark, Joseph Piza, Joe Fusco, Anthony Arasso and Phillip Kimmle, a former partner of Mike "de Pike" Heitler. Torrio's field general Al Capone was not present when the police arrived; he was already in hiding for the slugging of a policeman and a newspaper editor in Cicero. Records seized by the raiding officers revealed that John Torrio, John Patton, Al Capone, Jack Guzik and others were reaping an annual revenue amounting to millions of dollars from bootlegging and disorderly house operations. Four large breweries were operated by the syndicate to produce beer for Chicago's thirsty customers. Liquor was brought to the Windy City from New York, Miami and New Orleans. Carefully recorded were the names of police officers and Federal prohibition agents who were on the gang's payoff list. Complete customers' records were maintained. Everything was handled with the efficiency of one of the country's largest corporations. Torrio was a master at organization. The criminal syndicate which he had created was one of the most powerful in America's history.

With Al Capone's growing opulence came a corresponding increase in his political power. The gang leader fully understood the importance of strong alliances with the right politicians. In Chicago's First Ward Capone was on friendly terms with Hinky Dink Kenna and Bathhouse John Coughlin. Since the redistricting of the city in 1923, the First Ward's sole alderman was Bathhouse John. Hinky Dink remained the ward committeeman, however, which meant that he ruled over the political affairs of this important district. Al Capone recognized Hinky Dink as a masterful organizer whose ability could be useful to his criminal empire. It was not surprising therefore, that one of Al's favorite loafing places was Kenna's cigar store on South Clark Street. There Al also transacted much business—underworld business.

Dennis "Duke" Cooney, who had been the overseer of the disreputable hotels of the First Ward for Hinky Dink since 1916, now became an integral part of the Capone organization. The gangster placed Cooney in charge of his prostitution operations. Duke Cooney brought a wealth of experience and efficient methods into the brothel business. With Capone's backing, he increased the profits from established bawdyhouses, at the same time opening new places which still further swelled the ever-increasing revenue of the gang. Placing Kenna's right-hand man, Dennis Cooney, in one of the key posts of the Capone organization was evidence of the high esteem in which Hinky Dink was held by the underworld boss. And the deference shown him by Al Capone in turn served to increase Kenna's political stature. Chicago was passing through the disgraceful period in which politicians were fawning over the gang leader and seeking his favor. Insofar as the Democratic boss George Brennan was concerned, Kenna was then the political equal of Tony Cermak, president of the County Board since 1922 and later mayor of Chicago.

Al Capone marshaled the forces of the underworld as they had seldom been marshaled anywhere before. And as the vicious criminal elements and their political counterparts became more strongly organized, government was growing more and more disorganized, until it virtually fell apart and capitulated to a ruthless and defiant underworld. During the first four months of 1926 there were twenty-nine gang killings in Chicago, bringing the total to over two hundred within four years. On April 27, 1926, Assistant State's Attorney William H. McSwiggin, who had gained a reputation for securing death-penalty verdicts, left home in the company of two friends. One of his associates was Thomas Duffy, a beer peddler and a precinct captain in McSwiggin's faction of the Republican party. The third member of the group was James Doherty, a Capone gangster who allegedly had murdered Eddie Tancl of Cicero in November 1924. About 8:30 P.M. McSwiggin and his two associates stepped out of their automobile near a saloon operated by a friend. At this moment a car roared by. Its occupants emptied their guns into the prosecutor and his two companions. McSwiggin, Duffy and Doherty were killed. This gang killing created a furor. Even Al Capone, at whom the finger of suspicion pointed, found it expedient to flee the city until public anger subsided. Lengthy official investigations were conducted but of course they resulted in utter failure. The murderers represented an organization stronger than government itself.

The McSwiggin case was still fresh in the public mind when new gang violence broke out reviving the memory of Dion O'Banion's murder. At noon on September 20, 1926, eleven automobiles filled with armed gunmen, affiliated with O'Banion's former associate, Hymie Weiss, roared into Cicero. Twenty-second Street, the town's main thoroughfare, was filled with noonday shoppers and workers enjoying their lunch hour. In a restaurant next door to the Hawthorne Inn, the headquarters for Al Capone, the gang leader was having lunch. As the cars filled with Weiss gangsters neared the Inn, they reduced their speed. Suddenly from the passing cars, thousands of bullets and slugs from machine guns, pistols and shotguns went screaming into the Inn. Windows were shattered; plaster was ripped from the walls; doors were filled with bullet holes, and furniture was wrecked. When the attack started, Al Capone dropped to the restaurant floor. He was uninjured but one of his gunmen, Louis Barko, was struck in the shoulder by a bullet. Thirty-five automobiles that were parked along Twenty-second Street were raked by gun fire. One car, in which a woman was sitting with an infant, was hit thirty times. One of the bullets grazed her forehead and injured her eyes. The main business district of Cicero was thrown into a panic. A Chicago newspaper editorial blazoned, "This is War!"

Naturally, the Capone gang had no intention of allowing an armed invasion of its stronghold go unanswered. On the afternoon of October 11, 1926, Hymie Weiss and four companions stepped from their automobile near the flower shop at 738 North State Street where Dion O'Banion had been slain on November 10, 1924. As the five men were about to ascend the stairway leading to the second floor of the flower shop, bullets came screeching at them. Hymie Weiss and Patrick Murray, a beer peddler, were killed. W. W. O'Brien, a well-known criminal attorney, Benjamin Jacobs, a policeman of the bloody Twentieth Ward, and Sam Peller, the chauffeur, were riddled with bullets (but they eventually recovered).

Stray bullets from the assassins' guns crashed into the walls of the Holy Name Cathedral across the street. Both the chief of police and the chief of detectives accused Al Capone of responsibility for the double murder. But they did not even bother to question him. Capone offered to present himself at headquarters for interrogation but the head of the police department said that it would be merely a waste of time to talk with him. The law enforcement agencies were completely demoralized. The honest members of the police department no longer had the heart to fight back, and the balance were working hand in glove with the criminals.

Although the gangsters had no fear of the law enforcement agencies, they did have reason to fear each other. The bitter gang warfare which had been raging was proving costly to the underworld, and the time was considered propitious for a determined effort to bring an end to the gang killings. On October 21, 1926, therefore, a peace conference was held in a prominent downtown hotel within the shadows of City Hall. Maxie Eisen presided over this gathering of gunmen and plug-uglies who in the interest of self-preservation were attempting to reach an amicable agreement regarding territorial jurisdiction. Among those present were Bugs Moran, burglar, robber and ex-convict; Jack Guzik, the so-called brains of the Capone organization and a brother of Harry, the convicted pander; William R. Skidmore, Barney Bertche, Eddie Vogel, Vincent Drucci, Jack Zuta and many other prominent underworld characters. The conference allotted various sections of the city to the different warring factions insofar as beer distribution was concerned. Vince Drucci and Bugs Moran agreed to confine their illicit beer operations to the Forty-second and Forty-third Wards on the North Side, while all territory south of Madison Street was to be the domain of the Capone organization. When it came to gambling Al Capone apparently reserved the entire city for himself. Even the powerful North Side chieftains, William R. Skidmore and Barney Bertche, were told that in future they must obtain the approval of Al Capone as to all gambling and vice operations. Unfortunately, "honor among thieves" actually exists only in the minds of the literati. This time it disappeared almost as soon as the peace conference ended. Contrary to the solemn terms of the truce, there were territorial infringements followed by violence, while gang killings continued as frequent as before.

By 1928, the underworld was in the midst of one of its most prosperous eras. The political protectors of the gangsters were growing opulent and powerful. The hands of the honest police officers were tied; those of the dishonest kept grasping for more and more tainted dollars. And there were plenty to be had. Every few days reports of spectacular gang killings were flashed over the wires of the press services to all parts of the world. On September 7, 1928, a gang assassination occurred during the rush hour near State and Madison Streets, the busiest corner in the United States. Antonio Lombardo, who had been placed at the head of the Unione Siciliana by Al Capone in 1925, was shot and killed as he was walking with two bodyguards. Joseph Ferraro, one of the bodyguards, was also slain. The other, Joseph Lorlordo, escaped injury. The murderers, having completed their mission, quietly disappeared in the passing throng.

But Chicago had yet to witness its most bizarre gang slaying. On February 14, 1929, St. Valentine's day, seven of Bugs Moran's associates were awaiting the return of their leader in his headquarters, a garage at 2122 North Clark Street. Momentarily they expected Moran, Willie Marks and Ted Newberry to walk into the garage. Suddenly several men dressed in the uniforms of police officers entered the hideout. They purported to place the seven Moran hoodlums under arrest and ordered them to keep their hands up facing the wall. The commands were obeyed without strenuous objection. A brush with police officers was considered among the least of the worries of the criminal element—a temporary difficulty which could easily be fixed. The gangsters in full police regalia then raised their machine guns and mowed down their seven helpless rivals. The St. Valentine's day massacre stunned Chicagoans. It called the attention of the world to the city's lawlessness. Like virtually all Chicago gang killings it was never solved. It was known of course that Bugs Moran was an enemy of the Capone organization, but Al Capone had his usual airtight alibi. He was basking in the sun at his Palm Island estate just three miles from downtown Miami, when the assassination took place. His business manager, Jack Guzik, had been making daily long-distance telephone calls to the gang leader from the Congress Hotel in Chicago until three days before the mass slaying occurred. But for all the police ever found out, the calls may have related to the weather.

Actually, officialdom did not want to delve too deeply into the affairs of the underworld. Information concerning family secrets is usually kept within the family circle if at all possible. And the ties between the gangsters and political leaders were close; they were intimate. This was amply proved in the summer of 1929, when a member of Jack Guzik's family was married. Among the guests present at the wedding were Bathhouse John Coughlin, Alderman of the First Ward, William V. Pacelli, Alderman of the "Bloody Twentieth" Ward, Captain of Police Hugh McCarthy and Ralph Capone, a brother of Al. The gang leader himself was not present. Having run afoul of an unco-operative court in Philadelphia earlier that year, he was spending a few months in an eastern jail. It was evident, however, that members of the city council, high ranking officers of the police department and Al Capone's principal lieutenants were component parts of one big happy family —a family that ruled over the nation's second largest municipality for the benefit of rugged gunmen and ruthless racketeers.

The contempt in which Chicago's officials and law enforcement bodies were held by the organized criminal element had been demonstrated time and time again. Gangsters had attacked and killed an assistant state's attorney. They had bombed the homes of leading officials including those of the state's attorney, the city comptroller, a judge and a senator. And on June 9, 1930, they shot and killed a representative of the press. Alfred J. Lingle, a *Tribune* reporter, was the victim as he entered the busy Illinois Central Railroad subway at Michigan Boulevard and Randolph Street. The murder created a furor. Speculation was rife as to why "Jake" Lingle was assassinated, but investigation into his background and affiliations soon unraveled the mystery. Lingle was a gambling addict. On a newspaper reporter's salary he frequently made bets of a thousand dollars on a single horse race. He borrowed money extensively from gamblers including Jimmie Mondi. But Lingle was more than a "sucker" who made heavy donations to the gamblers. This was evident when it was disclosed that at the time he was murdered he was wearing a diamond-studded belt given him by Al Capone. This was a gift that the gang leader bestowed only upon those who were important to him. Lingle had become influential in the Capone gambling organization, particularly in Chicago's Loop area where he was somewhat of an unofficial mayor. He also had his finger in the racing news service. For a long time independent news services had waged warfare against Mont Tennes and the General News Bureau. About January 1, 1930, Jake Lingle had brought the warring factions together and they agreed upon a two-year truce. There were some indications that Lingle's activity in connection with the wire services may have been responsible for his murder.

The investigation of the Lingle slaying led in many directions. His connections with gangland activities were multifarious and numerous people could have desired his death. One of the gangsters logically suspected of having instigated the killing was the North Side gambling and vice lord Jack Zuta. On July 1, 1930, Zuta was about to be released from police headquarters at 11th and State Streets where he had been questioned concerning the Lingle murder. He confided in Lieutenant George Barker of the bomb squad that he feared rival gunmen were waiting outside the police building to kill him. The police lieutenant obligingly offered to furnish the gang leader with safe transportation, so Zuta climbed into the rear seat of Lieutenant Barker's sedan, insisting on sitting in the middle. He was flanked on one side by Albert Bratz and on the other by Leona Bernstein. With Lieutenant Barker in front was Solly Vision, another associate of Zuta. Lieutenant Barker left police headquarters and drove his car north on State Street to a point just beyond Quincy Street in the Loop, when it was observed that a dark blue sedan was following. Suddenly this car speeded up and when it was alongside the policeman's automobile, one of its occupants stepped to the running board, pulled a gun from his shoulder holster and fired seven shots at Jack Zuta. Lieutenant Barker stopped his sedan and jumped into the street, which momentarily diverted the fire of two assailants who were by this time emptying their guns at the Zuta party. Jack Zuta and his three associates quickly crawled out of the policeman's automobile and disappeared in the crowd of people walking along the street. Just back of Lieutenant Barker's sedan when he stopped, was a State Street surface car which was stalled during the gun battle. One of the bullets pierced the front of the streetcar striking the motor-man, Elbert Lusader, and killing him. Another bullet wounded Olaf Svenste, a night watchman, who was crossing the street on his way to the Standard Club where he worked. Following the attempted assassination of Zuta, the gunmen sped away in their car which belched forth a smoke screen and easily eluded Lieutenant Barker who started to give chase.

The North Side gangster appeared to be leading a charmed life. He had been virtually trapped. Two gunmen had fired upon him several times at very close range. Nevertheless he had managed to escape. Zuta's luck was very short lived, however. Only a month later, on August 1, 1930, he was in a dance pavilion near Delafield, Wisconsin. As he walked across the dance floor to drop a nickel into the electric player piano, five gunmen quietly sur-rounded him, and with gangland precision fired their weapons at close range. This time Jack Zuta did not have a chance. He was killed instantly.

The code of the underworld precludes a gangster from talking. But now that Jack Zuta was dead, the records and papers he left behind told an amazing story of the alliance that existed between politicians and criminals, of financial transactions between the underworld and the city rulers, of close relationships between the lawless and the law-enforcing bodies, of official corruption. For many weeks prominent politicians and police officials offered explanations concerning canceled checks which originally had been issued to them by the North Side gambler. Most of the explanations were weak and unconvincing. Judge Joseph W. Schulman of the Municipal Court received several thousand dollars from the slain gangster, between December 1921 and December 29, 1925. Schulman denied that the money came from the gambling king, although the checks were signed by Jack Zuta and were issued to and endorsed by the judge. Zuta had engaged in financial dealings with Emanuel Eller, a former judge of the Criminal Court, with George Van Lent, a former State Senator and Republican leader, with State Senator Harry W. Starr, with Louis L. Fisher, counsel for dog track interests and a former as-sistant state's attorney. Balance sheets reflected that a person designated as "M.K." received thousands of dollars from the profits of the Zuta syndicate. There was a strong indication that "M.K." referred to Matt Kolb, a politician-gambler known as the underworld representative of many county and city officials. The records established Zuta as one of the financial backers of the "Regular Republican Club of Cook County." The chairman of the Republican County Committee had issued to the slain gang leader a membership card in the William Hale Thompson Republican Club. And this committee was the one that named the organization candidates for the municipal, circuit and superior court judgeships. Charles E. Graydon who was the sheriff of Cook County in 1927 issued a card extending special police courtesies to Zuta, the public enemy. There were canceled checks and notes revealing that

Zuta had furnished money to police officials and members of the underworld such as "Dago" Lawrence Mangano, Tony Lombardo and Hymie Levin of the Capone gang, William R. Skidmore, the political fixer, Diamond Joe Esposito and Henry Finkelstein. There was a letter from the chief of police of Evanston, Illinois, requesting a loan of four hundred dollars from Zuta. The loan had been granted.

The names of prominent politicians on canceled checks, notes and other papers could not be dismissed with the customary denials accompanied by simulated indignation. While these men were busy explaining their dealings with the gang leader, Zuta's other acquaintances began to talk. His friends in Middlesboro, Kentucky, asserted that many Chicago politicians, including judges had visited the gangster there. A former county prosecutor stated that Mayor William Hale Thompson once visited Zuta in Middlesboro. To his Kentucky friends, Zuta had confided that he had raised $50,000 in the preceding Chicago mayoralty election in behalf of Thompson's campaign. In Probate Court hearings in Chicago, Senator Harry W. Starr stated that in a conversation with Zuta in 1926 in the Hotel Sherman the gangster told him of an organization he was forming in behalf of Thompson's candidacy for mayor. Senator Starr informed the court that "Zuta said he expected to be a power in city politics and he was going 'hook, line, and sinker' for Thompson because Thompson would go 'hook, line and sinker' for him." A woman who had been living out of wedlock with a Chicago police officer informed the state's attorney that Jack Zuta gave her $1500 to pay for the promotion of her patrolman friend to the rank of sergeant. The slain gambling boss had succeeded in bringing within the orbit of his influence, public officials in every stratum of government; police officers, judges, senators, the mayor, as well as the dominant political organization of the city, were all indebted to him.

As North Side gambling and vice lord, Zuta had often found it necessary to have property available to pledge as bail in connection with court proceedings. Following his death the Probate Court initiated hearings concerning his real estate holdings. Of particular interest to the court was a check in the amount of $2500 issued by the city after the gangster's death to pay the balance due him on property that had been subjected to condemnation proceedings. Arthur X. Elrod, who had suddenly left a job with the Corporation Counsel's office in 1929, after he was questioned about his connection with a slot-machine and punch-board company, was ordered to appear in court. Probate Judge Henry Horner issued a contempt citation for Elrod. The citation was finally dismissed when Elrod turned over to the court the deed to property valued at $20,000. Several years later Elrod was to become ward committeeman of the powerful Twenty-fourth Ward of Chicago and a member of the Board of Cook County Commissioners. From

his modest beginning as a bondsman for Jack Zuta, Elrod eventually became one of the most influential politicians of the city and county.

The Zuta case was featured by the press for many months. It had been
front-page news from the attempted assassination of the gang leader on
July 1, 1930, to his actual murder in Wisconsin a month later. It was November 15, 1930, before Arthur X. Elrod had cleared himself of contempt of
court in connection with Zuta's real estate holdings. By January 1931, testimony was still being given in Probate Court regarding Zuta's connection with
politicians in general and the Thompson administration in particular.

In the meantime, other incidents have occurred which further emphasized the close affiliation between the underworld and city government.
When the police raided a hotel at 2138 South Wabash Avenue searching for
Frank "The Enforcer" Nitti, one of Al Capone's chief lieutenants, they found
confidential police instructions calling for the arrest of forty-one gunmen.
Obviously someone in authority had provided the Capone organization with
secret police files. Capone and his henchmen had disapproved of eight names
on the list. Subsequent police instructions had accordingly omitted these
names without the knowledge of the police commissioner. Apparently these
eight gunmen were too occupied with gangland business to leave the city
while the police were ostensibly looking for them or to submit to the customary innocuous arrest.

Mayor Thompson's term of office was coming to a close. His administration was completely discredited. Even Republican leaders did not want Big
Bill as their standard bearer in the 1931 mayoralty race. From 1927 through
1930 two hundred and twenty-seven gang killings had occurred in Chicago
while rival criminal gangs were waging open warfare on the city streets.
During that same period only two defendants were convicted for implication
in a gang murder.

Thompson, however, refreshed after his two years of political inactivity,
was determined to seek a fourth term. He spoke glowingly of his accom-
plishments—of the boulevards, streets, schools and public buildings he had
provided for the city. His opponents talked of crime and gang killings. At
least the cowboy mayor could not be charged with having retarded the
city's growth. Its population had increased by almost a million since he was
elected mayor the first time in 1915. The United States Census figures for
1930 showed that 3,376,438 people resided in Chicago. This represented an
increase of over 600,000 in ten years.

Thompson entered the mayoralty race with his usual vigor and scathing
denunciations of his enemies. He was particularly hostile toward the *Chicago
Tribune* which had been one of the bitterest foes of his administration. Big
Bill had been in ill health. Perhaps that accounted for his foolish delusion
that *Tribune* officials had designs on his life. The publisher of the *Tribune*

learned that some of the mayor's followers had threatened to assassinate him if Big Bill met with foul play. With life then held cheaply in Chicago, the publisher bought an armored car and hired bodyguards. As Mayor Thompson raced through the city in his open car, he carried with him a sawed-off shotgun and other weapons. He was always accompanied by police guards and maintained an array of firearms in his residence. Chicago could properly boast of being one of the world's greatest centers of commerce, industry, finance and communications. But the publisher of the city's largest newspaper and the mayor found it necessary to arm themselves fully to provide for their personal safety during an election campaign. Chicago resented its reputation as the crime capital of the world. But who could say that this reputation was undeserved?

Section 17   THE CAPONE ERA

From *Chicago Surrenders* by Edward D. Sullivan, 1930.

The ides of March figured mightily in the bursts of assorted marksmanship in which Lingle was the most important victim. Al Capone, returning from the Eastern Penitentiary late in March, made his brief and closely guarded stay in Chicago the occasion for a grand get-together in gangland. Minor gangs, independent racketeers and new and bad blood from other gang-troubled cities joined with the great Capone organization. "Al for All, and All for Al" was the slogan of perhaps the greatest gang circus ever organized. They had the town licked and were proceeding in high.

Capone booze—and it has for years been good booze—was delivered on time, ninety dollars the case. Capone beer—not old but not green—rolled into the speakeasies on time invariably, fifty-five the barrel. Capone vice and gambling enterprises had nothing to fear. A deluge of money poured into the Capone coffers.

Back in gangland shadows the once powerful Bugs Moran-Aiello gang, its strong-armed roster depleted by a death list such as no gang ever survived, considered ways and means. Almost daily their minor gambling places, their alky cooking plants, their offices and their delivery arrangements were smashed up and invaded by the police. Repeated raids were made on the Zuta-controlled shady hotels and brothels of the North Side.

A racket without protection is no racket. The Moran-Aiello outfit could not get protection with money, by threat or through the usual political hook-up. They were out of luck; they knew why!

The situation was super "hot." Capone's vast bodyguard during his brief stay was the tip-off. He is seldom mistaken about anything in gangland. Soon he was in Florida, fighting for the right to stay there, making arrangements for the new $375,000 home with every requisite of a hide-away—or fort.

Bad as things were, the Moran-Aiello outfit, with the coming of April, had an ace in the hole. Their summer beer and booze business has been one of the greatest sources of income of the gang for six years and all the North Shore resorts, beyond Chicago police jurisdiction, have been acknowledged Moran-Aiello territory. No one had ever disturbed it. That is, not until the St. Valentine Massacre had taken seven men from the gang, five of them among the toughest "hoods" in Chicago. Not until constant raids had sent the gang skidding financially and caused a dozen desertions of "Big Shots" from its crumbling ranks.

In late April resort-keepers on the North Shore lakes were tipped off, brusquely and by tough tippers-off, that they had better get ready to take a new brand of beer. Because it was going to be delivered, they were going to like it and they were going to pay for it, without argument. That message was from Capone.

It was one of those spots which caused a Chicago speakeasy owner to wonder occasionally why he ever went into the business. The gang he takes his stuff from charges him for protection as much as for beer. They ought to protect him. The resort-keepers on the North Shore began to be aware that action was impending. It's something to worry about. If you reject *any* gang's beer you get it; if you reject both gangs' beer you are caught in a crossfire and if you ACCEPT both gangs' beer the best strategy is to get out and leave the place in charge of a bartender who doesn't know much. He'll learn.

North Shore resorts began to close. It was the last stand for the Moran-Aiello gang. High time to prove by action that no one could push that outfit any further. A few loads of beer headed from the West Side in Chicago were hi-jacked deftly by the Moran-Aiello top gunners. Twenty of them—plenty hard—set themselves at Cassidy's hotel, near Lake Bluff, during May. The effort to interfere with their resort business halted for a time. This was to be warfare!

Then on May 30 the strain was terminated by gunfire.

A group of the old Druggan gang, South Side beer runners, lately associated with the Capone West Side group, came to the North Shore for dinner. They had had no contact with the Moran-Aiello group personally, but they had secretly—until that night—been part of the "Al for All and All for Al" movement. It was no secret to the North Side gang, which, the police learned, had been tapping Capone wires all over town for a month when the invasion of the resort trade was threatened. So this stealthy invasion failed!

The visiting gang group had some women with them to indicate how casual the intrusion was. They ordered dinner at Manning's Hotel, Fox Lake, miles away from the Moran arsenal, at Cassidy's resort.

In the party were George Druggan, brother of the notorious Terry; Joe Bertche, racketeer, robber and "hood" recently released from Ohio State Prison; Sam Pellar, Druggan gangster and union racketeer; Michael Quirk, crack shot, labor slugger and extortionist; Eugene ("Red") McLaughlin, kidnapper; two women whose identity was never established and Mrs. Vivian McGinnis, daughter of Vincent G. Ponic, a well-known Chicago lawyer.

The party had spent money lavishly, had kidded the proprietor about the quality of the beer and liquor available and, having made a successful first "contact," were preparing to leave, at one-thirty in the morning, June 1.

Suddenly Manning, who was leaning over the table and fraternizing with them on the best of terms, threw his hands in the air and ran backward from the table. Behind the group and fifteen feet away a screen had noiselessly been taken out of a window. On the sill rested a machine gun.

In a moment slugs rattled about the room in which the echo of laughter had just dwindled. Quirk, Pellar and Bertche toppled from their chairs, dead. Druggan and Mrs. McGinnis, riddled with bullets, fell beside them. McLaughlin and the two unknown women ran wildly across the dining room, McLaughlin dragging a riddled leg and holding onto the women. Manning saw no more of the three who thus ran; perhaps very few people ever saw them again.

At least, that was true of McLaughlin, for on June 5, a tug threshing through the Sanitary Canal caught its propeller in a heavy wire and threw the body of McLaughlin to the surface. Weighted with fifty pounds of wire and one hundred pounds of metal his body had been thrown into the canal after he had been shot five times on a "ride." Nothing on him had been disturbed—keys, papers or eight hundred dollars in money. His slayers apparently thought the weights sufficient, and had neglected the usual removal of identifying articles.

Section 18   **THE ETHNIC SUCCESSION**

From *The End of Ideology* by Daniel Bell, 1960.

The Italian community has achieved wealth and political influence much later and in a harder way than previous immigrant groups. Early Jewish wealth, that of the German Jews of the late nineteenth century, was made largely in banking and merchandising. To that extent, the dominant group in the Jewish community was outside of, and independent of, the urban political machines. Later Jewish wealth, among the East European immigrants, was built in the garment trades, though with some involvement with the Jewish gangster, who was typically an industrial racketeer (Arnold Rothstein, Lepke and Gurrah, etc.). Among Jewish lawyers, a small minority, such as the "Tammany lawyer" (like the protagonist of Sam Ornitz's *Haunch, Paunch and Jowl*), rose through politics and occasionally touched the fringes of crime. Most of the Jewish lawyers, by and large the communal leaders, climbed rapidly, however, in the opportunities that established and legitimate Jewish wealth provided. Irish immigrant wealth in the northern urban centers, concentrated largely in construction, trucking, and the waterfront, has, to a substantial extent, been wealth accumulated in and through political alliance, e.g., favoritism in city contracts.

Control of the politics of the city thus has been crucial for the continuance of Irish political wealth. This alliance of Irish immigrant wealth and politics has been reciprocal; many noted Irish political figures lent their names as important window-dressing for business corporations (Al Smith, for example, who helped form the U. S. Trucking Corporation, whose executive head for many years was William J. McCormack, the alleged "Mr. Big" of the New York waterfront), while Irish businessmen have lent their wealth to further the careers of Irish politicians. Irish mobsters have rarely achieved status in the Irish community, but have served as integral arms of the politicians, as strong-arm men on election day.

The Italians found the more obvious big-city paths from rags to riches pre-empted. In part this was due to the character of the early Italian immigrant. Most of them were unskilled and from rural stock. Jacob Riis could remark in the nineties, "the Italian comes in at the bottom and stays there." These dispossessed agricultural laborers found jobs as ditch-diggers, on the railroads as section hands, along the docks, in the service occupations, as shoemakers, barbers, garment workers, and stayed there. Many were fleeced by the "padrone" system; a few achieved wealth from truck farming, wine growing, and marketing produce; but this "marginal wealth" was not the source of coherent and stable political power.

Significantly, although the number of Italians in the United States is about a third as high as the number of Irish, and of the thirty million Catholic communicants in the United States, about half are of Irish descent and a sixth of Italian. there is not one Italian archbishop among the 21 archbishops. The Irish have a virtual monopoly. This is a factor related to the politics of the American church; but the condition also is possible because there is not significant or sufficient wealth among Italian Americans to force some parity.

The children of the immigrants, the second and third generation, became wise in the ways of the urban slums. Excluded from the political ladder —in the early thirties there were almost no Italians on the city payroll in top jobs, nor in books of the period can one find discussion of Italian political leaders—and finding few open routes to wealth, some turned to illicit ways. In the children's court statistics of the 1930's, the largest group of delinquents were the Italian; nor were there any Italian communal or social agencies to cope with these problems. Yet it was, oddly enough, the quondam racketeer, seeking to become respectable, who provided one of the major supports for the drive to win a political voice for Italians in the power structure of the urban political machines.

This rise of the Italian political bloc was connected, at least in the major northern urban centers, with another important development which tended to make the traditional relation between the politician and the protected or tolerated illicit operator more close than it had been in the past. This is the fact that the urban political machines had to evolve new forms of fundraising, since the big business contributions, which once went heavily into municipal politics, now—with the shift in the locus of power—go largely into national affairs. (The ensuing corruption in national politics, as recent Congressional investigations show, is no petty matter; the scruples of businessmen do not seem much superior to those of the gamblers.) One way that urban political machines raised their money resembled that of the large corporations which are no longer dependent on Wall Street: by self-financing— that is, by "taxing" the large number of municipal employees who bargain collectively with City Hall for their wage increases. So the firemen's union contributed money to O'Dwyer's campaign.

A second method was taxing the gamblers. The classic example, as *Life* reported, was Jersey City, where a top lieutenant of the Hague machine spent his full time screening applicants for unofficial bookmaking licenses. If found acceptable, the applicant was given a "location," usually the house or store of a loyal precinct worker, who kicked into the machine treasury a high proportion of the large rent exacted. The one thousand bookies and their one thousand landlords in Jersey City formed the hard core of the political machine that sweated and bled to get out the votes for Hague.

A third source for the financing of these machines was the new, and often illegally earned, Italian wealth. This is well illustrated by the career of Costello and his emergence as a political power in New York. Here the ruling motive has been the search for an entree—for oneself and one's ethnic group —into the ruling circles of the big city.

Frank Costello made his money originally in bootlegging. After repeal, his big break came when Huey Long, desperate for ready cash to fight the old-line political machines, invited Costello to install slot machines in Louisiana. Costello did, and he flourished. Together with Dandy Phil Kastel, he also opened the Beverly Club, an elegant gambling establishment just outside New Orleans, at which have appeared some of the top entertainers in America. Subsequently, Costello invested his money in New York real estate (including 79 Wall Street, which he later sold), the Copacabana night club, and a leading brand of Scotch whiskey.

Costello's political opportunity came when a money-hungry Tammany, starved by lack of patronage from Roosevelt and LaGuardia, turned to him for financial support. The Italian community in New York has for years nursed a grievance against the Irish and, to a lesser extent, the Jewish political groups for monopolizing political power. They complained about the lack of judicial jobs, the small number—usually one—of Italian congressmen, the lack of representation on the state tickets. But the Italians lacked the means to make their ambition a reality. Although they formed a large voting bloc, there was rarely sufficient wealth to finance political clubs. Italian immigrants, largely poor peasants from southern Italy and Sicily, lacked the mercantile experience of the Jews and the political experience gained in the seventy-five-year history of Irish immigration.

During the Prohibition years, the Italian racketeers had made certain political contacts in order to gain protection. Costello, always the compromiser and fixer rather than the muscle-man, was the first to establish relations with Jimmy Hines, the powerful leader of the West Side in Tammany Hall. But his rival, Lucky Luciano, suspicious of the Irish and seeking more direct power, backed and elected Al Marinelli for district leader on the Lower West Side. Marinelli in 1932 was the only Italian leader inside Tammany Hall. Later, he was joined by Dr. Paul Sarubbi, a partner of gangster Johnny Torrio in a large, legitimate liquor concern. Certainly, Costello and Luciano represented no "unified" move by the Italians as a whole for power; within the Italian community there are as many divisions as in any other group. What is significant is that different Italians for different reasons and in various fashions, were achieving influence for the first time. Marinelli became county clerk of New York and a leading power in Tammany. In 1937, after being blasted by Tom Dewey, then running for district attorney, as a "political ally of thieves . . . and big-shot racketeers," Marinelli was removed from office by Governor Lehman. The subsequent conviction by Dewey of Luciano and Hines, and the election of LaGuardia, left most of Tammany clubs financially weak and foundering. This was the moment Costello made his move. In a few years, by judicious financing, he controlled a bloc of "Italian" leaders in the Hall—as well as some Irish on the upper West Side and some Jewish leaders on the East side—and was able to influence the selection of a number of Italian judges. The most notable incident, revealed by a wire tap on Costello's phone, was the "Thank you, Francisco" call in 1943 by Supreme Court judge nominee Thomas Aurelio, who gave Costello full credit for his nomination.

It was not only Tammany that was eager to accept campaign contributions from newly rich Italians, even though some of these *nouveaux riches had* "arrived" through bootlegging and gambling. Fiorello LaGuardia, the wiliest mind that melting-pot politics has ever produced, understood in the early thirties where much of his covert support came from. (So, too, did Vito Marcantonio, an apt pupil of the master: Marcantonio has consistently made deals with the Italian leaders of Tammany Hall—in 1943 he supported Aurelio and refused to repudiate him even when the Democratic party formally did.) Joe Adonis, who had built a political following during the late twenties, when he ran a popular speakeasy, aided LaGuardia financially to a considerable extent in 1933. "The Democrats haven't recognized the Italians," Adonis told a friend. "There is no reason for the Italians to support anybody but LaGuardia; the Jews have played ball with the Democrats and haven't gotten much out of it. They know it now. They will vote for La-Guardia. So will the Italians."

Adonis played his cards shrewdly. He supported LaGuardia, but also a number of Democrats for local and judicial posts, and became a power in the Brooklyn area. His restaurant was frequented by Kenny Sutherland, the Coney Island Democratic leader; Irwin Steingut, the Democratic minority leader in Albany; Anthony DiGiovanni, later a councilman; William O'Dwyer; and Jim Moran. But, in 1937, Adonis made the mistake of supporting Royal Copeland against LaGuardia, and the irate Fiorello finally drove Adonis out of New York.

LaGuardia later turned his ire against Costello, too. Yet Costello survived and reached the peak of his influence in 1942, when he was instrumental in electing Michael Kennedy leader of Tammany Hall. Despite the Aurelio fiasco, which first brought Costello into notoriety, he still had sufficient power in the Hall to swing votes for Hugo Rogers as Tammany leader in 1948. In those years many a Tammany leader came hat-in-hand to Costello's apartment or sought him out on the golf links to obtain the nomination for a judicial post.

During this period, other Italian political leaders were also coming to the fore. Generoso Pope, whose Colonial Sand and Stone Company began to prosper through political contacts, became an important political figure, especially when his purchase of the two largest Italian-language dailies (later merged into one), and of a radio station, gave him almost a monopoly of channels to Italian-speaking opinion of the city. Through Generoso Pope, and through Costello, the Italians became a major political force in New York.

That the urban machines, largely Democratic, have financed their heavy campaign costs in this fashion rather than having to turn to the "moneyed interests" explains in some part why these machines were able, in part, to support the New and Fair Deals without suffering the pressures they might have been subjected to had their source of money supply been the business groups. Although he has never publicly revealed his political convictions, it is likely that Frank Costello was a fervent admirer of Franklin D. Roosevelt and his efforts to aid the common man. The basic measures of the New Deal, which most Americans today agree were necessary for the public good, would not have been possible without the support of the "corrupt" big-city machines.

There is little question that men of Italian origin appeared in most of the leading roles in the high drama of gambling and mobs, just as twenty years ago the children of East European Jews were the most prominent figures in organized crime, and before that individuals of Irish descent were similarly prominent. To some extent statistical accident and the tendency of newspapers to emphasize the few sensational figures gives a greater illusion about the domination of illicit activities by a single ethnic group than all the facts warrant. In many cities, particularly in the South and on the West Coast, the mob and gambling fraternity consisted of many other groups, and often, predominantly, of native white Protestants. Yet it is clear that in the major northern urban centers there was a distinct ethnic sequence in the modes of obtaining illicit wealth and that, uniquely in the case of the recent Italian elements, the former bootleggers and gamblers provided considerable leverage for the growth of political influence as well. A substantial number of Italian judges sitting on the bench in New York today are indebted in one fashion or another to Costello; so too are many Italian district leaders—as well as some Jewish and Irish politicians. And the motive in establishing Italian political prestige in New York was generous rather than scheming for personal advantage. For Costello it was largely a case of ethnic pride. As in earlier American eras, organized illegality became a stepladder of social ascent.

To the world at large, the news and pictures of Frank Sinatra, for example, mingling with former Italian mobsters could come somewhat as a shock. Yet to Sinatra, and to many Italians, these were men who had grown up in their neighborhoods and who were, in some instances, bywords in the community for their helpfulness and their charities. The early Italian gangsters were hoodlums—rough, unlettered, and young (Al Capone was only twenty-nine at the height of his power). Those who survived learned to adapt. By now they are men of middle age or older. They learned to dress conservatively. Their homes are in respectable suburbs. They sent their children to good schools and sought to avoid publicity. Costello even went to a psychiatrist in his efforts to overcome a painful feeling of inferiority in the world of manners.

As happens with all "new" money in American society, the rough and ready contractors, the construction people, trucking entrepreneurs, as well as racketeers, polished up their manners and sought recognition and respectability in their own ethnic as well as in the general community. The "shanty" Irish became the "lace curtain" Irish, and then moved out for wider recognition. Sometimes acceptance came first in established "American" society, and this was a certificate for later recognition by the ethnic community, a process well illustrated by the belated acceptance in established Negro society of such figures as Sugar Ray Robinson and Joe Louis, as well as leading popular entertainers.

Yet, after all, the foundation of many a distinguished older American fortune was laid by sharp practices and morally reprehensible methods. The pioneers of American capitalism were not graduated from Harvard's School of Business Administration. The early settlers and founding fathers, as well as those who "won the West" and built up cattle, mining, and other fortunes, often did so by shady speculations and a not inconsiderable amount of violence. They ignored, circumvented, or stretched the law when it stood in the way of America's destiny and their own—or were themselves the law when it served their purposes. This has not prevented them and their descendants from feeling proper moral outrage when, under the changed circumstances of the crowded urban environments, late comers pursued equally ruthless tactics.

Ironically, the social development which made possible the rise to political influence sounds, too, the knell of the rough Italian gangster. For it is the growing number of Italians with professional training and legitimate business success that both prompts and permits the Italian group to wield increasing political influence; and increasingly it is the professionals and businessmen who provide models for Italian youth today, models that hardly existed twenty years ago. Ironically, the headlines and exposés of "crime" of the Italian "gangsters" came years after the fact. Many of the top "crime" figures had long ago forsworn violence, and even their income, in large part, was derived from legitimate investments (real estate in the case of Costello, motor haulage and auto dealer franchises in the case of Adonis) or from such quasi-legitimate but socially respectable sources as gambling casinos. Hence society's "retribution" in the jail sentences for Costello and Adonis was little more than a trumped-up morality that disguised a social hypocrisy.

Apart from these considerations, what of the larger context of crime and the American way of life? The passing of the Fair Deal signalizes, oddly, the passing of an older pattern of illicit activities. The gambling fever of the past decade and a half was part of the flush and exuberance of rising incomes, and was characteristic largely of new upper-middleclass rich, a significant new stratum in American life (not rich in the nineteenth-century sense of enormous wealth, but largely middle-sized businessmen and entrepreneurs of the service and luxury trades—the "tertiary economy" in Colin Clark's phrase—who by the tax laws have achieved sizable incomes often much higher than the managers of the super-giant corporations), were the chief patrons of the munificent gambling casinos. During the war decade when travel was difficult, gambling and the lush resorts provided important outlets for this social class. Now they are settling down, learning about Europe and culture. The petty gambling, the betting and bingo which relieve the tedium of small-town life, or the expectation among the urban slum dwellers of winning a sizable sum by a "lucky number" or a "lucky horse", goes on. To quote Bernard Baruch: "You can't stop people from gambling on horses. And why should you prohibit a man from backing his own judgment? It's another form of personal initiative." But the lush profits are passing from gambling as the costs of co-ordination rise. And in the future it is likely that gambling, like prostitution, winning tacit acceptance as a necessary fact, will continue on a decentralized, small entrepreneur basis.

But passing, too, is a political pattern, the system of political "bosses" which in its reciprocal relation provided "protection" for, and was fed revenue from, crime. The collapse of the "boss" system was a product of the Roosevelt era. Twenty years ago Jim Farley's task was simple; he had to work only on some key state bosses. Now there is no longer such an animal. New Jersey Democracy was once ruled by Frank Hague; now there are five or six men each "top dog," for the moment, in his part of the state or faction of the party. Within the urban centers, the old Irish-dominated political machines in New York, Boston, Newark, and Chicago have fallen apart. The decentralization of the metropolitan centers, the growth of suburbs and satellite towns, the breakup of the old ecological patterns of slum and transient belts, the rise of functional groups, the increasing middle-class character of American life, all contribute to this decline.

With the rationalization and absorption of some illicit activities into the structure of the economy, the passing of an older generation that had established a hegemony over crime, the general rise of minority groups to social position, and the breakup of the urban boss system, the pattern of crime we have discussed is passing as well. Crime, of course, remains as long as passion and the desire for gain remain. But the kind of big, organized city crime, as we have known it for the past twenty-five years, was based on more than these universal motives. It was based on certain characteristics of the American economy, American ethnic groups, and American politics. The changes in all these areas mean that, in the form we have known it, it too will change.

Section 19   **THE RACKET AS IDEAL**

From a statement submitted by Harry E. Barnes to the "Racket" Subcommittee of the Committee on Commerce, U. S. Senate, 1933.

The "something-for-nothing" ideals for the age of finance capitalism have borne fruit in an appalling development of crime and racketeering. Crime represents antisocial action, obviously beyond the pale of the law and clearly punishable by the force of the State. Racketeering embraces a wide variety of practices on the borderline between crime and shady business practices. It rests primarily upon fear and consists of diversified forms of extortion of money without any corresponding services rendered.

Both crime and racketeering of today have derived their ideals and methods from the business and financial practices of the last generation. The basis for our crime orgy has been comprehensively laid by the developments of the last 20 years. It is a law of social psychology, formulated by Gabriel Tarde and others years ago, that the socially inferior tend to ape the socially superior. The latter capitulated pretty thoroughly to the prevailing "something-for-nothing" psychology of the era of speculative finance capitalism. Freebooting in railroads, banks, utilities, receiverships—and other high-toned racketeering—becomes shockingly frequent.

It was inevitable that, sooner or later, we would succeed in "Americanizing" the "small fry"—especially the foreign small fry. Their ancestors, if they lived in this country, had usually made an honest living conducting shoe-shining parlors, clothes-cleaning establishments, fruit stands, restaurants, and the like or at hard labor on roads, streets, and railroads. The younger generation looked with envy, not at the bowed backs and wrinkled brows of their parents, but rather at the achievements of the American financial buccaneers who had made away with their millions, with little or no service to society. If our usurers of high estate could get theirs, why should anybody drown himself in perspiration? This was the question they asked themselves.

About the time this something-for-nothing psychology was filtering through the skulls of the small fry, along came the "noble experiment." This provided a perfect set-up for the budding racketeers. Nothing could have been consciously designed which would have suited their purposes more perfectly. Public opinion in many sections of the country was very definitely against prohibition, and not a few regarded the bootleggers as crusaders for the old American liberties. Prohibition promoted other rackets—the hijacking racket among the wet outlaws, rackets in foods, milk, transportation, building construction, and the like. All was relatively safe, since the legal profession was already ethically impaired through its affiliations with the reputable racketeers.

The depression further stimulated the growth of racketeering since it threw out of work millions who might otherwise have preferred to earn an honest living. From these millions it was easy to recruit a few thousands needed as the underlings of the master minds of the racket world. Revelations of the doings of our financial moguls by Mr. Pecora and others only strengthened the conviction of the racketeering element that they should get theirs, get it quick, and get it good and plenty.

The idea that when prohibition is ended the racketeers and criminals who have made millions in illicit selling of booze will meekly and contritely turn back to blacking shoes and slinging hash is downright silly. They will apply the technique they have mastered to the dope ring, kidnaping, bank robberies, hijacking of legitimate liquor supplies, and the like. They will find crafty lawyers all too willing to defend them from the "strong arm" of the law for value received.

The combined crime and racket bill has been estimated by the latest competent students as running between $12,000,000,000 and $18,000,000,000 a year. Of this total, the racketeering bill amounts to around $4,000,000,000 to $5,000,000,000. This appalling crime bill is produced primarily by organized criminal gangs and racketeers, for the total depredations of isolated criminals—the lone wolves of the underworlds—are slight by comparison. The criminal types of the last generation have all but disappeared. Once in the great majority of all crime, the thefts and pocket picking now pale into insignificance when compared to the achievements of the racketeers and gangsters. The acts of the latter include a great variety of antisocial acts—

bank robberies, train robberies, looting of warehouses, and thefts of securities; the rackets in connection with liquor, dope, food, milk, the building trades, laundries, cleaning and dyeing establishments, garages, taxis, and the like; the use of gangsters in labor troubles; the swindles of the bucket-shop operators; and a host of lesser offenses against life, property, and personal liberty.

Suppose we take the total crime and racket bill of our country to be $15,000,000,000. Such a sum is impressive, but it is almost meaningless by itself. It is hard for the average man to comprehend the extent of a million dollars to say nothing of fifteen thousand million dollars that our overt lawlessness costs us each year. It may help a bit to set this $15,000,000,000 off against what is involved in some of our major public problems or necessities, national and international.

Perhaps the most staggering sum is the total fixed debt of the hard-pressed American farmers. This is $9,000,000,000. It threatens to drive the formerly proud and independent American farmers into penury and servility. Yet it amounts to only about half of our annual crime bill. Many hold that the fate of the world depends upon our canceling the war debts owed to us by European States—"cancelation must precede recovery." But these debts amount in their present value to only $5,873,636,000—roughly a third of our crime bill. It is estimated by leading economists that an expenditure of $4,000,000,000 for public works would furnish enough purchasing power on the part of newly employed laborers to set us decisively back on the road to recovery. This is a quarter of our crime bill. The cost of running our national Government staggers us when we contemplate a budget of over $4,000,000,000, but this again is no more than 25 percent of what it costs us to indulge our love for lawlessness. The bonus was held by many to be a threat to our very financial integrity, but it involved only $2,225,000,000 about one seventh the cost of crime. The deficit in the last Federal Budget amazed and terrified us, but it was only about the size of the proposed bonus payment. The Farm Board has been denounced as a scandalous national extravagance, but its operating fund amounted to only a paltry thirtieth part of our crime bill. The Reconstruction Finance Corporation has at its disposal less than a quarter of what we pay for depredations on our life, liberty and property.

Here, then, is a problem over which we may well pause and start to work to save America. From a purely economic point of view alone, the suppression of crime and rackets constitutes a most promising field for retrenchment in order to provide funds to save our social order. We could cancel all the war debts, put on a giant public-works project, deal with all the immediate problems connected with the hardships of American agriculture, pay the bonus, make up our Federal deficit and still have money to spare if we could free ourselves from unnecessary crime.

A main danger lies in the tendency of many to link crime and racketeering exclusively with prohibition and its abuses, and to expect that modification and repeal will make us over into a national Sunday school. Settling the prohibition muddle will help, but to give America a crime rate low enough to suggest a civilized Nation will require far-reaching changes in our national psychology and our political methods. So long as the lawless can get protection in return for keeping corrupt politicians in office, we shall not be free from the crime millstone about our necks.

Section 20 **THE RACKET DEFINED**

> From "Racketeering" by Murray I. Gurfein, *Encyclopaedia of the Social Sciences.*

Racketeering, a term loosely applied to a variety of criminal schemes, has not yet received exact legal definition. It usually designates, however, the activity for profit (in connection with the sale of goods and services) of an organized group which relies upon physical violence or an illegal use of group pressure to accomplish its end. It thus applies to the operation of an illegal business as well as to the illegal operation of a legal business. It cannot be confined to extortions in business alone, for it includes the use of violence to enforce the rules of illegal activities, such as distribution of narcotics and prostitution. In common parlance also the term is often applied broadly to organized crime or to any easy way of making money.

The word gained currency in the early 1920's, but its origin remains obscure. The first instance of its use has been ascribed to "Big Tim" Murphy of Chicago. Another theory holds that the term was first employed about 1885; two Chicagoans had organized a teamsters' union in New York and an official investigating it is supposed to have said, "This is not a noise but a racket." According to a third theory, racket has entered the modern vocabulary by way of the vaudeville stage, where it means the type of entertainment in which a performer specializes, and hence a special method, generally an easy one, of getting along in the world. There is still another explanation, which is perhaps the most plausible. The word racket has long been used to describe a loud noise and hence a spree or party or "good time." In the 1890's social clubs of young men in New York City, under the auspices of political leaders, gave affairs called rackets; since among their number there were members of neighborhood gangs, it was found easy to coerce local tradesmen to buy tickets. Local gangsters soon improved upon the idea and formed "associations" for the sole purpose of selling tickets in this manner.

The practise of extortion by officials and private citizens has been recorded in many civilizations, although perhaps it was never as well organized as it is under modern conditions. Whenever evidence of organized extortion is found, historical analogy exists. Pertinent instances are the practises of the Greek sycophants and the Roman delators, who, in systems where a private citizen could prosecute for crime, extorted money from guilty and innocent alike under pain of exposure. The Rhine and Danube barons in medieval times, the Barbary pirates, the African and Asian chieftains who preyed upon caravans, the Scotch and English outlaws described in the Waverly novels, the Mafia in the agricultural regions of Sicily—all were virtually racketeers. The levying of periodic tribute against their own depredations marks their status.

Coercion and insistence upon cuts in profits through threats of violence were fully established in the late nineteenth century, as indicated by the practise of "protecting" small storekeepers and peddlers from visitation by the gang itself. Gambling houses and brothels were long subject to extortion by gang leaders, and many murders were traced to disputes over an unearned cut in stuss and other games of chance. The business racket was known early in the century; a study in Chicago in 1904, indicated several rackets in the trucking and clothing industries and during the incumbency of Mayor Mitchell in New York rackets in the foodstuffs, building and clothing industries were exposed. But it was not until the close of the World War and the beginning of national prohibition that the rackets, as they are now known, became widespread.

The racket pattern is not the same in all industries. The simplest type is that in which a monopoly is set up by the racketeers with no other aid than protection by politicians. Illustration is found in rackets in some perishable foodstuffs, where the technique is to coerce retailers through suggestion or ready example of violence to cease buying from the wholesalers and to buy from a new and unnecessary middleman—the racketeer himself. In this type of racket the numbers are few and the investment small, as credit is easily obtained from the wholesalers.

Almost as simple a type of racket is found in the direct association racket, where tradesmen in a market or neighborhood are given "protection" against violence to person and property in return for the payment of "dues" to an "association" organized by the racket. Failure to pay dues results in visitation by a henchman of the rejected "protector." The more complex the industry, the more intricate is the association racket, functioning through collusive agreements between business men, racketeers and labor leaders. In such rackets the primary object is usually price fixing and the elimination of undercutting; the racketeer is initially called in to enforce the sanctions which under the antitrust laws the association itself could not lawfully assert. The tradesman who refuses to join finds not only that he is subjected to physical violence but that his laborers are "pulled" from the job or assaulted, the movement of his wares is stopped and often his offers to buy goods are rejected, as explicit testimony in New York and Chicago has shown. In some industries the collusive agreements are detailed and ingenious, involving the cooperation of a number of labor leaders and of both wholesalers and retailers; the associations have boards of directors, systems of fines and carefully formulated rules.

Certain of the labor rackets are not operated as part of an association, but the prime movers are the labor leaders themselves. Violence in unions is not new; at times as a matter of self-preservation it has been essential in the struggle of labor for survival, particularly where labor has been rendered powerless by sweeping injunctions. Since the use of force by both sides at the time of the famous Molly Maguires in the post-Civil War period the resort to violence in labor disputes has resulted in the hiring of professional gangsters by both employers and unions.

Strictly speaking, this is gangsterism rather than racketeering; on the other hand, the "shakedown" racket developed by some labor delegates comes close to official extortion. Money payments are demanded and received on threat of pulling jobs for fancied minor grievances or of "breaking" new unions struggling for a foothold or of sending back to work, in breach of trust, men who have legitimate cause to strike or of permitting organized laborers to work at a lower wage scale. From the laborers a "kickback" is exacted for the privilege of working, and contumacy is met with fine and suspension. Some delegates have working arrangements with companies selling construction machines or materials, resorting to sabotage and strikes to combat sales resistance; at times the delegate himself is a contractor on the side. In order to insure iron control over the union democratic processes are destroyed. Sluggers are brought into the union to keep elections from getting out of hand; soon local elections are abolished and a supervisor responsible only to the international president is appointed. Not all such appointments are to foster corruption, but the method is adaptable to such a purpose. Union funds dwindle away on "swindle sheets" which record their payment merely for "the good of the local."

The technique of enforcement in racketeering is familiar—personal violence including murder, destruction of goods and premises, kidnaping, bombings and incendiary fires. The methods employed by the Black Hand have been accepted and modernized. The use of bombs is alarmingly great; according to one estimate, in Chicago from the period from January 1, 1928, to October 1, 1932, 500 bombs had been planted, resulting in more than $1,000,000 damage. By underworld gossip there are set scales of fees for bombing; the Illinois Crime Survey in 1929 reported an interlocking system for bombing in different fields and in the case of one bombing crew in Chicago the fees were actually revealed.

Although gangs are employed for special acts of violence, including professional killings, the racket itself must be distinguished from the old fashioned gang. Even the terminology of the underworld makes the distinction; a group of racketeers is called a mob rather than a gang. The older racketeers were in many instances former members of old neighborhood gangs. But the earlier gangs were much larger than the mob; some of the famous neighborhood gangs of New York and Chicago mustered hundreds and even thousands of adherents. The modern racket is generally smaller for a number of reasons. Since it exerts pressure where resistance is weakest, it does not need mass demonstration of strength; its power is not often challenged. The code does not require that a victim be met face to face, any more than a legally condemned prisoner is expected to seek vindication by ordeal of battle; there is greater safety from the police in smaller and more trusted numbers. An exception of a limited kind applies to the beer and liquor rackets. In these the syndicate managers and "front men" have been comparatively few but the employees of the racket, if truck drivers, brewers and salesmen are included, are many. In some of the rackets there are hangers on who render important service without sharing in management.

The modern racket as distinguished from the gang is scarcely a neighborhood affair, for the territories covered are much larger, and with few exceptions (notably in specialized rackets) the members of the racket do not seem to be racially homogeneous. In the type of racket, however, which preys largely upon business owned by a particular ethnic group, the racketeers are themselves almost exclusively of the same group. Examples are found in certain fresh vegetable rackets which prey largely upon Italians, in the kosher poultry racket directed against Jews and also in certain labor rackets aimed primarily at Irishmen.

The focal points of racketeering are the larger cities, where its interstitial growth is easiest. Chicago and New York City have held the limelight, but rackets are operated in other large cities as well. Detroit and Kansas City and Cleveland with its lugubrious "funeral racket" have been exposed as racketeering centers. The farmer too is often a victim of the racketeering, for his goods pay tribute as they come into the city. "Legs" Diamond, for example, operated a beer racket in a rural county of New York and in his sales arguments included some of the more refined forms of torture.

The general inactivity of police and prosecutors in the face of racketeering is unquestionably related to connections between politics and the underworld, although some part of the breakdown may be laid to inefficiency. The difficulties confronting honest and efficient law enforcement officers cannot be overlooked, for extortion is more difficult to prove than holdup, and witnesses are reluctant to testify because of fear, satisfaction with the racket or lack of confidence in police and district attorney; in order to secure convictions of racket leaders great energy and a persistent use of the John Doe grand jury investigation are required of the district attorney.

The connection between politicians and the underworld is old; in New York the alliance goes back at least to two decades before the Civil War. The use of gangs for election frauds and intimidation of voters, in return for which "protection" is given by politicians, has never ceased, particularly where elections and primaries are closely contested, as exposures in New York, Chicago and Cleveland have dramatically shown. But it is probably a mistake to attribute the rise of the racket in Chicago to intense political factionalism in that city or to assume that the alliance is disrupted when one political machine is firmly entrenched; racketeers contribute to political campaigns directly, and also indirectly through distribution of foods to the poor of a neighborhood under the auspices of a district leader. Often the real appointing power, the district leader, is in politics for reasons of business and mutually advantageous alliances are part of the game.

The relation between politics and racketeering, although difficult to prove, has been revealed in important instances. The Illinois Association for Criminal Justice reporting on the Municipal Court of Chicago found, for example, "a definitely established relationship between the underworld and some feudal lords." The Magistrates' courts inquiry in New York City exposed the common practise of intercession by district leaders on behalf of criminals and the acceptance of a large loan by a magistrate, later removed, from a notorious leader of the underworld. The murder of an assistant district attorney in Chicago, with its subsequent exposure of close connections between officialdom and racketeers, as well as the use by professional gamblers of district clubhouses in New York furnishes other striking evidences. Amazing too are the criminal records of notorious racketeers—discharge after discharge by the lower courts for "lack of evidence"—as are the astonishing "leaks" of information from the offices of prosecuting attorneys. But it is unlikely that all the political "fixing" is due to outright corruption of public officials. Some, as Moley has recorded, are "money honest but politically crooked." In the practise of this official immorality the release of no single criminal is considered a menace to society.

Political corruption was greatly stimulated by federal prohibition. The public conscience was softened by widespread opposition to the attempted regulation of personal habit, and large sums came into the hands of bootleggers. The step from political protection of an illegal traffic in liquor to protection for other crimes was but a short one. Many former gangs were absorbed into the beer and liquor rackets, as pre-prohibition criminal records disclose. The illegal nature of the enterprise itself compelled violence and murder. As the sanction of force became routine it was an easy transition to find subsidiary fields of action, as, for example, where the anti-trust laws barred legal attempts to combine. Because of a general disrespect for law the racket found its respectable partners in crime, business men, prepared for the partnership.

From the functional point of view the wholly parasitical racketeer must be distinguished from the racketeer who performs a measure of service by acting as a stabilizing force in industry. The parasitical racketeer is big brother to the juvenile gangster, who in return for tribute refrains from stealing from the pushcarts and stores of the neighborhood, and whose services are valuable merely to the extent of the self-restraint he exercises. His contemporary counterpart injects himself into the economic scene in the same fashion but on a larger scale. Choosing a weak spot in the industrial structure he proceeds to occupy the point of vantage to his own profit. His operations are most likely to begin where the victims are of foreign origin and ignorant of the laws and where small capital is required. Fruit dealers, cleaners and dyers, truckmen, fish, vegetable and fresh poultry dealers, are the most likely subjects for exploitation. The field is more fertile when the supply of the product is relatively small and easy to monopolize or where the time element is essential to the victim, as in the "shakedown" of building contractors working under heavy contractual penalties for delay or as in "loading" and trucking rackets, where the movement of perishable foodstuffs is essential to prevent decay.

The racketeer as a type is a natural evolutionary product of strict laissez faire. Society lays no restriction upon the number of middlemen who may enter a field. There is no challenge to the middleman to prove his economic usefulness; no certificate of convenience and necessity is asked or given. The parasitical racketeer, no more or less useful than many jobbers and wholesalers, personifies economic individualism in its farthest reach. He grows in a porous economic organization, giving no reason for his being except that he is a seeker after gain. For the ethics current during the era of prosperity that was almost excuse enough. The American scene, in broad perspective, showed tolerance toward the acquisition of riches at the expense of moral restriction. In an era of unrestrained competition the touchstone of morality was success. The pegged market in stocks, the manipulation of subsidiary

companies, the reckless puffing of securities, the taking by corporate manage-
ments of inordinately large bonuses, the rather widespread evasion of taxes,
the easy connivance of politicians in grabs—are a few illustrations of the
temper of the times which furnish a key to the parasitical racketeer.

The attitude of the typical victim is not unrelated. Even though the motive of fear is primary, there is often the feeling too that when the tribute
can be passed on to the consumer the extortion is not inherently wrong. Some
long for freedom of action, but many covertly approve methods that bring
greater stability to their own businesses. Certain commission merchants, for
example, have admitted that selling directly to a racket monopoly instead
of to many retailers is a boon because it eliminates many detailed bookkeeping entries.

On the other hand, the stabilizing racketeer, while he is in purpose
and method a criminal, is in function perhaps an illegal police force. He is
more powerful than injunctions and suits for damages; he executes the man-
dates of his associates with dispatch and by direct methods. These associates
are legitimate business men, and the racketeer's problem is often a sensible
limitation of production. His methods, however, are violent, and the power
he wields is uncontrolled, for he has no concern with the tests by which his
victims are selected. This alliance between business and the underworld is
attributable in substantial respects to the antitrust laws; yet the entire burden
cannot be made to fall upon these laws, for even if voluntary combination
for price fixing were legal, the recalcitrant individualist would still be a
problem for discipline and the cost to the consumer, perhaps, would remain
equally high.

The racketeer sometimes called in to organize an association often remains to head it by intimidating his employers. With armed force at hand
and with a reputation it is not difficult for him to find new spheres of influence. As the activities of the rackets are broadened, large sections of the
community thus find themselves paying an unofficial sales tax to powerful
lords of the underworld. A Capone is able to offer civic peace to Chicago
through his own police methods, to protect a labor union against parasites
and to break a powerful association racket by the prestige of his name.

An invisible government is set up, linked to the invisible government of
the political machine. Its existence, like that of lynch law, is inimical to
government, for the reservation of the exclusive use of force by the state
is fundamental to an ordered political society. Sharing with the state the use
of force the illegal organization also becomes a coordinate taxing agency,
for it levies a tribute upon sales and services.

Estimates as to the cost of racketeering are little more than guesses.
Many direct payments can never be determined; losses by extortion are not
reported to the police as are thefts. The indirect costs to the community in

higher prices and association dues are difficult to assay, for the higher prices
are sometimes partially compensated for by the saving of marginal entrepreneurs from costly bankruptcy or by the prevention of forced liquidations.
Accurate comparison of average prices before and during the advent of the
racketeer is a complicated task, since many other market factors may enter.
Added elements of costs which must be considered of course are increased
insurance rates for plate glass; arson, burglary and bombing risks; as well as
the expense involved in added police protection and prosecuting expenses.
The New York State Crime Commission in 1931 reported that racket
costs to the nation were estimated to range between $12,000,000,000 and
$18,000,000,000 annually, while the attorney general of the United States
stated in 1933 that the national tribute to racketeers amounts to $1,000,000,000
annually. As the Wickersham commission concluded, "the data prerequisite
to any estimate of racketeering losses are nonexistent."

In the face of the challenge of racketeering society must take action
by direct police methods and perhaps by a reappraisal of legislation. The
repeal of federal prohibition is already accomplished, and proposals to repeal
the anti-gambling laws and to modify the rigors of the antitrust laws are
being discussed. Public opinion must be made to feel that the dispensation
of favors through political "pull" is vicious. The press and the bar must exert
pressure for the appointment of able men to prosecutors' staffs for the dis-
barment of lawyers who grow rich as advisers to the underworld.

While the problem of law enforcement as such is essentially a local matter, the federal prosecutions of racketeers are also important. The federal
government has followed two principal methods, that which makes use of
the income tax and that which relies upon the antitrust laws. A third method
coming into increasing use is applicable where extortion is attempted through
use of the mails. Violation of the anti-trust laws is clearly subject for federal
action since interstate commerce has been restrained; the mailing cases likewise are properly federal. But the use of the oblique attack of the income
tax law has met with some criticism. The objection based upon constitutional
demarcations in the field of criminal jurisdiction is, however, only theoreti-
cally applicable, for the complexities of modern conditions were not foreseen by the founders, and the tendency of Congress and the courts has been
toward an expanding view of the constitution in the designation of new
federal substantive crimes. It is clear moreover that since the government is
legally entitled to share in the profits from many forms of criminal endeavor,
a separate crime—against the revenue—has actually been committed. Again,
the danger that prosecutors will have too free a hand in the selection of
defendants, although it is in theory disturbing, has in practise been found
illusory, for in most income tax prosecutions commission of other crimes—
extortion, bribery and the conduct of illegal business—has in point of fact
been incidentally proved.

Not only does the success of the federal prosecutions demonstrate the possibilities of action by local agencies when freed from political pressures, but the methods of federal investigation themselves should foreshadow the technique to be followed by local authorities. The tracing of criminal relationships by means of bank accounts, often under fictitious names, and the close scrutiny of corporate books are important features. The use of the John Doe grand jury investigation where crime is known to exist but where the racket leader is not yet definitely linked to any provable conspiracy is valuable. The application to duty which calls for the summoning of hundreds of witnesses from an industry, sometimes for merely informal preliminary conversation, points the only way in which the few good witnesses competent to prove cases of racketeering will be found.

Recent legislation has strengthened the federal attack on kidnaping and the powers of state officials to proceed against business racketeering. The immediate remedy, however, is to be sought not so much in new laws as in the selection of able enforcement officials, divorced from political pressure. The repeal of prohibition has already caused the liquor racketeer to turn to new fields; but adequate defense ought to come from a change in the public attitude toward law-breaking and from the pressure of lower standards of living, impelling political revolt against "unofficial sales taxes." A fearless and free officialdom is the preliminary answer to the challenge.

Section 21 INTO THE TRADE UNIONS

From a statement by Steve Sumner at a hearing before a subcommittee of the Committee on Commerce, U. S. Senate, 1933.

Mr. Sumner. I did not come with any prepared talk. I do not know that I can do better than to just tell the committee here of the troubles that we have had.

The racketeering started here in Chicago several years ago. It was first brought in by big business. The men to whom we generally look as being above the average were the very men that were the lowest. They brought them in. They brought them in, and they prospered very nicely under the prohibition regime, and it was the man who drank that made them possible. It was not the men or the women that tried to make the country clean and decent for people to live in. It was the drunkard, the man who drank, that made the racketeer in the first place, and big business that brought them in here, employed them, and they got a start.

Then when prohibition began to dwindle out, they had to fall to something else, and they figured that the labor movement was the next best bet. They came into our place and they politely said, "We are coming in, and when we do, you are going out." As they said several times, "When we walk in, they will run out."

Well, they walked in. They told us plainly that the milk business looked to them like a good business for their boys to engage in after prohibition, whiskey, and beer and all that stuff had gone down. Of course, we argued with them. We tried to persuade them that there was no chance in the milk business for racketeers, that we had been organized 30 years, that we had gone on and taken care of our men as best we could, tried to look after the families of the milk drivers. But they said, "No, the milk dealers have been getting away with murder and we are going to show you old fogies over there on Ashland Avenue how to run the business." I said, "All right, but I think you have come to the wrong place." So in time they offered $100,000 for us to step out and for them to step in. To that we told them nothing doing. Finally we said, "All right, if it is fight you want, we will give it to you."

We appealed to the chief of police and we got aid. We went to the State's attorney, and we did not get very much support at that time. That was not under our present State's attorney. So then we got busy and elected a new State's attorney and then we got support, and he has gone along and done wonderful.

It got so bad that we had to fortify our office. The office is now fortified with steel. Senator Murphy here looked it over. We have prepared to take care of ourselves. We are going to do it. If they want anything from us they can come our way. We are not out hunting them, but if they come our way we are going to take care of ourselves, and them, too, if we can.

Racketeering is just because the people have got in the frame of mind that they are afraid of those fellows. Whenever you say anything about Murray Humphreys, or "Three-Fingered" Jack White, or Al Capone, the majority of people begin to shiver. They said, "Why, you can't cope with those fellows. There is no good of saying anything against them. If you do, your life is in danger."

Now, when the human family, the citizens of the United States, have gotten into a frame of mind where they are afraid to say anything against crime, I think it is time that we should fingerprint every child when it is born and every man and woman in the United States.

Some complain about that. "Oh, yes, fingerprint, like in the old country." Well, if we have to adopt the rules of the old country in order to be safe here, we better adopt them. I believe that every man and woman should be pictured, should be fingerprinted, and their history gotten, by the Federal Government.

That is going a long way. There are men here who say, "Oh!" and give a holy horrible cry. If a man is going along decent and honest, he need not care where his fingerprints are. It is only those who are afraid that they might do something to break the law who are afraid of being fingerprinted.

I believe that the fingerprint is a good thing for the safety of the people. I might be murdered, for instance—and that is liable to happen to me at any time.

The Chairman. I hope not.

Mr. Sumner. I hope not, too, but it might. Now, if you have my fingerprints you might find out who I am, not that it makes much difference after a fellow is dead, but kind of like to have a record of how you, died, anyhow. (Laughter.)

It is my opinion from what I have found with these racketeers—and believe me, we have met up with a lot of them in the last 18 months—it is my belief that they are the lousiest, most cowardly skunks on the face of the earth. (Laughter and applause.)

I am determined as long as I live—and I hope it will be 50 or 60 years longer—to devote my life to helping the Government chase down these racketeers. Some gentleman from Ohio—by the way, I am a Buckeye, too— has given you enough information and has read out a plan there which if it were closely followed would clean this all up. But I want to say this to him: That there are some cases here where you cannot afford to take time off. We do not like to have our enforcing officers break the law, but when you are dealing with those birds I don't know as it is any great crime. Suppose you do break the law, if you are dealing with a bird like Murray Humphreys. What we want is to have those fellows curbed. We don't want their cases sent to the supreme court and then have them turn out people like Murray Humphreys, turn out "Fur" Sammons, and "Three-Fingered" Jack White. Why, it is no use for the courts here to try to run down a criminal. The police here endanger their lives to get them, and then because of some kind of sob stuff these birds get off. I don't know what that sob stuff is anyway, but I hear them talking about it. I guess it is where they cry and plead and beg for leniency. Isn't that it?

Senator Murphy. Yes.

Mr. Sumner. Then I got it right all along.

The Chairman. I think you knew all the time. (Laughter.)

Mr. Sumner. I wasn't dead sure, but I kind of had an idea. Now, the police run a man down. They go to a lot of trouble and expense to convict him, and the juries, a great many of them, haven't got backbone enough to say yes, the fellow is guilty, when they think he is. Finally, we get a jury that is honest enough to convict the bird, and then his case is taken up to the supreme court. Then the birds down at the supreme court turn him loose. I say birds, because I mean just what I say. A lot of them are no good, and don't care a whoop about the welfare of the people. Just pay attention to some technicality.

I think it would be wise to kind of overlook some of these technicalities and get down to the thing that will protect the people. That is my opinion. You send a man to the supreme court and then they will turn a fellow loose like "Fur" Sammons, and then the police go to work and get him back in again and then Ed Shurtleff, up here in Woodstock, turns him loose again, and then they arrest him and put him under $20,000 bonds, and then he jumps the bond and God knows where he is now. The worst kind of murderer that this country ever saw is now at liberty on account of a fool trick by Ed Shurtleff.

I say that people have a right to kick, and I am going to kick and holler against these fellows as long as I am able to, and I am in earnest about it.

There are many more things I would like to say but you have got a lot of witnesses you want to hear from and you can call on me any time you want and I will be here. If I can drive a nail into those fellows' coffin, I am glad to do it.

The Chairman. You have done it today. You have helped a lot, Mr. Sumner.

Mr. Sumner. I hope I have.

The Chairman. I want to ask you a question while you are here apropos of some testimony given last night. What is the wage now of a milk driver in Chicago?

Mr. Sumner. $40.

The Chairman. It is not $65, is it?

Mr. Sumner. No, it is $40; and it does not amount to much over $30, because he has to pay for a lot of dead beats and people that he will trust out of the goodness of his heart and then they are not able to pay. A lot of them are willing to pay but not able to pay.

The Chairman. He is charged with all the milk on his wagon, is he, and then he has to pay for what is not returned?

Mr. Sumner. Not exactly that. He is charged with all the milk, but the employer carries the charge account. But if the employer says, "Don't trust any further," and if the driver, knowing the people a long time, continues to give them milk, he is held for that bill. If they don't pay, he has to pay it. So if the men get out with $35 a week clear, that is as much as they are making now.

The Chairman. I made the statement last night that there was not a milk driver in the United States who gets $60 or $65 a week.

Mr. Sumner. I doubt it.

The Chairman. You do not believe there is such a man?

Mr. Sumner. No; I do not believe it.

The Chairman. Thank you very much.

Mr. Sumner. Indeed, you are welcome.

The Chairman. We are much obliged to you.

Mr. Sumner. Any time I can help nail those birds, let me know. They are no good and we are better off without them.

The Chairman. Thank you very much, Mr. Sumner.

Section 22   **THE LABOR SKATES AND I**

From *The Stolen Years* by Roger Touhy and Ray Brennan, 1959.

Back in 1932, I began getting a two-way squeeze. On one side were my friends in labor unionism. On the other was the Chicago mob. The federal government put Capone into prison for income tax cheating, but The Enforcer, Nitti, stepped into his place. And Nitti was looking around hungrily for fresh money.

Repeal was on the way, and the syndicate's big profits from gagging whiskey and watery beer soon would be ended. The great depression was settling down for a long stay. People didn't have the money for gambling. Business in the Capone brothels fell off, even after the price was cut to one buck in some of the dives, with the girl getting forty cents and the house taking the rest.

Banks closed. The Insull utilities empire fell apart. Insurance companies went bust. Brokers jumped out of their skyscraper windows so often that somebody suggested paving Chicago's La Salle Street with rubber.

In the late 20s and early 30s the biggest and most solvent treasuries in the world were in the labor unions. Some of the old-time labor skates didn't trust banks. They socked the union's cash away in safe deposit boxes or invested in U. S. Government bonds. The top American Federation of Labor unions in the Chicago area had about $10,000,000 in their treasuries.

Chicago gangsters long had been nibbling at the unions around the edges. For years Al Capone was in the business of providing thugs and scabs to break strikes for employers. In breaking a strike, Capone would weaken the union involved and then put his own thieving men into the organization.

Public opinion was against unionism, generally, and the labor men could expect a minimum of protection, if any, from the cops and politicians.

To a union trying to build up its membership, the racketeers had a novel approach. One of them would call on the local officers with a pitch like this: "Let us put one of our men in your office. We'll help you get members. All we want is a job for one of our boys." A union that fell for this sucker bait was through. Once a mobster got any authority, he took over the local, emptied the treasury and stole the monthly dues.

In the late 1920s, my friends from my days of organizing telegraphers came calling on me. They were getting steamroller pressure from the syndicate. Three or four of them wound up murdered or kidnaped. They were afraid to live in Chicago with their families. A couple of their homes were bombed. They wanted to move into my quiet area.

I gave them the okay. What else? They were my friends, and they were safe in the suburbs. The suburban police and town officials wouldn't hold still for any gangster killings or other violence.

Patrick "Paddy" Burrell, a Teamsters' Union International vice president, settled down in Park Ridge and some other union bosses followed him. One of Burrell's business agents, Edward McFadden, was a sort of real estate agent for the labor skates—renting houses for them under assumed names, buying furniture, putting in supplies of groceries and hiring housekeepers.

I had known McFadden, an elderly character with long white hair, since my boyhood. He was called "Chicken" because he once had been connected with a union of poultry pluckers in Chicago.

All of the union officials brought their bodyguards with them to the country to live, and it made quite a collection. The bodyguards carried guns, as their profession required, and they represented the alumni groups of about every penitentiary in America. Things were lively around our quiet suburban saloons for a while. I sent word, through McFadden, that the bodyguards were asking for trouble with the local law, and the rowdiness eased off.

In 1929, the syndicate had offered to cut my brother, Tommy, and me in on a multimillion-dollar union racket. Out to Tommy's home in suburban Oak Park came Marcus "Studdy" Looney, a Capone pimp who had graduated into labor muscling. The big dealers of the syndicate had sent Looney. Tommy, who was just out of the Indiana State Penitentiary at the time, telephoned me to join them.

Now, I'm not going to pull any punches in telling about Tommy. I'm his brother, and I'll still do everything I can for him. But he did get into a lot of trouble. He did time for burglary and mail robbery. The sensational newspapers got to calling him "Terrible Tommy" Touhy, and I inherited the nickname after the Factor hoax.

Tommy paid a heavy price for the things he did, and he never complained. He was partly paralyzed back in 1929, and years later he became an almost helpless, hopeless invalid. He finally went to one of the western states to live out his days.

Studdy could hardly read or write, but he was a whiz at arithmetic, particularly at subtracting—subtracting money from people. He brought a list of Chicago area unions with him to Tommy's house with the amounts of money in their treasuries. It added up to about $10,000,000, as I have said.

One top prize to be stolen was the union of Chicago milk wagon drivers, with a bankroll of $1,300,000, and an income of about $250,000 a year in dues. The boss of that local was tough Robert L. "Old Doc" Fitchie, then in about his 65th year. He had been a friend of my father and he had been fighting union racketeers all of his life.

Other labor skates and their unions on Looney's list included Art Wallace of the painters, Johnny Rooney of the circular distributors, Mike Boyle of the electricians, Tom Reynolds of the movie projection booth operators and Mike Norris, a teamsters' man. Many of them were to be murdered or to knuckle under to the syndicate in the years that followed.

Looney brought word that the Teamsters' International, of which Burrell was a vice president, had about $8,000,000 in strike funds in Indianapolis and Cincinnati. The Chicago mob planned to knock off the teamsters' locals one by one and finally to grab the treasuries. At that time, Jimmy Hoffa was still in knee pants and Dave Beck was slugging it out on strike picket lines.

After dangling the prospect of big money in front of us, Looney made his proposition to Tommy and me: "You guys can each have a union, the boss says. Which ones do you want?"

His meaning was plain. If we would double-cross the labor leaders, some of whom had been our friends for years, we would get rich quick. I could be a lot of help in the swindle, because the labor leaders trusted me. I would be able to persuade them to put some Judases—to be picked by the syndicate, of course—into the locals.

Tommy and I told Studdy that we wanted no part of the scheme. We were polite about refusing, but firm. Looney did some blustering, warned us to keep our mouths shut about the mob's plans, and left. He wasn't a block away before Tommy and I were on the telephone warning our friends in the labor movement. I was building up a houseful of bad will from the syndicate.

Paddy Burrell called a meeting of unionists in his Park Ridge home and invited us. Tommy went, but I stayed away. After the conference, Tommy and Jerry Horan came to my house. I was working on my fishing tackle in the basement rumpus room.

Horan slapped a cow-choker sheaf of money on the bar and explained:

"We union guys have started a war chest to protect ourselves. Burrell put up $75,000 for the teamsters. I kicked in $50,000. We want you to be treasurer. When money is needed, we'll draw it from this bankroll."

I never liked the idea of holding anybody else's money, and I said so. Horan insisted. They didn't want to put the cash in a bank because they wanted it ready at hand, nights or days or holidays. I agreed, at last, but I tacked on a few reverse conditions:

"I'll keep the money for you, but I'm not going to pass it out to any slob who comes asking. You name one man who is eligible to draw from the fund. I'll give the cash to him, and he'll have to sign a receipt for every dollar he takes. Okay?"

Horan said that was all right and we agreed that Burrell's man, Eddie McFadden, would make all withdrawals. I put the money in a fireproof safe behind a sliding panel in the basement. Then we had a bottle or two of my special beer.

The Chicago mobsters learned soon, of course, that I was handling the labor skates' bankroll. The syndicate had stool pigeons everywhere. Another black mark had been checked up against me, and the syndicate never forgot. As the months passed, I began hearing rumbles that my family and I might get hit by a bomb in our home.

I hired two guards, Walter "Buck" Henrichsen, a former county highway cop, and Eddie Schwabauer. Both of them were good shots, and it developed later, they were even better at lying under oath.

One or another of the guards sat in our back yard playhouse with a shotgun while the kids, Tommy and Roger, were at the swimming pool. Clara drove the youngsters to and from parochial school, about two miles away, or else I did. I kept a man on duty outside the house all night.

We never let the boys know of any possible danger. When we discussed anything like that, we remembered our old Western Union days together. We would hold hands and signal each other with Morse code by pressure of our fingers.

On a sunny spring afternoon, I was in the basement, making ready for a fishing trip to the Wisconsin lake country. The time came to pick up Roger and Tommy at the school. Clara called down the stairway that she was leaving on the errand.

The telephone rang in fifteen or twenty minutes. It was one of the boys' teachers, and she was screaming with hysteria.

Two men in a car had tried to grab Tommy and Roger as they left the school. The boys had jumped into the car with Clara and she had driven away toward home.

"Mr. Touhy, those men are following," the teacher yelled. "I'm terribly frightened."

I grabbed a deer rifle off the wall and loaded it as I ran to one of our other cars. I rolled along the highway toward the school at ninety miles an hour. I met a couple of cars, but not the one Clara was driving.

A dozen teachers were on the school grounds, some of them crying. They waved frantically and pointed back the way from which I had come. I drove back, slowly this time, but cursing and raging. I thought for sure that the syndicate had snatched my family.

Halfway home, a car I recognized came out of a driveway ahead of me. In it were Clara and the boys. She had stopped off to buy fresh eggs and milk from a farmer, a by-chance thing that had saved them all.

Clara hadn't noticed anything, but the teachers said two men had jumped out of their car as the boys came out of school. They ducked back when Tommy and Roger ran toward Clara's car, parked at the curb in the direction of home. She got away because the men had to make a U-turn to follow her.

I increased the guards around the house and on the kids. I assigned Henrichsen, the former county cop, to watch the school to be certain that the boys didn't get grabbed at recess or lunch time. And I made sure that anybody who tried it wouldn't live long.

A friend loaned me a laundry truck, one of those panel body jobs with a rack to hold bags of wash on the top. I put peepholes in one side of the body and then hinged it so the panel would drop down. I parked the truck— with myself and three other guys in the back—across the street from the school. All of us had guns.

Section 23 **INTO HOLLYWOOD**

From *Crime on the Labor Front* by Malcolm Johnson, 1950.

The United States is still suffering from some of the evil effects of the Prohibition Amendment, perhaps the most thoroughly ignored law ever written on the national statute books. The "noble experiment," as Herbert Hoover called it, introduced an era of lawlessness such as this country had never known, marked by wholesale murder, open warfare between rival bootleg gangs, and a complete cynicism and disregard for law and order by a large segment of the public, which saw gangsterism and politics closely allied. It was a period of political corruption on a national scale, with legislators, judges, and other public officials bought and sold with gangster money like so many sacks of potatoes. It was a period in which professional murderers, as typified by the bootleg gangsters, came to be regarded as colorful heroes whose exploits were celebrated in the movies and in the newspapers. Some of the top gangsters and racketeers in the country today first rose to power during that period of machine-gun law. With the passing of prohibition they turned inevitably to other lawless activities. One of these was the labor racket.

Of all the gangsters who flourished during prohibition, none attained such power and wealth as Scarface Al Capone. This deceptively mild-looking little man with soft brown eyes migrated from Brooklyn to build an empire of crime in Chicago with influential underworld connections throughout the country. It was one of the ironies of the times that Capone enjoyed complete immunity from the law for the reign of terror he invoked. He was never brought to trial for any of his major crimes, including innumerable murders committed by his paid gunmen on orders from himself. When the law finally nailed Capone it was for income-tax evasion. He was convicted in 1931, served seven years in prison, then retired to a life of luxury in Florida until his death, of paresis, in January, 1947. Capone's gang lieutenants carried on his organization, which is still active in Chicago.

Though its chief source of income during prohibition was from the sale and distribution of liquor and beer, the Capone mob owned brothels, gambling establishments, and night clubs. In addition, the mob perfected the "protection" racket as it is now known—the device of levying tribute from businessmen for the privilege of staying in business. The protection, of course, was from the gangsters themselves; if the victim did not pay, a bomb, or "pineapple" in the mob vernacular, was exploded in his place of business. The racket usually was worked through a trade association, so-called, to which the victims were compelled to belong.

When the Capone gangsters invaded the labor field after the death of prohibition in December, 1933, they applied the technique of intimidation against the unions and their members. One of the gang's first and most successful ventures in labor forms an almost incredible story of extortion in the motion-picture industry. The story is now a matter of public record through the court testimony of a convicted labor racketeer who squealed against his gangland bosses. It is a story with strong political implications, with hints of bribery in high places. It is a story of how the most notorious gang in the country, working through union officials, brought the entire Hollywood movie industry to its knees.

The story properly begins in Chicago in 1932 as the prohibition law was on its way out. It was a bleak year in the depth of the nation-wide depression: a year of soup kitchens, bread lines, bank failures, shuttered factories, and of jobless, despairing men tramping the street in a vain search for work.

It was a bad year even for labor racketeers. Nevertheless, a paunchy little man of boundless cupidity named Willie Bioff was doing his best to turn a dishonest dollar by organizing and preying upon Chicago's kosher butchers. Bioff was a panderer, a thief, an extortionist, and an all-around racketeer and gangster. His name a few years later was to strike terror in the hearts of the Hollywood movie moguls.

In that year, 1932, Bioff met a professional unionist, one George E. Browne, business agent of Local 2 of the International Alliance of Theatrical Stage Employees, an American Federation of Labor union with jurisdiction over motion-picture-theater projectionists and allied theater workers. As a sideline, times being what they were, Browne was organizing chicken dealers. It was a fortuitous meeting—for Bioff and Browne. Both had only one interest in the labor movement: to gouge money out of it. Each was quick to appreciate the talents of the other. As a labor leader, Browne, tough and thoroughly corrupt, was more than willing to accept the aid of a smarter racketeer. He found one in Willie Bioff. While Browne was a good front man, Bioff was the schemer, the planner, the strategist with an utterly ruthless talent for extortion. Bioff and Browne joined forces, abandoned the kosher market, and concentrated on the theatrical union as offering greater possibilities. Nominally, Bioff became Browne's assistant. Actually, he was the brains of the combination.

Browne's union local was in a bad way. Out of 400 members, 250 were unemployed. There was no profit for Browne and Bioff in unemployed union members. They decided to mix charity with business by setting up a soup kitchen where the unemployed could eat free. They persuaded politicians and theatrical celebrities to drop in frequently for meals and contribute $20 to $50 to a good cause. The contributions served the double purpose of keeping the local alive and providing Brown and Bioff with a small income. The contributions also gave Browne and Bioff the idea for their first successful shakedown. In 1934 the pair went to millionaire Barney Balaban of the Balaban & Katz theater chain with a demand that he restore a pay cut imposed on IATSE members in the Balaban & Katz theaters in 1929. They had no illusions about getting the cut restored, nor did they want it. Their interest never was in the welfare of the workers except when it was a means of extorting more money from them in dues, initiation fees, and assessments.

Balaban appeared to give their request serious thought. He said he might be willing to comply, but was afraid that if he did so, other unions would jump in with similar demands. That would be too costly. Browne and Bioff then casually mentioned the soup kitchen, observing that it cost $7,500 a year and was serving a humane cause. Balaban got the point. He saw immediately that paying for the kitchen would be much cheaper than restoring the pay cut. His attitude reflected that of many businessmen who paid off labor racketeers. In permitting themselves to become extortion victims they nearly always were seeking some advantage for themselves, usually at the expense of the workers. Obviously the large sums paid to labor gangsters were never passed on to the workers. In any event, Balaban volunteered to pay for the soup kitchen in lieu of restoring the pay cut. He quickly discovered that Browne and Bioff had no intention of letting him off so lightly.

"I figured right then I might as well kill a sheep as a lamb," Bioff boasted in court. "Barney turned out to be a lamb. When he agreed to our suggestion I knew we had him. I told him his contribution would have to be $50,000 unless he wanted real trouble. By that I meant we would pull his projectionists out of the theaters. He was appalled, but we turned on the heat. He finally agreed to pay us $20,000. The restoration of the pay cut was forgotten. We were not interested in that then or at any other time. We didn't care whether wages were reduced or raised. We were interested only in getting the dough, and we didn't care how we got it."

From the day that Balaban coughed up $20,000, Browne and Bioff knew that they were on top of a lucrative racket. Joyously they celebrated the knowledge by spending $300 at a night club and gambling resort operated for the Capone mob by Nick Circella, alias Nick Deane. As they wined and dined on the money that they had extorted at the expense of their members, they boasted of their recent good fortune. A few days later, Frank Rio, a leader in the Capone gang, accosted Browne and demanded to know how the union was making out. Up to this point the mob had let Browne alone; the "take" wasn't enough to interest it. But the first big shake-down changed the picture entirely. Browne spun a woeful tale of his union's impoverished state, but Rio was unimpressed. "From now on," he said, "we expect 50 per cent of the take. Everything you get. Understand?"

Browne and Bioff understood perfectly. The Capone gang had muscled in on them, as it had on so many other union locals. It was a case of the big fish swallowing the small fish. Brown and Bioff knew that they had been served with the usual "or else" proposition. They agreed to cooperate, for they had no choice. On the one hand they hated to surrender half of their union booty. On the other hand they were smart enough to know that, with the Capone mob's backing, the "take" should be much larger and that future expansion would be made easier. The gang's reputation for terrorism, built up over the years, would take care of that.

It should be remembered that the mobsters at no time had any official connection with this or any other labor union except insofar as they were able to plant their own stooges in union offices. Their sole interest in a union was the profit in it for them. They operated behind the scenes, issuing orders and directing policy through their captives in the union. In this instance they took over by intimidating two thieving union officials who were not too unhappy about being taken over. The capture of Browne's local was just the beginning. The mob was determined to expand and gain control of the international union. They intended to do it by using Browne as a front man. A meeting was held. Present were Browne and Bioff; Frank Nitto, or Nitti; Louis Campagna, Paul DeLucia, and Rio—all top men in the Capone circle. Nitto, a first cousin of Capone was known as the Enforcer. When Capone went to jail on income-tax charges, Nitto was regarded as the number one man in the gang's underworld enterprises. Campagna was one of Capone's ex-bodyguards.

The gang chieftains knew that Browne had been defeated in 1932 for president of the international union. They told him he was to run again and get elected. There must be no mistakes this time. Where were the weak spots, the places in the national organization that had failed to support him? New York City, New Jersey, Cleveland, and St. Louis, Browne said. The gangsters explained that their out-of-town connections would help this time—Abner (Longy) Zwillman, racket boss of New Jersey; Louis (Lepke) Buchalter and Charles (Lucky) Luciano in New York, and lesser known gangsters in Cleveland and St. Louis. For another meeting, two weeks before the June, 1934, convention of the IATSE, Lepke was summoned from New York. Nitto gave Lepke a message for Luciano, New York's vice overlord and member of the syndicate: "Local 306 (the New York projectionists) was to vote for Browne for president."

"I won't have to see Lucky on that, Frank," Lepke replied. "I can handle it myself. I'll also see Kaufman of New Jersey (Louis Kaufman, business agent of the big Newark local) and see that Longy (Zwillman) delivers that outfit."

The campaign went exactly as planned. The Capone syndicate's representatives in the key cities spread the word: "Vote for Browne." As a final gesture to insure success, the syndicate's far-flung representatives gathered in Chicago and from there descended on the international union's convention in Louisville. The presence of the nation's top gangsters and their gunmen at the convention, circulating among the delegates and openly backing the candidacy of Browne, created such an atmosphere of intimidation that opposition wilted. Browne was elected without a single dissenting vote. Democratic processes were forgotten and the best interests of the dues-paying union members were ignored. Everybody at the convention knew that the Capone gang had made a successful bid for power and was now in control of the union.

President Browne's first official act was to announce that Willie Bioff was his "personal representative." The convention delegates knew what that meant too: Bioff was giving orders for Browne and through Browne. Backed by the Capone gangsters and their powerful out-of-town connections, Bioff and Browne were quick to solidify their control of the entire union. The Capone syndicate appointed Nick Circella to oversee their activities and to report back to the syndicate. Browne and Bioff were warned against double-crossing the syndicate unless they wanted to retire feet first. From then on they were tools of the mob in a major racket venture, and the stakes were high.

When Bioff and Browne departed for New York to chart a campaign of extortion and to "confer" with theater owners and other union officials, they were told to feel free to call upon Luciano or Frank Costello any time they needed help. "They are our people," gangster DeLucia explained, according to Bioff's testimony. This was long before Costello, gambler, ex-convict, and slot-machine racketeer, had become such a controversial and influential figure in New York City politics.

In Chicago the mob, through Browne and Bioff, extorted $100,000 from motion-picture theater chains by threatening to force them to hire two projectionists in each theater booth instead of one. The Balaban and Katz circuit paid $60,000; Warner Brothers $30,000; and an independent chain, the S & S., $10,000. Here again the racket fee was at the ultimate expense of the union workers. There would have been more work for more members had the union's demand been on the level. When one theater representative protested bitterly that putting two projectionists in a booth would drive him out of business, Bioff replied, "I can't help that. If this is going to kill drama, then drama has got to die." After this shake-down, the Capone mobsters gave Brown and Bioff the bad news that henceforth the gang's take was to be 75 per cent instead of 50 per cent; Browne and Bioff could divide the remaining 25 per cent between them.

The mob's brazen method of operation was further demonstrated in the case of a burlesque-theater owner named Jack Barger. When Barger opened a new theater in Chicago, Bioff called on him and calmly announced that Barger would have to surrender half his profits. "Barger raved and said it wasn't fair, but I told him that was the way it had to be if he wanted to stay in business," Bioff recalled in court. "He went along."

On orders from Bioff, the wages of union members were slashed and stagehands were laid off so that the profits would be bigger for division with the mob. This was during the worst part of the depression, when work of any kind was hard to get and good men and their families were going hungry through no fault of their own. Yet a union whose ostensible purpose was to better the living conditions of its members was deliberately and pitilessly throwing men out of work and cutting wages. Not content with this abuse of the members, Bioff milked another $200 a week from the theater owner, Barger, when he discovered that Barger was drawing that amount for himself in salary. The gang promptly put one of its own men on the payroll for a like amount for doing nothing. They closely scrutinized Barger's books to see that they got their full share of the money. In fact, they ran the business. Everytime Bioff saw Barger, he would taunt him by asking, "How's *our* business, partner?"

Like other labor racketeers before and since, Bioff and Browne extorted money from their victims by a variety of methods. They sold "strike prevention insurance" for whatever they thought the traffic would bear. They threatened wage hikes and shorter hours, demands which were promptly withdrawn and forgotten when payment was made directly to them. They ruthlessly sold out their members by agreeing to wage cuts or longer hours. One of Bioff's greatest triumphs in the field of "strike prevention" was the $150,000 he extorted from Charles Moscowitz of the Loew's theater chain in New York in 1935.

By 1936, two years after seizing control, the Capone gang's power in the union was such that it was ready to launch a daring offensive against the billion-dollar industry of Hollywood itself. Millions in extortion fees were the stake. The union had only a small membership on the West Coast, but that did not deter the mob. They persuaded the West Coast studios to give the IATSE jurisdiction over labor by exerting pressure against movie outlets, notably the Balaban & Katz theater chain, a subsidiary of Paramount Pictures.

It was necessary, however, to close every theater from Chicago to St. Louis before the theater officials saw the light and influenced the West Coast companies to give the IATSE jurisdiction. That done, Bioff in the fall of 1936 went to Nicholas M. Schenck, president of Loew's and spokesman for the movie industry in dealings with the union.

"You have a prosperous business here," Bioff told Schenck. "I elected Browne president of this union because he will do what I say. I am the boss and I want $2,000,000 out of the movie industry."

"I was shocked," said Schenck, recalling the conversation. "At first I couldn't talk. But Bioff said, 'You don't know what will happen. We gave you just a taste of it in Chicago. We will close down every theater in the country. You couldn't take that. It will cost you many millions of dollars over and over again. Think it over.'"

The movie bigwigs, including Schenck, the late Sidney Kent of Twentieth Century-Fox, and Leo Spitz of RKO, thought it over and decided to pay. An agreement was reached by which the major companies were to pay $50,000 a year and the minor companies $25,000 a year to the racketeers. The payments were to continue indefinitely—forever, if Bioff and the mob had their way. A first payment of $75,000 in cash was made to Bioff and Browne in a room in the Hotel Warwick, New York. Schenck brought $50,000 and Kent $25,000. Bioff and Browne dumped the money on a bed and carefully counted it, while Schenck and Kent watched, squirming.

The full story of the audacious Hollywood shakedown is a matter of court record today because Willie Bioff out-smarted himself. Otherwise the conspiracy might never have been revealed. Juggled bookkeeping and a dummy loan finally started Federal investigators on his trail. Bioff, like Capone before him, first attracted the government's attention in connection with income-tax evasion on a transaction of $100,000.

Bioff's talent as an extortionist had won him a bankroll of $100,000 which he was anxious to conceal from the government. He yearned to buy a ranch in California, but knew an investment of that kind would arouse the curiosity of the tax agents. So in 1938 Bioff pretended to borrow $100,000 from Joseph M. Schenck, the chairman of the board of Twentieth Century-Fox and a brother of Nicholas M. Schenck. Bioff realized that it would look curious for Schenck to make him a loan of that amount. Therefore he arranged with Schenck for the latter's nephew, Arthur Stebbins, to give him a check for $100,000. Bioff gave Stebbins the cash in return. On the books, however, the transaction appeared as a loan, guaranteed by Schenck, with Bioff giving a note. In the eyes of the government it appeared that Schenck had derived an income of $100,000 in a deal he had not reported. In the chain of investigations which followed, other irregularities were discovered. Schenck was indicted for income-tax evasion and sentenced to three years in prison. The sentence was reduced to one year and a day for perjury after Schenck gave evidence against Bioff and Browne leading to the discovery of the extortion conspiracy and the union's backing by the Chicago mob.

Browne and Bioff were indicted for extortion and conspiracy, tried, and convicted in 1941. Bioff was sentenced to ten years in prison, Browne to eight years, and each was fined $10,000. In prison the two racketeers squealed on their gangland bosses. The mobsters were indicted by the government on March 18, 1943, on charges of conspiracy, extortion, using the mails to defraud, and of having extorted more than $2,500,000 from union members and motion-picture producers.

Frank Nitto, the Enforcer, named in the indictment, committed suicide. Nick Circella pleaded guilty. Frank Rio had died in 1935. The defendants brought to trial were Louis Campagna and Paul DeLucia (mentioned previously), Phil D'Andrea, Francis Maritote, Ralph Pierce, Charles Gioe, John Roselli, and Louis Kaufman. Except for Kaufman, they were all members of the Capone group. Each had a long police record. Maritote, for instance, had been arrested twenty-seven times.

The gangsters were tried in New York. Willie Bioff was the principal witness against them. He testified with gusto, his hard, pig-like eyes gleaming from behind thick glasses. For days Bioff was on the stand, spilling out the story of the mob's control of the union and of the extortion plot. Obviously relishing his role, he boasted of his own part in the plot and implicated all the defendants. His attitude was that he was a gone goose anyway and that the gangsters deserved punishment, too. He, Bioff, was going to see that they got it. The gangsters listened impassively as Bioff, smirking and leering at them, gave evidence that was to convict them. Browne, though less flamboyant, corroborated Bioff's testimony.

Section 24 **THE LEPKE ERA**

From *Treasury Agent* by Andrew Tully, 1958.

When Louis Lepke Buchalter, the nation's most wanted criminal, gave himself up on a New York street corner the night of August 24, 1939, America heaped well-earned plaudits on the shoulders of J. Edgar Hoover, boss of the FBI, and Columnist Walter Winchell. After all, it was Hoover and Winchell, the intermediary, to whom Lepke surrendered in the soft gloom of the intersection of Fifth Avenue and Twenty-eighth Street.

But before all the history books have been written, somebody should make a motion to divide at least secondary billing between a woman scorned and a coldly efficient agent of the Federal Bureau of Narcotics named Andy Koehn. The lady, a comely redhead who will remain anonymous as long as the Treasury Department can manage it, put the Narcotics Bureau on Lepke's trail. And Andy Koehn, a merciless sleuth, so harassed Lepke's pals with his hard-mouthed attentions that they threatened Lepke with sudden death unless he turned himself in.

Lepke died in the electric chair in New York State's Sing Sing Prison on March 4, 1944. Specifically, he was executed for the slaying of a Brooklyn candy-store owner named Joseph Rosen, whom Lepke had driven out of his job as a garment trucker and then ordered killed to keep him from talking to the law. This was ironic because in the criminal empire Lepke had built, Joseph Rosen's death was a minor incident.

Lepke was probably the greatest criminal in the nation's history, a tycoon who bossed a veritable General Motors of crime. For years he was undisputed ruler of the fur, garment and baking industries in the New York City area, a role which enabled him to extort from these businesses at least $50,000,000. He was the director of at least 250 criminal enterprises with 300 so-called "foremen," and a herd of accountants, bookkeepers, professional killers and industrial wrecking crews. As chairman of the board of Murder, Inc., he ordered the deaths of between sixty and eighty persons. He was a silent partner in a dope-smuggling ring which between October 1935 and February 1937 smuggled into the United States more than $10,000,000 worth of narcotics.

Yet Hollywood would have despaired of Lepke. Despite the violence he administered, he was a shy man, almost apologetic, who draped his slender five-foot seven-inch frame in suits of quiet hues and looked upon the world with warm, soft brown eyes. Burton Turkus, who prosecuted him for the murder of Joseph Rosen, once described Lepke's eyes as "like a deer's." While other gangland big shots roared along their flamboyant way, Louis Lepke Buchalter sat at home with his English wife and a stepson reading magazines or playing a little pinochle. Occasionally he shot a round of golf and he liked to sit on the beach in Miami. He rarely had more than one drink at a sitting.

Louis Buchalter was the name listed in the records when he was born on New York's Lower East Side on February 6, 1897. The family—ten other children besides Louis—lived in a crowded flat over a small hardware store operated by Papa Buchalter. Louis got the name which was to become notorious from his mother, who used to call him "Lepkeleh," meaning "Little Louis."

Little Louis got better-than-average marks in school and seems to have behaved himself. But he quit school at the age of fifteen after having been graduated from the eighth grade and went to work as a delivery boy at three dollars a week. The next year his father died, and the family had to break up. A sister, two married half-sisters and an older half-brother of Lepke's migrated to Colorado, and Louis went to live with his mother and two brothers in Brooklyn. By the time Lepke was eighteen, his mother and his two brothers had moved to Colorado; Louis' older brother out West offered to send him to high school and college, but Louis wasn't interested. He stayed East and moved into a furnished room on the East Side.

In this brawling neighborhood, Lepke shortly embarked on his criminal career. He picked pockets, robbed pushcarts and generally pursued the fast buck. Here, too, Lepke struck up a friendship that was to endure most of his life with one Jacob Shapiro, a vulgar little hoodlum known as "Gurrah Jake." The name came from the cry pushcart peddlers used to set up when Jake descended on their merchandise with larceny in his heart. "Gerrarah here, Jake!" they'd scream, meaning, "Get out of here, Jake," and Jake's pals soon shortened it to "Gurrah."

Lepke did the usual illegal errands for the big-time hoods—mugs like "Gyp the Blood," "Little Augie," "Kid Dropper" and "Yoske Nigger." He robbed a few neighborhood sweatshops, and just after he reached his twenty-first birthday he was sent up to Cheshire Reformatory for making off with a salesman's sample case in Bridgeport, Connecticut. Paroled in July 1917, he was back in prison the next year on a larceny charge and was stashed away again, for two years, in 1920. By this time Lepke was an accepted mobster in the East Side underworld, a dangerous kingdom where thirteen men were shot to death between 1919 and 1927. Lepke wanted a dodge that was both a little safer and a lot more profitable.

He decided, in the mid-twenties, to make his mark in labor racketeering. It already was a going business, on a small scale. Thugs like Little Augie collected flat fees for calling out their henchmen to beat up striking workers. Lepke wondered why the boys didn't muscle in on a kind of retaining fee basis; he had ideas how it could be done, but Little Augie was in his way. So Lepke took the approach direct. On a fine October day in 1927 a car pulled up alongside Little Augie and his bodyguard, a slender youth with long legs whom some knew as Jack (Legs) Diamond. Little Augie was shot dead. Legs Diamond was found full of lead but recovered to become a big name in the underworld.

Now Lepke took over the labor rackets, slowly but surely. He let it be known that he had organized a corporation of goons, and shortly both union officials and factory bosses were knocking at his door. After his thugs had cowed union rebels who had asked embarrassing questions of the labor brass, Lepke would keep them on the job to intimidate the officials themselves and eventually to oversee the election of a new slate of officers pledged to the financial support of Louis Lepke. Similarly, manufacturers who had used Lepke's organization as strike-breakers soon found that Lepke had voted himself in as a full partner.

Dissenting union members either were beat up or murdered. Factory owners who objected to sharing their profits with the mob found their plants wrecked or their stocks ruined by a special Lepke task force expert in the art of acid-spraying. By 1929, Lepke employed a force of fifty assorted hoodlums, bookkeepers and "foremen," the latter assigned as watchdogs in plants where Lepke had reason to distrust the legitimate management. Professional killers started out at twenty-five dollars a week and progressed, by a display of their special skills, to a top of $150.

Nobody has ever managed to figure out Lepke's gross from this far-flung empire. Fifty million dollars was as close as law-enforcement accountants could come, and this was considered a conservative figure. By the early thirties, Louis Lepke dominated a widely assorted number of industries, including bakery and pastry drivers, milliners, garment workers, leather-workers, motion-picture operators and fur truckers.

By that time, too, Louis Lepke was "The Judge," to his admiring mobsters, a quiet, dark-complexioned man with thick black hair and a long nose thick at the tip. In 1931, he had married a stocky brunette named Mrs. Beatrice Wasserman, whose husband had died a couple of years earlier. Four years later, Lepke adopted his wife's son, Harold, and was known to be deeply attached to the boy.

The police knew plenty about Louis Lepke but he was tough to catch. Lepke, Gurrah Jake and "Little Hymie" Holtz were arrested for the Little Augie murder but were released for lack of evidence. In June 1933, Lepke and "Trigger Mike" Coppola were pinched in a fashionable Manhattan apartment, but no weapons were found in the place. They tried a vagrancy charge, but it was dismissed when Lepke produced a roll containing $800. In October 1935, everybody knew that Lucky Luciano had used three of Lepke's killers to liquidate a beer baron named Dutch Schultz, but there was a paucity of the kind of evidence that convinces juries.

By that time, also, the name of Louis Lepke Buchalter occupied a prominent place in a document on file in the Washington headquarters of the Federal Bureau of Narcotics. He was listed as Number 3 in the Confidential List of Suspected Major Narcotics Violators, and as an associate of Jack Legs Diamond and of Sam Bernstein, a notorious dope pusher. It would not be until the summer of 1937, however, that Narcotics would get a strong lead on Lepke.

Meanwhile, enough of Lepke's labor-racketeering victims had summoned up their courage to make an antitrust case against him. On November 6, 1933, a Federal grand jury returned two antitrust indictments against Lepke, and two weeks later Lepke was arrested. Released on bail to await trial, Lepke went back to his desk and not only continued his labor racketeering but in 1935 took over the leadership of a gang of international dope smugglers whose operations later were described by Narcotics Commissioner Harry J. Anslinger as the most extensive in the nation's history.

Lepke was given plenty of time to pursue his latest criminal dodge. He didn't come to trial on the antitrust charges until October 26, 1936. Two weeks later, he and Gurrah Jake Shapiro were convicted on both counts and later were sentenced to two years in the penitentiary and fined $10,000. Lepke appealed and was released on $3,000 bail, whereupon he slipped out of New York and became a fugitive.

"The Judge" may have acted precipitously, for on March 8, 1937, the Circuit Court reversed Lepke's conviction. The government, however, decided to try Lepke again, and the case was called for trial the second time on July 6, 1937. Lepke remained in hiding, his $3,000 bail was forfeited, and cops all over the country started looking for him. As a matter of fact, Lepke never left Brooklyn, where he moved from hiding place to hiding place while he continued to run his empire. There were some loose ends, though, and one of them started Louis Lepke Buchalter on his downfall.

One day in late June 1937, Narcotics Commissioner Anslinger received a letter in female handwriting. It was unsigned, but it suggested that if the Commissioner wanted some information on Lepke's activities in the dope racket the writer would be glad to oblige. A couple of days later a woman phoned the Commissioner, identified herself as the writer of the letter, and invited him to meet her for a drink at the Carlton Hotel. "And come alone, Buster," she told him. "I may have to trust you, but I don't want no round-table conference."

Anslinger, a man of unquenchable curiosity, went alone to meet his informant. She turned out to be a woman of about thirty-five, with dark red hair and a grievance. A mug she knew as a close friend lately had been romancing another doll. Worse, he had presented this rival with a new mink coat. The mug was an employee in one of Lepke's subsidiary corporations—a dope-smuggling venture—and the redhead was prepared to tell all.

What she told Anslinger was so well prepared and well documented that by December 1937 thirty-one persons, including Lepke, had been indicted for conspiracy to smuggle drugs into the port of New York in the baggage of gang members posing as round-the-world tourists.

The conspiracy had been born in January 1935, shortly after an explosion had rocked a clandestine heroin plant operated by three guttersnipe hoods named Yasha Katzenberg, Jake Lvovsky and Samuel Gross.

Seeking a new source of supply and some ideas on running the stuff, Lvovsky and Katzenberg sought Lepke's ear at a dinner party in the apartment of a mutual friend. Lepke was interested. He suggested the boys get in touch with one Joe Schwartz in Mexico City "and tell him you're friends of mine." Lepke also said he had some ideas about how to get the stuff into the country, which he would divulge later, after Katzenberg and Lvovsky had set up an organization through Schwartz.

"You've got to work from within," Lepke told his new associates. "You've got to be smart."

Katzenberg went to Mexico City and signed up Schwartz. He and Schwartz then took off for Shanghai, where Schwartz contacted a couple of Greek expatriates representing heroin dealers. Meanwhile, Lvovsky and Gross interviewed and engaged a crew of carriers who would transport the junk from Shanghai.

Now Lepke divulged his master plan. It was to bribe United States Customs inspectors in New York to sell the gang a supply of Customs stamps to affix to the baggage containing the heroin. Lepke assigned a couple of his men to handle this end of the matter and assured Lvovsky and Gross they could start sending the "tourists" back with the junk as soon as they could book passage.

As the brains of the conspiracy, Lepke made no cash investment; he simply muscled in. His share, voted by Lepke, was 50 per cent of all profits from the original importation, plus 50 per cent of all profits following their secondary distribution to addicts. Lepke ruled that this secondary distribution would be made by an old pal of his, whom he ordered to buy up every grain of heroin the gang got into the country.

The scheme worked beautifully, from October 1935 to February 1937. Six smuggling voyages were made on such respectable ships as the *Queen Mary, Berengaria, Majestic* and *Aquitania*. More than $700,000 worth of pure heroin, worth $10,000,000 on the retail level, was smuggled into the port of New York in trunks bearing appropriate Customs stamps.

The procedure never varied, because there was no need to monkey with success. In China, the heroin was stashed away in two wardrobe trunks which accompanied the carrier as passenger's baggage to France via the Suez Canal. In order to escape the prying eyes of French Customs officers, the trunks were transferred from Marseille to Cherbourg to a ship sailing for the United States. Then, in the U. S., the final stage was accomplished through the co-operation of two venal U.S. Customs inspectors.

The inspectors sold Customs clearance stamps to the gang for $1,000 per trip. (Lepke had feared they might hold out for $1,500.) The stamps were printed in eight colors, and they had to be bought the morning the ship docked because different colors were used for different days, and one thing Lepke couldn't buy was advance notice on the color scheme to be used on a given day. The trunks were not declared on the passenger's baggage declaration but were placed on the dock under his initial. Lvovsky, the stamps in his pocket, would mingle with the pier visitors and locate the trunks containing the contraband. Then he would casually sit down, first on one trunk and then on the other. When he left, the trunks bore the proper stamps.

Once safely through Customs, the trunks were delivered to the home of one of the gang members; the heroin was picked up later by a representative of the retailer. Lepke got his cut the same day.

Nor did Lepke suffer when the last load of heroin, worth $126,000 wholesale, was mysteriously hijacked from the pier. He insisted on being paid off, not only on what he would have received from the wholesale disposal to his pal but also his share of the retail distribution. Some of the more suspicious members of the gang suggested that it was one of Lepke's men who had hijacked the shipment.

By the fall of 1937, Narcotics agents had got their hands on a kilogram of heroin with Shanghai markings which they could prove had been part of a shipment which had arrived on the *Aquitania* in May. Some people talked, hoping a good word would be said for them in court. As a result, in December a grand jury handed down indictments against thirty-one persons, including Lepke, who was named on ten counts.

Lepke, of course, was still in hiding, but he was wanted by practically everybody. He also had been indicted for extortion, along with Gurrah Jake and Max Silverman, Lepke's "foreman" in the bakery racket, and District Attorney Thomas E. Dewey had offered a $25,000 reward for his person, dead or alive. From his hideout, Lepke directed the dispersal of key witnesses to various points west of the Mississippi River. For witnesses who were uncooperative, Lepke decreed death, usually by ice pick.

Max Rubin, a Lepke mobster specializing in the garment industry, was shipped to Salt Lake City, then to the Catskills, then to New Orleans. But Rubin always got homesick for his wife and two children and came back to New York. Once, after returning from New Orleans, Rubin was picked up by one of Lepke's men, who drove him to the corner of Amsterdam Avenue and 150th Street. There Rubin was ushered into the presence of Louis Lepke, standing under an awning. Lepke wanted to know why Rubin had returned.

"I got homesick," said Rubin.

"How old are you, Max?" asked Lepke.

"I'm forty-eight."

"That's a ripe old age."

A few days later Rubin caught a slug in the neck. He was on the danger list for several days, but he survived to testify with cruel competence at Lepke's murder trial.

Lepke shifted his hideouts often. For a while he lived in a Coney Island joint called the Oriental Dance Hall. Then he moved to a Brooklyn waterfront flat, where he grew a mustache and took to wearing dark glasses. In a house on Foster Avenue in Brooklyn he posed as the paralyzed husband of his landlady. Here he raged about a mistake made by his gunmen: they had accidentally murdered an innocent music publisher whom they had mistaken for Phil Orlovsky, a potential Dewey witness.

About this time Andy Koehn, the Narcotics agent, entered the picture. Commissioner Anslinger had assigned Koehn to devote his exclusive talents to the search for Lepke. Koehn was a tall, strapping man of about fifty, with curly blond hair and cold blue eyes that matched a machinelike efficiency.

Dewey was relentlessly parading witnesses in and out of the jury room, hammering at them with questions designed not only to sew up his case against Lepke's mob but to get them to tattle on the boss's hiding place. Koehn figured the underworld was getting nervous, that the boys might be starting to think that Lepke was a nuisance whose continued freedom was imperiling them all. He believed he could add to their nervousness.

For nearly three months Koehn went visiting. He popped in regularly on Lepke's pals and racketeering associates, including some citizens who enjoyed a respectable reputation in the public prints. He wanted to know where Lepke was hiding, and when the boys laughed and said things like "Search me, Buster," Koehn resorted to psychological warfare.

To a labor union official, he would remark that "this sure is a nice apartment you have here. Nice family, too." Then he would remind the unionist that nice things are of no use if a man is in jail for harboring a fugitive. "This guy Dewey means business," Koehn would say, fixing his cold eyes on his squirming host. "He wouldn't care much if a guy like you got hurt."

Koehn visited Lepke's relatives and his enemies. He talked to mugs who might feel it would be to their own legal advantage if Lepke gave himself up and thereby put an end to the fuss the cops were raising. He reminded the mob that the law eventually would catch up with Lepke, and while waiting to catch him the constabulary might employ its time harassing minor hoodlums.

Finally, early in August 1939, an underworld contact phoned Koehn and suggested a meeting in a Lower East Side spaghetti joint. As the two sat down in a booth, Koehn fixed the mug with a cold stare and asked his nagging question: "Where's the Judge?"

The mug squirmed. "Listen, Andy," he said, "lay off. I wanna tell you something. Lepke's gonna surrender. He's trying to fix it now. Some of the mob got to him. They told him they were getting tired of all this heat, and either he gave himself up or he was going to be dumped on the courthouse steps very dead."

About ten o'clock on the night of August 24, 1939, a man with a mustache and wearing dark glasses got out of a car on Fifth Avenue at Twenty-eighth Street. He walked over to a sedan parked at the curb. In the sedan was Walter Winchell and a husky man named J. Edgar Hoover.

"Mr. Hoover, this is Lepke," Winchell told the FBI boss.

"How do you do?" said Lepke. "Glad to meet you. Let's go."

Lepke was wanted for murder and for practically everything else. But the Narcotics Bureau got first crack at him. Now forty-three, and a little stouter than in his palmier days, Louis Lepke Buchalter went on trial in the Federal Court of the Southern District of New York on December 5, 1939, on a charge of conspiracy to violate the narcotics laws. He was convicted after a fifteen-day trial, and on January 2, 1940, he entered pleas of guilty to nine other indictments charging him with the unlawful importation of heroin, failing to make dutiable entry for certain pieces of baggage and with bribing a Federal employee.

He was sentenced to twelve years in the penitentiary and fined $2,500, on these charges and subsequently was sentenced to another two years on the antitrust indictment and to thirty years to life on thirty-six extortion counts. Off he went to Leavenworth, saddened by the thought that he would be deprived of the company of his old pal, Gurrah Jake Shapiro. Gurrah Jake had surrendered in 1938 and already was serving time in a Wisconsin pen.

In the same narcotics case, Jake Lvovsky got seven years and a $15,000 fine; Sam Gross, six years and a $15,000 fine; Yasha Katzenberg, ten years and $10,000; Joe Schwartz, three years and $3,000. The two corrupt Customs inspectors also were sent to the pen.

Lepke would remain in Leavenworth only seventeen months before being returned to New York to face trial for the Murder, Inc., killing of Joseph Rosen, the garment trucker Lepke had driven out of business. The government charged that Lepke had ordered the killing, that Emanuel (Mendy) Weiss had fired the actual shots and that Louis Capone, no relation to the late Al, had assisted in the getaway.

Louis Capone was a nondescript hoodlum, strictly a glorified errand boy with a curiosity about violence. But Mendy Weiss was one of the most evil men ever to harry society, a man who boasted, "I love to kill." Both Customs and Narcotics agents had a fat book on Weiss.

Customs thought they had a case on Weiss years before when agents seized a suitcase containing heroin in the possession of one Jacob Gottlieb as Jake was trying to smuggle the bag into the United States from Canada. Gottlieb made a statement naming Weiss as one of his partners, but a few days later he committed suicide in his jail cell.

Weiss was nabbed by Narcotics agents early in 1940 on a charge of operating an illicit morphine plant in Manhattan and was indicted with several others. Weiss subsequently jumped his bail of $17,000 and was still at large when he was indicted on narcotics charges in Dallas in May 1940. He finally was picked up in April 1941 in Kansas City, where he had been posing as a Colorado gold-mine owner and whiling away his evenings playing poker at an exclusive club with, among others, a couple of local judges.

With everybody rounded up, the State of New York opened its murder case against Lepke, Weiss and Capone in Kings County Court, Brooklyn, on October 20, 1941. The boys had nine defense lawyers, but they were a fragile dike against the torrent of unfriendly testimony poured forth by such old Lepke standbys as Max Rubin and the Oriental-like Allie Tannenbaum. Through thirty-five witnesses and fifty-seven exhibits, Prosecutor Burton Turkus all but pulled the switch on the three defendants. They were convicted, and on December 2, 1941, all three were sentenced to death in the electric chair.

Lepke and his two pals sat down for the last time in that ugly chair in Sing Sing Prison on March 4, 1944. Lepke was unmoved, as he had been on that Sunday morning when Mendy Weiss had boasted to him of how efficiently he had dispatched Joseph Rosen. "What's the difference?" Lepke had said then. "What's the difference as long as everyone is clean and got away all right?"

Section 25 **MURDER INC.**

From *Murder Inc.* by Burton B. Turkus and Sid Feder, 1951.

Mobdom did not like the approaching demise of Prohibition. Alcohol always was a good buck, as they say. The hoods wondered which way to turn for new and lucrative illegalities.

It presented a serious problem to the suave underworld millionaire who operates under the name of Frank Costello—except when the boys call him the Prime Minister, as they do. Prohibition had been good to Frank C. On the stepping stone of alcohol, the little paisan climbed out of the tenements of Harlem and the slums of Greenwich Village, where the Bohemian idealist mingles with the practical politician, to a swank seven-room apartment overlooking Central Park. He advanced to ownership of Wall Street skyscrapers, to oil lands in Texas and Oklahoma, to plush gambling operations heaven only knows where, and to remarkably close association with many ranking political figures in various parts of the country.

Costello had early realized the opportunities in alcohol. He was chummy with Bill Dwyer and Big French Lemange, Owney Madden's pal. They had put together as lavish an alcohol operation as the era produced. There had been a mix-up with the Law in 1927. Several coast guardsmen, admitting their guilt, called Costello the payoff man. The jury did not believe that of Frank. Not all the jurors, anyway, and nothing came of the charge. That occurred only a short time after Costello became a citizen, too. (Incidentally, the "Prime Minister's" application for citizenship carefully avoided any reference to a 1915 conviction, with its one-year sentence, for possessing a pistol.)

Like Costello, most of the boys had problems, with repeal on the way in 1931 and 1932. A man has to keep busy. As the recently-appointed ruler of Unione, Charley Lucky had some investments with excellent returns. He had become acquainted with the numbers, for instance, and moved into dope on a wide scale, and launched an occasional foray into industrial stuff. But alcohol was still the big revenue-producer.

Lepke already had a neat "gimmick." He was developing labor and industrial extortion in the garment trade, in flour and trucking, from all of which he exacted tribute. Most of the boys, however, were in the same boat as Costello. In New Jersey, Longy Zwillman and his first lieutenant, Willie (Moretti)

Moore, had made fortunes during Prohibition. They were now at liberty, too, and could use something to keep the pot boiling.

Dutch Schultz, who had been in beer, found an answer faster than most of them, in the everyday institution of the restaurant.

Frank C., though, was the direct antithesis of Dutch Schultz. The "Prime Minister" deplores violence. Such things as mob wars and gang shootings cause him to shudder. Indeed, violence has been so abhorrent to him that in 1929 Costello even called a convention in Atlantic City to talk about cutting down on the rough stuff, and similar economic improvements. Al Capone came to that one. After it was over, Al took the train home. In Philadelphia, almost before the train came to a stop, police hauled him off to the station house for toting a gun among his belongings. The scar-faced thug got a year in jail. No one has ever been certain whether it was Al's own gun that put him behind bars—or, as was whispered, someone else's gun looking for Al. Such as Bugs Moran, for instance—Al's chief business rival in Chicago. Capone was simply placed "on ice" for safe-keeping.

By the time Prohibition was ready for burial, the new lineup was already in the game. The batting order in the East looked something like this:

Frank Costello—gambling (Frank Erickson, bookie boss and Florida representative; Dandy Phil Kastel, bucketshop specialist, as New Orleans general manager; section chiefs in other places).

Lucky Luciano—narcotics, numbers, prostitution (although he set up a mighty cry that the latter was a wrong rap, even after he was convicted of it).

Joey Adonis—bail bond, arbitration and "contacts" for above groups; political connection specialist; Brooklyn waterfront enterprises.

Lepke and Gurrah—industrial and labor extortions in flour, clothing, trucking, bakeries, fur, motion picture theaters, ad inf.

Buggsy Siegel & Meyer Lansky (Bug & Meyer Mob)—dirty work and enforcement specialties, particularly for Lepke; varied Philadelphia enterprises.

Abner (Longy) Zwillman—assorted New Jersey operations. (Willie Moretti, or Moore, chief deputy, and Florida operative.)

Dutch Schultz—restaurant racket; Harlem numbers banks; general protection extortion; beer. (Bo Weinberg, chief assistant and trigger.)

For group purposes, this set was known as the Big Six, since Dutch Schultz, an insane individualist, had little in common with the others. But the entire set-up was still practically isolationist in form—"every man for theirself," as the boys sometimes put it. In spite of the modern trend toward lessening violence, each had his own organization, lined up his own protection and declared mob war when he felt like it. It was, largely, the horse-and-buggy way of the Al Capones, the Legs Diamonds. Across the river, too,

Reles told me afterward, he and Happy and Pittsburgh Phil and Louis Capone lived in a crime world of their own. It was the same celluloid collar isolationism.

Nevertheless, 1932 was a big year all around. Except, perhaps, toward the end, for Dutch Schultz. The Treasury Department detected an odor about The Dutchman's income tax returns. Schultz left rapidly. "Bo Weinberg is the boss while I'm away," he stipulated, as he tossed his other shirt into a bag.

In spite of Schultz's absence—or because of it, since Dutch was strictly a hothead—things went along swimmingly, as they say. The new rackets brought out such profits that the bosses hardly had to reach out to pick them up. Then the natural reaction set in. Human nature is easily the most unfathomable of all phenomena. The bosses became eager for power and insured security to go with their plunder. What they wanted was some development to guarantee their edge—to prevent any slip-up.

Actually, the "gimmick" was so obvious that it is amazing it took until 1934 for someone to finally come up with it. It was there all the time—the blueprint which converted the scattered mess of unconnected mobs in New York and Chicago and Kansas City and here and there into a smooth-going, tightly-bound business.

According to the mob's most reliable "recording secretaries," Lepke had the germ of the idea as early as the end of 1931, and Lucky saw the possibilities even before Joe the Boss was impeached. But credit for really pointing out the way goes to Johnny Torrio, a round little man who started out as a saloon-keeper.

Johnny Torrio always was a sharp guy. 'Way back, even before Prohibition, Johnny showed how sharp he was. That was when the Italian Society was expanding onto the Brooklyn waterfront. Johnny closed up his Manhattan saloon and opened one in Brooklyn, just to be near the center of business.

There, he hooked up with Paolo Vaccarelli, who was known to the underworld as Paul Kelly and was one of the first to combine a position as an official of the longshoremen's union with manipulation of dock control. When Prohibition came, though, Johnny Torrio headed west and took over Chicago from Big Jim Colisimo. En route, of course, he called on his old school chum, Frankie Yale, to come out and remove Big Jim. When half a dozen bodies were found on a railroad track, Johnny imported another old buddy from Brooklyn as his bodyguard, a hoodlum with a scar on his face, name of Al Capone.

Prohibition took hold, and the first thing you know a man couldn't even go out in his garden to pick a rose, without someone with an unfriendly implement like a sawed-off shotgun, blowing holes in him. Then Johnny really demonstrated his astuteness. He could not see the fun in living in a shooting gallery. He had all the money he needed. So, he said, "Here you are, Al—I'm handing it over to you and I'm getting out." And he "delivered" Chicago to Capone.

Johnny took a trip to Italy, stayed for several years. When he came home, he bought real estate in Miami and Maryland. At this writing, he is still in real estate. His most recent recorded transaction, in fact, was with the sheriff of Hillsborough County (Tampa), in Florida. As for Capone and Yale and the rest who stayed to pick the roses—they wound up being buried under them.

By 1933, Johnny was dealing in millions. He ranked with Lucky and Joey A. They said he was the biggest thing since Arnold Rothstein, the gambler-boss, as a bankroll man for underworld enterprises. After repeal, Johnny acquired a strictly legal and legitimate licensed liquor concern—one of the largest ones in the field.

You might say, in fact, that the only time Johnny Torrio wasn't on his toes was when he tried some flim-flam with fake stamps and juggled books in his liquor business. The Government asked a lot of questions about $68,000 in unpaid taxes. Ironically, the same Al Capone to whom Torrio handed Chicago as a gift, helped send the round little ganglord up. Al was a doddering has-been by then, serving time himself for tax evasion. He had fallen so far, by underworld standard, that he pleaded to turn stoolpigeon. That made them laugh—mighty Al Capone, who used to shoot guys for the same thing, begging with tears in his eyes for permission to sing. He thought it would make him look good to his keepers, and win privileges. In his babbling, Al mentioned Torrio's income. Uncle Sam already had been checking on Johnny's books.

When they sprang it on Torrio, he was still quick on the pickup. He knew they had him, and that a trial and accompanying legal loop-the-loops would only waste time. Besides, testimony often involves friends. So Johnny pleaded guilty. He served two and a half years, and was out and around again in 1941.

It was long before that—back in 1934, actually—that Torrio got the brainstorm for streamlining crime. The idea had to be presented first to the East's Big Six. The reaction of Lucky was required, and of Lepke and Buggsy Siegel and his partner, Meyer Lansky, Frank Costello's friend. New Jersey's rackets ruler would have to be consulted, too. The stoolpigeons told us the first discussion meeting was held in a fashionable New York hotel, with all mobs represented.

"See what you think of this," Johnny was quoted as saying, and he proceeded to outline the method that would not only provide the sought-for power, but would guarantee security of the mob bosses, with it. There is, of course, no verbatim report on the conclave. No one was keeping the minutes. But according to the mobsters who talked, the following is close enough to exhibit the proposition:

"Why don't all you guys work up one big outfit?" the mob moguls were asked. Immediately, the old antipathy to "hooking up" could be felt. "Wait now," they were advised. "That doesn't mean throwing everything into one pot. Let each guy keep what he's got now. But make one big combination to work with."

The new ventures, it was pointed out, would involve far more risk than the well-oiled machinery of bootlegging. In planning for the future, a prime item must be proper recognition and evaluation of the common foe: Law enforcement. It would be different than during Prohibition's happy heyday, when every mob had its individual protection and connections. A lot of the contacts would die with repeal. Why not pool surviving connections, then?

First and most important factor to be faced was the fighting among themselves—the gang warfare that marked every difference of opinion.

"One guy gets hit, and his troop hits the outfit that did it," the protagonist went on. Reprisal in mob murder always cost valuable manpower. But more: it exposed the underworld's most vulnerable spot—it brought heat from the Law. In the end, it helped no gang, for good men were being lost continually. Why not an organization, then, which could eliminate this weakness, simply by dealing with such matters to the interests of all?

There was sudden interest among the magnates at that. Each had been plagued by—and participated in—such costly clashes. These, remember, were the new order moguls. In spite of envies and ego, they were administrators and businessmen. There is no intent here to hand them unwarranted credit; these are simply the facts as our investigation found them. These gang leaders appreciated prospects never admitted by the isolationist torpedo of the Joe the Boss ilk.

It was quickly realized, of course, that no one of them would ever stand for one single boss—one czar over all. Each regarded himself a big shot, and was fanatically jealous of his position. But it was explained how there could be central control based on co-operation, without sacrifice of individuality. A board, or panel, of all the bosses themselves—that was the gimmick Johnny Torrio had in mind. Such a board could arbitrate inter-mob disputes by meeting and talking and deciding who was right and who was wrong. That was the key that finally convinced them.

Enthusiastically, the ganglords agreed on this board of directors, to include all the individual mob leaders, each with equal say, each with equal power. The board would dictate policy, handle all negotiations on the inter-mob level. And on that principle, they organized. On that conception, the Syndicate was born.

Each boss remained czar in his own territory, his rackets unmolested, his local authority uncontested. In murder, no one—local or imported—could be killed in his territory without his approval. He would have the right to do the job himself or permit an outsider to come in—but only at his invitation. In fact, no lawlessness, on an organized scale, could take place in his domain without his sanction and entire consent, unless he was overruled by the board of governors. And even then, he would have a say in the discussion. It was State's rights in crime!

Basically, it was a gilt-edged insurance policy. Every mob leader now had behind him not just his own hoods, but a powerful amalgamation of all mobs. Every gang chieftain was guaranteed against being interfered with in his own area—and against being killed by a rival mobster. The structure was definitely not a corporation. Had any of them known the word, he might have called it a cartel—a confederation of independent business concerns working toward the common goal of insured crime, and profits from same.

Soon, the criminal bands from beyond the East saw the strength of the union. The Brooklyn stoolpigeons told us a second meeting was called in Kansas City, to hear from the Western executives. The Capone crowd from Chicago and the Kansas City mob liked the idea. Reports came from Cleveland and Detroit that the Mayfield Gang and the Purple Mob wanted in. Boston and Miami, New Orleans and Baltimore, St. Paul and St. Louis—all flocked to the confederacy of crime, until it was nation-wide.

Thus, the Syndicate came into being. And, incredible as it may sound, the incessant, indiscriminate toll of gangsters lost through mob rivalries came to an abrupt end almost immediately!

A century and a half before, men of noble purpose had gathered from separate colonies to form a more perfect union. Here, a handful of evil delegates met, inspired by no nobility at all, but just as intent on a more perfect union—for crime. In each case, the result achieved a sovereign government made up of several sovereign "states." Perhaps no other analogy more closely fits the national Syndicate and its thriving organization to this day.

The Law never had or never will have insurmountable difficulty with unorganized crime. Some cases are always bound to go unsolved, certainly. But graveyards hold uncounted headstones heralding the quick dispatch by law and order of unattached criminals.

Up to 1934, with mobs separate and individual, no matter how swiftly the underworld traveled, the Law overtook it sooner or later. But when the gangster discovered organization, when he converted from unorganized crime to Syndicate operations on the national scale, he developed an edge that law and order has not entirely matched, even yet.

The vast majority of lawbreaking, from burglary to murder, is against local law—state, county and municipal. All are bounded by jurisdictional limits. On the other hand, nationally-organized crime knows no limitations of boundary. A county or state prosecutor, hemmed by jurisdictional boundaries, can hardly turn up an organization functioning in forty-eight states. A District Attorney, armed with just ordinary crime fighting weapons, has no means of penetrating this tightly-knit body. He can get lowly members of the mob; the higher-ups who pull the strings are always well covered.

The confederation of the mobs resulted in so powerful an antagonist that, until the Brooklyn informers enabled us to attack Murder, Inc., from within, not a single top-notcher in the Syndicate ever had been harmed. And, except for that one temporary break, not a single top-notcher has sat in the electric chair before or since. It remains today the same mighty adversary. If Kid Twist had not turned a light on it, there is no telling how long it would have been before the Law could even have surmised the existence of such a set-up. No one would have believed that these self-exalted cut-throats would ever cede even the smallest scrap of personal power to a syndicate.

Once it was agreed, back there in 1934, the government of crime was quick to get its machinery under way. Already established gang territorial lines became kingdoms inviolate against murder or muscling. And for seventeen years now, this national ring has governed the underworld through that policy.

Whenever a body is found in the gutter or a doorway today, it is still more or less casually dismissed by press and public as the result of a difference of mob opinion, just as it was in the trigger-happy twenties. It doesn't work that way any more. Not one top boss in the underworld has been slain since 1934, unless the execution was sanctioned, approved and, in fact, directed by the ganglords of the nation. That goes—from Dutch Schultz in 1935 to Buggsy Siegel in 1947 and Charlie Binaggio in 1950.

There has been virtually no internecine warfare in gangland in that period, other than that ordered by the Syndicate itself. This is exactly what the organizers had in mind when they combined to eliminate the economically unsound flare-ups in which gang had difference with gang, and settled it with guns. In the statute book of the new order, it was made absolute that there must be arbitration before blood spilled between rival jurisdictions —whether both are in New York or one is in Detroit and the other in Los Angeles. Murder for personal reasons is flatly banned. Majority rule decides all issues, and all gang moguls are charged with responsibility for seeing that the code is lived up to—to the letter and the punctuation.

Each member of the board of directors, at the top of the new government, was a boss of a member mob—the head hoods in the major cities. The succession has followed that form. They hear all business disputes, decide all policy and operational methods after listening to all sides.

"That is the democratic way," they said then. It never has been a one-man decision.

Along with the legislative and executive branches of crime, the gang planners also set up a judiciary, just as in any "democratic" government. They devised the Kangaroo Court of the underworld, with "justices" from the board of governors. Charges serious enough to warrant the death penalty for any high echelon gangster are called before it—cases, which in the deadly non-co-operating days of the gang vs. gang, would have meant immediate no-questions-asked mob warfare. Like the Supreme Court of the United States, the Kangaroo Court is a court of last resort. Its word is final; its decisions irrevocable. Thus, when the court ruled, in 1935, that Joey Amberg, extortionist and dope peddler, must die, die he did, although he was a protégé of Buggsy Siegel, and his cause was pleaded by the highly-placed Joey Adonis.

Even such prominent powers as Dutch Schultz and Buggsy Siegel had no appeal from the verdicts. When each of these characters was rubbed out, it was the formal execution of a death sentence officially decreed by the kangaroo court—and after regular trial, at that. Nor does the kangaroo court know no other verdict than "guilty." Reles told me of at least two acquittals, in cases in which conviction would have carried the death penalty with as much enforcement power as any duly constituted court of criminal jurisprudence.

Hand in hand with the new set-up, too, came an accent on "connections"—political, protection connections. One of the suggestions for co-operation at the original organization meeting, at which Johnny Torrio had outlined the whole idea, had been for interchangeable use of each mob's contacts. Under the Syndicate such protection worked perfectly, right from the start.

There are various methods of accomplishing this end. On the basic level, is the prosaic paying of "ice." Then, too, top-ranked bosses are always on the lookout for friendships that produce valued contacts. They weasel themselves into political campaigns and into close association with public officials wherever and whenever possible. Corruption is a cancer that spreads all too easily under the careful nurture of criminal chiefs avid for power.

One snatch of testimony during the Kefauver Committee hearings in New York in March, 1951, expressed it especially succinctly, even though protection or corruption were not mentioned. O'Dwyer was on the stand at the time, telling of a visit he made to Frank Costello's apartment, and of seeing several top political leaders of the city there:

> Q—A funny thing what magnetism that man (Costello)
> had. How can you analyze it; what is the attraction he
> has?
> A—It doesn't matter whether it is a banker, a businessman
> or a gangster; his pocketbook is always attractive.

The racketeer regards himself as a businessman, with politics every bit as sound as those in legitimate enterprise. Take good will, for instance. The grocer, the manufacturer, the mail order house build up good will in order to keep customers coming back, to prevent a competitor from taking customers and to convince potential customers to deal with them. That, says the mobster, is exactly what murder does. Assassination, therefore, has always been given as careful consideration by the gang magnate as good will ever has received from the decent businessman.

With the advent of the national organization, and the banning of "unnecessary" killing, sanctioned eliminations became a matter for experts, strictly. It took more than just pulling a trigger to carry out the purpose of the Syndicate—the furtherance of the new national rackets business.

Each outfit had always taken care of its own eliminations. A few of the gang bosses, whose multiple activities required it and whose affluence could afford it, sometimes hired special slayers at so much the throat-cutting. But mostly, each mob used its own triggermen.

When the Syndicate opened for business, however, it became vital that there be no slip-ups, no loose ends, in such matters. There were occasions when one or another mob had a job to be done which, for security reasons, could not be efficaciously handled by its own members. The local boys, for instance, might be so placed that such a slaying would point directly toward them, or, perhaps, the selected victim was wary of them. That made it desirable to bring in a new face to do the work. As time passed, this custom became more popular. In a businesslike manner, it advanced to importation of killers from a mob in another city or state, with the approval of the boss of that outfit.

Early in the growth of this practice, the Brooklyn executioners were summoned, like any others, for, through Joey Adonis, Brooklyn was on the Syndicate's national map. It was soon noted that the Brooklyn killers always were proficient. The precision-like technique they had perfected came to be looked upon with great respect and approbation by mob moguls the country over, for its painstaking attention to detail and its neat finality of accomplishment.

"Those kids in Brooklyn got it taped real good," said one gang boss. And another praised: "That Reles and Pittsburgh Phil, and that Maione know how to cover up a job so nobody can find a thing."

No matter what the assignment, their talents functioned with art and skill—even to labor disputes and eliminations, which were the most hazardous. Hence, since every mob, the country over, had the right to call on any other for co-operation and assistance, gang bosses far and near took to inviting the Brooklyn assassins more and more frequently. It was no more the duty of the Brooklyn troop than of any other mob in the cartel. But so adept were the Brownsville thugs that, before very long, they were being used almost invariably from the Atlantic to the Pacific, from Florida to the Canadian border. Eventually, they were recognized as the more-or-less official execution squad for the Syndicate, on call at any time. They worked so many contracts so successfully that Lepke, before long, practically adopted them en masse.

"Lepke would send in $12,000 flat a year for his work," Reles revealed to us. The Kid had but one complaint about the set-up. "Their accountant came with the proposition," he related ruefully. "His name is Simon Lepasco. He would bring the money down to us. He's no accountant. He's a shakedown artist."

The Brooklyn experts were not for hire. Their outside work was solely on contract service for other Syndicate gangs—the same as a garbage disposal company contracts to haul off the refuse from a suburban block every day; not just one garbage can from one house that summons it on one particular day.

That put the last nail in the Syndicate's construction. It completed Murder, Inc., a coast-to-coast crime co-operative, dealing in everything from nickel-and-dime thievery to murder, and comprising every mob that meant anything in the underworld of the United States. It was a going concern, and for the next six years it went where it pleased. All in all, it was the biggest thing to hit crime since Cain invented murder and used it on Abel.

The new lineup, with the Brooklyn troop as enforcement squad, proved a huge success immediately. The upper echelon mobsters were openly and audibly appreciative.

"Lepke was satisfied real good," Reles preened to us in 1940. "Lep give us eleven contracts for witnesses when he was on the lam. We knocked off seven of them before Dewey put him on trial last year."

Lucky, too, took to the set-up at once. In fact, one of the first Syndicate contracts the Brooklyn troop undertook was at the behest of the notorious dope-peddler with the droopy eye.

Muddy Kasoff, a small-time narcotics hustler from lower Manhattan, was meddling with Lucky's territory, and he was granted permission to take the proper reprisal. He contacted the Brooklyn firing squad.

"This bum is cutting in on my play with the stuff," Lucky briefed them. "You guys take him."

The boys learned that Muddy had some good friends—and the friends had money. They figured here was a golden opportunity. They "snatched" Muddy. (Kidnaping was popular back there in 1934.) They took him to a hideout and they bound him and stood guard over him.

"Get your pals to get up five thousand, or we knock you off," they demanded. Muddy was impressed naturally. With no quibbling, he told his captors how to contact his friends. Two or three days later, the return contact was made.

"We can only get up twenty-seven hundred," the friends reported sorrowfully. "Here it is. If you hold off a little while, we can dig up the rest."

To the hoodlums, though, the request for time sounded like an obvious stall. Besides, $2,700 was a fair night's pay, anyway. Muddy was blindfolded. His hands were roped behind his back. He was loaded into a car. Muddy felt relieved. Evidently, his kidnapers were preparing to release him. They drove him far out on Long Island—to Island Park, a pretty seaside spot, where the fishing is good not too far offshore. The car was stopped. Muddy was led to the edge of a vacant lot, and his hands were freed.

"We're turning you loose, punk," the captive was informed. "Take a hundred steps before you touch the blindfold. If you touch it before, we'll grab you again. Now get!"

Muddy walked nine paces. He could feel the grass under his soles. He took ten strides more, into the weeds. He heard no sound, and he wondered if his abductors had gone. He counted off half the distance, with stumbling unseeing steps. As he got that far, the hoods raised their pistols and blasted away. Next morning, what was left of the dope peddler who meddled with Charley Lucky was found at the foot of a billboard—which pleaded for motorists to drive safely.

"Sure . . . all the big shots were satisfied," sneered Reles, when he told of the Syndicate, and Brooklyn's death-dealing function in it.

The national network rooted deep. It has been subject to devastating attack since 1934. The industrial and numbers extortions of the 1930's were throttled by Governor (then Prosecutor) Dewey when he nailed Lucky and Jimmy Hines, the Tammany boss. In 1940 and 1941, our convictions of the murderers who made the rackets click eliminated some of the highly ranked operatives. But the organization remained. The blueprint, the methods of the rackets, the gang killings—these are the signs that it is still with us.

As a matter of fact, our convictions could not even completely obliterate the Brooklyn branch, despite the loss of the seven killers I had the pleasure of putting into the electric chair. The troop had dug in too long to be altogether uprooted. Just how long, Reles related next, after he had completed painting the picture of the national organization. He went all the way back, to the flowering of the Brownsville branch—and its birth in blood.

PART V
ANATOMY OF THE UNDERWORLD

MURDER INC. was the instrument through which the underworld established a *pax romana*. The warring lords were curbed. The individualist outlaw was liquidated. A co-ordinating council was established. A central authority—more a court of jurisdictional claims than a directing body—was recognized. And all this was possible because armed power—Murder Inc.—was overwhelmingly in the hands of the merged mobs.

There were standouts, of course, who resisted easy absorption. There was Vincent ("Mad Dog") Coll, who earned the nickname of which he was proud. There was Dutch Schultz, one-time ruler of a beer dynasty, who stood aside from the Syndicate, even while seeking its co-operation. And there was Buggsy Siegel, who had his own ideas about establishing a bookie empire on the West Coast, since he refused to merge his wire service with the national network. And there were others. But they all learned the "corporate" lesson and they learned it the "hard way."

A Mad Dog Coll was a greater menace to the underworld than to the law-abiding citizen. To the innocent bystander who might be cut down on one of Coll's forays, the tragedy was personal; to the underworld, the same act was a threat of social and communal importance, since it endangered the entire "business" of the Syndicate. To a public that did not distinguish between a psychopathic killer, like Coll, and a cool businessman, like Costello, the wild gun play of the Mad Dog was an incitement for a "cleanup," and for "action" against the gangsters. Such public furor threatened the entire underworld operation. The Mad Dog had to be cleared off the streets. And if the police could not do it, by due process, the underworld would and did do it without undue delay.

Commenting on the demise of Coll, Richard O'Connor writes: "He had become so dangerous that the underworld, both for its own protection and as a public relations gesture, coldly and precisely sent him to his death."

Dutch Schultz, at one time, represented a similar and even greater menace to the underworld. Under an income tax indictment, handled by Thomas Dewey, Schultz proposed that the most efficient way to eliminate his own difficulties and to get Dewey off the back of the Mob was to liquidate the persistent District Attorney. The motion was put before the highest council of the Syndicate, which decided against any such brash action on the theory that the murder of Dewey would so stir the nation that the entire crime corporation would be in danger, and that it was the better part of valor to let Schultz and/or the Eastern end of the business "take the rap" or even to close shop on the Atlantic Coast for a while rather than risk the whole works. Dissatisfied with the decision, Schultz decided to take the law in his own hands and "rub out" the DA with his own murder machine. When word about the Dutchman's plans leaked to the Syndicate—with its highly efficient network of information—it beat Schultz to the punch and privately eliminated this troublesome freebooter. Ironically, the same Dewey, whose life was thus saved by the Syndicate, later sent some of his saviors to the electric chair. (The account of how Schultz was handled appears at length in *Murder Inc.*)

Buggsy Siegel was, likewise, eliminated because he crossed corporate purposes. The vast retailing empire of bookmaking is dependent upon a national wire service that, through its speedy, accurate, and confidential reporting gives the bookies an unethical, but highly profitable, edge against their gullible customers. One of the great struggles within the underworld was the campaign to wrest control of these services from Mont Tennes and then Jim Ragen. When the Syndicate was finally set for national consolidation, it found that one of its own boys from Brooklyn, who had outgrown his britches on the West Coast, was insistent upon sovereign status. The Bug was exterminated!

A major function of Murder Incorporated was to establish quiet, to use overwhelming force to win positions of power so that, by using the new levers of economic and political influence, open violence would be rendered unnecessary. In effect, the Syndicate is responsible for reducing the amount of gang warfare and haphazard crime, in the same way that a monopoly or cartel eliminates the amount of cutthroat competition in industry. This means that the extent of underworld operation can not be measured by the ordinary crime statistics on beatings, shootings, murder. Indeed, quite the reverse may be true! The crime cartel may well help lighten the load on the police blotter.

To the individual who chooses crime as a career—not some amateur motivated by a passing hunger or a wild urge—affiliation with the corporation is preferable to lone-wolfing. The corporation offers security!

In this era of the "organization man," the underworld—like most institutions that prosper within an established culture—has learned to conform. Its internal structure provides status for those who would plod along in workaday clothes. In its external relations, it affects all the niceties of a settled society, preferring public relations and investment to a punch in the nose or pickpocketing. Affiliation with such an organization is almost irresistible to the youth who would choose crime as a way of life.

To begin with, "organized" crime offers a steady job—with excellent opportunities. Contrast the unhappy plight of the free-lance thief with a member of the mob—in terms of present income and future outlook The "independent" crook lives in a constant state of insecurity, ferreting out his next victim, researching the joint to be "heisted," uncertain ot the police, short on accomplices, without funds for legal protection. He must envy the "organization" man, who is given a carefully delineated assignment, guaranteed a given income, operating among "bought" police, surrounded by well-trained accomplices, backed by a fund for the finest legal talent. The former lives amidst all the jeopardies of free enterprise. The latter is socialized, a reasonably safe and secure segment of our total social structure. The former lives from hand-to-mouth. The latter is a salaried man, living on a guaranteed annual wage. The former can see little ahead of him but a life of endless crime, flight, and ostracism from society. The latter can look forward to rising in the hierarchy of his organization to become top man in a company—a real legitimate company, perhaps with a recognized standing on the stock market—drawing a regular legal income in his later years. Such advancement is not merely from low salary to high income but from violence to peace, from dodging the cops to evading the income tax. As part of the underworld, an ambitious youth can rise from bodyguard and hood to a pillar of the community, giving to charities, dispensing political favors, sending his boys to West Point and his girls to debutante balls.

But the young ruffian, even if he lacks the imagination to see what affiliation with the "organization" can mean for his *future,* must still appreciate the practical advantages of the corporate endeavor in terms of the *immediate* operation. For "organized" crime means criminality with maximum impunity. If a "job" has to be done, that "job" is handled as a mission by the "organization," projected with thought and planning.

Consider a typical gangland *murder*—the ultimate sanction in enforcing the will of organized crime. Such murders would baffle Sherlock Holmes with his endless pursuit of "motive" and "clue." The "organized" killer has no motive—at least, no personal motive—any more than a soldier has a personal motive in killing an anonymous enemy. And he leaves no clues, because a vast, intricate, and efficient outfit is at his side systematically erasing all clues—to protect the business.

The killer is generally an imported "gun." He comes from some other part of the country—or some other country. He does not know the name of the victim. He does not know the reason for the murder. He does not act in hot blood; he waits his time, watching for the opportune moment. He arrives to perform a mission and he departs when the mission is completed. He is as impersonal as a salesman selling a commodity, this time a commodity known as death. What the impact of this commodity is on the ultimate consumer—whose name may be blazoned in the next day's headlines—is of no concern to the peddler. It's all part of a job.

The victim is pointed out by the finger man, who plays no part in the killing per se. This finger man knows only two things: the face (not necessarily the name) of the victim and the face (not necessarily the name) of the killer. If the finger man is accurate, the right victim is "hit"; if the finger man is inaccurate, the wrong person is "hit," an occasional mishap in underworld killings.

Before the "job" is done, the victim is "cased." Sometimes this is the work of the killer, or of the finger man, or of third parties. The best victims are those with the most regular habits, for regularity leaves less to chance. A man like Thomas Dewey was a perfect pigeon for a Dutch Schultz, because the Dutchman found Dewey so predictable. Each morning, the same hour of departure from home, the same drug store, the same phone call, the same line of walk, the same mode of travel. The planners of the murder could think ahead, setting place and time, reasonably certain that the victim would be there for the appointment.

The killer appears on the scene with an appropriate murder weapon. He does not purchase it. The weapon is not in his name and is not traceable to him. The gun was probably stolen, as often as not from the arsenal of the United States armed services, from some crate pilfered off a dock where "organized crime" has been known to lift items and cargoes by the carload. Should someone try to trace the murder weapon, his trail might well end with the Secretary of Defense.

Before use, the weapon is "treated." At one time, it was sufficient to file down the number on the gun. But after it was discovered that the police had ways of submitting the gun to scientific analysis to discover the original numbers, the underworld took to chiseling out the markings in depth. Now the gun was as anonymous in origin as the killer himself. After the murder, the gun could be discarded—and that was the end of the trail.

The auto—and most gangland killings do involve an auto—is likewise rendered anonymous. The car is generally stolen. The purloined murder vehicle is not delivered directly to the killer; it is parked at a set location to be picked up by the murderer at a given time. The license plate is also stolen, so that if a witness notices a plate number, this clue will lead to the wrong car. And after the murder, the car is dumped, turned over to a specialist whose sole job is to junk cars and to junk them beyond recognition. (In the good old days of Murder Inc. in Brooklyn, the cars were turned over to Oscar the Poet, a premature beatnik type who practiced his own form of parasitism on the "mob" by getting a few pennies per car out of the junkies to whom he turned over the vehicle. In between such scavenging, Oscar would while away his time in Brooklyn parks reading belles-lettres.)

The murder car is driven by a specialist—not the murderer. The killer, it is assumed, has plenty on his mind, without the bother of driving a car under stress. In addition, the killer is a "foreigner" who is unacquainted with streets, traffic, cops, and the local terrain. The driver specialist, moreover, has already practiced a few trial runs, at the proper hour, and—if necessary —could keep driving the car while the killer made his exit.

Behind the murder car is an interceptor car—an innocent vehicle, un-used in the commission of the crime, but useful in blocking pursuit, in ob-structing visibility, in providing a rescue squad where needed. (In a case of high priority, the "interference" car might also carry a killer to dispose of the original killer if that is called for by the script.)

The script, while conceived by an engineer of murder, is generally sub-mitted to approval of a narrow committee. In the planning, the legal mind is important. The smart lawyer can supply each of the participants with a handy reason for being where he is at the time he is there. The murder is planned with the possibility of apprehension in mind. If caught, what then? The alibi, the reason, the case are prepared before the crime.

Finally, after the production of the commodity is engineered in every detail, the underworld thinks through the appropriate trade-mark. The killer MUST BE KNOWN. While the name of the individual killer must be hidden, the name of the corporation must be advertised. The reason for the killing in most cases is not to get rid of an individual who may have balked at the orders and extortions of the underworld but to serve notice ON OTHER INDIVIDUALS that the word of the gang is law. Hence, the killing of a per-son would be a great waste, unless it were established publicly that this particular individual was killed because he defied the demands of the under-world. And so the gang leaves its trade-mark on the victim. The trade-marks vary from time to time and place to place, but every knowing crime investi-gator knows the mark of the mob. This mark is the "commercial," the brand, the means whereby one killing becomes a means of perpetuating a going business. The underworld has found that it pays to advertise.

Hence while the underworld has an elaborate system for seeing to it that the murderer will not be found, it simultaneously sees to it that the murder will out. In this way, the underworld—as organization—can claim credit for the crime while the individual murderer—as organization man— goes unpunished.

Sometimes, despite elaborate preparation, something goes awry—and the killer is apprehended. When this happens, the underworld defense moves into new level. And at this second line of defense, organized crime has a great deal to offer the young man who chooses the corporate criminal way of life.

The underworld has its links with the police, the individual copper who walks his beat. His pay is low; his life is dull; his future is limited. But in an entente cordiale with the underworld, he can find new horizons: highly increased pay; women and wine; a quick financial killing. The temptation to make a deal with the underworld, especially when it appears to harm nobody, is as alluring as it is common. Starting with a weekly stipend for closing one eye at a gambling joint, the sum—and the involvement—multiply as the cops and robbers convert traditional antipathy into mutual assistance. When, on occasion, the operation of the business calls for violence, the local constabulary is cast in the role of accomplice *in absentia*.

More important than the cop on the beat, however, is the DA. It is the District Attorney who must gather the evidence, make the case, push the prosecution. If the DA can be reached—indeed, if the underworld can put its own man in the DA's office—then the crime organization can guarantee a high level of security to its employees.

Where police and District Attorney can not be bought—and, in most cases, they can not—then the underworld must get to the witnesses. Some of these can be intimidated, some can be bought, and some must be liquidated. In all such cases, the troublesome witnesses are the "outsiders," the innocent bystanders who saw a crime in commission. The "insiders," the members of the organization who are involved, are little trouble. Their code calls for "no ratting." They live by this code. The punishment meted out to them if they do turn state's evidence is merciless and virtually inescapable. The troublesome witness is the "outsider." And to handle these obstinate witnesses is one of the continuing chores of the violent end of the crime business.

If the case ever comes before a jury, the underworld goes to work on the twelve peers of the accused. Skillful lawyers pick them with care, of course. But after that comes the usual round of bribes and threats.

This vast legal operation—bribery, lawyers, elections, threats, disposal of witnesses—is a costly enterprise. And for this purpose the underworld has its defense and lamming fund. This slush fund can enable the accused to disappear—take it on the lam—or make a superb defense. Precisely how this chest gets its funds is still unrecorded. One interesting clue is the "fine" allegedly imposed on one of the "guests" at Apalachin for violation of corporate discipline. Into what coffers did this "fine" go? There are other rumors and speculations about "assessments" on those able to pay to meet "legal" fees and to finance escapes.

Whatever the method of fund-raising and disbursement of this emergency chest, its existence is one of the major fringe benefits for a member of the mob.

Despite this defense in depth, members of the mob are repetitively hailed into court and found guilty. Sometimes, that is the way the mob plans it. Thus, for minor crimes, such as gambling and pushing dope, the "big shot" in the racket arranges for a stand-in. Sometimes, a small fish is allowed to fry so that the big fish may go free. Occasionally, a man high in the organization may be turned in and allowed to be taken—either to take pressure off the total business or to get rid of an ambitious rival within the hierarchy. (There is reason to believe that when Lepke surrendered to J. Edgar Hoover, the underworld overlord was led to believe that there was a "deal" with the FBI. It took Lepke only seconds to find out that no such arrangement had been made. Lepke's death in the electric chair took some of the heat off the Syndicate and, simultaneously, made room for a power shift within the organization.) Now and then, a top figure in the underworld is taken and tried and found guilty—as if he were just another criminal.

But when a member of the mob goes to jail, he carries with him the protection of the organization. Behind the prison walls, there is a structured society among the inmates. There are the lords and the lackeys among the convicts; there are gangs and gang leaders; there are kangaroo courts, fines, levies, and punishments. When the "organzation man" moves behind bars, the organization goes with him. The "home office" protects him against bullies, gets him preferred cells and the softer job, works on parole—and, most important, takes care of his family. Even in the jails the underworld is a power.

The excerpt entitled "Behind Prison Walls" is semifictional, based on the experiences of a low man on crime's totem pole who spent time in jail. As told to James D. Horan, author of this chapter, the convict depicts the power of the mob even in a high-security prison.

One fringe benefit of affiliation with the "organization" is medical care. To the freebooter, a serious knife or bullet wound in the abdomen becomes something more than an injury requiring medical treatment. The operation often has to be surreptitious, handled by quacks and drunks, without benefit of sanitation, hospitalization, nursing care. If for no other reason than the medical and surgical benefits usually available in the corporate setup, the criminal should prefer working for the big outfit. At one time, especially when constant violence created a long roster on the "most wanted" list, the medical arm of the service gave many a criminal not only a new life but also a new face. J. Edgar Hoover complained bitterly some years ago that "the increasing use of surgery by criminals in an effort to conceal identity undoubtedly placed added responsibilities upon the practitioner" of law enforcement.*

These, then, are the positive advantages of "organizational" affiliation on the part of the starting criminal. Despite these "securities" there are free-lancers, true to the American spirit of enterprise. And these latter, so long as they confine themselves to housebreaking, holdups, and other little under-

* John Edgar Hoover, "Plastic Surgery and Criminals: The Surgeon's Responsibility," *American Journal of Surgery*, Vol. XXVIII (April 1935), p. 156f.

takings, will be tolerated by the "organized" giant. But, if the "independent" attempts to invade established territory, he will face quick extermination: first, he will find himself plagued by the police, who were probably turned loose on the intruder by the underworld; second, he will find himself threatened with violence; third, if he is a success, he will be offered a merger; and, if all else fails, he will find himself clad "in a wooden kimono."

In this vast "organization," who is the top man? This question is asked repeatedly and, curiously, it is answered repeatedly—but the answers are rarely the same. For a while the top name was Capone, although according to a few journalists there was a highly cultured fellow known as "The Camel" who was viewed as Capone's boss. Then there was Lepke, the cool, sober, judicial chairman of the New York, perhaps the national, board. Then, during the Kefauver hearings, Frank Costello carried the sobriquet of "Prime Minister of the Underworld." But even then there were those who insisted that Lucky Luciano, exiled in Italy, was running the show by remote control. In more recent years the title "King of Crime" has been given to Vito Genovese, and—by one magazine—to Joe Profaci. For a time there was the game of naming New York's "Mr. Big," a waterfront figure who through portside gangs was alleged to have vast hidden control. Some sleuths say that the trail leads to a politician of national fame, while still others whisper about various union leaders and bankers.

If there were some one man at the top, holding all the strings in his hands, it is likely that he would have been discovered before this. And with his discovery, all his power would have had to fall apart, for this is one operation that can hardly continue in the cleansing glare of publicity.

What seems most probable is that the underworld is organized along feudal lines: robber barons and their retainers. Their sovereignties are roughly defined. Sometimes they clash, and when they do there is blood or a council of the elders to avoid blood. The top man, if there is such, is no more than *primus inter pares*. And whatever crown he wears rests uneasily on his bloody head.

A small insight into the types and relationships of the "organization" men was provided by Federal Judge Irving R. Kaufman when he pronounced sentence at the Apalachin trial. In prescribing penalties, the judge offered thumbnail sketches of the guilty, delineating "top dogs," and "strong-arm" men, business type, counsellor-at-law, and respected politician. The excerpt entitled "Thumbnail Sketches" is a rare statement in the annals of criminal and legal literature.

The rise of two men—from rank and file to middle bureaucracy—in the underworld is related briefly in the excerpt entitled "On the Waterfront." The full story of "Cockeye" Dunn's influence, methods, and final comeuppance, as told by William Keating in *The Man Who Rocked the Boat,* is one of those "stranger than fiction" accounts out of the files of an assistant DA.

One of the most discerning descriptions of the underworld hierarchy and most sensitive portaits of a "top dog" appears in Joseph Dinean's *Underworld USA*, a portion of which is reprinted here under the title "The Hierarchy of Crime." The central figures of this book, Fingers Tolland, a field representative of the "organization," and Earl Connor, the superexecutive, are both semifictional, although the author leaned heavily on known persons for his model. For the student of organized crime, the most penetrating and challenging section of this chapter is in the final pages where Connor reveals himself not only as a wise executive, in the model of a Carnegie, but also as a tolerant philosopher, in the manner of The Ecclesiastes.

Although Earl Connor, like many composite characters, may be too flawless to believe, there is little doubt that the leadership of the "organization" is a worldly crew. Within the collective leadership of organized crime must reside vast working knowledge of our institutions, deep insights into human behavior, executive capacity, financial skill, and political know-how. In many respects, these men must have the qualities of leaders in a revolutionary movement, organizing the rebels against law, infiltrating institutions, assigning and removing lieutenants, planning operations, establishing new authority, imposing their will through a process of violent gradualism. Any one angle of the business operation requires skill: to supervise the total system requires genius.

A number of excerpts focus on various operations in the far-flung empire of the underworld. The two excerpts on the numbers racket—the first an excerpt from *The New York Post* entitled "The Numbers Racket," and the second from the memoirs of a DA's man, entitled "Fixing the Clearing House" —deal with different facets of one gambling enterprise. The first details the complexity of the operation, the vast army of employees, of customers, the minutely careful system of collections and disbursements, the national network of information, the relationship of little banks and big bankers and the underworld's own Federal Reserve. The second reveals the kind of contacts organized crime holds in its hands, a frightening, amusing, true tale— with a Hitchcock ending.

The excerpt entitled "Into Seventy Businesses," by Senator Estes Kefauver, gives a blow-by-blow description of how one underworld type muscles into one little business in recent years and how the business expands, with the original owner transformed into an impotent "partner" and lists some seventy industrial and commercial fields into which the underworld had penetrated in the 1950's.

Between the Kefauver investigation of 1950 and the McClellan investigation of 1960, the underworld proved its ability to move forward into the second half of the century. In an interview with Robert Kennedy—counsel to the latter committee—the magazine *Nation's Business* asked bluntly, "Do you see this as a new surge of crime?" And Kennedy answered flatly, "I see it as a new surge by the people in the underworld. Organized crime is far more widespread now and far more serious than during the days of Al Capone."

The fact that the 1960's continue and amplify the pattern of the 1950's in the development of the underworld does not mean that the Kefauver investigation, exposés, and pressure had no meaning for organized crime. The concentration of the TV cameras on Costello may well have caused the subsequent prosecutions, convictions, and loss in status for the "Prime Minister." But the embarrassment to any one individual or group of individuals did not prove an embarrassment to the organization. The new situation called for new faces, new ways, new measures—and new blood with new vigor. The continuing vigor of the underworld into the 1960's is attested by the report of a Kansas grand jury on the deal between organized crime and the police in Kansas City. This appears as the section entitled "Police-Syndicate Deal."

The corners into which the underworld creeps are not always the obvious enterprises, as may be noted from the excerpt dealing with operation of organized crime in stock speculation. This exposé of underworld figures, with their boiler-room tactics in the stock market, conceals more than it reveals, for this account talks about known "outlaws" who were out in front as investment brokers. But all this leaves untouched the obviously far more difficult area of "pressures" exerted on investors outside stock-selling offices to place their orders through favored firms.

In these sections appear the names of men who, while kingpins in their own jurisdictions, are also part of a total "organization," with their names repeatedly linked with the other prominent names of the American underworld.

Probably the most shocking display of underworld power appears in the excerpt on the underworld in the War. The incident discussed in this piece has been described and rewritten dozens of times because of its bizarre quality, placing the vast might of the United States government in a position of dependency on the underworld. Curiously enough, the "organized" gangs come out as partial saviors of the nation; the government appears in the role of petitioner and client of the mob.

The endless probe that has collected the clues, hints, rumors, and deductions composing this episode arises from the fact that Lucky Luciano, one of the top dogs in New York's and perhaps America's underworld, was released from prison by Thomas Dewey, his nemesis, on the proviso that Luciano return to his native Italy. Through numerous campaigns in New York City and New York State, Dewey's opponents repeatedly asked the question: "Why did Dewey let Lucky go?" Repeatedly, there were dark hints that this was all part of a political deal. The section on "The Underworld and the War" by Frederic Sondern is presently the most widely accepted line of speculation on why Lucky was paroled.

A companion piece, also derived from the crime-infested waterfront, is the excerpt from *Waterfront Priest* by Raymond Allen. This section, "Pattern of Power," selects one man in a key spot, analyzes his ties, and notes the links between the upper world and the nether world of our culture.

The twelve excerpts in this section on the underworld today do not pretend to be a coverall of the "organization's" operation. These pieces focus on facets that outline, even if they do not complete in scope and detail, the anatomy of the underworld.

The two conclusions that are inevitable are these:

1. No corner of American life—government, sports, commerce, industry, labor, gambling, investment, or even defense—is immune to underworld penetration.
2. The underworld is no longer an ugly hood, a muscle for hire to any master, but an independent power, vying with other great classes and movements in America for wealth and influence in our culture.

Section 26   BEHIND PRISON WALLS

From *The Mob's Man* by James D. Horan, 1959.

The name came from a prisoner who was being sentenced downtown. When the judge said he was to serve his time in Clinton Prison at Dannemora, the con cried, "Oh, God, no, Judge! Not Siberia!"

Whether or not the story is true, it describes how every con on his way to prison feels about Dannemora. It really is Siberia, both in weather and conditions. Situated in the bleak section of New York State where the mercury drops as far as twenty below zero, this century-old institution strikes terror in any man at first sight of its dirty stone walls.

I saw it on a gray November day in 1933. I was in a draft of forty-five cons, the scum of the earth, the trouble-makers, the killers and the morons. We were shackled one to another with leg irons and confined to the last car of the train. Each of us had a burlap bag with a few personal articles. When we got to Dannemora we hobbled onto a bus which took us to the prison. The light was growing dim as we approached the pen where I would spend the next ten years of my life. My heart sank like a stone when I saw it. The man I was shackled to, a skinny runt named Mickey just groaned out loud.

That guy's groan of despair expressed the feelings of all of us.

After we shuffled into the prison we were handcuffed and assigned cell blocks; I was sent to Southhall.

In the mess hall, where we were given a sandwich and coffee, I met Black Charleston, a towering Negro whom I had seen a few times around the Four Queens. I had heard he was in for rape and was a four-time loser.

I was mighty glad to see a friendly face.

"Man, I feel sorry for you," he said.

"Why, Charlie?"

"You assigned Southhall?"

"What's wrong with that?"

"You must be on somebody's list. That's the worst place they have here. That's where the riot guys are."

"What riot guys?"

"The guys that started that riot in 1930. They burned the whole place and held off the troopers for three days. Ain't you guys heard about it down the river?"

"We heard there was trouble, but not that bad."

Charlie shook his head. "Those guys are real mean. They beat up the guards, almost killed one, then made a bonfire with mattresses. They acted like they were crazy. Me, I stayed in my cell. I want no part of them babies." He shook his head. "Andy, I feel real sorry for you."

When he went away I just stared down at the coffee. It was one of the lowest points in my life. I seriously wondered if there was any more point in going on.

After eating we were separated; I was marched to Southhall. I could hear cots creak as cons rose to give me the eye. Then the hack pointed with his club to a cell. This place, just six paces wide, was now my home. It was cold and damp, with one dirty window.

The next day, I became a part of the prison routine; up at 7:00 A.M., march to breakfast, then to the cotton shop, where we were locked in until nightfall. Back to dining room, and in the cell by 7:30 P.M.

Every Thursday we took our clothes off in our cell and were marched one by one to a shower.

The third night I was jerked out of my sleep by an inhuman scream; it rose and fell, rose and fell. It sounded like a man under torture.

"What the hell's that?" I asked the con next to me.

"Some guy's blowing his top. Happens every night."

And usually it did—men no longer able to stand the cold, the dirt, the feeling that you were a caged animal, went mad and screamed at the top of their lungs until the hacks dragged them off to the nuthouse, which was conveniently across the street. To enter the Dannemora Prison for the Criminally Insane was the end, the living death. I found myself praying at night, praying that my sanity would hold and I would never make that trip. . . .

The prison, I soon discovered, held the most vicious criminals and the nation's top racketeers. They were five times worse than the guys at Sing Sing, which some of them contemptuously called "The Country Club." Here were Lucky Luciano and his henchmen, Little Davey Petillo, Jimmy Frederico, Ralph Laguri, and smaller hoods like Richie.

I saw Richie the first day I was permitted in the yard. He knew that I was in from the prison grapevine, and he was on the lookout for me. I was wondering where I would find a friend, when I saw him grinning at me. It was the first good thing that had happened to me since my arrival. We hugged each other like lost brothers. Then he started to introduce me to his mob, headed by a giant Negro named Big Sasso, who I think is still there. Sasso was over two hundred pounds, and strong as a wild bull. He really belonged to the jungle. Once I saw a man smash him over the head with a baseball bat. Sasso only laughed and, with the blood streaming down his face, grabbed the con, lifted him off his feet and was choking him to death when the hacks came. It took six of them to tear his hands loose. Sasso got isolation for three months; it only made him more savage than before.

As Richie explained it, there were several combinations in the prison: Big Sasso's mob, Luciano's mob and an Irish mob headed by a burglar from the West Side.

Each gang had its favorite spot in the yard and also its stable of homosexuals. Whenever there was trouble it was usually over the homos. For example, there was the gangster nicknamed "Little Piggie," because his personal habits disgusted even the cons. He had as his boy a young kid who was doing a robbery rap. To keep the kid happy he supplied him with cigarettes, groceries and other items. When a new draft from Sing Sing arrived, the kid started following a new guy. Piggie caught him in the ball field and slashed him terribly. It took thirty-two stitches to close the wounds. Piggie, in turn, was smashed over the head with a rock and almost killed by the new guy. This led to other isolated fights, until Big Sasso and the Italian warned the others—any more trouble with the hacks and somebody would get burned.

A kangaroo court ordered the kid to share his affections with both cons.

I soon found out that in every prison there are what we call peddlers; they're always selling something. It started when I sent my clothes to the laundry for the first time. They came back a mess.

Richie tipped me off.

"You got to pay, Andy."

"Pay who?"

"The guys in the laundry. Two packs of butts gets your shirt ironed. Three packs and they put in starch. Four packs will take care of your sheets and pillowcase. If you have ten packs the shoeshop will put on soles and heels. Fifteen packs and the tailor shop will give you tailor-made prison pants."

I soon found that the mess hall jobs were the peddler's choicest offering, since food is the priceless commodity in prison. Prison fare is atrocious. After a year of that slop a man will sell his soul for a good feed. But the food isn't as bad as the way it's prepared. If you could steal mess hall food before they got their hands on it, you could cook it yourself and sell it for a carton of cigarettes. This is obtained from the commissary, where an inmate's money is held for him.

The other lush jobs are nurse in the hospital, porter, ground keeper, steward in the warden's house, and so on. The hospital nurse is tops, because an inmate has access to goof balls and 190 proof alcohol. Both of these items are in great demand: they help a man forget. And anything that will help an inmate in Dannemora escape reality, even for an hour, is priceless.

These jobs are not given to anyone. Wardens will deny this, but there are pay-offs anywhere from a C-note to three hundred. Usually a top mobster in stir decides who gets the job. He sends in the name of a favorite lieutenant to the officer in charge. This officer in turn makes the recommendation to the PK, who always goes along.

Do you wonder why ex-cons are the most cynical people in the world? Even in stir you have to pay or have connections. . . .

After I realized what the choice jobs were, I worked as hard as I could to get one. I never gave any back talk; I even volunteered, which is unheard of.

The work in the cotton shop to which I was assigned was hard and miserable. The favorite cons who acted as stool pigeons were given muzzles and masks, but the rest of us had to work without them. All I had to do was look at my handkerchief to know what color we were running.

But I knew if I kept on my good behavior I could butter up the guard who was in charge of my section. He was a middle-aged, white-haired man, strict, but not unfair. After I had volunteered a few times I caught his eye.

"You're a good worker, Andy," he said. "Keep at it and I'll get you transferred to the mess hall."

It took me eight months, but I finally made it. My experience in Sing Sing's mess hall came in handy, and in a few weeks I knew my way around. The first thing I stole was four eggs for Richie and Big Sasso.

Before long I was bringing out food every day. Richie and I would cook it up and sell it. We split the dough with the others and soon had a smooth-working combination.

It lasted for six months. And then another con who worked in the mess hall thought I was too cocky. He was a short, husky Italian named Salami, who I heard later died in the chair for killing a cop in a Brooklyn holdup.

One day he accused me of taking his coffeepot off one of the burners. I denied it and he went for me. I floored him. He came up with a dirk and I smashed a coffeepot over his head. When the hacks came, he told them the dirk was mine and that I had started the brawl.

Whether they believed him or not, I lost the setup and went back to the shop.

The first day in the yard, I joined Richie and the others.

"You going to take care of him, Andy?" Sasso asked.

"I'll take care of him in my own way."

"We heard you were set up," Richie said.

"What do you mean?"

"The other mob wanted one of their boys in there. They got Salami to set you up."

"You get him today or don't hang around with us," Sasso said.

I knew what he meant. If the other mob thought for a minute they could get away by strong-arming us, they would go even further.

I went looking for Salami.

I didn't get him where I wanted until two days later. He was going into Easthall when I grabbed him. He was no pushover, but I was out for blood. No holds were barred. Because I had caught him off guard and kneed him before he could do it to me, I had the advantage. I belted him from one end of the corridor to the other.

"Enough—enough," he kept saying. But I didn't even hear him. When he went down I stomped him. I realized what I was doing when I found two guards were almost twisting my arms off and Salami was on his way to the hospital.

This time I went to the rock pile. But the other mobs in Dannemora had their warning. Maybe we didn't have a big shot like Lucky Luciano, but we had fists and shivs and we weren't afraid to use them . . .

The rock pile near Easthall was the toughest job in Siberia. From 7:30 to about 4:00 P.M. you fed rocks to a crusher. I did this for eighteen months. In a way I'm glad now; at least it hardened my body and left me so exhausted I didn't have the energy to think.

Then I was put on another gang. For two years I dug holes one day and filled them the next; piled dirt on one side of the yard and the next day took it back to the other side. It was just like the WPA.

In 1936 a new figure appeared at Dannemora who would have a great deal of influence on my life and Richie's. This was Bumpy Johnson, the enforcer for the numbers mob in Harlem. Today Bumpy is serving a long term in Atlanta on a narcotics rap.

He is a man of about medium height, stocky, with a round face. When he smiles he shows a gold tooth. A bump on the back of his head gave him his nickname. Although he is a veteran criminal and racketeer, he is not well known to newspaper readers. But ask the Feds or the cops about him.

Bumpy is a far cry from the usual mobster you see on TV or in the movies. Although he never went beyond the fourth grade, he is a self-educated man. During the time he was in Dannemora the cons used to call him the Professor. The mob outside made sure he was well staked, and he was always getting magazines on world affairs. In the late thirties when the Nazis were starting to move, Bumpy used to entertain us in the yard with discourses on world affairs.

It was Bumpy who insisted that I start reading. For that I'll always be grateful. At first I read grudgingly; then as the years went by I found myself reading anything. A whole new world, which I never suspected existed, opened for me. I'll never forget the excitement I felt when I discovered *The Three Musketeers*. I couldn't wait to finish it. In the yard I used to explain to the cons what had happened in the last chapter. After a while they expected me to give them a book report. Before I left Dannemora I think I had read every book in the library twice over.

I had my first talk with Bumpy in the barbership, where the cons were taken one by one every Tuesday and Friday. A guard stood `he left and one at the right of each man. Half the time the damned barbe.. never sterilized the razors, and we broke out with sores.

"How's the setup here, Andy?" he asked.

"No good."

"What's wrong?"

"Too many mobs. The Italians are the bosses."

"We'll see," he said. "We'll see."

Bumpy moved in with Big Sasso, whom he knew, and between them they soon had the toughest cons in the yard with them.

In 1938 the prison was split into two big combinations, the Italian mobsters under the strong arm of Little Davey Petillo, and the others under Bumpy and Sasso.

Things came to a head on the football field one day. We were playing when some of the others, led by Petillo, came and announced this was their field.

Bumpy and Little Davey squared off. Petillo is a rough character, and when he told a con to walk on the other side the con jumped. But not Bumpy.

Davey jabbed Bumpy with his finger.

"You may have a rep outside, but not in here," Davey said.

Bumpy jabbed him back. "I'm going to start making one right now. Want to help me?" But the hacks saw trouble brewing and came up on the run.

Petillo's mob struck back the next day; Bumpy was found unconscious in his cell. He had been badly beaten.

One of Petillo's men got it next. Three of our mob caught him in Easthall and left him a battered mess.

This mob war behind prison walls went on for a long time. The guards knew it and were uneasy. But they couldn't do anything. The beaten men never squealed, and now the stoolies were afraid to squeal. They knew it wasn't a simple fight between individuals, and if they talked they would be burned by either mob.

These are the ground rules of the underworld in prison—they kill and beat among themselves but don't want any interference from the outside.

A truce unexpectedly came about when Little Davey turned on his boss, Lucky Luciano, and tried to kill him. I don't think it has ever been published, but Davey had cornered Lucky and was just about to clobber him with a baseball bat when a big prisoner fought him off. I understand the con got an early release for this. You can imagine how relieved the warden must have been that his most celebrated prisoner wasn't dead in his cell. Luciano at the time was a tremendous power in Dannemora. He ruled the place like a king, from his cell on C Block. When he first arrived, he was put in what we call the Flats—the first gallery in Westhall. Here he had an electric stove, curtains on the door, and a canary. He stayed for eight months before he moved to C Block, one of the best and cleanest blocks. It was there that I met Davey. I had permission to press my own clothes in the laundry, and was working at it when Davey came in with some stuff.

"Hey, kid, press this for me, will you?"

I knew I would get something out of it, so I agreed. Davey liked the job and took me to see Lucky, whose clothes they were.

To me Lucky looked the part of the rap he had been sent up for: pimping. He had wavy dark hair, manicured nails, and razor-sharp creased pants.

"Want to clean my cell every day, kid?" he asked.

"Sure, what's the rate?"

He waved his hand. "Davey'll take care of you."

And Davey did. For mopping and cleaning the cell I was never without cigarettes, candy, cake or Italian salami.

I used to see at first hand how the Italians in there would come up with their family troubles or their money troubles for Lucky to take care of. Even Italians on the outside would come up to see him to mediate arguments or decide things.

Luciano was supposed to work in the laundry, but he paid a con to do his job. Instead of the rough prison wear he wore a silk shirt and black shoes which glowed with polish.

He went to the mess hall every day, but never ate there. Little Davey cooked his food, and served him at night with a thermos of coffee—that is until Davey tried to kill him.

After that try, Lucky made sure he was always surrounded by a ring of tough hoods he hired as bodyguards. He could generally be found up on the hill in the handball court, drinking coffee and playing rummy, a game he played day and night with either Jimmy Frederico or one of his bodyguards.

It was an open secret that Lucky was angling for a transfer to Comstock and its chicken farm or Great Meadows, where a con can sleep outside the farm.

I'll never forget the second Joe Louis–Max Schmeling fight. Lucky was the big bettor and won. He had twelve pillowcases of packs of cigarettes, and all day his flunkies were giving them out.

The case of Luciano, I believe, underscores my point that any big-time racketeer who is sentenced to prison can buy his ease inside. No matter what the warden or the guards say, rank in the underworld has its privileges behind bars.

Section 27 **THUMBNAIL SKETCHES**

> From the statement of Federal Judge Irving R. Kaufman, *The New York Times*, 1960.

In sentencing each defendant alphabetically, Judge Kaufman gave a thumbnail sketch of the man and expressed his opinion of him. The defendants, their sentences and Judge Kaufman's characterization of each follow:

R. A. B., 58 years old, of Kingston, Pa.—five years in jail and $10,000 fine. "A man devoid of conscience. One who poses as a legitimate business man. Everything in his record indicates that society would be better off if he is segregated."

I. C., 35 of Endwell, N. Y.—three years, no fine. "A rather intelligent fellow who played a minor role in the underworld. Loyal to the criminal element and could be trusted by the underworld."

P. C. C., 49, of Brooklyn—five years, no fine. "Marked with anti-social patterns. Willingly spent one year in jail in order not to answer any questions, even though given immunity."

J. F. C., 59, of Dallas, Tex.—five years, no fine. "A high-ranking criminal who cloaked himself with the facade of legitimate business."

F. D., 50, a lawyer of Downey, Calif.—four years, no fine. "Hostile and arrogant toward law enforcement and his bar associates. Lived with individuals of ill repute, and after Apalachin resided in the home of such an individual."

N. J. E., 54, of Brooklyn—five years, $10,000 fine. "A most important member of the underworld. His five-year sentence to be served following the ten-year sentence imposed last year after a Federal narcotics conviction."

L. A. L., 34, of Linden, N. J.—four years, no fine. "A person devoid of emotion, whose first loyalty was to the underworld."

C. L., 46, of Brooklyn—five years, $10,000 fine. "His probation report reads like a Who's Who in crime. An important member of loan-shark and gambling rackets in Brooklyn and an associate of premier criminals for most of his life."

J. M., 62, of Brooklyn—five years, $10,000 fine. "He was arrested in Chicago at a similar meeting thirty years ago. A member of the criminal hierarchy and elite."

F. T. M., 58, of Elizabeth, N. J.—five years, no fine. "A bootlegger and gambler who would do anything for a fast dollar."

M. A. M., 64, of Forest Hills, Queens—five years, $10,000 fine. "Elected to serve sixteen months in civil jail rather than betray his loyalty to the criminal elements. A close friend of the top dogs of the underworld."

J. C. M., 66, of Buffalo, voted Man of the Year of Buffalo in 1956—four years, $10,000 fine. "Apparently an important factor in the political life of that city. Was apparently leading a double life, which was exposed by events at Apalachin, Respected on the one hand, some law enforcement agencies suspected him of being a power in the underworld. His presence at Apalachin apparently confirmed that suspicion."

J. O., 47, of Lido Beach, L. I.—five years, $10,000 fine. "Has several narcotics convictions. A veteran criminal with nothing but contempt for constituted authority."

J. O., 46, of Pittston, Pa.—five years and $10,000 fine. "A strong-arm man and associate of high-ranking members of the underworld."

J. P., 62, of Brooklyn—five years, $10,000 fine. "Has tried to present himself as a much-maligned and humble man, when he is in fact a notorious member of the underworld. The perfect example of the trinity of crime, business and politics that threatens the economy of the country."

A. P. R., 63, of West Orange, N. J.—four years, $10,000 fine. "Shrewd, cunning and conniving."

J. T. S., 47, of Cleveland, Ohio—five years, $10,000 fine. "Feels that everybody has a price, including public officials. Tried to bribe a probation officer. A high liver, contemptuous of society."

A. J. S., 35, of Wyoming, Pa.—five years, $10,000 fine. "An important man in the underworld since 1946. Has attempted to cloak himself in legitimate business. Tried to invade the union field by using force and violence."

S. S., 59, of Rosemeade, Calif.—five years, $10,000 fine. "Has made a mockery of the law since he arrived in this country as a stowaway in 1923."

P. T., 53, of Endwell, N. Y.—five years, no fine. "Had two prior convictions for illegally manufacturing alcohol. A man with little respect for lawabiding citizens."

Section 28   **ON THE WATERFRONT**

From *The Man Who Rocked the Boat* by W. J. Keating and R. Carter, 1956.

In defending the public against the underworld, neither prosecutors' offices nor police departments see fit to compile facts about the enemy. The orderly, efficient dossier from which the storybook detective gets so much information is practically unknown in real life. There is no such thing as pressing the buzzer and instructing the blonde to dig out everything on John Dunn.

The police offer a sheet listing Dunn's local arrests, plus those out-of-town arrests known locally. The list includes dates, types of crime charged, name of arresting officers and eventual disposition of the cases, but this is watery milk for an investigator who needs to know the man's background, his methods, his associations and his standing in the criminal community. The prosecutor's own files contain nothing, unless the criminal happens to have been a defendant in a trial which took place in the prosecutor's own jurisdiction. The trial folder is useful, because you can find in it not only the transcripts and appeal briefs but other material pertinent to the prosecution case. For instance, the folder on Johnny Dunn's coercion conviction had given me a glimmering of his story. Had there been no such trial, I would have had to rely on what I could learn piecemeal from friendly cops, from other district attorneys' offices which might have had dealings with the man, and from agents of various Federal enforcement agencies. Nowhere in Federal, state, county or municipal government could I have found a centralized, comprehensive body of information about Dunn or any other member of the underworld. Unbelievable though it may seem, the same remains true in 1956. An investigator with limitless patience can sometimes patch together a decent file on a prominent criminal by consulting upward of two dozen separate official agencies, but he rarely has the time to do so.

The reason for the general lack of data, by the way, is the indifference of law-enforcement agencies toward conducting intelligence operations in the underworld. Presumably if agents and other detectives were keeping tabs on the leaders of organized crime, it would be worth while to maintain files, if only to have some place to put the information. But crime in our country is fought almost entirely on a complaint basis, after the horse is stolen, and preventive criminology is practiced only by one or two police departments and two or three well-staffed, privately financed citizens' anti-crime commissions, of which more later.

It took me months to assemble an adequately clear picture of Johnny Dunn, Andy Sheridan, and the other unique characters important to my investigation of the Hintz Shooting. Much of the information came from records which had been compiled before the war by Tom Dewey, when he began but did not complete an unprecedented inquiry into the affairs of the Port of New York. Much of the rest came from old magazines and newspapers and the prodigious memory of Detective Lieutenant Joe Sullivan.

I located the old Dewey files in a forgotten corner of our Rackets Bureau but, under office regulations, was not permitted to take them out, and spent night after night sitting in the deserted Rackets Bureau, making notes. Finally, with Jack Grumet's help, I negotiated a transfer of the files to my own office. Meanwhile I dug up probation and parole reports on Dunn, Sheridan, McGrath, and colleagues. Among other things, I learned that, in planning to prosecute Johnny Dunn for murder, I was playing pioneer. Since World War I, several dozen waterfront murders had been reported. None had been solved. The explaining was frightening.

The Port of New York is the richest in the world. Each year, cargoes valued at fifteen or sixteen billion dollars pass across its piers, including more than a third of the country's foreign trade and about half of the furs, jewels, watches, appliances and other luxury cargoes of that trade. At least one New Yorker in every ten earns his bread in port commerce or ancillary occupations. Shipping companies make millions in transporting the cargo, and stevedoring companies make millions in loading and unloading the ships.

In order to maintain his foothold in competition for these fruitful piers, a stevedoring entrepreneur is well advised to interest himself in the politics of the city. For decades, the political machines have relied on the munificence of waterfront magnates at campaign time and have repaid the generosity by nominating candidates whose reformist zeal does not extend to the docks. Similarly, the police department has long played only the most passive role in waterfront affairs. The stevedoring companies prefer their own unofficial cops, who frequently turn out to be gunmen like Johnny Dunn.

The function of Dunn, I found, was to maintain order among what very likely was the most disorganized and heavily exploited industrial labor force in the United States, the longshoremen. A guiding principle in waterfront economics was the principle of the large reserve labor force—at least two men competing for every job. On most piers, only the executive and supervisory personnel could actually be spoken of as having jobs. The work itself was performed by casual labor, men who never knew from one day to the next whether they would work or where they would work. To get this employment in an industry only slightly less hazardous than mining, the men were required to submit to fantastic speed-up, a total absence of safety precautions and a variety of cash kickback rackets. On all but a few piers, they were hired and their labors were supervised by hoodlums, because hoodlums had demonstrated to the stevedoring firms that they made the most efficient foremen.

Each day, twice a day, whenever there was a ship to be loaded or unloaded on the Hudson River piers of the West Side or Hoboken or Jersey City, or the East River and Bay piers of the East Side and Brooklyn, longshoremen would shape up on the street like roustabouts and wait to be picked for work by the hiring boss. There seldom were more than twelve thousand jobs to be had, and there always were at least twenty thousand applicants. Jobs went to the most co-operative and docile.

A union, the American Federation of Labor's International Longshoremen's Association, enjoyed what amounted to a closed-shop agreement with the stevedoring and shipping companies. The union locals were controlled by hoodlum partners of those who held supervisory positions on the docks, and the organizing weapons were gun, fist and blackball. At the top level, where the figurehead was a florid plug-ugly named Joseph P. Ryan, the union was a political auxiliary of Tammany and an economic auxiliary of the Shipping Association. Like any good company union, the I. L. A. maintained no defense fund: no longshoreman ever got a penny of strike benefits and all of the union's strikes had been denounced as "wildcat" by its officers and had been broken with their active, unconcealed help.

As compensation for their heroic work in keeping men from organizing themselves, the gangsters of the union drew nominal salaries from the treasury, adequate salaries and bribes from the stevedoring firms and *carte blanche* to conduct whatever pierside rackets they chose. Aside from penny-ante propositions (which ran into millions a year), such as wage kickbacks, crap games, bookmaking, policy lotteries and the like, these rackets included formidable business undertakings such as highjacking of cargo and exorbitant fees for the loading and unloading of pierside motor trucks.

Large-scale theft was rampant. The shipping companies were accustomed to hearing from foreign consignees that goods had not arrived. The stevedoring companies were accustomed to getting the resultant inquiries from the shipping companies. The insurance companies were accustomed to paying for the "losses." None acknowledged any stake in modifying conditions on the piers. When insurance rates went up (thereby increasing the incomes to which certain city politicians were accustomed in their private positions as insurance agents), the added cost to the exporter or importer was simply passed to the consumer. Nobody has ever been able to provide an accurate figure for the needless cost to Americans of pillage and bribery in the Port of New York, but I have heard it put at one hundred and forty million dollars a year and I am not disposed to quarrel with the estimate.

This, then, was the background against which John Dunn had been performing with my night-club companion, his brother-in-law, Eddie Mc-Grath. From the Dewey files, probation reports and other sources, I learned that McGrath was unanimously regarded as the brains behind Dunn. He had come from a respectable family, had sung in the choir at St. Stephen's and, in adolescence, worked for the telephone company as a clerk. In 1927, when eighteen, he pleaded guilty to acting as lookout in a grocery-store burglary which had netted him forty-seven cents. He was given a suspended sentence. He then turned tough and, during the next two years, was arrested four times on stick-up charges. Each case was dismissed for lack of evidence. In 1930, when Officer Dan Mahoney arrested him in another robbery, he was sent to Sing Sing under a five-to-ten-year sentence. While in keep, he became good friends with Johnny Dunn. He was paroled in 1933 and, less than two years later, was accused with Dunn of having murdered another parolee, John McCrossen. They beat the case easily. It never came to trial, but in the backwash Eddie was returned to Sing Sing as a parole violator. He emerged in less than a year and found his way to the waterfront and a pier job which required only that he show up once a week to collect his pay. The Parole Bureau got repeated tips that, for a man supposed to be working, McGrath was spending an inordinate amount of time with big-shot gangsters at Hot Springs, Arkansas, but he was never caught at it. Once he arrived at the pier in a convertible driven by a handsome woman, dashed into the washroom, splashed water under the armpits of his work clothes to simulate honest sweat, and walked out just in time to greet the gumshoe from the Parole Bureau.

After the investigator left, Eddie rejoined the lady in the convertible and drove off.

After a few months of such labors, McGrath was awarded official recognition by Joseph P. Ryan, who appointed him a salaried international organizer of the International Longshoremen's Association. In light of the fact that the new organizer had never handled a baling hook for pay in his life, Ryan's gesture indicated mainly that McGrath had achieved prestige in the underworld.

In 1936, when Eddie discovered the waterfront and the labor movement, Johnny discovered the trucking industry and the labor movement, obtaining from Joe Ryan an I.L.A. charter for something called Terminal Checkers and Platform Men, Local 1346-1, and preparing to set up shop as a leader of the masses. Before he was able to get far underway, Dunn was called upon to exercise a high degree of statesmanship in order to save Ryan from embarrassment. The A.F. of L. Brotherhood of Railway, Steamship Clerks and Freight Handlers and the I.L.A. had been having some jurisdictional difficulties and Johnny's new "union" was salt in the railway brotherhood's wounds. When the dispute went to William Green, president of the A.F. of L., Johnny quickly delivered a bona fide of good intentions toward the House of Labor by liquidating his union. Green, no mean statesman himself, thereupon awarded the gangster A.F. of L. Federal charters for three new locals affiliated not with the I.L.A. or any other international union, but directly responsible to the A.F. of L. executive board. The new organisms were called 21510, 21511 and 21512, Motor and Bus Terminal Checkers, Platform and Office Workers. The first had jurisdiction over New York, the second over Pennsylvania and the third over New Jersey. Dunn placed the Jersey organization under the stewardship of the murderer, Andrew Sheridan, and began looking for employers to sign up. Naturally, he had not yet bothered to sign up any workers.

His first contract was with the Highway Transport Association, which later became the Motor Carrier Association of New York, a mutual-aid society of some five hundred trucking firms. Under the contract, workers at the inland freight terminals of the association's members were to get fifty-five cents an hour. Dunn made plain that they would be docile about it. Since the workers either had to sign with him or be dealt with by his thugs, he soon had two thousand members, none with a voice in the affairs of the union. He also had access to a thief's dream come true—warehouse upon warehouse full of expensive import and export merchandise.

Thus, in 1937, we find Eddie a labor leader on the docks and Johnny a labor leader at the truck terminals. They also took over the truck loading racket at the lower West Side piers. For every item of merchandise removed from a pier and placed on a truck, the trucker had to pay a fee which varied according to the type and weight of the cargo. Minimum rates ranged between five-and-one-half and eleven cents per hundred pounds, on millions of tons of cargo. It mattered not whether the trucker's own employees attended to the loading or whether these chores were performed by some of Dunn and McGrath's strongarms—the fees had to be paid. A trucker who required special service, such as getting loaded ahead of turn, paid premium fees. A trucker who balked at the shakedown did not get this merchandise, and his driver came home bloody. A similar shakedown was exacted when trucks unloaded cargo for overseas export. The take ran into hundreds of thousands of dollars a year, and, because a pier was useless unless cargo could be trucked onto it or away from it, the rulers of the loading and unloading racket found themselves able to exercise power in determining who would work on the pier, and who would run the petty rackets.

Dunn and McGrath now were men of substance, men worth cultivating. They moved like feudal princes through the streets of the West Side and put their elbows on ringside tables in the fancy night clubs operated by other gangsters uptown. They mingled with judges and makers of judges, the cream of New York political and industrial life, at the annual testimonial dinners of the Joseph P. Ryan Association, where bankers and murderers broke bread together in honor of the stumblebum who kept things so nice and peaceful in the harbor. In 1937, Cockeye was important enough to be a member of the banquet arrangements committee, serving under William J. McCormack, a former drayman who now did all the stevedoring for the Pennsylvania and Erie Railroads, dominated the trucking industry, the tugboat industry, the sand and gravel industry and made errand boys of state and city officeholders. McCormack was the biggest man in the port, and there sat Dunn on his committee.

Dunn even became eminent enough to merit political recognition. In 1938, when a Tammany sachem named Michael J. Kennedy was running for Congress in Joe Ryan and Bill McCormack's waterfront district, the campaign manager was John A. Coleman, chairman of the Board of Governors of the New York Stock Exchange. And working under Coleman on a "Labor for Kennedy" committee was Johnny Cockeye.

One might suppose that all this glamour would have worked a change in Dunn and McGrath's approach to making a buck. For instance, one might expect that they'd have begun to let others do the dirty work. But it just wasn't so. In 1939, Johnny and Eddie were arrested in the robbery of a Staten Island brewery. Eyewitnesses identified them to the cops. But the case never came to trial, because the eyewitnesses changed their minds.

In October, 1940, Eddie, who had been socializing more and more with national mobsters such as Joe Adonis, was charged with first-degree murder. It all was a perhaps excusable mistake on the part of police in Key West,

Florida, who fished out of the ocean the remains of a New York loading-racket hoodlum named Leon Tocci and thought they had reason to believe that the former choirboy had done Leon in. Eddie was found in Boston (by now he had become a confirmed traveler) and was taken back to Florida, where the case, of course, failed to stand up.

In the Dunn-McGrath mob the main killer was the business agent of Local 21512, Andrew Sheridan, who had not always been a labor leader but had almost always been a gunman. A fat, hulking man with the mentality of a twelve-year-old and eyeglasses as thick as milk bottles, Squint Sheridan started life as a petty larcenist, graduated to stick-ups and, by age twenty-six, had served at least eight years in various reformatories and state prisons. He became a trigger man for Dutch Schultz, the beer baron, and after a duel with a cop, went back to prison for six more years, including time out for an escape. In 1937, he made his way to the waterfront, was adopted by the Dunn mob, and became a salaried organizer for I.L.A. Local 856, as well as head of one of Johnny's locals. He also was given a piece of the loading racket, and took home as much as eight hundred dollars a week. He had been murdering for pay on and off through the years, but now he became busier then ever, enforcing labor-management amity on the docks.

A longshoreman on Pier 14 named John (Mutt) Whitton had begun questioning the system under which he sweated out his day's wages and had been brash enough not only to take a couple of courses in labor relations but to shout his new knowledge to all who would listen. One afternoon Andy Sheridan came onto the pier, asked Whitton to step into the toilet for a conference, fired three shots into the man's brain, stuffed the body down a drain and walked away. A warehouse platform worker named Joe Moran had not bothered to study labor relations but had made unflattering remarks about the tendency of his union—Dunn's union—to sell him and his colleagues down the river. One night Andy Sheridan drove up in a car, stepped out, walked to the platform and, squinting near-sightedly through his thick glasses, said to the first man he could see, "Who's Moran?"

"Me," said Moran.

"Okay," said Sheridan, pulling a gun. He fired one shot through Moran's forehead and one through his body, killing him instantly. He then left.

Had any of the several witnesses to either murder dared talk to police, Sheridan would have been executed. But nobody talked. The waterfront was governed by a code of silence which had its roots in the instinct of self-preservation. A longshoreman who turned rat could count on turning corpse. Nor would he have any assurance that his talking might bring the murderer to justice. The organized underworld was altogether too chummy with police, and vice versa, for any longshoreman to take chances.

The Whitton and Moran murders were only two of literally dozens committed by Sheridan, but they suffice as examples of the true nature of his employment as a labor leader. Dunn, who undoubtedly admired Sheridan's craftsmanship, used to spend a lot of time in the hulk's company. They were particularly fond of grabbing a sandwich in a certain small restaurant on West Eighth Street, which is the main thoroughfare of Greenwich Village. In time they got to know the owner of the place, and when they let it be known that they were labor leaders he said, "I'm glad to hear that. Maybe you can help me. I've been having some trouble with my help. Maybe you can advise me."

"What kind of trouble?" asked Dunn.

"Oh, the grievances and stuff. The delegate from the restaurant union enforces every letter of the goddamned contract and it's a pain in the neck. Every time I step out of line on the goddamned contract the help squawks to the union. Is that reasonable?"

"No," said Dunn. "Who is this delegate?"

"He comes around," said the restaurant man. "He'll be here tomorrow again."

"We'll handle him," said Dunn.

"You'll talk to him for me?" cried the owner joyously. "Oh, boy! One union man to another! You'll straighten it out for me!"

"We'll straighten him out," said Dunn.

The next afternoon the owner introduced his friends to the delegate from the restaurant union and watched happily as they walked into the rear of the place for a conference. In a minute or so he heard piercing screams from the rear, rushed toward the sounds and found the union delegate on his knees, with Dunn and Sheridan holding pistols to his head.

"What are you doing?" shrieked the owner.

"I thought you wanted this bastard straightened out," said Dunn.

"Not like that!" howled the owner.

"Make up your mind," said Dunn, pocketing his pistol and walking out, with Sheridan in trail.

These, then, were the men who had shot Andy Hintz. Criminals of the worst order, but organized criminals with friends in high places, criminals who could muster political support. What kind of political support would they be able to command now?

Section 29   **THE HIERARCHY OF CRIME**

From *Underworld U.S.A.* by Joseph F. Dinneen, 1956.

When big city newspapers refer to "Gangland" or "the Underworld," readers sometimes conceive it as a place, a definite area, the slums or multiple-separated slums within a city. Successful gangsters never live in the slums, nor do they recruit their associates, assistants or members of their gangs from the slums. Successful gangsters usually live in beautiful homes or apartments in respectable, even upperclass neighborhoods.

It is true that slums are a reservoir from which crime manpower is drawn, but the criminal (usually a delinquent) must work his way in crime out of a slum proving ground and into a gang. He must learn the trade by starting at the bottom; nor are the slums the only source of manpower. Middle and upper classes furnish their quotas—much smaller than the slums, it is true, but nevertheless they do produce criminals. The criminal mind can occur in any environment. The climate and soil of slums are more favorable to its development.

Gangland or the Underworld is, in fact, a segment of population made up of an insignificant number of independents and a large number who coalesce and cooperate. The criminal population of any city is determined by national and local economy, by national or local prosperity and recession; by the size of the city and the character of its business and industry, its government whether reasonably honest or abnormally corrupt, local political behavior, the size and character of its police force, the efficiency of its administration and the character of its courts and jurists. There are other factors—chiefly social, racial or religious—where any discussion of opinion is bound to be violently disputed.

Roughly, criminals account for 1 per cent of the total population. Whether a city or any congested area goes above or falls below this norm is determined by the factors involved. Crime incidence in standard reporting statistics will rise or fall sharply when any factor is changed or suddenly disturbed. The abandonment of a shipyard employing forty-five thousand persons will cause a delayed or sleeper rise in a graph. A horrendous crime involving multiple murders or an enormous sum of money will bring about such a tightening of police protection that the graph will take a steep dive.

The degree of fluctuation depends upon the violence of the disturbance in the factor.

It may be unbelievable—or more accurately, incomprehensible—to the average law-abiding, respectable person that a boy could grow up, marry, have children and spend his whole life from childhood to death in crime. A law-abiding businessman reads a news report of a bank teller who embezzled $300,000 over a period of three years. He wonders how he got away with it for so long in spite of all safeguards and precautions, periodic visits of bank examiners and audits. He is satisfied to read that the culprit has been arrested and is now in jail. The important point is that he got away with it for so long.

A gunman goes to jail for armed robbery. How long had he been getting away with it before he got caught? How many armed robberies did he commit? What would the total amount of money he stole add up to? The reader is apt to think that this was his only crime, or at best one of very few. He rarely contemplates him as a career criminal busy week after week, month after month, or year after year in the business of stealing. If the gunman has a record, a measure of how long he got away with it is the lapse of time from his release or parole from jail to his next capture. How many persons he robbed in that time only he knows (if he hasn't lost count) and he won't tell.

Fingers Tolland's real education in crime was begun in reform school. In that respect he was typical of thousands of career criminals. Their universities are reform schools and county jails. There they meet the experts in their chosen callings. They discuss procedures and techniques at continuing seminars. This is hardly the fault of superintendents, wardens, or jail administrations. They do as much as they can to prevent it, but the only positive prevention is an inhuman, barbarous, solitary confinement for all prisoners. In most cases, wardens and superintendents can do little or nothing about political interference in their administrations. The shining lights in all of them are the chaplains of all creeds, universally untouchable, who have the courage to turn up graft and corruption wherever and whenever they see it.

There is a caste system among prisoners in most jails where guards (screws) and sometimes the jail officials divide prisoners according to their financial or political importance outside the walls. How will a guard behave toward a prisoner who first promises to have him upped a grade in his civil service rating (which means an increase in salary) and next delivers the goods? Will the guard close his eyes to violations of prison rules by that prisoner? Will he allow him extra privileges? Suppose other guards are similarly rewarded and in time the prisoner with political influence puts guards on his personal payroll, having checks delivered to their homes each week? Will the political prisoner then be able to smuggle liquor, narcotics, barbiturates into the jail? Jail riots and strikes found seed in such a system.

Within the jail, specialists in various departments of crime discuss their common problems. Top rating among criminals goes to gunmen, triggermen, the rangers and commandos who risked their lives for huge stakes in planned robberies of payrolls, banks and money carriers. They take the biggest chances, the possibility of facing guns fore and aft. A guard might be hidden or facing them. He might walk in unexpectedly. Police might close in from behind. They might be chased in a hail of bullets. They are rough, tough. Lesser and younger prisoners look upon them with awe, and some hope to be like them. They are listened to with respect.

Next are the yeggs, safecrackers, a highly specialized group who usually work with gunmen; B&E boys, sentenced for breaking and entering—porch climbers, second-story workers, fur loft thieves, lock pickers (the word has another connotation when applied to ticketless medical quacks); "paper-hangers" (forgers); "cons," confidence men, skilled in every variation of Badger and Chief rackets, including selling Brooklyn Bridge; glib, fast talkers, always good storytellers and among the most entertaining of all criminals; dips, pickpockets who work independently, but useful to have around on some jobs that require them; the automobile boys, independents or members of a ring, skilled in stealing cars by jumping the ignition either with wires or a silver quarter placed in the right spot under the dash. Some of them can open what appears to be a securely locked automobile merely by inserting a stenographer's celluloid erasure shield in a door crack. The skills of specialized criminals compare with and sometimes excel those in legitimate crafts.

From these can be picked a team to do any criminal job for a specified price or on shares to be divided. In some cases they are hired by a "brain," a leader who determines their "cut" or pays an agreed price satisfactory to the participants.

Such jobs usually involve "inside control" by a confederate working in the bank, plant, office or place to be robbed. In such a case, the confederate takes a great, and sometimes the full, risk of being caught and would take the rap and go to jail without involving the participants.

At the bottom of the scale are footpads and bag-snatchers, hoodlums who roll drunks in parks or deserted places. They are looked upon with contempt. They take small chances for what the experienced criminal terms "peanuts." The motive for murder among career criminals is primarily robbery. Only the trigger-happy among them kill for any other purpose and after the first time he is usually marked "poison" on the books of those who make a living at crime. The professional criminal usually kills to make an escape; to immobilize opposition; in self-defense, through misunderstanding or accident or for vengeance upon a double-crosser. Necessity or motive almost always is clear. His interest in those who kill for jealousy inside or outside an eternal triangle is just as keen as that of the law-abiding outside prison walls and for the same reasons. He wonders if, under the circumstances, he would have done the same thing.

Among criminals a man is measured by the same yardstick as in legitimate business. How successful has he been in his past ventures and how much money does he make? What is his personal standard of living? Does he have a wife and children? How well does he take care of them? If he is not married, does he keep a woman? Or women? How much can he afford to drop in a dice or poker game or at a roulette wheel without wincing or borrowing? How much and how often does he bet at the track? Is he a good spender, quick to pick up a tab? Does he drink? If so, can he hold his liquor and his tongue? As a gauge of competence and success the kind of car he drives is of little importance. It might have been stolen.

The next yardstick applied is: Against this continued success how often has he been in jail or in danger of going to jail? This requires some equating. If his terms were short ones—three to six months in a House of Correction or at a colony country club penal institution—it indicates either political influence or superb legal talent. Successive nol-prosses or dismissals for want of prosecution confirm it. Taken together this means that he has kept himself busy at crime. He would have to in order to pay such fees. A busy man in any trade or profession must be competent and efficient. Such a criminal would be in demand among other criminals and could command his own price or cut. He has the experience and the knack of getting away with it.

In a city that averages eighteen holdups or robberies a month and two captures, obviously somebody got away with it sixteen times. If a gunman or robber of any class goes out twice a month, picking his jobs carefully with a reasonably accurate idea of what the haul will be and takes an average of $2,000 a month, he is averaging about $460 tax free per week. Inevitably he carries the pitcher to the well too often. He is rated tops, good or poor on the number of times he gets away with it. Any consistently good operator must expect some unlucky breaks that cause or lead to arrest.

The successful gangster, racketeer, or predatory bandit is easy to spot. If he is married, he usually lives in an expensive house in a respectable, if not exclusive, area. He does considerable entertaining but rarely, if ever, has his neighbors in as guests. He has a high-priced car, perhaps two, sometimes a chauffeur and domestic help. If he is single, he has an expensive apartment on the drive, the avenue, the hill, an excellent address where he lives just as lavishly. Show girls and beautiful women are among his guests; but he has no visible means of support.

He is inclined to be indolent and lazy. He works hard and efficiently and is under a strain while he is about it, but he relaxes quickly when it is over. He leaves his house or apartment at no regular time each day. Nobody in the neighborhood knows where his office is or what he is supposed to do there. If his name and picture have been in newspapers frequently, gossips see to it that everybody in the neighborhood or in the apartment building are told about it immediately. Route or squad car beat patrolmen learn about it quickly and the place is listed for periodic surveillance. The racketeer learns this quickly too, but it rarely disturbs him. He anticipates it. If his calling makes him an undesirable neighbor, there is little the residents can do about it. He has seen to that by lease and contract.

Perhaps the greatest handicap to crime prevention, suppression and control is the common concept of highly successful racketeers and gangland overlords as grown-up hoodlums, a phenomenon of moron minds directing various sized groups of other moron minds. Few stop to think of the brains and intelligence it takes to rule and govern big crime in a national syndicate, or of the nature and character of men who do so.

Married or single, a man must have a home, a place he can call his own; a place where he can rest, relax; a place to keep the things apart from money that he values. There are big shot racketeers, like the self-made men in business, who acquire outside interests, even cultural hobbies they can well afford to indulge. They become collectors of art, rare books—and surprisingly, some of them come to learn and know what is in the books. A man can hardly achieve eminence in any field and remain stupid. The Lucianos, Costellos, et al., did not get where they are by sheer luck, bull-headed determination, and the power of weapons. It takes much more than that. A crime syndicate that covers as many criminals as there are employees in the Post Office Department cannot be administered by a dumbbell or a board of dumbbells. A top racketeer must be a general and a diplomat; able to grasp a national picture, to comprehend millions; to effect treaties, agreements, and understandings between sectional groups; and to compose problems involved in vast sums of money and exchange. His survival depends upon his ability to do so. It is hardly a job for a moron. It requires superior intelligence.

In the public eye, for example, Earl Connors was a vague but reprehensible character. He never posed for pictures or gave newspaper interviews. Only his intimates, and they were few, knew anything of his private life. For more than half a century he was a shadowy, fearsome figure in the background. When the Kefauver Committee was investigating the syndicate, Earl was not called.

This was unfortunate. He might have added tone to the proceedings and the natural TV spectacle. Connors was not a college man. He was entirely self-educated. Because of the focus of national attention on crime, a professor from the crime laboratory of a local university and a well-known criminologist, both Ph.D.s, sought an interview with Earl. They wanted to talk to him strictly in confidence. After some negotiation through a newspaper crime reporter (who had talked to Earl only on rare occasions himself) a meeting was arranged. They found a tall, strapping, well-tanned man, sixty-eight years old, with silvery hair and sharp blue eyes. He met them in his library. It was lined with books. They found some of the titles astonishing.

They found common ground immediately. The meeting stretched over four hours. Earl had them to dinner. He was an interesting and gracious host. They still had not covered enough ground. They enjoyed Earl's conversation. He enjoyed theirs. Another meeting was arranged, and then another until it became a habit. In the beginning, Earl disconcerted them; and then he fascinated them. He disconcerted them because they discovered him to be a scholar, a conversationalist who spoke flawless English, a profound student of government, a man familiar with Plutarch, Cicero, Pliny, Machiavelli; one who could discuss More's *Utopia*, Bacon's *Atlantis*, Adam Smith's *Wealth of Nations*, Voltaire, Emerson, John Stuart Mill, Lowell, the Bill of Rights, or Karl Marx. He showed them rare volumes, samples of early American printing art, all of them on political subjects, and was proud of his collection of classical recordings.

When sincere friendship no longer made personal questions impertinent, and they could forget what he was and what he represented, they pinned him down on his intellectual pursuits. "Like most people," he said, "you've been led to believe that people like me are an assortment of crude, ignorant louts who have acquired a lot of money. Some of us are crude," he nodded his head in agreement, "but we are neither ignorant nor louts. Some of us don't speak the English language very well. Some speak with an accent, but for my part, when I meet and associate with a so-called 'gang leader' of some stature, I remember what I have long since learned: Beware of the man who pronounces words as they are spelled because you may find to your chagrin that he knows more about the subject matter defined by the words than you do.

"You can't obliterate crime or minimize it or control it by pitting against it the only kind of forces for law and order now available. It is absurd to confront men of their intelligence by district attorneys elected to office because they are good-looking, popular, or good vote-getters. That kind of equipment is hardly suitable and entirely ineffective in a war against organized crime, and so the cities can do nothing about it. Obviously they don't want to, or the people of a city would not elect an incompetent like that to the office. The conclusion is that people of the cities object to organized crime, but they don't want to end it.

"It is just as absurd to confront organized crime in a state by a jackass attorney general elected to the office with the help of a political machine. He knows nothing about crime or criminals or about the crime syndicate. He's just another political wheelhorse, not a brilliant, intelligent lawyer capable of leading a fight against crime. The conclusion is that the people of the state are not sufficiently disturbed about organized crime to do anything about it.

"The ideal choice, the perfect man in any public office, is usually a political miracle—an almost unbelievable surprise that comes too rarely. How can you expect an attorney general who owes his appointment, perhaps, to his able fund raising or political organizing in behalf of a presidential candidate, to be transformed suddenly into a fighting leader organizing existing forces and supplementing them with reinforcements and reserves in a fight to the finish with organized crime? Why should he? The people are not demanding it. They seem to be satisfied with organized crime.

"Senatorial, congressional or joint committees won't do it. The Kefauver Committee hearings provided a good TV show. It sent a handful of persons to jail. When it ended, public interest in organized crime ended. Crime has always been with us. Organized crime has been with us now for some time. It is better organized than in a state of confusion. At least the organizers keep it within bounds and under some sort of control. In any case, there's nothing you gentlemen can do about it now—except live with it."

Section 30   THE NUMBERS RACKET

From "The Numbers Racket" by Ted Poston, 1960.

This is the story of the Pad.

It is the story of a multi-million dollar collaboration between members of the police vice squad and powerful policy barons, many of them with Mafia connections, to control and perpetuate the numbers racket in the five boroughs.

It is the story of day-by-day, week-by-week, month-by-month graft which is so vast as to stagger the imagination of the men actually on the take.

Before we tell the story, let us make one point clear. Not all police officers in the various divisions of the Police Dept. are venal. Most of the men are honest enforcers of the law—even in areas where the policy racket flourishes. But this is not to minimize the effect on department morale where the minority fattens on graft in the open view of honest policemen—and the public.

Veteran police officials told The Post during this newspaper's investigation of the policy racket that there are men who have accumulated so much money from The Pad that they can scarcely find ways to spend it without getting in trouble. There are others who are trying desperately to get out of the department before the bubble bursts, but their superiors won't let them.

And there are others, these officials say, who never rose above the rank of plainclothesman before they retired but now own prosperous businesses in the South and West—businesses set up with their own capital.

What is The Pad?

The Pad is the police-approved list of spots or locations where "official protection" is guaranteed in the six-day-a-week operation of the numbers racket.

A spot might be a grocery store or a tailor shop, a luncheonette or a poolroom. It might be a bank of elevators in a Wall Street office building. It might be an elevator or a newsstand in the Garment Center.

It can be any agreed-upon place where a numbers player can openly place his daily wager without being molested by the cops. It might be even a specified hallway in a Harlem tenement.

A spot or location, however, is not to be confused with a policy bank. A bank may—and many of them do—have a score of spots in just one police precinct. But each spot must be approved by the police for The Pad. And each spot on The Pad must be paid for in cash.

And who shares in fixed fees collected for this "legal" operation of an illegal racket? The payoffs are not limited to vice squad plainclothesmen assigned to the suppression of vice and gambling but are distributed regularly to sergeants, lieutenants, captains and, in many cases, to some of their superiors.

This is how the cash flows:

The cop on the beat—low man on the totem pole—collects from each "spot" on The Pad in his area daily. There are three daily shifts; each cop on each shift makes his own collection.

The two men in the squad car whose patrol includes The Pad collect their "blanket payment" weekly. This frees them from the task of daily collection.

The men on the take in the precincts, the divisions, the borough commands and the special squads, on up to officials in Police Headquarters itself, receive their share of the payoffs from their own special pick-up men once each month.

To operate on a "Full Pad"—that is, to buy protection from the bottom to the top—costs each spot, even if it's just a tenement hallway, about $2500 a month. The tariff is scaled proportionately higher for those spots and locations where the daily play is greater.

And here is why veteran police officials call the graft take "astronomical":

The Post investigation of just 90 "approved" spots in a single section of Harlem indicated that specified payments to the police involved exceeded $220,000 a month, or an annual take of more than $2,500,000.

"But you must remember," one official expert told The Post, "that, contrary to popular belief, the numbers play in Harlem comprises only a fraction of the daily play in all boroughs. You have to multiply the Harlem take many times to get anywhere near the real figure for the 'ice' paid out by policy.

"There are 80 precincts in New York City, and in my experience in all five boroughs, I have not found a single one in which a Pad for policy isn't maintained in one form or another.

"Of course, Harlem is the happy-hunting-ground for the boys who get greedy. They can get their regular take from the operators of The Pad and their shakedown from some of the small fry for an additional taste-something-extra-without risking too much of a squawk."

The Post began digging into the numbers game in January after Rep. Adam Clayton Powell Jr. charged that the police in Harlem were running Negro bankers out of business and turning the game over to whites—mainly Italians, although Powell also spoke of Jewish policy racketeers in one speech from his Harlem pulpit.

The inquiry spread to all sections of the city as it became apparent that Harlem furnished only a fraction of the astounding sums bet daily on a sucker's game.

The Post team established that the gross numbers business written every day on the waterfront—in Manhattan, in Brooklyn, on Staten Island—exceeds Harlem's "action" on its best days. They also found that it was easier to "get down on the figure" in any section of the Garment Center at that moment than it was to get similar action on, say, Lenox Av. (*The heat happened to be on uptown, of course, as a result of Powell's blasts at the police from his pulpit and on the floor of Congress.*)

In staid Wall St., few people had to walk further than a designated elevator or a newsstand in his building or around the corner to make a daily bet. Such big numbers bets are placed in the financial district that the total play there appears to exceed the entire take in the Bedford-Stuyvesant section of Brooklyn.

The Bronx—once the stamping ground of the late Dutch Schultz—was found to be organized into a tightly closed duchy which probably would have made the Dutchman himself proud.

Most New Yorkers are vaguely familiar with the numbers game, certainly one of the simplest forms of mass gambling ever devised.

The bettor takes a 1,000-to-one chance that he can pick a set of three digits anywhere between 000 and 999 which will appear in an agreed-upon tabulation at a race track, clearing house, or elsewhere. If he wins, the most he can get is 600-to-one (really 599 to one, since the original wager is included in the payoff). Some banks pay as little as 300-to-one in the case of certain numbers which the policy operators consider "hot" at a given time.

The general conception (or misconception) is that numbers racket is a harmless little game dreamed up in Harlem and played only by poor people who hope to cash 600-to-one bets on pennies and nickels filched from their relief allotments. The newspapers down through the years have fortified this conception by calling the game "poor man's policy," "the welfare client's Wall St.," "the dream of the destitute" or "the opiate of the paupers."

Nothing could be further from today's truth. And no one knows it better than those Vice Squad cops who profit by it.

For more than a quarter of a century, the police brass has been "estimating" that New Yorkers bet an average of $100,000,000 a year on the numbers. That figure may have been valid back in 1935; the gross at that time did contain a lot of penny, nickel and dime bets on the daily lottery.

But those days are gone forever.

Today's numbers bets usually begin at a quarter. A flat, $1 bet is no longer unusual. Regular $10 bets are accepted by some collectors, and the sky is the limit where the larger banks are concerned.

(*Of course, a long-time addict can get down a nickel or dime bet, or even a series of bets for pennies, but most banks' regular operators scorn such wagers whenever possible.*)

One authoritative source, who has watched the phenomenal growth of the game over the past quarter century, said frankly:

"Nobody can really know how much money is bet on the numbers yearly, not even the big operators or the police themselves.

"But it is my opinion that the annual take in the five boroughs here is closer to a quarter billion dollars than to the $100,000,000 figure so commonly used."

He cited reasons for his conclusion.

"Back in 1935," he recalled, there was only one official number for all boroughs. It was based then, as now, on the three figures derived from the total parimutuel bets on the third, fifth and seventh races at a specified race track (Hialeah now).

"But in Brooklyn, for instance, the player can bet on two sets of numbers every day—the usual one based on the third, fifth and seventh races, and a brand new number based on the total parimutuel handle at the track that same day."

This Post informant cited another reason why he believed that the daily take from numbers had doubled or even tripled during recent years.

"In the old days," he said, "there was only the 'day number' available.

I mean that the wagers were only paid off on races run during the daytime. Now there is also a 'night' number for a large part of the year.

"I think this is almost exclusively a New York development, but night numbers are taken daily for the full run of the trotting races at Yonkers and Roosevelt Raceways.

"Again, no one except the policy banks which book the night number can know how much is wagered, but the night numbers, for the months they run, probably take in almost as much as the day game took in in 1935."

There is also a variation of the numbers game which has added to the "racket's" gross. This innovation, first popular around 1940, is called Single Action and permits the player to make individual bets on each of the three separate digits composing that day's full figure.

Say, for instance, that the player has already made his bets for the day on the number 671. He then can make Single Action bets—the payoff is 8-to-1—that the first number that day will be 6 or the second number will be 7 or the third will be 1.

Single Action is most popular in areas of Negro and Puerto Rican concentration and is often banked and operated by the runners and collectors in the employ of the big policy banks.

One former policy banker, forced out of business by the rising costs of The Pad, operated recently on Single Action alone. He estimated that Single Action, controlled mainly by Negroes, grosses between $15,000,000 and $25,000,000 a year.

"The big white banks haven't moved in on Single Action," he said, "mainly because it's too complicated to handle and they're afraid they might get cheated. There's nothing too complicated about it for the cops, though. Nobody cheats them. You've got to get on The Pad to stay in business. And if the bite gets so big it drives you out of business, that's just too bad for you."

"If you write $1,000 worth of numbers a day," a recently retired policy operator said bitterly, "then the first 12 days of the month you work for the cops.

"The cops are the only ones who are guaranteed to make their taste (profit, that is) no matter what happens."

The operator was discussing The Pad, the list of spots and locations in all five boroughs sanctioned by corrupt policemen, where the mobs behind the numbers racket are permitted to operate wide open six days a week in return for specified payoffs totalling millions upon millions of dollars a year.

Here, in detail for the first time, is what policy operators must pay crooked cops to operate just one "full open spot"—that is, an agreed upon location where numbers bets may be handled without police molestation:

$300 a month to a squad connected with high-echelon officialdom, with $25 of this going to the "bag man," who is usually a retired cop like ex-Sgt. Joseph Luberda.

$300 a month to the group connected with the next highest official, again with $25 going to the "bag man."

$300 a month to the ranking squad in the department hierarchy. This sum may often be picked up by a member of the squad, obviating the $25 cut for a "bag man."

$300 a month to a group operating out of a top office, based on geographical location.

$350 to $615 a month to a smaller geographic subdivision office.

The $350 figure is the basic sum for all such groups in the city, but the $615 figure was cited as the current Pad in one group which covers several precincts.

Police operating from the smaller subdivision, which now has some 30-odd plainclothesmen, originally set their price at $350 monthly also. But the bite has gone up twice—first to $470 and then to $615 a month because of policy scandals and a wholesale transfer of members of the old squad in one of Police Commissioner Stephen Kennedy's periodic shakeups.

But back to the monthly payments for the operation of a "spot," which, not to be confused with a policy bank, may be merely a Brooklyn grocery store, a Staten Island tailor shop, a Wall Street newsstand, a Garment Center elevator, or even an agreed-upon hallway in a Harlem apartment.

To be on The Pad for a "full open spot," the operators must also pay, on top of what is listed above:

$250 a month to be divided among detectives in the precinct where the spot is located.

$10 a month for each of the precinct lieutenants involved.

$100 a month to be split among the racket precinct sergeants.

If a precinct captain must be paid, the sum varies, but it is usually about $75 per month per spot. And from this sum, the captain must take care of his own "bag man" and a precinct warrant officer.

But this doesn't end the payments. For each spot—and some banks have as many as 20 spots or more in a single precinct—the cops also collect $35 a week to be split between the two patrolmen assigned to the squad cars on the beat. These men pick up their own take at a specified place in person weekly.

The final "official" payment for The Pad goes to the cop on the beat.

It is $2 a day, accepted personally, and paid to each of the beat cops on the three shifts from Monday through Saturday. Thus, a cop with only a half dozen spots on his beat is assured of at least $12 each day in "legal payments."

One policy operator, who discussed The Pad, was asked why the cop on the beat had to be paid.

"He knows you are on The Pad," the reporter said, "and he knows his superiors may raise hell if he arrests you. So why pay?"

The policy man smiles at the question.

"Of course he knows he can't arrest me," he said, "and I know it too. But he doesn't have to. All he needs to do is just stand in front of my spot and nobody is going to come in and play any numbers as long as a uniformed cop is standing out front.

"So you just slip him his two bucks and send him on his way. After all, he's got to visit other spots on his beat for his taste also. You don't want to be a bad fellow by delaying this messenger on the swift completion of his appointed rounds."

It was not easy to flush out the exact details of The Pad, although Post reporters learned about it shortly after Rep. Adam Clayton Powell charged that Harlem police were turning the Negro bankers' business over to whites —mainly Italians.

The 10-week investigation started in Harlem but quickly extended to all five boroughs since even preliminary study showed that the numbers game, like the organized graft and corruption which it spawned, was not just a Harlem pastime but citywide.

The existence of The Pad was well known throughout the multi-million-dollar industry. Even before Joseph Luberda, the retired cop, was picked up drunk with The Pad for one section of Harlem, everyone in the industry knew that such lists existed.

And Luberda, now serving a contempt term in prison for refusing to name the police squads and officials for whom he had been collecting, admitted that much when asked before the grand jury:

"In other words, police officers would go around to different places and visit these people who are operating these gambling places and collect money in return for their refraining from interfering with their operations?"

"Yes, sir," said Luberda, "could be."

But few known policy operators in Harlem or elsewhere were willing to go into details on the actual Pad in the early days of The Post's investigation.

Even men who had spent their lives in the game only to be reduced from bankers to controllers and even down to runners because of increasing vice squad demands were reluctant to discuss The Pad.

Similarly, HONEST members of the Police Dept.—and the vast majority on the force have little opportunity to get on The Pad—would admit the existence of the organized graft and corruption involving the numbers racket, but would give no details.

One police official said frankly:

"If you knew the actual amount of money involved, you wouldn't believe it. And even if you believed it, The Post wouldn't dare print it. The thing is just that big."

One long-time former banker whose bank has been taken over by the East Side Harlem mob, which now dominates the citywide game, asked a reporter half-jokingly:

"You want to be killed?"

Then, more soberly, he remarked: "Look, this thing is much bigger than you think. Anybody who talks about it too much is out of business for good. And I'm too old to learn anything else now."

As The Post team continued digging, however, it became obvious that the police too had learned of their inquiries.

Two men who had discussed the payoffs quite frankly with reporters suddenly decided to leave town—one on an extended Caribbean vacation. A former banker who now has a legitimate business was called in by a member of a vice squad inspector's staff and questioned about the passing presence of a Post reporter in his establishment.

"If any of you fellows go around shooting off your mouth," he was told, "we are going to close down the whole operation."

The suspected men reportedly retorted: "and then what will *you* do? Starve to death?"

A few days after this incident, a source close to an influential police official called one Post reporter to inform him that his home telephone had been tapped.

"There's nothing you can do about it, but just be careful," he said. "It's not a legal tap and nobody in the department or the Telephone Company will admit that it exists, no matter how much hell The Post might raise about it. But the boys know what you are doing and they want to know how much you know."

The Post reporters were able to obtain Pads first from one source in one borough and then from two other sources in another and the payoff lists checked in all major details.

Once confronted with the actual schedule of police-set payments, several policy operators confirmed the figures. Then well-informed sources familiar with the department not only confirmed the "official" Pad but filled in other details of the vice squad's lucrative participation in the rich numbers game.

A police-connected source, who had never denied the existence of The Pad but had refused to discuss its operations until The Post obtained the "official" list of graft payments from other sources, explained how the money is distributed to members of the ring.

"Beginning in the precinct," he said, "and extending on up the line through the special squads, the take is divided on the basis of shares. The plainclothesmen involved each get the basic share with two or more shares being given monthly to their superiors.

"Take the _ _ _ _ _ _ Division, for instance, where the monthly take is listed at $615 per spot. There are some 30 plainclothesmen there now and each gets a basic share of $15 per spot. The lieutenants' share comes to $25.

"Now take the _ _ _ _ _ _ Division, which covers three precincts, has 50 spots on its pad—and you and I both know that there are far more than 50 spots involved in that area. But take 50 spots as an example. That means that each of the plainclothesmen who are on the take there gets $750 each a month for these 50 spots alone and the lieutenants involved are in for $1,250 each."

The source, stressing the point that not all policemen share in the policy graft ring, added:

"I'm not saying that every man in the _ _ _ _ _ _ Division is in on The Pad. But that makes little difference to the operators of the approved spots. The pay-off must be made on the basis of the personnel assigned to the division, to the precinct and to the special squads above them. How it is split up in the squad is sometimes another matter."

Another source familiar with another borough furnished further light on the matter as he described "pay day" in one station house.

"I had gone there on a matter not connected in any way with vice or gambling. I had to see a plainclothesman who once had been assigned to my precinct and who had some information about a suspect in a burglary ring.

"We were sitting there in the squad room discussing my case when a fellow pushed open the door and yelled 'pay day!' And everybody stopped what they were doing as this fellow went around the room calling out each name and taking sealed envelopes from a box under his arm.

"The plainclothesman with whom I was talking broke off our conversation and took his envelope. He split it open right in front of me and started counting the crisp sheaf of $10 and $20 bills. I stopped counting when he passed $180. But he finally finished his count and resumed our conversation as if nothing had happened."

The source added:

"Of course this happened several years ago. I don't think they are quite as open about it now, especially when the heat is on. The fact is, the take has grown so large now that they are forced to take more precautions, for they all know that a real bad break can eventually blow them and the whole department sky high."

One retired banker—and most of them claim retirement in any discussion of the racket—reinforced the suggestion that the police are not always honest with The Pad.

"For several months when I was active," he recalled, "they had me down for 31 men in the Division office. One of the plainclothesmen involved was a good friend of mine. He finally felt that they were cheating him on his share, so he came and told me the truth.

"There were really only 26 men on my Pad for that Division, and either the boss or the bag man had been taking me every month for an extra $75 a spot, and I had several going then.

"I tried to see the brass about it but that was no dice. The big guys always avoid any kind of contact which would tip their hands. But the next time the bag man came around, I squawked to him. He denied that he was ringing in 5 extra shares a spot on my Pad but the next month he only picked up for 26 men."

Other policy operators pointed out that only the real big banks can afford the "full open spot" payments for their various spots because of the amount of police graft involved. One Harlem banker, also claiming retirement, complained:

"I don't think that there has been a Negro banker—what few there are of us left—on a full Pad for the last few years.

"Most of us are down from the beat cop on through the precinct, and in some cases, most cases I would say, for the Division also.

"I'm told you can still make a living at this—if you don't get too big, although you are still liable to raids by all of the guys on the special squads above the Division level if they are not getting their taste.

"There was a time when you could make a personal Pad with individual members of these squads, but the big boys cut that out. Now all contracts must be made with the squad itself in behalf of all those involved and any plainclothesman making a personal deal will find himself busted to uniform in a minute.

"But the real danger in being on only a partial Pad is that you can't afford to expand too much. If the local cops find you've got a real good business, they'll try to force you to give the business to one of the East Side mob."

This former banker, a Negro, was reminded of Powell's charge that the cops were hounding Negro bankers while protecting the Italian big shots.

"There's some truth in what he says," the source observed, "but I don't think it's just racial. You see, these cops know that the East Side mob can afford a full open Pad for each of their spots. And in many cases the banks will collect the pay-off in a lump sum and give it in bulk to the pay-off men.

"No, I don't think it's all racial. From the cop's point of view, it's just more efficient business."

One inevitable result of the operation of The Pad—the multi-million-dollar police-protection set-up in the numbers game—has been to give major control of the policy racket to the underworld here.

Call them what you like—the East Harlem Mob, the Syndicate, the

Mafia—The Post's investigation of policy showed that these are the people who now control what once was a comparatively harmless, penny-ante lottery and is now a major racket.

Today, for the first time in the 150 years that it has existed here in one form or another, the numbers game is now a means as well as an end.

The end is obvious—the once-fabulous profits reaped by numbers bankers from suckers who take a 1,000 to 1 chance on picking a number in the hope of getting a 600 to 1 payoff if they're lucky enough to win.

The profits are still there but the rigidly organized graft of dishonest vice squad policemen has made a heavy dent in the take enjoyed by the policy banks.

The means became equally obvious when Post reporters began a two-month investigation of the numbers game here in the wake of Rep. Adam Clayton Powell's charges that Negro numbers bankers were being forced out of the game by the police so that whites—mainly Italians—could take over.

For the numbers industry—with its thousands of collectors, hundreds of controllers and other thousands of full and part time employees—provides an already established apparatus for other uses by unscrupulous racket bosses.

Here is what the Brooklyn Grand Jury reported last year after its investigation of gambling and police corruption:

"If you scratch the professional operator of gambling ventures you will find the narcotics peddler, the loan shark, the dice game operator, the murderer.

"Brooklyn has been the scene of a number of unsolved gangland homicides over the past few years. Almost every one of those killings is involved with gambling ventures in one form or another.

"In one case where seven leading narcotics dealers were convicted in Kings County last year, six were actively engaged in gambling activities, including bookmaking and policy, which they used as the source of funds for their deadly trade in narcotics."

A veteran numbers banker who insisted on using an obviously fictitious name told The Post a story which vividly illustrated the Grand Jury's findings.

"It happened around Christmas a year or so ago," this man said. "I was paid up on The Pad (the list of police-protected policy spots) and would've been in good shape if all the cops on The Pad, past and present, hadn't doubled back for a 'Christmas taste.' I had to shell out.

"And then, just before New Year's, I get hit heavy by some of my biggest players. I was out about $18,000 and I just couldn't raise that kind of money. Then the bag man for one of the special squads set up a meet for me with the East Harlem boys. He said they'd let me have the money until I got back on my feet.

"But when we finally had our meet, I found they wanted something in return. They said that if I would use my setup to handle about $18,000 worth of hoss (heroin) that I wouldn't even have to pay any interest on the $18,000 they were lending me.

"Well, I wasn't going to get mixed up in that kind of rap this late in life. So I just walked out. They didn't like it a bit, and the bag man told me later I was a fool. Of course, they took over my bank anyhow—and they've still got it."

Unfortunately, other bankers pressed to the wall by limited capital and mounting vice squad graft demands, evidently have taken the other road. During its investigation, The Post found strong indications that at least one major "independent" bank in Manhattan is closely allied with the narcotics trade, as is another in Brooklyn and at least two in The Bronx.

The connection is becoming increasingly evident as narcotic agents more frequently find themselves tracking down dope peddling suspects only to find them also employed in numbers operations.

The Syndicate, or Mafia, has long been active in the numbers game on the waterfront, but policy then was only an adjunct to such other activities as loan sharking and other waterfront rackets.

It was not until 1949 or so that the late Albert Anastasia, chief assassin of Murder, Inc., decided to expand from the waterfront and take over the policy game in other profitable areas.

First to feel the weight of the new decision was Louis Weber, Brooklyn's then admitted policy king and a pal of James Moran, Mayor O'Dwyer's right-hand man and a political power in his own right in Kings County.

One night in 1949, Weber received a visit in a South Brooklyn tavern from Anastasia and Frank (Frankie Shots) Abbatemarco, who had handled the policy operation for Anastasia's syndicate on the Brooklyn and Staten Island waterfronts.

The conversation was short and to the point. Weber was out; Frankie Shots was taking over.

Weber was a man of standing. He had a vice squad payroll nearing that of Harry Gross' still-to-be-exposed bookmaking empire. He had defied a long list of District Attorneys (when defiance was necessary) and could depend on the immense political power of Moran in the O'Dwyer Administration.

But Weber knew this was all to no avail when the Syndicate decided to move in. So he gave up a life-long policy empire in Brooklyn without an argument and fled to West Harlem to try to re-establish himself. He never attained his former eminence.

For the next decade, Frankie Shots, a boastful, high-living thug, became Brooklyn's biggest policy operator, although the real power for the borough's operation was held by Carmine Lombardozzi, a representative of the East

Harlem mob which even then was consolidating its spreading policy power.

Lombardozzi, soft-spoken and unobtrusive, was only faintly known to the public until his participation in the 1957 underworld conclave at Apalachin put him on the front pages.

Brooklyn underworld sources said that Lombardozzi was demoted after Apalachin, presumably for not being diligent in pushing the Syndicate to take over all the major policy banks in Brooklyn, and Mike Miranda, still a major policy figure in Brooklyn, took over his behind-the-scenes role.

(Frankie Shots, loud-mouthed to the end, wasn't as lucky as Lombardozzi. Suspected of holding out on the Syndicate, he was mowed down in Brooklyn by two gunmen on Nov. 4, 1959 in the very same tavern where Louis Weber had been handed his walking papers.)

The Syndicate's plan, duplicated in other boroughs, was quite simple. The major banks were swept up by the mob, with all direction coming from the East Harlem empire of Vito Genovese, Anthony (Fat Tony) Salerno, Trigger Mike Coppola and Joseph (Joe Stretch) Stracci.

The remaining "independent" banks, run mainly by veteran Negro and Puerto Rican bankers, were to be supervised by the Syndicate at a flat fee of 1 per cent of the gross take.

Each "independent" bank had to permit a Syndicate representative to check its "ribbon" (the daily adding machine tabulation of the total play) so that the Syndicate could be assured of its 1 per cent "off the top."

At the same time, the mob undertook to put all policy spots and locations on The Pad—the vice squad's list of police-protected places.

The conquest of Brooklyn by the Syndicate was almost complete by early 1958 when District Attorney Edward Silver began a secret two-month investigation which in April of that year led to the smashing of the $5,000,000 bank of Angel F. Calder, the city's largest Puerto Rican policy banker. The raid also revealed an open connection between Calder's bank and what Silver called "the Manhattan Syndicate."

Working so quietly that even the clerical staff in his office didn't know when he planned to act, Silver assembled 82 detectives and picked plain-clothesmen on April 1, 1958, and made a series of simultaneous mass raids which netted Calder and 67 of his associates, along with policy paraphernalia, the day's play and several thousand dollars in cash.

The prize catch of the raid proved to be an obscure East Side mobster, Emannuel (Nappy) Frazetta, 40, of 160 Mott St. Frazetta was seized in the basement of a three-story brownstone at 693 Lafayette St. in Bedford-Stuyvesant, which Silver said was the temporary headquarters of Calder's main bank. The raiders found Frazetta holding the "ribbon" for the day's policy play and surmised that he was checking for the Syndicate to guarantee its 1 per cent take.

Frazetta would only admit that he was "a messenger" sent over from Manhattan to "pick up something" to turn over to "somebody" in a subway.

Urbano (Benny) DeMucci, 41, seized while checking the take there at a Calder annex, also was suspected to be a Syndicate representative.

Calder himself, along with his son, Angelo, and his brother, Julio (One-Eyed Red) Calder, was charged with contriving a lottery—a felony—and released in $25,000 bail each.

Forty-four other persons seized among the 68 with the Calders were also booked and released on bail. Most of them went directly back into business.

On April 9, just eight days after the big April Fool's Day raid, Silver's Rackets Bureau detectives struck again—in the absence of any action by the police who regularly covered the area.

The DA's men seized Otis Spain Jr., of 110 Cambridge Pl., and charged him with possession of 22 numbers slips containing 1,800 plays. One of the 45 booked in the big Brooklyn raid, Spain had been plying his trade industriously since his release on bail.

With Spain in custody, the Rackets Bureau detectives struck again that night at 924 Lafayette St., just three blocks from the basement at 693 Lafayette where Calder's main bank had been smashed.

The raiders acted on information that 20 of Calder's controllers and runners were assembled there to set up a new operation, but apparently the policy boys had been tipped by their own sources, for the DA's squad found just two men there.

But the raid was not in vain. One of the two men turned out to be the aforementioned Angel Calder himself, a durable veteran of 22 years in the business and the other was Fitz Sealy, 70, another old time policy operator.

The 45 men seized in the Calder ring are still awaiting trial after two years.

Silver and Asst. DA Koota told The Post this week that the trial was being held up awaiting clarification of a 1957 U. S. Supreme Court decision which indicated that evidence obtained by wire-tapping might not be admissible in local courts.

One year after the raid, the State Court of Appeals upheld the use of wiretap evidence in state courts, but Koota pointed out that the Court of Appeals did not rule on the legality of wire-tapping under Section 605 of the Federal Communications Act, on which the Supreme Court based its ruling.

"We are still concerned," Koota said, "about the possibility of having a policeman admit to an act which the U. S. Supreme Court has held to be illegal. Such testimony by a policeman might expose him to possible indictment by a Federal Grand Jury."

Meanwhile, it can be assumed that the Calder bank is back in business as usual—probably trying to lay up a reserve for the day when the court showdown finally comes and Silver—as he expects—sends most of the 45 to jail.

But a Brooklyn Negro policy banker, whose operation was once closely associated with that of Calder, predicted that there wouldn't be much reserve left.

"The only boys who made anything out of the Calder business," he said, "are the vice squad boys on The Pad. They were around the day after the first raid to say that everybody's payments had to go up because 'We're taking more chances now.' And I'll be damned if they didn't try to get a second hike just 8 days later when Calder was picked up again.

"So the old man will be lucky if he can keep his head above water until the trial comes up. I doubt if they'll leave him much more than that."

Section 31 **FIXING THE CLEARINGHOUSE**

From *The D.A.'s Man* by Harold R. Danforth and James D. Horan, 1957.

From celebrated murder cases our office swung into the case of a huge gambling racket which I believe has no peer when it comes to the fantastic, Hollywood-type investigation we used to break it.

I believe in this case, more than in any other, District Attorney Frank Hogan proved that wire taps, legally used, are necessary to break up any criminal combination. Without our taps this syndicate, which reaped more millions than Dutch Schultz ever dreamed of, might never have been found out.

The investigation began in a quiet way. Our office was interested in gambler Tony Bender, later to be described by Hogan as "one of the top underworld figures in the East." We discovered that Bender and several ex-convicts, gathered almost nightly at a check-cashing center on West 35th Street.

"Put a wire in," District Attorney Hogan ordered. "Let's find out what they are up to."

A Supreme Court order was obtained and a tap was put on the telephone. I was sitting on the wire with other investigators, and I can still remember how bewildered we all were when we went over our notes at the end of the day. The dialogue seemed to have come right out of the Mad Hatter's tea party.

For example:

Man's voice: "Thanks for the 35 bucks but you still owe me seven."
Out: "Okay."
In: "I've decided to give my wife a divorce on the 25th and give her custody of the two kids."
Out: "Okay."
In: "This is a 12-horse race and I'm betting position three."
Out: "Lay 300."
In: "I'll meet you at 25th Street and 7th Avenue for lunch."
Out: "I'll be there."
In: "It's a funeral—43 cars but no coffin."
Out: "No body, heh?"
In: "I broke my leg in two places, lucky it wasn't nine pieces."
Out: "Got it."

Although the calls appeared to be gibberish, a pattern began to emerge; the calls were made at exactly the same time and the figures each day were in groups of three digits. It was evident that they pertained to some sort of a lottery, but these figures did not jibe with those played at the pari-mutuels. Day after day the messages were funneled through Tom Fay to the Chief of the Rackets Bureau, Al Scotti, to be studied. Scotti reported the latest findings to Hogan.

The Bureau of Investigation put the check-cashing office under round-the-clock surveillance. Finally we came up with one concrete piece of evidence; the outgoing calls were being made to a Tony Bender in Hackensack, New Jersey.

After a conference with Scotti, Assistant District Attorney Andrew Seidler, Chief Investigator Fay and Chief of the Accounting Bureau Joseph M. Gasarch, it was agreed that some form of the numbers racket was the core of this operation—just how it worked and just what it was remained to be determined. Gasarch and his assistants, Alex Finkelstein and Sam Lachter, began scanning newspapers each day, looking for three numbers which would fit in with those in the coded messages. Finally, after reading and rereading hundreds of daily newspapers, it was established that the first two digits were taken from the daily noon bond sales. The source of the third digit was still a mystery until one of Gasarch's boys found it in the daily figures released by the Cincinnati clearinghouse.

On the wire the coded calls kept coming in almost at an exact second. Now we sat glued to the tap, carefully noting each word that came over; now the conversations were beginning to make some sense.

From the wire tap we found that calls were being made from a man named Irving Bittz, a Prohibition hood and a former member of the Lepke-Gurrah gang, who also played a minor role in the Lindbergh kidnaping investigation, and a man named Abe Goldberg; both were employed in the circulation department of a New York newspaper. At a certain hour one or the other would call and give the cryptic message.

The pieces of the puzzle now began to fall into place; these two men were part of the scheme and their part was to pass, by coded messages the figures about to be printed. They were then passed in code to Nat Levinson, another member of the ring, who had offices in New Jersey.

Numbers, of course, are the heart of the policy racket—it is traditional that three digits are used—in which the player bets on a sequence of figures appearing daily in newspaper statistics. They may be Stock Exchange figures, bond sales, pari-mutuel totals—or they may be a combination of these numbers. There are no ground rules in the numbers game; each mob makes its own. The players, of course, assume that the numbers which they are playing are beyond the control of the persons operating the game.

For a numbers mob they had a perfect setup; they apparently knew the winning number long before the clearinghouse figures were released. We have just seen how they got the first two digits. But how did they get the third? While we were working on that, the calls from the newspapermen were abandoned. Calls began to come in from a Broadway bowling alley. The messages were still cryptic:

To the alley: "You have a date for me at 2:00 p.m."

From the alley: "Got it."

Then, we learned, Kane put in a toll call to a number in Cincinnati.

The calls to Cincinnati were of the same pattern.

Outgoing: "I'll meet you at two—can you make it?"

Incoming: "Two it is. I'll be there."

The following day after this conversation Gasarch and his accountant-sleuths walked in with a newspaper.

"There's your answer," he told Scotti. The number 2 was the last digit of the financial statement issued by the Cincinnati clearinghouse.

We found that by taking the second and third digits of the daily bond sales up until noon as the first two digits of the key number, and the second digit in the Cincinnati clearinghouse figures as the third digit of the key number, they would match the figures heard on the wire tap. For example, if the noonday bond sales amounted to $1,580,000 the second and third digits were 5 and 8, and if the clearinghouse figures for the day were $38,000,000, then the second digit would be 8 making the number 588.

What was crystal clear and yet rather unbelievable was that the gang had some high official of the clearinghouse on its payroll. This man, who obviously had the authority to release the daily number to the press, could rig the last digit to fit the purposes of the mob.

It is important at this point to pause a moment to examine the so-called "innocent nickel-and-dime numbers game" and the average player who has made it a multi-million dollar racket. Down through the years we have collected evidence that this supposedly innocent game has financed underworld infiltration into unions, supported loan-shark syndicates and organized crime of every description. The dossier of almost every big-time racketeer shows some affiliation with the policy, or numbers, game. It is their financial stepping-stone to more vicious activities.

Who is the typical policy player? He or she—women are heavy bettors —is usually about 40 or older. Mostly, they are embittered, frustrated, shiftless and superstitious. The nickel, quarter or dollar they bet daily represents a dream; a crock of gold spilling into their laps. With one swoop they can retire to luxury and a life of ease. It never occurs to a bettor that he has less than a 1000 to 1 chance of winning. The odds never count, it's the dream, the escape from the humdrum, monotonous, abrasive daily life that must be lived day after day. Sometimes he comes close—if only he had bet 432 instead of 423! The near miss spurs him on. Finally the daily bet is a habit which is never broken. During the Depression we found case histories of men and women who played their relief checks on the numbers. Some spent the money usually set aside to pay a weekly insurance policy premium.

Our office now had the gang's *modus operandi,* but it wasn't sufficient legal evidence to lay before a grand jury. What we needed was proof that the game was being played and a conspiracy was operating to rig that game of chance. Many more hours of surveillance and more wire taps followed; conference after conference was held in Scotti's office.

The biggest problem was to find the mob's office—not the check-cashing drop that was only a message center—but the heart of the policy game—the banks. This is the most difficult part of the whole policy setup to locate. Police congratulate themselves if they find three or four a year. Few operators know their locations, which are visited only by the mob's top bosses. This is not only to protect them from the law, but also from rival mobs, gun-crazy juveniles and stickup men who know the haul may prove as high as $75,000. Of course, no complaints ever reach the police.

What made it doubly difficult was that the numbers rackets in New York are based on local pari-mutuels and as far as any of us knew, there were no policy drops operating on the Cincinnati clearinghouse figures. I contacted some of my informants, who said there were a few spots in the city where you could play a policy based on the Midwest figures, but even my underworld informants looked blank when I asked where they could be located.

"Who wants to play the numbers on the Cincinnati combine when you have pari-mutuels in the city?" they asked.

We found the western figures were used by New Jersey policy drops, but that wasn't New York County.

Anthony Perone was assigned to find out where in New York this particular policy ring had its drops. It was a question even the underworld had difficulty in answering.

Tony disappeared for weeks. Because we had a record of a few Staten Island telephone numbers, he decided to strike out there first. He adopted a whole new life; he took a room, walked around with a scratch sheet in his pocket and looked mysterious. He paid visits to bars, grills and restaurants. Tony has a quiet, easy-going nature and it wasn't hard for him to strike up conversations. If he thought he had a likely prospect he would draw him out slowly, then casually wonder where he could play a number.

"Four seven two," he would murmur almost to himself. "I saw the combination on a truck. I just got a hunch I can hit if I can find a spot to lay a buck . . ."

Then one night a milkman with whom he was drinking slapped him on the shoulder.

"Hell, Tony," he said, "that's easy! I got a guy on my route that takes numbers. Let's see . . ." He took out his wallet and finally a scrawled address fell out. "Sure, here it is . . ."

Tony placed his first number that day. He got to be known as a steady player and before long was an accepted customer. From this spot he found others scattered across the island.

Then one night Scotti received a call from Tony, "I have it wrapped up, boss," he said quietly. "We can start knocking off some places tomorrow."

The following morning Tony drew up a list of policy drops to be raided. From these small fry we hoped to get the bigger ones.

In cooperation with the police—the police who were to stage the raids were not told of the purpose or location of the raids until a few minutes before they started out—we staged a series of raids across the island.

When news of the raid appeared in the papers I could hear the puzzled voices of the mob's bosses. . . .

Incoming: "Hear the news?"

Outgoing: "Yeah—so what? Usual stuff."

They were puzzled for a few days, then apparently their fears died down and business went on as usual.

While Gasarch and his accountants studied the records we had seized in the raids, Tony was assigned to shadow a new figure who had appeared in the case; William Tiplitz. Tony found him in the customer's room of a

Newark brokerage house at the dot of 11:30 a.m. At 12:05 p.m. the total bond sales appeared on the screen. Tiplitz hurried to a hall phone booth. Tony slipped into the adjacent booth and heard him call a number which we traced to the headquarters of a policy bank operated by Dan Zwillman, a relative of the well-known racketeer, Longy Zwillman. Tiplitz gave the person who answered the phone the noonday bond figures. Apparently the mob had discontinued the arrangement with the newspapermen and now obtained the bond sales figures through Tiplitz.

The way the racket worked was now clear. All policy bets had to be in by 11:30 a.m. At 12:10, after Tiplitz's call, the mob knew the first two digits. Then clerks studied the day's tickets recording the bets to find out which third digit had the lowest play for the day. For example, if the bond sales amounted to $1,580,000, they knew at 12:10 p.m. that the first two numbers would be 5 and 8. They would then hunt for the third number that, combined with 5 and 8, had received the smallest play.

Tony found that Tiplitz would call the policy bank back and receive the third number. Let's say that 583 received no play or very little play, then Tiplitz would be informed by code that 3 was the number the mob wanted.

Tiplitz then returned to the brokerage office and at 12:45 would receive a call from Kane's Broadway bowling alley. Kane's position in the ring now became clear; it was his job to receive from Tiplitz the number the mob thought would receive the lowest pay.

The muffled conversation went something like this:

Tiplitz: "There's nothing here (the code that the mob wanted 0)."

Kane: "Okay."

or

Tiplitz: "You got a date at six (the number the ring wanted rigged)."

Kane: "I got you."

I was sitting on Kane's wire and could hear him put in a call to Cincinnati seconds after that.

Kane: "Bill there?"

Bill: "Bill speaking."

Kane: "Charlie wants to see you at six."

Bill: "I'll be there. Goodby."

When Tony made his report we checked the clearinghouse figures and the figure six was the rigged total.

More conferences were held in Scotti's office. It was decided to set our sights for the mysterious Bill. Tony was selected to go to Cincinnati and run down Bill, and if possible, be with him when he called or answered the New York call—clearly a very difficult assignment.

We first checked the Cincinnati number Kane had called and our suspicions were confirmed; it was the official number of the Cincinnati clearinghouse. In Cincinnati Tony carefully made a study of the entire building at different hours. Around noon each day he saw a tall, distinguished, white-haired man enter what seemed to be an empty Board of Directors' meeting room.

Just about the time the call from Kane was due Tony slipped into the building and followed the man into the empty room. The man turned as Tony entered. "What can I do for you, young man?" he asked.

Tony said very earnestly, "Well, sir, I'm looking for a job."

The man smiled in return. "I'm afraid you have the wrong office. You want the Personnel Department."

Tony stalled. He wanted to make sure this was Bill, and if it was he wanted to be near when the New York call came in.

Tony said, "I have some brokerage experience and I thought I would fit in nicely here."

The white-haired man nodded. "I'm sure you will, son. Now if you just go down the hall . . ."

Tony interrupted, "Could you tell me, sir, what the starting salary is?"

Although he seemed impatient the man courteously answered all questions. Six minutes passed. Then Tony, who feared he was becoming conspicuous, left to go to "Personnel."

Outside, he carefully lighted a cigarette and waited a moment. The phone rang and Tony re-entered the room to hear the man say, "This is Bill. At six? I'll be there."

Tony hid his exuberance by apologizing and explaining he wanted to make sure on what floor the Personnel Department was located. "Bill" carefully explained.

"Are you the president, sir?" Tony asked with wide-eyed innocence.

The man smiled. "No, son, I'm Dennison Duble, the secretary."

Tony was stunned but masked his feelings and left. For the next few days he cautiously investigated Duble's background. He found the man had been for 20 years an honored resident of the community. He was a popular brokerage-house partner before succeeding his father in the office of secretary of the clearinghouse. When Tony arrived he was being considered as a candidate for mayor of Mariemont, a suburb. He was the father of two children and had an impeccable background. As the cliche goes, "everyone spoke well of him."

Through surveillance Tony found that Duble walked into the empty room at the exact minute every day to take the New York call. It was his job to alter for the mob the clearinghouse figure in his daily report which he released to the press, to fit the desired number which had the lowest play. For example, if the actual total cleared through banks for the day was $38,000,000 and the mob wanted the number six to appear he would release

$36,000,000. For this service, we later learned, he received $1,000 a month from the mob.

We now had the members of the gang, their *modus operandi* and proof of a conspiracy to rig a lottery. Back in New York, Tony gave his report and Scotti, under Hogan's direction, organized a huge dragnet which would take in suspects in New Jersey and New York, besides Duble in Cincinnati.

Excellent co-operation was given by Essex County Prosecutor Duane E. Minard, Jr., and the schedule of raids was worked out by Tom Fay, Scotti and Captain William Grafnecker, with all of us assigned to teams.

On July 26, 1949, after a year and a half of intensive undercover and wire tap investigation, our office moved in on the gang. One team picked up Tiplitz, another raided Zwillman's policy bank just as he was hanging up on Kane in New York. That very moment Detective James Canavan walked in on Kane, who, for some unknown reason, had decided to use the phone service in the lobby of the building that day instead of his business phone.

In the lobby a telephone operator took the number you wrote on a slip of paper, then assigned you to a booth to make your call. Canavan, who stood behind Kane, wrote his home number down under the one Kane had written, an invaluable bit of evidence for the grand jury. As the Cincinnati call was coming in Canavan arrested Kane.

While Kane was being pulled out of the booth in New York, detectives in Cincinnati walked in on Duble, who surrendered peacefully. He waived extradition to face arraignment in New York. So perfectly were the raids synchronized that the entire three-state operation took only 13 minutes.

Duble's arrest shocked Cincinnati. The city's leaders refused to believe this pillar of respectability could be on the payroll of Eastern gangsters. The shocked Police Chief of Mariemont said, "I just can't believe it. He is the last man in the world I would think would do anything like that."

Duble removed all doubt of his guilt. Two hours after his arrest he confessed and resigned from his office. He immediately became a state's witness.

Nine men were arrested in the roundup and indicted on charges of conspiracy to contrive a lottery. In January, 1950, eight of the nine were fined and sent to jail for from six months to two years.

Duble, because of his cooperation, received six months and $1,000 fine. Only Tony Bender escaped punishment. He put up $35,000 bail and refused to leave New Jersey without an extradition fight.

The investigation showed the mob could have made millions without cheating their players but they were too greedy; they wanted everything. On some days, because of the rigged numbers, they didn't have to part with a penny.

Section 32 **INTO SEVENTY BUSINESSES**

From *Crime in America* by Estes Kefauver, 1951.

Midway in its investigations of what the late Lincoln Steffens aptly characterized for all time as "The Shame of the Cities," the Senate Crime Committee directed its attention momentarily to a special phenomenon of national scope. We wanted to take a look at black market operations—the ugly racket that had plagued American economy in the price control and rationing days of World War II and that was again threatening to become a menace. We realized we could not explore the entire field of black market operations, but because of the timeliness of the subject—the Korean war then was a few months old, and Congress was being asked to vote price control over certain items—we felt it would be both useful and healthy to dissect at least one example. There was reason to suspect that racketeering money once again was in the black market field, creating a condition that was wrecking an important part of the mobilization program planned by Congress and the Administration; and we wanted to know about it.

The black market investigation, of course, tied in squarely with our investigation of another major threat to American life—the infiltration of legitimate business by members of the organized crime syndicate. If the disciples of Frank Costello, the late Al Capone, and their local counterparts in every major city of the country get a strangle hold on even a minor portion of American business, all I can say is God save America. One of the principal aims of the Senate Crime Committee was to expose the extent of this already dangerous penetration and to suggest protective legislative countermeasures.

For our black market investigation we singled out a particularly flagrant and ugly case involving illegal sugar operations. It was a case that came within the committee's scope for two principal reasons: (1) these particular black marketeers had cut freely across state lines; and (2) there were hints of possible connections with the organized underworld—i.e., the national crime syndicate.

It was a shoddy, dirty story in which none of the principals was particularly clean—though one was very sorry. The case was that of Eatsum Food Products, a candy company owned by a manufacturer named David George Lubben, of Woodcliff Lake, New Jersey. Originally Lubben had been a legitimate businessman, but he admitted he had made the mistake of deciding to cheat on the wartime laws of the land for the sake of personal profit. Before he was through he had been taken for a financial cleaning—and in the course of it had been given the scare of his life—by a clever New York operator who had an ex-convict for a partner.

Lubben had been a merchandiser for a Cincinnati bakery. He came to New York during the war years to go into business for himself as a candy wholesaler and manufacturer. The Eatsum company which he acquired, however, had not been in business long enough, under existing OPA regulations, to have any appreciable sugar quota, so Lubben tried everything he could think of to remedy the situation, including coming to Washington to confer with expensive attorneys and "public relations" counselors who, in Lubben's words, claimed "they knew a man who knew a man who knew a man who knew a man who knew a man who knew Harry Truman . . . or something of that sort." Eventually he fell in with some sharp characters in New York City and soon found himself over his head in the black market.

Then Lubben met up with some new characters, namely, William Giglio, the smart operator, and Frank Livorsi, the ex-convict, who had acquired a jelly factory which had a sugar quota of 14,000,000 pounds a year. As Lubben himself told us, all he could think was that "14,000,000 pounds would make me as big as Hershey." Soon the operator and the ex-convict were his partners in Eatsum, and then came the inexorable finale: Lubben was out and they were in.

The public hearing on the black market sugar case, which had been preceded by preparatory executive sessions in New York City, was conducted in Washington. We began with an examination of Livorsi, the forty-seven-year-old ex-convict, who has had an abominable record as a member of society. An admitted friend of such underworld characters as Frank Costello, Willie Moretti, Trigger Mike Coppola, Little Augie Pisano, and others, Livorsi has been arrested, according to his own recollection, at least ten times, including twice on charges of homicide with a gun. The only conviction, however, was a two-year sentence for importation and transportation of narcotics in 1942. The low ratio of convictions to arrests in the cases of known hoodlums, incidentally, was a phenomenon found all over America that gave the committee much concern.

Could Livorsi think of any legitimate business he ever was in, Counsel Halley asked, before he went to jail? "I can't think of any legitimate business," Livorsi sullenly replied. On being released from prison, Livorsi went to work for two dress factories, one of which was owned by a man who also had been a narcotics convict. In 1945 Frank Livorsi teamed up with smart, smooth-talking William Giglio, then thirty years old. They acquired ownership of the Tavern Fruit Juice Company, a jelly manufacturing business.

Livorsi, who never had been in the jelly business before, glibly told us that he "borrowed eight or ten or twenty thousand (dollars) . . . I am not sure about that" to enter the deal. With the company came the precious sugar quota of 14,000,000 pounds.

In executive session Counsel Halley asked Giglio why "a bright young man like you" would choose a convicted narcotics peddler and thorough-going hoodlum as a partner. Giglio, alternately an articulate, sarcastic, or injured witness, protested that Livorsi had "paid his debt to society . . . If he were my brother I could love him no less . . . He is a very dear friend of mine and if I had the opportunity tomorrow to take him into business with me again and if I could make the man a wealthy man, I would do so." At the public hearing Giglio added: "The reason I took him in is because Mr. Livorsi has a very lovely family. He has three lovely daughters and a lovely wife, and he is a lovely fellow and entitled to a break."

Anyhow, Livorsi testified, the Tavern Company prospered, and there came a time when "Bill Giglio told me . . . that we were going to buy into the candy business." "Whatever he told me," Livorsi added, "was all right with me because I knew he was a capable fellow." So the ex-convict became a partner with Giglio in Lubben's Eatsum candy company. Livorsi insisted that Eatsum was in the "candy business" and entered stubborn denials when Halley, in a series of questions, asked if Livorsi had not been aware that Eatsum actually was buying and selling large quantities of corn syrup in transactions in which the parties concerned passed "large sums of money in cash payment at black market places."

In his new role as jelly manufacturer, Livorsi said, he gave jobs to a number of paroled convicts, including another ex-narcotics dealer, a man known as Big John Ormonte who had been in jail with Livorsi. Big John was paid $100 a week, supposedly to work at the candy factory, but as we later heard from Lubben, he was such a disturbing influence that Lubben had to appeal to Giglio to take him out of the plant. Big John's salary continued, however, and Livorsi insisted that his old buddy "did his part." As Livorsi explained Big John's duties, "If I wanted to take off and go away from the plant, he would be around the plant seeing that the men did their work . . ."

There was considerable confusion and debate about just how much Livorsi did draw out of the various jelly, candy, syrup, and sugar operations. He admitted his salary was $1000 a week, but when Halley produced an income tax return "showing you got $290,000 in 1946," Livorsi demurred, saying, "I wish I had seen it." Finally he conceded that the figure "must be right if you have it in front of you." He did recall that on two occasions partner Giglio handed him packets of $100 bills—about $35,000 in all. "He told me," Livorsi explained, "this is from Eatsum dividends or something." He also said he was able to buy a country home for $50,000 which he later sold for $85,000.

The end of the sugar ride, so far as Livorsi was concerned, was when the little empire founded by Giglio "went broke." There were a lot of unpaid creditors clamoring at the door. "You didn't even pay your income tax, is that right?" Halley asked him. Livorsi replied: "I went broke with it."

> HALLEY: What have you been doing for a living since 1947?
> LIVORSI: I have been following the horses. . . . I go from track to track. I go from New York to Florida.

Senator Tobey, in his inimitable manner, inquired of Livorsi if he wasn't ashamed of his lifelong illegitimate activities. Livorsi shot back: "Betting horses, shooting craps, or playing cards is illegitimate?" Livorsi further declared, "I am a good American in every way."

When Mr. Lubben took the witness chair the story of the web into which he had fallen—admittedly through his own desire for profit—became clearer and more orderly. It was a tragic story, one that is well worth retelling here in the hope that it may point up a moral to any other potential Lubbens who, in these unsettled and inflationary times, may be teetering on the border between honesty and avarice. There can be no excuse for Lubben's actions, but he has paid dearly, and at least he was man enough to tell the story of his misdeeds to the committee without any attempt at self-justification. Admitting freely that he bought sugar on the black market, he said: "But nobody asked me to go into business. I can't look for anybody to feel sorry for me. I just did it."

Eventually Lubben met up with a man named Ronald Stone, a former attorney who, as Halley pointed out, had been disbarred in connection with subornation of perjury. "The fact that he (Stone) had had this trouble—" Lubben fumbled, "I mean, Jesus, who am I to judge? He was always very nice with me. . . . Everybody was in the act and everybody had an angle. Ronnie Stone was very valuable in getting supplies to us. . . ."

> Q. (*By Halley.*) He also helped you get the black market sugar, did he not?
> A. Yes, he did.

Lubben told us of having given Stone $10,000 in cash on one occasion to give to a man, supposedly an East Orange, New Jersey, attorney who would be able to get him a legitimate sugar quota. "It was worth almost anything to get a quota . . . not to have to worry about using black market sugar," he said. So he passed over the $10,000, but nothing happened. "We never did hear any more about it." (Stone, in his testimony, claimed the amount was only $1000.)

Explaining why he didn't go to court and try to get his money back, Lubben exclaimed: "How could I go and say I gave somebody $10,000 to use their influence with the government? You have your $10,000 licking and you have to take it and leave it alone." He went on to say that he had "paid two other people since then"—two men in Washington whose names he couldn't recall but which he would "dig up" for the committee.

At this point there was a bit of drama in the hearing room. Senator Tobey, always eager to ferret out information on alleged "influence peddlers," shouted: "I wish you would dig it up! I would like to get hold of these vermin if I could!" Lubben replied, "One of them is in this courtroom now." As Lubben started to point, a well-dressed man, who was heard by newspaper reporters to exclaim that the witness was "lying," stood up and said: "He is referring to me." He identified himself as a Washington attorney named Frank S. Ketcham, whereupon the irrepressible Senator Tobey, who mixed puns with his denunciations, demanded: "Did you catch him or did you not?"

Ketcham went on to say that he had been consulted by Lubben on how he could get a quota, and that he gave him advice and worked on the case approximately six to eight months. "It was a very difficult job to attempt to do and I could not produce any results," Ketcham said. For this, the attorney said, Lubben was charged "fairly and reasonably" a fee of $2500.

Then, Lubben testified, he consulted another man in Washington who "was supposed to have been Harry Truman's campaign manager in Missouri." "How much did you pay him?" Senator Tobey inquired. Lubben answered: "I think the first time we gave him one thousand bucks, sir, but we weren't the big time for the man. He had more pictures in his office of more of you senators shaking hands with different people than any place I have been in this town.

"If you were just ordinary John Q. Public," Lubben went on, "and you wanted to get something done and you went into this man's elaborate suite of offices and saw a lot of beautiful pictures in the office—a gorgeous place— you would think this man was very successful because he certainly didn't get all those pictures staying home at night. I thought really truly that this was a man who was going to get a job done for me. I would have paid anything to get a sugar quota, sir, gladly."

Finally Lubben, whose memory was "bad" on the subject, remembered after much urging and a recess of the hearing that the man with the pictures on the wall was named Victor R. Messall, a public relations counselor with offices in one of Washington's newest and fanciest buildings. We called Messall to the hearing and told him what Lubben had said. "Is David Lubben here? . . . I don't even know that I know the gentleman or not," Messall parried. Lubben stood up and told Messall that they certainly had met; that a Lieutenant Frank G. Harris had taken him to Messall's office to discuss the sugar quota and that Lubben had paid Messall a retainer. Messall denied knowledge of the whole thing; then Counsel Halley produced a letter to Lieutenant Harris on Messall's business stationery, purportedly signed by Messall, discussing the Eatsum matter and saying that the writer had "been given to understand that this allocation will be very substantially increased shortly. . . ." Messall then said that the letter probably had been dictated and written by an employee of his, and that he had so many accounts that he "couldn't, of course, keep up with all of them."

As a further exploration into the sometime ways of Washington, Halley asked Messall: "Do you say you did or did not ever hold yourself as having been a campaign manager for President Truman?" Messall replied: "I suppose if somebody asked me if I had been—a lot of people come to my office and say, 'I understand that you used to be with Mr. Truman.' I don't advertise the fact, but I am certainly proud of it. I was his secretary for six years, from the day he came to Washington in 1935 until his re-election in 1940. I left him in March 1941 to go in private business. I did manage his campaign in Missouri in 1940 when he was elected to the Senate."

In justice to Mr. Messall, there was no evidence that he personally tried to sell himself to Lubben as a wonder-worker or that he attempted to trade on his rather ancient connection with Mr. Truman. The incident, however, does illustrate the extreme care which people in his position should exercise to avoid embarrassing their former associates by giving the impression that they have "inside connections."

Some time after the $10,000 episode, Lubben continued, Stone introduced him to Louis J. Roth, an accountant, of 166 West Thirty-Second Street, New York City. Roth was presented, Lubben said, as "somebody that really has connections." Roth in turn, the manufacturer continued, represented himself as being connected with William Giglio's Tavern Fruit Juice Company; Roth said, Lubben testified, that Giglio had a connection with one of the largest baking corporations in the United States, and that Tavern itself had just secured the 14,000,000-pound sugar quota. This figure overawed Lubben, as he had been scrabbling for black market sugar in quantities as low as twenty-five 100-pound sacks at a time.

So Lubben paid a visit to the office building wherein were located the offices of the huge corporation which he claimed Roth had mentioned; he said he had the impression that there was a definite tie-up between the corporation and the parties he was going to see. He walked through the corporation offices and "met a great many people" who were told that "Dave is coming in with us," Lubben said. They finally wound up in an office on the same floor, occupied not by an official of the corporation but by an attorney who represented the corporation, and there was Giglio. Lubben made a deal to transfer a fifty per cent interest in his company to Giglio and Livorsi; it was his understanding that a relative of Giglio's, one Frank Loperfido, also was in the deal. The sale price was around $40,000, but Lubben claimed his new partners actually paid nothing until they had drawn enough profits out of Eatsum to effect a "paper" liquidation of the purchase price. In exchange for half of his business, Lubben said, his new partners "were to see that I got some sugar." But, he mournfully related, he "never got so much sugar that you could sweeten your coffee with" out of his new partners.

Soon after he acquired the new partners, Lubben went on, a number of things began to happen, all of which added up to grief for him. Giglio, he said, insisted that Eatsum move out of its modest uptown offices, for which Lubben paid $135 a month, and into a new place which was "a regular Hollywood suite," the unhappy manufacturer went on. Everybody had "gorgeous" big private offices and Giglio had a fancy bar in his. In all, the move cost Eatsum about $14,000. Then began a series of unpleasant and threatening visits from various OPA investigators, some of whom, Lubben said, later went to jail. There also was an infiltration into the firm of characters such as Big John Ormonte and another chap identified as Big Louie, who wore a "racetrack suit" and scared off the women buyers. Lubben said he also began hearing from various sources, including Louis Roth, that Frank Costello, the New York underworld king, was the "real boss" of the Giglio organization. Whether it was true or not Lubben never found out, but on one occasion, he testified, he did in fact see Costello at the Copacabana night club with Giglio and Livorsi.

Lubben himself was no angel, as was made abundantly clear by his testimony. He confessed that it was he who, in the relatively short period he stayed in business with Giglio, set up the intricate arrangements for buying a vast quantity of corn syrup in the Midwest by making under-the-table black market payments to farmers and selling it pretty much on the same basis. Everything was done for cash and in five months of 1945 more than $400,000 in cash was received from these transactions, Lubben testified. The money, he went on, was kept in "a little green cashbox" hidden in "a panel in back of the bar in the wall" of Giglio's office. Lubben had the key to the cashbox for the first ten days of the operation, then, he said, it was turned over to Giglio's cousin, Frank Loperfido. "The last time I knew about it there was $140,000 in there," said Lubben.

The denouement was that Lubben, after staying in business with the Giglio group for about nine months, lost both his nerve and his taste for the fantastic deal and decided he would get out at any cost. But he had a harder time getting away from Giglio & Co. than Br'er Rabbit had with the Tar Baby.

The business at that time, according to Lubben's figures (disputed by Giglio), was worth $940,000—including the $140,000 allegedly in the green box. Lubben claimed he took back the lease on the plant and machinery he originally had in the Bronx and turned everything else over to the Giglio group, with the understanding "that they would pay my income tax for the nine months in which I was a partner." In fact," said Lubben, "they later on charged me back about $23 because they claimed that some raisins I had in the warehouse shrunk a little bit. They were that methodical."

Senator Tobey asked Lubben if he had not had "a sense of apprehension and fear that if you did not play ball and do what they said, they might do physical harm to you?"

"I did, yes, I did," Lubben fervently replied. "That was the reason I wanted to get away from them." He went on to say that he had counted on receiving half of the money in the cashbox the day he broke up the partnership. But when he asked Giglio about it, Lubben testified, Giglio coldly told him, "You know we had OPA trouble."

"I said," Lubben continued, " 'I don't know anything about it, but certainly you had not $140,000 worth.'

"In that office that day were Frank Livorsi, John Ormonte, and a couple of other people. I looked around there and Giglio said, 'You are not going to get my money. You are lucky we don't charge you for some other things around here. We ought to get more back. You are getting too good a deal.' "

So Lubben, letting discretion be the better part of valor, "walked out and . . . never went back into that office" until some months later when he said Giglio called him down to close out some details. The final snapper to the whole tangled mess was that Lubben never got his income tax paid by his ex-partners, either.

When he went back into business on his own, Lubben concluded, he still fooled around with black market sugar until he finally was able to buy out a company that had a legitimate quota. "From then on I was free . . . I felt . . . like I had just made a good clean confession," he said. "For the first time in a long time I was able to sleep." At this point Senator Tobey epitomized the feelings of all of us by remarking:

"You make me kind of sorry that I voted for price controls last night, opening up this vista again. History might repeat itself."

What we heard from William Giglio was a different story. He was an evasive and disputatious witness, as the record plainly shows. But step by step Counsel Halley led him through an absorbing recital of the career that Giglio, who gave his address as Ocean Port, New Jersey, had managed to achieve in his thirty-five years.

He began as the owner of a liquor store; worked during World War II as an "expediter for a company manufacturing collapsible masts"; became interested in the syrup business through helping a friend in the Bronx; then, with his ex-convict friend Livorsi, bought into the Tavern Fruit Juice Company. Tavern engaged in a pretty sharp operation, about which Halley and Giglio tangled tartly. The year before Giglio and Livorsi had bought in, the company had had its sugar quota raised to 14,000,000 pounds because, as Giglio himself explained it, all jelly manufacturers were being encouraged by OPA to make as much jelly as they could, for the reason that "in 1944 fats and oils and butter were in short supply and OPA requested of all jelly manufacturers to manufacture more spreads, more bread spreads." Tavern manufactured great quantities of imitation-flavored jellies from the sugar it received under OPA allotment, but—again in Giglio's own words—"all of our imitation-flavored jellies were sold to a very limited number of customers, only the top customers in the country." These customers, it developed, were large cooky manufacturers, short on sugar themselves, who were buying Tavern's products as "baker's jelly" and paying, as Halley charged, a "premium price."

I asked this remarkable young promoter what he thought of the ethics of taking sugar, which the government wanted him to manufacture into jelly in order to save butter and margarine, and selling the jelly to bakeries which turned right around and used it as a substitute for the sugar which they could not get at the time. "Senator," he answered, "this was perfectly one hundred per cent legal."

There was considerable dispute as to how much money Giglio and Livorsi actually had made from their participation in the Tavern and Eatsum ventures. Halley suggested that the figure was more than $500,000 in the year 1946 alone, but Giglio insisted it would be nearer $400,000 for all operations. Giglio also maintained that Lubben was wrong about many details to which he had testified, and, in defending his relationship with his ex-partner, Giglio claimed that he had enabled Lubben's Eatsum company to earn better than $250,000 by wholesaling jellies made by Giglio's Tavern outfit. The brash young man even seemed rather proud of the cozy arrangement, which he described to us as follows:

"Tavern would sell to Eatsum; Eatsum would mark the material up fifteen per cent, which was the legal wholesale markup, and they would, in turn, sell to National Biscuit and Sunshine Biscuit, and so forth. So Eatsum earned some $200,000 or $250,000, not on Eatsum's efforts, but on the sale of materials that I was already selling."

As a sidelight, Giglio related how, toward the peak of his operations, he was able to purchase the estate of the late Senator Barbour in New Jersey. He said he paid $100,000 for it—$50,000 of which was "borrowed" from a new corporation he had organized. Halley asked him if he had any gambling equipment at his country estate, and Giglio admitted there were two roulette wheels.

But he wanted to explain this, the glib young man said, because "roulette wheels are normally considered as gambling equipment and I would not like to be supposed here to be a gambler, because that is something I have never been." What really happened was that a "Panamanian gentleman whom I met in Florida" had made him a proposition whereby Giglio would get a "legal license to run a gambling casino in the country of Panama." Gambling in Panama, of course, is legal. Giglio "rushed out," as Halley put it, and bought the two roulette wheels before he ever had any kind of contract. But the deal "never panned out," Giglio told us, and "that equipment lay on my property for three years until it was warped and useless" and "I finally burned it to get rid of it."

The grand finale to the Giglio saga was the pyramiding of the assets he had after Lubben was frozen out into an even bigger corporation called American Brands. There was a period of fantastic expansion and great affluence; then a whopping bankruptcy. The whole mess still is in process of litigation, including, as this was written, a federal income tax investigation. Irving Saypol, U. S. Attorney in New York, credited the committee's work with helping the tax probe enormously.

American Brands was a big thing while it lasted, the young promoter explained to us. It had a lot of interests, including a huge research project directed by Giglio himself (who was neither a scientist nor an engineer), aimed at developing methods of manufacturing sugar from blackstrap molasses, citrus waste juices, grapes, and other products. "I was the only stockholder of American Brands," Giglio said; it did a business of approximately $3,300,000 in 1946. Giglio's salary was $1000 a week, and on top of it he traveled around the country, spending huge sums on "research." Halley, who had studied the books of American Brands, suggested that the cash spent by Giglio on these trips "ran to several hundred thousand dollars," but Giglio, with perfect aplomb, said "I don't believe that." How, I asked him, had he managed to spend even $100,000 traveling around the country in a short time? Giglio earnestly answered:

"This was not for me alone, Senator. I traveled . . . and carried with me eight or ten men, engineers and chemists. We went to New Orleans, eight and ten of us at the time. We went into the Florida citrus region . . . out to Sacramento. . . . It was a failure. It didn't work out."

At another point Giglio said: "I made one big mistake. I attempted to go too far too fast. That was my error." Counsel Halley, agreeing with the witness for once, said, "I will admit you went far and fast. . . ."

At the time he testified before us Giglio—his American Brands Corporation in bankruptcy and under investigation by the Internal Revenue Bureau—had found a new position as general manager, he said, of a pharmaceutical firm known as the Heparin Corporation. Heparin, a heart drug, is "one of the great boons to medical science today," Giglio explained. Personally, I viewed with some alarm Giglio's next assurance that "the Army and Navy procurement division could explain that one to you (the Senate Committee). They buy great quantities of it."

Throughout our investigations the committee discovered evidence of infiltration of legitimate business fields by crimesters and their associates. We saw it in Chicago, where Joe Fusco, once labeled a "public enemy" by the Chicago Crime Commission, became the city's largest wholesale liquor dealer; we saw it in Miami, where hoodlums took over hotels; and we were to see more of it in every city where we conducted hearings. The committee found more than seventy separate types of businesses into which countless hoodlums had infiltrated, as follows:

Advertising, amusement industry, awnings, automobiles, bakeries, ballrooms, banking, baseball, bonding, bowling, boxing, candy, catering, cheese importing, cigarettes and tobacco, cleaning and dyeing, coal, construction, copper, dairies, dress manufacturing, dress sales, drug manufacturers, drugstores, electrical equipment, fishing, florists, foods of all types (meat, groceries, and fruit, etc., both wholesale and retail), furniture, gambling casinos (legal in Nevada), gambling equipment manufacturers, garages, gas stations, haberdashery, hardware, hotels, ice, importing, insurance, jams and jellies, juke boxes, junk, laundries, linen supplies, liquor (wholesale and retail), lithography, loans, manufacturing (miscellaneous), oil prospecting, olive oil importing and wholesaling, paper, printing, publications (both racing publications and scandal sheets which posed as legitimate but whose operations verged on blackmail), racing operations and race tracks, race news wire service, radio, ranching, real estate, restaurants (including taverns, bars, and night clubs), rubber, shipping, slot machines, steel, surplus property, tailoring, television manufacturing and sales, textiles, theaters (stage and movies), trucking, transportation, unions, and washing machines.

The pattern of legitimate infiltration by the hoodlum element is a familiar and often a vicious one. It begins with the hoodlum finding himself with more money than he knows what to do with, accrued, of course, from his illegal ventures in gambling, narcotics, bootlegging, prostitution, or what not. A good example of this was established in our interrogation of the Newark, New Jersey, gangster, Abner (Longie) Zwillman, a confessed rumrunner and strong-arm man of the prohibition era, named by former District Attorney William O'Dwyer of Brooklyn in his testimony as one of the old leaders of "The Combination" which ran Murder, Inc. Zwillman's close associates, O'Dwyer testified, were the late Louis (Lepke) Buchalter (electrocuted), the late Bugsy Siegel (murdered), Lucky Luciano (deported), Albert Anastasia (now in the dress manufacturing business), and Joe Adonis (as this was written, in jail). Zwillman wound up the prohibition era with a fortune. Now he is a participant in a tobacco vending machine company

(Michael Lascari, who took money to Lucky Luciano in Italy, is one of his associates); a truck sales and parts agency; a trading company that buys and sells auto equipment and used machinery; another company that deals in scrap iron, and a company that places and operates some 700 washing machines in apartment buildings. He also has investments in properties and business held for him in the names of other persons acting as his trustees; he declined to give us information about these trusteeships, stating that he had set it up in that manner because "sometimes my name kills a deal."

I cannot overemphasize the danger that can lie in the muscling into legitimate fields by hoodlums. None of us on the committee would deny the right of an honestly repentant wrongdoer, who has paid his debt to society, to go straight in a legitimate field; indeed, this should be encouraged. But there was too much evidence before us of the *unreformed* hoodlums gaining control of a legitimate business; then utilizing all his old mob tricks—strong-arm methods, bombs, even murder—to secure advantages over legitimate competitors. All too often such competition either ruins legitimate businessmen or drives them into emulating or merging with the gangsters.

The hoodlums also are clever at concealing ownership of their investments in legitimate fields—sometimes, as Longie Zwillman said, through "trustees" and sometimes by bamboozling respectable businessmen into "fronting" for them. Virgil Peterson of the Chicago Crime Commission testified that "hundreds" of hoodlum-owned businesses are successfully camouflaged. He told us of having been consulted by a friend of his who had been offered a $25,000-a-year job to head a "new corporation." Peterson investigated for him and found that "the fellow who had contacted him was part and parcel of the Capone Syndicate."

There are other obvious dangers of having criminals in control of legitimate businesses. For one thing, a legitimate business is a very convenient front for a gambler or criminal: it can be used as a "cover" for the profits of his illegal operations, thus enabling him to defraud the government of taxes on many hundreds of thousands of dollars of income. Another drawback is the basic unwholesomeness of having gangsters in control of companies that perform vital services or distribute necessary commodities to the public. I am thinking particularly of instances we uncovered where men with criminal records own interests in transit and taxi companies, and where they sell and manufacture food products and even vital medicines. I, for one, do not like to think of food products necessary to the health of my children, or of medicine that can mean life or death to a great many people, coming from plants controlled by gangsters whose code of ethics is the dollar sign, and who do not care if that dollar sign is stained somewhat with blood. As one possible means of remedying the situation, I favor passage of legislation which would expose such operations by giving the Securities and Exchange Commission authority to require public listing of names of all large investors in corporations whose interstate operations affect the public welfare.

Section 33 **THE NEW SURGE**

From "The New Surge" by Robert F. Kennedy, 1959.

A new surge of racketeering is strangling businesses across the country. The situation is more critical than ever before. It will get worse.

You as a businessman, as well as public officials and union leaders, are involved.

Establishment of a national crime commission to deal with this growing problem is under study on Capitol Hill. Such a commission will likely be recommended to Congress by the Senate Rackets Committee, headed by Sen. John L. McClellan, Democrat of Arkansas.

The commission would take over when the McClellan Committee winds up its work this year, and would attack corruption that is beyond the reach of the Committee.

Even so, new laws beyond those now being considered in Congress will be needed to check the mounting trend of gangsterism.

These are the views of Robert F. Kennedy, chief counsel of the McClellan Committee during the almost two and a half years of investigations into improper activities in the labor-management field.

For the details on how unions get and use their power, how you can avoid being trapped by hoodlums, and what you could be doing about the situation, read this exclusive interview by the editors of *Nation's Business:*

Mr. Kennedy, are businessmen being hurt by infiltration of racketeers into business?

In my estimation, based on two and a half years of investigations by our committee, the situation is far more critical now than it has ever been. In some communities in the United States local law enforcement is completely under the control of gangsters. A large number of businesses are controlled by the underworld.

Gangsters have taken complete control of a number of industries to obtain a monopoly, often with the help of dishonest union officials.

Could you tell us about some of these situations?

First, although businesses of all sizes are concerned, the so-called service industries have been particular targets; the providing of linen to hotels and restaurants; the paper towels that are provided to restaurants; even the silverware; the providing of laundry; the handling of cartage, where a few companies in one city began to exercise complete control over the industry.

Once the gangsters get their foot in, once some businessman makes a deal, he finds that, in two or three or four years, the racketeers come back and extract a little bit more, and a little more, until ultimately they control everything.

That is the great danger. And they are getting stronger and stronger.

How does this happen as far as businessmen are concerned?

I think initially they make the deal because these gangsters come to them and say, "If you make this arrangement with us, instead of 10 per cent of this particular industry in this community, we will make sure you have 50 per cent." This sounds very lucrative, so the businessman brings them in as partners possibly. Other businessmen make "sweetheart" contracts with some union official. A few years after the initial deal, the businessman doesn't control the industry any longer. The gangsters can blackmail him, threaten his family. Sometimes the businessman has become so corrupt himself that he plays along. We found that happening again and again.

The gangsters infiltrate the political ranks of the cities and counties?

Yes, they have. A number of communities even at present are completely under the domination of gangsters.

Often the difficulty is that the prosecuting attorney and the law enforcement officials are corrupt. There isn't much anybody can do unless the governor sees fit to step in. In some states he can't, and in some states he won't.

So you have a situation where the people really can do nothing about it.

Do you see this as a new surge of crime?

I see it as a new surge by the people in the underworld. Organized crime is far more widespread now and far more serious than during the days of Al Capone.

Will the surge continue?

It will continue and get much worse, in my estimation.

Why is that?

I think the gangsters have gotten smoother in their operations. From prohibition they learned about operating in interstate commerce. They set up a transportation system to operate with other groups throughout the country, obtaining sugar and other ingredients.

The second thing, they obtained a great deal of money during and immediately after the war. They have a great deal of cash available, so when they move into an area the legitimate businessman can't compete. As we have just been seeing, they can pay a greater bonus for placing their juke box, or their pin ball machine, for instance, than the ordinary businessman can afford.

What can be done about it?

I think that public knowledge and interest would be extremely important. I think the federal government must take a more active interest in organized crime—and I think they are doing that now. I think we need some new legislation dealing with organized crime.

I think that judges and courts in some areas must become more realistic about what the problems are. I think that the individual's liberties and freedom are extremely important. I think, however, we should put some emphasis on the public interest and public security.

Section 34 **POLICE-SYNDICATE DEAL**

From a Kansas City Grand Jury report, 1961.

By far the greater portion of the jury's time was spent investigating the operations of the Kansas City Police Department and its connection with organized crime in Kansas City. Some of the findings of this investigation can now be told. They reveal a shocking situation that should cause every member of this community great concern.

Our findings must not be interpreted as a condemnation of the entire membership of the police department, most of whom are, unquestionably, men of integrity and ability.

It is an indisputable fact that the professional criminals in Kansas City are highly organized. This criminal group is ruled by an "inner circle" commonly called "the syndicate." The "syndicate" functions like a board of directors, formulating policy and giving orders to the other members.

Within the total criminal organization there is also an "outer circle," composed of persons who possess specialized criminal talents.

Based on sworn testimony it is the belief of this jury that the Kansas City "syndicate" is probably connected with the Mafia or Black Hand Society.

Beginning in Kansas City in the early 1900's there was a small group of thugs, mostly of foreign descent, who started by preying upon members of their own national group. By means of threats of arson, bombing, beatings and murder, this parasitical element established a flourishing extortion racket.

With the coming of prohibition, the Kansas City "syndicate" turned to bootlegging and the operation of "speakeasies."

When prohibition was repealed, several members of the organization began an extensive traffic in narcotics. Other members continued their gambling and prostitution activities.

In 1943 the Federal Bureau of Narcotics successfully cracked the narcotics ring, sending several members of the organization to prison.

From the days of prohibition the "syndicate" has had an active interest in politics and exerted considerable influence in both city and county elections. Many citizens of this community will still recall the "bloody" election of March 27th, 1934, when "syndicate" hoodlums roamed the city in unlicensed black sedans slugging and killing. According to the Kansas City Star of the next day the result was four dead, 11 critically injured and countless numbers severely beaten.

The political power of the "syndicate" probably reached its zenith during the days of Charles Binaggio. Following his assasination in 1950, it became necessary for the "syndicate" to form new alliances to insure the continuation of their criminal activities.

Based on sworn testimony presented to this jury, it now seems apparent that sometime in 1953 a "deal" was made between the "syndicate" and certain members of the Kansas City, Missouri, Police department which led to the "syndicate" being permitted to operate a number of gambling and after-hours liquor establishments, control prostitution, and fence stolen merchandise in Kansas City. In return the "syndicate" supposedly promised to commit no major robberies or burglaries within the city limits.

It is the belief of this jury that it was because of this deal with the underworld that the Downtown Bridge Club, located at 1425 Baltimore, was permitted to operate for nearly five years as a gambling establishment with little or no interference from the Police Department. Although frequent police "raids" were conducted on this establishment, it is now apparent that one or more members of the Kansas City Police Department were tipping off the operators of the Bridge Club when a raid was forthcoming. Books of account kept on the Bridge Club operation reveal that on days when the Vice Squad conducted a "raid," gambling activity was usually interrupted for only a short time. In fact, some of the days when "raids" occurred were among the most profitable so far as gambling income was concerned.

The Downtown Bridge Club was only one of several permanently located "syndicate" gambling establishments here in Kansas City.

The jury also received testimony that at least five permanently located Negro commercial gambling establishments have operated here 24 hours a day, seven days a week, 365 days a year, for a number of years.

After-hours "syndicate" liquor establishments were also apparently "off limits."

    o   o   o   o   o   o   o   o   o

It further appears that "syndicate" stolen goods were not considered "hot" unless transported across state lines thus invoking a Federal violation. The "syndicate" thieves operated with considerable immunity so long as they fenced within the confines of Kansas City proper.

Prostitution, always a lucrative source of income for the "syndicate," also became highly controlled under the 1953 deal.

Based on the foregoing it appears that for the last seven or eight years the "syndicate" and its affiliates have had a "criminal playground" in Kansas City at the expense of the public.

Competent officials, with many years of experience in law enforcement, have repeatedly testified before this jury that in their opinion crime could not flourish in Kansas City to the extent that it has flourished without the connivance of some members of law enforcement agencies. It is the opinion of this jury that such connivance could only take place in exchange for a consideration over and above the mere "guarantee" by the criminal element that major crime would be kept out of Kansas City.

Section 35   **ON WALL STREET**

From "On Wall Street" by Sylvia Porter, 1959.

The gangsters of the underworld have moved into Wall Street on a scale never before known.

Mobsters with links traced to the dreaded Mafia, the Lindbergh kidnaping, the notorious "Gangland Convention" at Apalachin, N. Y., in 1957—these and others have been discovered in firms selling securities to the public in the past 18 months!

"Never has the danger to the naive little investor from the criminal element been as great as it is today," warns Louis J. Lefkowitz, the crusading, hard-hitting Attorney General of N. Y. State.

"The securities profession is one of the most honorable in New York. Millions of Americans in every State and city are now interested in buying stocks. The criminals have decided this is a perfect setup for them and are using money they've made in bootlegging, prostitution, narcotics, in so-called legitimate financial enterprises to make more quick, dirty money. The danger these elements pose must be recognized."

Just as New York is the heart of the securities business in our nation, so Lefkowitz' office is the heart of the state's securities policing system. The Attorney General's office is within walking distance of Wall Street's skyscrapers. The staff of the state's securities bureau is now working around the clock in a crash attack on known and new racketeers. To find out what is going on, I've just completed a series of interviews with Lefkowitz and his chief lieutenants. Here is the first of five reports.

The mobsters have infiltrated many securities firms and are placing in jeopardy legitimate houses headed by financially weak or unwary but still honest men.

Hundreds of thousands of gullible Americans in states across the nation have been defrauded out of many millions in recent months.

Confidence in the vitally important securities business is being undermined by the criminals. Suffering particularly are the over-the-counter firms, which in the overwhelming percentage of cases are, of course, 1,000 per cent honest.

Sounds dramatic? Sure. For it is.

The fact is, says Lefkowitz, that "a network of ex-criminals has been operating and the public must be warned!"

How could a mob take over such legitimate firms?

In the past several months, men with criminal convictions ranging from arson to kidnaping, mobsters tied to the Mafia and the 1957 "Gangland Convention" at Apalachin, N. Y., have been discovered operating in the securities business in New York.

These criminals have obtained control of established financial houses. Through these fronts, they have sold millions of dollars of worthless or near-worthless stocks to gullible victims the nation over.

"A criminal network has been successful in muscling into Wall Street in a shocking number of cases," warns New York Attorney General Louis J. Lefkowitz. "This network exists."

In yesterday's column, I named actual names of some of the hoodlums caught in crooked securities deals in the past 18 months. With understandable incredulity, I asked the Attorney General "how do they manage to get in?" Here is the pattern he gave me.

1—A first and common move by the mobsters is to seek an established, legitimate front which is vulnerable to a takeover.

The gangsters may find a firm which is in financial difficulties and arrange to have a seemingly respectable outfit lend the firm money.

Or the gangsters may move in by threatening employees with bodily harm. This was the procedure reputedly followed in the case of Lincoln Securities Corp. of 42 Broadway. Said Lefkowitz, "we received testimony from persons apparently in fear of their lives."

2—A second move of the mobsters is to put one of their own hoodlums in control of the firm.

3—A third move by the mobsters is to collect a staff of "loaders"—or high-pressure salesmen.

"This is done just by 'talk on the Street,'" Lefkowitz revealed. "These loaders have regular meeting places in key office buildings in Wall Street and uptown Manhattan. Word gets around that so-and-so needs loaders and has a hot deal and they come to be screened by the top man and told what the deal is. A top-notch loader can make as much as $3,500 a week. They're all paid in cash, all use fictitious names."

4—Then the swindlers set about getting themselves a block of worthless or near-worthless stock to promote to the public.

"The pattern is to locate a dead or near-dead corporation shell and arrange to take over the stock for a minimum amount."

So now the gangsters have a front, high-pressure salesmen, stock to sell. Now they're ready to create a market and pull in the suckers.

"How do the racketeers distribute their valueless stock?" I asked Lefkowitz and the chief of his now feverishly active securities bureau, Assistant Attorney General Carl Madonick. This is the gruesome procedure.

A first step by the swindlers is to build up a glowing picture of the company. Brochures are printed, press releases and "progress" reports are prepared. A whole library of appealing literature is set up for distribution.

Another immediate step is to get the sucker lists in readiness for later phone calls from the salesmen and perhaps for receipt of some preliminary mouth-watering material. The best salesmen come equipped with their own sucker lists. Any person's name can be on a list of prospects if he has shown he is susceptible to buying by mail or phone.

Now the big step is the creation of a national market price via fictitious quotations, phony transactions. "We had one a few weeks ago," revealed Madonick, "involving a Los Angeles promoter of the stock of Alaska Dakota Development Co., Inc. The promoters induced New York brokers to list fictitious quotations on the stock which then appeared in a publication of the National Daily Quotation Service. Stock was supplied to a securities firm in Denver which in turn supplied stock to two firms in New York. A market was made to appear for the stock at the prices quoted—which, of course, was all the salesmen needed."

And now comes the salesmen's pitch . . . Usually they gather in the New York firm around 6 p.m. to put through long-distance calls to names on their sucker lists . . . In, for instance, Iowa, a physician will pick up a phone, hear a charming and yet authoritative voice say something like:

"Dr. ——? This is Mr. So-and-So calling from New York. A friend of yours asked me to call to let you in on a hot stock my firm has at $1.25 a share. I'd like to sell you 1,000 shares but I have only 200 I could possibly allot you at this $1.25 price . . ."

If the doctor is a typical sucker, after he has listened to the loader tout the stock's prospects, he'll grab the 200 shares.

A few days later, a glowing "progress report" on the stock probably will come to the doctor's office and soon the phone will ring again.

"Dr.? Did you hear? Your stock is now $1.75!" And after a few minutes of the new spiel, the doctor is likely to be eagerly thanking So-and-So for the privilege of buying another 200 shares at $1.75 . . . And so it will go until the doctor is "loaded."

But what if the doctor wants to sell and take some "profits"?

He may get no answer when he calls So-and-So's number in New York. Or if he does reach So-and-So, he'll either be talked out of selling or told "there are no customers for your stock now."

"No customers?" . . . "Not now, we'll call you" . . .

Too late, the doctor realizes he has been taken. What happens when he complains to his banker or lawyer will be told tomorrow.

When Carl Madonick, New York Asst. Attorney General in charge of the State's Securities Bureau, and five of his staff members burst into the Wall Street office of a bunch of stock swindlers one early evening a short time ago, all they saw was a room about 15 by 18 feet in which were sitting a man who identified himself as the president of the firm and a girl receptionist.

In back of the man, though, was a wood panel and it was obvious that something was going on behind that wall. Madonick announced "This is a raid!" and specifically requested he be allowed to investigate. When the man finally consented to open a concealed door in the panel, revealed was another room about 20 by 18 which had an unmarked separate entrance. In this room were 12 telephones being used by that many men.

Racket-hating New York Attorney General Louis J. Lefkowitz' men had found another "boiler room"—so called because the noise of the men using the phones and the pressures of their sales spiel are reminiscent of a boiler.

From the phones in this boiler room, the high-pressure touts were calling all over the United States to unload hundreds of thousands of dollars of worthless stock on countless gullible investors.

Section 36 THE UNDERWORLD AND THE WAR

From *Brotherhood of Evil* by Frederic Sondern, Jr., 1959.

On a cold February evening in 1946, the S.S. Laura Keene, a tired Liberty ship, was making ready to sail from New York for Italy. It was a historic evening for the brotherhood, one which no one who witnessed it will ever forget. Charlie Lucky Luciano, former overlord of New York City's rackets and organized vice, was being deported by the United States government. No departure of royalty could have been more impressive. In front of the entrance to the pier in Brooklyn at which the Laura Keene was berthed stood a double row of burly longshoremen shoulder to shoulder with bailing hooks hanging like policemen's sidearms from their belts; they were the guard of honor. When Charlie Lucky arrived he was surrounded by a phalanx of agents of the Bureau of Immigration and Naturalization who had brought him over from Ellis Island, where he had been held for several days. It seemed that the heavy federal bodyguard was there more to protect him from the press than to prevent his escape. The big longshoremen scanned the official party, permitted it to pass. There were shouts of "You'll be back, Lucky"—"You keep punchin', boss." Then the ranks closed again to prevent newsmen from following.

What happened during the next few hours before the ship sailed still seems incredible. Big cars kept arriving with members of the top echelon of the brotherhood. Their bodyguards lugged out great baskets of wine and delicacies which grinning stevedores wheeled carefully onto the pier. Frank Costello and Albert Anastasia came to pay their respects to Don Salvatore and wish their old *compadre* well. There were others of almost equal underworld rank including prominent Mafia satellites such as Meyer Lansky, the great gambling organizer, and Joseph (Socks) Lanza, boss of the Fulton Fish Market and the Lower East Side docks. Tammany Hall was also prominently represented. The party aboard—with champagne, caviar and lobster, as reported by a federal agent—was very gay, while the longshoremen and their bailing hooks, city police and dock patrolmen kept newsmen and all others at bay. Finally the Laura Keene blew her whistle, an impressive group of cheerful gangsters gathered on the pier to wave and shout a last good-by and Don Salvatore was on his way to Italy, a new life and, supposedly oblivion.

From Washington the infinitely patient Commissioner Anslinger had watched the whole bizarre business of Charlie Lucky's parole and deportation with misgivings. Don Salvatore, even after nine years in prison, was obviously still a capo mafioso of great influence. The files of the Bureau of Narcotics on important criminals are unusual in their attention to basic traits of character. From the record the commissioner was pretty sure that he would hear from Charlie Lucky again.

The early career of the extraordinary gangster who was second only to Al Capone in organizational genius has been told many times with varying degrees of accuracy. But in even the most factual, well-informed accounts he has never been shown as the mafioso of the purest water which he is. He is and always has been the personification of the brotherhood of evil, in American dress, with all of its ruthlessness, savage cruelty, sentimentality and peculiarly twisted ideology toward God and man. He is a modern mafioso —like Adonis, Costello and the rest. But he might as well have lived in Sicily a hundred years ago—as might all of his old friends who were snared at Apalachin.

Salvatore Lucania was born in 1897 in the little Sicilian town of Lercara Friddi near Palermo. His father, Antonio, was a hard working, thrifty laborer in the sulphur pits close by. When Salvatore was nine, Antonio Lucania had saved enough to realize his ambition of years—America. By the time he was ten, young Salvatore was on the streets in the toughest section of New York City, the Lower East Side around Brooklyn Bridge. The teeming tenement district where hundreds of thousands of recent immigrants huddled in poverty and squalor was the city's center of vice and crime. Both of the boy's parents worked long hours and had little time for him, he disliked school intensely, was often a truant and a criminal career began. At 15 he was already a petty thief, an expert gang fighter with knife and stone and chief runner for an important narcotic peddler. He was caught delivering a parcel of heroin and served six months of a year's sentence in jail. This made him eligible for underworld promotion. He applied to the Five Point Gang which terrorized Little Italy around Mulberry Street, for admission. They had been watching him. Young Lucania was small for his age, with delicate hands and feet, but he was very quick, shrewd, hard and always seemed to use his head. His application was accepted.

From here on, others far more important began to watch Salvatore Lucania. One in particular, a capo mafioso named Giuseppe Masseria, saw the young man's possibilities and qualifications. First of all, he was born in Sicily, and this is still important in the brotherhood's upper echelon. Various reporters have written that this tradition has long since been wiped out; that the old "mustache Petes" have disappeared. This is not true, as the Apalachin meeting conclusively proves. They don't wear handlebar mustaches any more but the mentality of the mafiosi has not changed a bit. To this day they regard the paesano—the fellow countryman—as the most reliable associate. Secondly, young Salvatore had convincingly demonstrated on many occasions the cardinal virtues of the true mafioso: he had an iron self-control. No matter what the provocation or the emergency, the hoarse voice never rose in pitch; the cold, seemingly unblinking eyes showed no emotion whatever. The sensitive hands might flutter slightly, but that was all. Always penetratingly alert to the emotional reactions of others, he was an underworld diplomat of the first order who believed in using brains and mediation first, guns only when absolutely necessary. Even as a junior member of the Five Pointers he had been able to calm down the explosive young hoodlums, and the older ones as well, who liked a fight for the battle's sake, and without seeming to, had begun to guide them into disciplined and lucrative racketeering.

By the early 1920's, Salvatore Lucania had emerged as Giuseppe Masseria's chief of staff and, at a remarkably early age, a power to be reckoned with in the grand council of the brotherhood in New York. A few bloody years followed, as in Chicago, while the bootlegging empire of the eastern seaboard was being organized. After at least a hundred murders and untold mayhem of various kinds, Giuseppe Masseria was established as the area's principal capo mafioso and Lucania as his crown prince. It was a powerful team. The squat, crude, older man with little pig's eyes, who could consume three heaping platters of spaghetti at one sitting, had great seniority in the brotherhood and a fearsome reputation for ruthless and efficient killing that went back to 1905. Young Salvatore became his brains, his memory and his constant companion—but always, as far as the police and public were concerned, in the shadows. Very few, even in the underworld's upper reaches, knew of the great influence that he was beginning to exert on the New York mafioso's thinking and operations. Like Al Capone, he was a businessman of crime and a superb executive. He had the same sense of tidy organization and orderly chain of command. But unlike the noisy Neopolitan, the basically austere Sicilian preferred anonymity—not only for business reasons but from personal preference.

With the weight of Don Giuseppe Masseria's influence behind him and his own uninhibited imagination, he—again like Capone in Chicago—started a gradual expansion of the brotherhood's activities from bootlegging into other fields of Prohibition. He had two friends who were also growing power-

ful, Joe Adonis and Albert Anastasia, the coming boss of Murder, Incorporated. The three Sicilians had all sorts of projects for organized gambling, a
chain of brothels, large-scale narcotics peddling, "protection" extortion on
New York's docks, in the garment industry and the big food markets. The
aging capo, Masseria, didn't like it. He thought that the boys were going too
far too fast and said so with all the authority of a don. They refused to obey
and he began putting obstacles in their way. The inevitable happened.

An ancient rule of the brotherhood requires a capo mafioso to step down
when age impairs his initiative. If he retires gracefully, as many have, he
can look forward to a peaceful twilight of life with the position of a respected
elder statesman who is consulted by the new executives and often acts as
impartial arbitrator in their disputes. If he does not withdraw voluntarily,
he is traditionally given one warning—the assassination, generally, of a minor
assistant. Don Giuseppe had his late in 1930 when one of his bodyguards
was cut down in ambush from which he himself could not have escaped if
his death had been decreed. But the capo was stubborn; he had no intention
of laying down the reins. One day in April 1931, therefore, Charlie Lucky
invited him to dinner at Scarpato's, an excellent Italian restaurant in Coney
Island. The capo liked plenty of food and wine; it was late before they
finished and the dining room was almost empty. Charlie Lucky went to wash
his hands. He was unquestionably and probably in the men's room when
three men materialized behind the tiddly don's chair, methodically emptied
their revolvers into him and as rapidly disappeared. By the time Lucania
dashed out, as he told the police a few minutes later, the killers were gone
and his beloved old patron was very dead. None of the restaurant's staff could
give even the vaguest description of the men. All they did know, and very
definitely, was that Mr. Lucania had been in the washroom. It was the perfect example of a Mafia execution carried out in the traditional manner. By
ancient custom a ranking mafioso when condemned by his own brotherhood
must be killed, if at all possible, humanely and unexpectedly, and preferably
after plenty of food and wine. It has always been so, and still is.

Salvatore Lucania by succession was now a capo mafioso of the first
class. His extraordinary rise to racketeering and political power during the
next years was less spectacular than that of Capone in Chicago had been,
but it was more careful and thorough. With the flexibility of a new generation
of mafiosi which had grown out of American influences on the brotherhood's
original exclusiveness, Charles Luciano, as he now began to call himself,
realized that he had to work out a system of peaceful coexistence with the
non-Italian gangs of New York; until they could be subjugated or sup-
pressed, that is. Various reporters who have written about the brotherhood
believe that the Mafia as such came to an end during this period; that its
membership became simply a part of a nationwide syndicate of criminals of

all races and kinds. This seems, on the basis of much evidence, an incorrect assumption. The story of organized crime in the United States from Luciano through the Apalachin meeting up to this writing indicates that the brotherhood has not deviated from its essential principles by a degree. Capone and Luciano changed its methods, modernized them, but basically Salvatore Lucania was just as much of a mafioso as Giuseppe Masseria of the previous generation.

Before long Charlie Luciano had working arrangements not only with his fellow mafiosi, but also with such un-Sicilian associates as Louis (Lepke) Buchalter, dictator of the garment center rackets; Meyer Lansky of New York gambling; Longy Zwillman of various New Jersey gangs and very powerful; the Scalici brothers of the Brooklyn docks (they were Sicilians) and others. It was the first of the big racket syndicates perfected by Luciano in the post-Capone period. Its members quickly realized the advantages of this sort of arrangement and subscribed to it. In New York the destructive internecine warfare stopped abruptly. The idea of large-scale economic dividends—developed by Al Capone and worked into a permanent pattern by Savatore Lucania—spread through the country's racket combines from coast to coast. Meetings of gang leaders not only of states but from whole sections of the nation became increasingly frequent; so did long distance telephone calls, as recent investigations have shown.

Many writers have lumped these groups together and called them The National Syndicate or just The Syndicate. Actually, what Capone and Lucania inspired by their examples is a number of syndicates, all continually in touch with each other. On careful examination, one finds that almost every one of them is either dominated or strongly influenced by a group of mafiosi. Senator Estes Kefauver after many months of investigation wrote that "the Mafia is the cement that binds organized crime." And the men who perfected this peculiar kind of cement were Capone and Lucania.

Salvatore Lucania made another important contribution to the top bracket of the brotherhood and its associates. He radically changed their dress and their manners. He became the underworld's exemplary Beau Brummel, in a quiet way. His suits were conservative and well tailored; his shirts, ties, shoes and accessories were expensive but not ostentatious. The wide-brimmed fedoras and odd overcoats which had been the mafioso's uniform for so long had already begun to disappear, and the quietly elegant Mr. Luciano carried the trend further. Everybody who worked for him, as he is reported to have once said to his immediate staff, "has to look legit." This precept has been maintained by the brotherhood ever since. He influenced the brotherhood's manners in the same way. Under his chairmanship a meeting of the heads of various cartels at the Waldorf Astoria—where, as Mr. Charles Ross, he lived for a number of years in an apartment suite—

became a far more austere gathering than a convention of industrial executives in the same hotel might have been.

The detailed story of the rise and fall of Charlie Lucky Luciano—his nickname stems from his extraordinary luck in gambling with cards and horses—has been told so often that only the barest chronology of it seems necessary here.

By 1935, "Mr. Charles Ross" in his elaborate headquarters in the Waldorf Astoria was one of the most powerful capi mafiosi which the brotherhood has ever produced. He was master of the most lucrative of the New York rackets. No gambling operation, no important dock or garment extortion could be organized without his permission and a provision for his cut. He had ironclad protection from Tammany Hall which extended from New York City to Albany. Frequently, members of the New York judiciary and sachems from the Hall would attend his morning levees, which as the hotel staff later testified, had a regal air. Don Salvatore had reached the pinnacle. He might have stayed there for quite a while had he not made, despite all his caution and perspicacity, two very serious mistakes.

Prostitution has been a specialty of the Sicilian brotherhood for two centuries. It is regarded by the mafiosi as a business as inevitable and reliable as that of the mortician, in which they have always been interested. Charlie Lucky as a youngster on the Lower East Side had been, besides thief and narcotics runner, a messenger and solicitor for a number of brothels. He had learned the business from the ground up, its economics and personnel problems. As he rose to the New York overlordship, he realized that organized prostitution could earn almost as much as gambling, narcotics or extortion. With three stalwart mafiosi as field generals, he put together the largest combine of brothels in the history of this or probably any other country. At the height of its operations, more than 200 madams and well over 1,000 girls were paying tribute to Charlie Lucky's organization from a business which grossed approximately $10,000,000 a year. Charlie Lucky, however, was too greedy. The madams had to pay too much for protection, and the girls had little take-home money. The strong-arm methods of Davey Betillo —Charlie Lucky's executive officer for this division—which produced brutal beatings and slashings for the slightest defection or failure to pay was finally more than the girls could take, and rebellion began to simmer. "Mr. Ross" in his luxurious eyrie at the Waldorf, surrounded by obsequious assistants, did not sense the growing unrest and its menace. "Whores is whores," he said on one occasion over a tapped telephone. "They can always be handled. They ain't got no guts." This was his first mistake.

Charlie Lucky liked the company of prostitutes and constantly had them in his entourage. That was his second mistake. He regarded all of them as "dumb broads" and thought nothing of making telephone calls and conducting business with his assistants in their presence. Unfortunately for him, several women like Nancy Presser, Cokey Flo Brown, and Mildred Harris were neither stupid nor without courage. He had abused them all, finally, with contempt. Their peculiar prostitute's pride was offended. They all had excellent memories.

In 1935 New York City went through one of its infrequent revulsions against chronically inefficient and dishonest government. A special grand jury brushed aside the regular district attorney and demanded a special prosecutor. Thomas E. Dewey was appointed. He soon found that Charlie Lucky Luciano was his main objective; that almost all of New York's organized crime stemmed from the sleek, apparently untouchable Mr. Ross of the Waldorf. Dewey's brilliant investigation and prosecution of the great capo mafioso is history. Charles Lucania was indicted for the crime of compulsory prostitution, tried in General Sessions Court and found guilty on sixty-two counts. The prostitutes that Charlie Lucky had regarded as such harmless trash were superbly convincing witnesses. Dewey could also have prosecuted for narcotics trading and extortion on a huge scale, but the white slavery charge was the easiest to prove, aroused the greatest public indignation and would bring the most severe penalty. Before pronouncing sentence Judge McCook fastened the cool, immaculate don with his eyes. "You are," he said quietly but with venom, "one of the most vicious criminals that has ever been brought before this court. It is the sentence of this court . . . 30 to 50 years . . ." The judge thought that he was handing down the equivalent of a sentence for life. He did not reckon with the don's ingenuity, lawyers, connections—or his position as a capo mafioso.

Charlie Lucky disappeared from public view in the State Penitentiary at Dannemora, a maximum security prison known to New York felons as "Siberia." It is an interesting fact that a big-time racketeer maintains his prestige and certain privileges even behind the walls. Many chores are done for him by fellow convicts, he becomes an arbiter of disputes, his advice far more sought than that of the chaplain. "He practically ran the place," a guard who saw much of Charlie Lucky told us once. "He used to stand there in the yard like he was the warden. Men waited in line to talk to him. Charlie Lucky would listen, say something and then wave his hand. The guy would actually *back* away. It was something to watch. The real mob boys when they were about to be discharged would always have a last talk with the Boss, as they all called him. He was sort of philosophical about the whole thing. He thought he was going to be there for a long time and tried to make the best of it." The coming of World War II did not excite Charlie Lucky. He had no idea of what it was going to do for him or that it was going to make him, at least for a while, an asset to the United States government.

The value of Don Salvatore's war effort has been the subject of much controversy. Some writers have claimed that it was outstanding, others that it was negligible. The truth seems to lie in between.

In 1942 an unusual group of men gathered in the headquarters of the Bureau of Naval Intelligence for the 3rd Naval District, which covered New York, New Jersey and the largest and most important eastern seaports. Among them were former prosecutors, FBI and Treasury agents, city detectives—all handpicked for the almost superhuman job of protecting the miles of docks which were the anchor of our lifeline to Europe, and of stifling the sources of information which Hitler's intelligence services had set up in the New York area. Sabotage on the piers was increasing. The huge French liner *Normandie,* which was being converted into a troopship capable of carrying an entire division, burned and sank at her Manhattan berth. Accurate information on sailing dates and cargoes of ships leaving New York was reaching the cordon of German submarines which then virtually controlled the eastern seaboard and sank our and British shipping almost at will. At a meeting of the harassed Naval Intelligence staff at 90 Church Street one day, someone advanced the idea of enlisting the tightly organized New York-New Jersey dock underworld in the struggle. The Annapolis professional police officers saw the possibilities at once. No force could patrol the vulnerable piers and ships as effectively as the tough, alert longshoremen, truckers and watchmen who knew every inch of them. The waterfront prostitutes and their pimps could be a counter-intelligence corps, if properly organized, of the first order. An unusually shrewd and courageous officer, the late Lieutenant Commander Charles Haffenden, USNR, appointed himself coordinator of the whole extraordinary operation.

It was not easy to pick an underworld autocrat of the caliber that the Navy needed. He had to be a patriotic reliable crook. Haffenden and his staff finally chose Joseph (Socks) Lanza, an immensely energetic organizer whose predominantly Italian gangs controlled the huge Fulton Fish Market and the docks on Manhattan's Lower East Side. Lanza, who was under indictment at the time for extortion, accepted and proceeded to do an excellent job. Longshoremen, under orders from Lanza, became among the Navy's most vigilant patrolmen and agents. The fishermen who supplied the market and knew the offshore waters as only they can, formed a first-class observer corps. The organization was so successful that Haffenden wanted to expand it to the critical piers of Brooklyn, the West Side of Manhattan and Jersey across the Hudson. Here, however, the planners at 90 Church Street ran into a wall of underworld resistance. Even Lanza, with all his power and connections, was unable to breach it. The racketeers in control, many of them mafiosi, regarded the Navy—war or no war, and despite the fact that they hated Mussolini—as part of government and law, and therefore anathema. Lanza had a suggestion. There was only one man who had sufficient authority to solve the problem—and that was Charlie Lucky Luciano. The more conservative elements at 90 Church Street had misgivings, to say the least. The idea of the United States Navy approaching the exwhoremaster-general of New York— in prison at that—seemed too fantastic. It was done nevertheless.

Most of the details of what happened from here on are still classified information in unapproachable Pentagon files. An angry Senator Estes Kefauver, with all the authority of a congressional investigating committee behind him, tried to get at the facts in 1951. He had little success. The Navy, members of District Attorney Hogan's office and everybody else who really knew anything were and remain vague for a good reason. It was a very embarrassing business.

The main features of the story are clear enough. At the Navy's request, Charlie Lucky was suddenly transferred from Dannemora, in the farthest corner of New York State, to the equally secure but more accessible Great Meadows Penitentiary just north of Albany. Every few weeks a small group of naval officers in civilian clothes headed by his old friend and lawyer, Moses Polakoff, would go to visit him. These conferences were arranged with utmost caution and secrecy. Various writers have published quotes from the conversations—all entirely spurious. But there is no doubt that Charlie Lucky unlocked doors for 90 Church Street. A few words from the capo mafioso to such mighty *compadri* as Joe Adonis, Vincenzo Mangano—dictator of the Brooklyn docks—and Albert Anastasia of Murder, Inc. would have brought immediate compliance. Most of these messages were probably carried by Counselor Polakoff, who has long occupied a unique position of trust among New York's racketeers, having defended the most prominent of them over three decades. Others went out over the extraordinary communications system which powerful gangsters seem to be able to maintain with the outside in even the most closely guarded prison. The details are conjecture and always will be. In any case, the arrangement seems to have been effective. There was surprisingly little sabotage or any other trouble on the docks of the 3d Naval District during the remainder of the war. Various Nazi intelligence officers interrogated in Germany after the war, incidentally, commented on the extreme difficulty which their agents had in doing any damage in New York at all. They had thought that the teeming port would be an easy sabotage target, with plenty of American *Bund* members to place incendiaries and delayed-action bombs. It wasn't. According to the German chiefs, some of whom we interrogated, their men were discouraged by the vigilance of a very tough and violent, as they put it with amazement, group of Italians.

In 1945, counselors Polakoff and Wolf brought the case of Charles Lucania before the New York State Parole Board. It was a long and difficult hearing. The witnesses—racketeers, law officers, lawyers and Charlie Lucky himself alike—were all amazingly mute when it came to details. Finally, however, the board came to several conclusions. Charles Lucania had definitely made a contribution to the war effort. It was customary in New York to deport a criminal alien after he had served a substantial part of his sentence, and that under the circumstances nine years should be regarded as such. And finally, the board thought, Charlie Lucky exiled to Italy for life could do no further damage to the United States. Governor Dewey, although as district attorney he had convicted Charlie Lucky in the first place and should have known his character as well as anyone, concurred. The governor granted parole and the federal authorities ordered deportation. Charlie Lucky, like many mafiosi, had never bothered to become an American citizen.

Section 37 PATTERN OF POWER

From *Waterfront Priest* by Allen Raymond, 1955.

For almost a generation, before the arrival of Father Corridan at the Xavier School, the one man along New York's waterfront who typified untouchable power to veteran West Side longshoremen was William J. McCormack. "Big Bill" was a multimillionaire industrialist, born of lowly origin within their own neighborhood. Their eyes followed his rise.

The one man who symbolized to those old-timers a somewhat smaller power was their union president, Joseph P. Ryan, or "Joe." He also had been brought up in their neighborhood and they had watched him climb.

These old-timers knew that McCormack and Ryan had worked together as political and business allies on both sides of the harbor, in New Jersey and New York. They knew that of the two men, McCormack had always been the stronger, the tougher, and the smarter. "Big Bill" was the leader and Joe Ryan the follower.

For most of these years McCormack was seldom in the public eye. His climb to great riches drew very few newspaper headlines. Ryan, the follower, was often in the news as a labor-union leader and politician. Although McCormack admits today to 64 years of age and might be even five or six years older than that, the newspaper reading public heard very little of him until the great scandals uncovered officially by the New York State Crime Commission in the early 1950's began to reveal themselves. Then suddenly he became known as the harbor's "Mr. Big," or, by his own words, "The Little Man's Port Authority."

According to a brief biography of McCormack, for which he paid a press agent in 1952, New York harbor's "Mr. Big" was born in New York in 1890. He was the son of one Andrew McCormack who migrated to New York from County Monaghan, Ireland, after the Irish potato famine of 1849. His mother was Julia Moran, a second-generation Irish-American, whom Andrew McCormack married here after his arrival.

The elder McCormack was a wagon driver. He never emerged from poverty. After 39 years of work, six days a week, ten to 12 hours a day, he was hospitalized for a while. His employer let him go and paid him only seven dollars and one half of his final week's pay, since he had only worked three days.

Then and there, young Bill, the youngest of four children, two boys and two girls, vowed he never would let such a thing happen to himself. When he grew up he was going to be one of the bosses, and independently wealthy. He had gone to work when he was ten years old, delivering meat before and after school and on Sunday mornings for two dollars a week. At 13 he quit school to become a wagon boy. A juvenile Hercules, he became a wagon driver at 15. At 16 he owned his own one-horse truck. By that time his family had moved to Jersey City. He and his older brother, Harry, went to work as teamsters in the perishable vegetable market in Jersey City, known as the "Peach Yard."

In those days fights and physical violence were a normal part of the teamster's life along the waterfront: The two McCormack brothers soon became known on the Jersey City piers as two of the hardiest brawlers in the neighborhood. They were always ready to use their fists to reinforce their words in any argument. They also had business acumen. When Bill McCormack was 20 he owned three teams of horses. When he was 23 he bought out a trucking company which had 15 wagons and 30 horses.

In those years he became a close friend of Frank Hague, who for many years was mayor of Jersey City, undisputed boss of Hudson County politics, and one of the most influential Democratic Party politicians in the eastern part of the United States. He also became a stanch friend of Dan Casey, who for many years was Mayor Hague's chief of police. Before they were 30, both McCormack brothers were stout pillars in Frank Hague's political machine, and their trucking business grew prosperous.

By the time World War I had rolled around, their trucking concern was large enough to handle most of the meat shipped to the AEF. In 1920, right after World War I, McCormack joined with several other truckers in forming the U. S. Trucking Corporation, installing himself as executive vice-president in charge of labor relations. The then-Governor Alfred E. Smith had just been defeated for governor by Nathan L. Miller, Republican. McCormack, and his friends, made Al Smith the president, or front man, for their company. Thereby they showed an acute perception of the value of political prestige to any concern which wants to grow rich along the New York waterfront.

When Smith was re-elected governor in 1922, he made McCormack, his former business associate, chairman of the New York State Boxing Commission's License Committee. This committee had absolute authority over licenses to everyone, fighters, managers, handlers, referees, judges, and promoters, in professional boxing.

By 1927, when a great building boom was under way in New York, McCormack sold out his interest in the U. S. Trucking Corporation. He went into the sand and gravel business. He was a great friend of the late Sam Rosoff, builder of many New York subways—an occupation which also requires political connections of a very high order. He also became a great friend of an Italo-American newspaper publisher and politician who was in the sand and gravel business, Generoso Pope. Soon after entering the business, McCormack began supplying ready-mixed concrete to builders of all kinds.

In 1930, through contacts, partly political, which he had formed while in the trucking business, he obtained the contract to handle all the stevedoring business of the Pennsylvania Railroad, largest shippers into the metropolitan area. This contract brought him back into the handling of a large part of the city's perishable food products, along the piers of the Hudson River, where he had worked as a lowly wagon driver's helper when a boy of 13. In 1932 he organized the Jersey Contracting Company which took over the handling of all the Pennsylvania Railroad's work on the Jersey side of the harbor. Entry into the oil-distribution business followed swiftly. Today a chain of McCormack-owned filling stations is the largest independent chain in New York. Bill McCormack's business enterprises in New York today include the following:

The Transit-Mix Concrete Company; Penn Stevedoring Company; Jersey Contracting Company; William J. McCormack Sand Company, which dredges sand from the bottom of Long Island Sound, and the Morania Oil Tanker Company, which is named for Julia Frances Moran, his mother. He also is president of the Lincoln Fields Race Track in Chicago, but is said to serve this institution without salary. All told, his enterprises are said to gross some 20 million dollars a year, and McCormack personally is reputed to have rolled up a fortune of many millions.

Joe Ryan, the protégé and friend of Bill McCormack, although neither so tough nor so smart as the man above him, was tough enough to manage most of the men on the docks, because of the gunmen under him or political pals.

Ryan, the child of Irish immigrants, was born in Babylon, Long Island, May 11, 1884. Both his parents died before he was nine years old. A stepmother brought him to Manhattan, where he lived through his early years in Chelsea.

Chelsea and Greenwich Village are close enough together on the Lower West Side so that they merge into each other almost imperceptibly. Ryan and McCormack are known to have been acquaintances in boyhood. Their friendship only ripened as Ryan became a labor-union leader, after World War I.

Ryan went through several of the primary grades in the Xavier Parochial School. He left school when only 12. For a time he swept floors, was a stock boy and clerk in several stores, and then became a conductor on a cross-town trolley car. He was 28 years old before he got his first job on the docks. Like McCormack, Joe Ryan was then a big and powerful man, known to be handy with his fists.

He worked on the docks for less than a year. Then while he was working the hold of one of the ships, at 15 dollars for a 60 hour week, a load of lead ingots was dropped on his foot, so that for a short time he was sent to a hospital. He had bought a membership in the I.L.A. in 1916 for only two and a half dollars. That was the going rate for a union book. In later years he was wont to jocularly refer to this purchase as the finest investment he ever made.

A friendly official of the old I.L.A., knowing Ryan to be penniless and liking him, as countless acquaintances have liked him since, got him the post of financial secretary for the Chelsea local of the I.L.A. No. 791. This was then a part-time job. Soon afterward he was advanced to full-time work as an organizer at 30 dollars a week. It was the most money Ryan had made in all his life. He then discovered his natural talent. He was good at a certain type of sentimental and humorous oratory, and he was grand as a politician—meaning a go-between, or fixer. He made himself solid as a faithful henchman of the Democratic Party organization of Manhattan known as Tammany Hall.

By 1927 Ryan became president of the I.L.A. by favor of local leaders who controlled its inner politics. He was never popular with the rank and file. By 1943 the local leaders made him president for life, at a salary of 20,000 dollars a year, plus 7,200 dollars for expenses. This money was only a small part of the financial rewards of his office, as the public hearings of the New York State Crime Commission were to reveal in 1953.

Ryan, like McCormack, was always a good churchman. In New York politics that is an asset. He has for years been a trustee of the Shrine Church of the Sea, where his good friend, the Right Reverend Monsignor John J. O'Donnell, is pastor. Monsignor O'Donnell, as honorary member of Ryan's I.L.A. and as chaplain of the port, has been stanch in Ryan's defense at all times. Ryan with a wife and two daughters is also known as a good family man. He also has been capable of outbursts of generosity toward poorer acquaintances during his own times of affluence.

A big, burly barrel of a man, fat in his later years but with plenty of brawn, Ryan in affluence went in for Cadillacs and suits and shirts of the finest tailoring. He developed a penchant for dining and wining long and heartily at such restaurants as Toots Shor's in midtown Manhattan, and Cavanagh's on West 23rd Street. Cavanagh's has been a hangout for influential Tammany politicians as well as a haunt for discerning gourmets for more than a generation. Ryan also became a member of the Elks, the New York Athletic Club, and the Winged Foot Golf Club in Westchester County.

Beyond all else he became the so-called "standard-bearer" of the Joseph P. Ryan Association. This was a political club with two paramount and intertwined obectives: to advance the fortunes of Tammany Hall and Joseph P. Ryan.

The Joseph P. Ryan Association, with the aid of the Central Trades and Labor Council, waxed fat in political power. It gave an annual dinner and dance for many years, either at the Hotel Commodore or the Waldorf Astoria. This dinner-dance was a great deal more than a festive occasion. It served to dramatize, once a year, the great power and influence which Ryan and his closest associates wielded in New York City's government; their affiliations with businessmen of undoubted means and some respectability; and their influence over thugs and murderers. A sprinkling of murderous hoodlums was always at these Ryan dinners in close proximity to judges of the courts, district attorneys, heads of city and borough governments, and ranking bureaucrats in the city's many governmental departments. For many years the chairman of the committee of arrangements for this festive occasion was Ryan's great and good friend, Big Bill McCormack.

Although these dinners were given always in Ryan's honor, the real insiders of New York politics knew since the middle 1930's certainly, that Big Bill McCormack, the rising industrialist, was a bigger man than the guest of honor, Chairman of the committee on arrangements was a very good title for him. Back in 1931 there were two chairmen of the dinner, Mayor Jimmy Walker of New York and Mayor Frank Hague of Jersey City.

In 1937 the late Mayor F. H. La Guardia and his police commissioner, Edward P. Mulrooney were listed as guests at Table 26. The late "Cockeye" Dunn, murderer, was a member of the committee on arrangements. Philip Mangano, another murderer now gone to his reward but then a flourishing member of the Anastasia-Adonis mob, sat at Table 80.

In 1938 Mayor La Guardia stayed away. But Mayor O'Dwyer was at the dinner in 1950, sitting at Ryan's own table. Mayor Vincent Impellitteri was a regular attendant at the dinners for years. In 1948 the listed diners included Police Commissioner Wallander, United States Attorney McGohey, District Attorney Miles McDonald of Brooklyn, District Attorney Frank Hogan of Manhattan, District Attorney Foley of the Bronx, and District Attorney Sullivan of Queens. Charles Yanowsky, the Alcatraz graduate who was then running the Jersey City waterfront, sat at Table 115.

The dinner of 1951, on the very eve of the State Crime Commission's investigations, was as good as any. Its committeemen and guests, drawn from political and business life and the underworld, suffice to show the pattern of power which has governed the New York harbor for two generations. Once again, McCormack headed the arrangements committee. Harry M. Durning, Collector of the Port, was a vice-chairman. Members of the committee included Harold Beardell, president of J. T. Clark & Son, a stevedoring concern, who testified openly before the New York Crime Commission of his money payments to union officials. Frank Nolan, president of the Jarka Stevedoring Company, since then convicted of commercial bribery; Eddie Florio, Ryan's old bootlegger henchman from Hoboken, later in prison on a perjury rap; William J. Tracey, a big tugboat magnate; and Hugh E. Sheridan, impartial chairman of the trucking industry.

The dinner-dance committee was equally eminent. Its chairman was John J. Casale, a boss trucker. Vice-chairmen? The five borough presidents of Manhattan, including Robert J. Wagner, now mayor.

Others on this committee were Mike Clemente, the perjurer now serving five to ten years, Inspector McQuade of the New York Police Department, and John Mangiamelli, an I.L.A. leader who later pleaded guilty of stealing union funds. Also "Connie" Noonan, who refused to answer questions at the Crime Commission hearings on the ground his answers might tend to incriminate him.

The chairman of the entertainment committee was Colonel Ivan Annenberg, circulation manager of the New York *Daily News*. The vice-chairman was the Honorable Albert Goldman, United States Postmaster. Members of their committee included Harold Bowers, business agent for the I.L.A. "Pistol Local"; and Anthony V. Camarda, head of one of the Anastasia locals in Brooklyn who was later jailed for stealing union funds.

The two chairmen of the reception committee were the Honorable Hugo E. Rogers, a former leader of Tammany Hall, and the Honorable Charles W. Culkin, a great Tammany power. Two of the members of their committee were Willie Cox, a pier loader who once served a term in Elmira for biting off an opponent's ear during a brawl on a New York excursion steamer, and Inspector Herbert Golden of the New York Police Department.

Guests at this dinner included Chief Magistrate John Murtagh, John A. Coleman, former governor of the New York Stock Exchange, Carmine De Sapio, current boss of Tammany, and "Joe the Gent," I.L.A. leader in Newark.

The dinner of 1952 was the last of the dinners. In 1953 Father Corridan was speaking on waterfront problems at a dinner of hotel executives in the Hotel Commodore. He was introduced as the man who had knocked the Joe Ryan dinner out of the city's social life.

"As a result of this," the toastmaster said, "the grand ballroom of the Commodore is now available next Saturday night."

Reporters for years got chuckles from these dinners, because of the odd mixture of businessmen, politicians, and widely known thugs to be found there. In recent years reporters were not welcome. But as recently as 1950 Governor Thomas E. Dewey of New York was sufficiently cognizant of the political power represented on these occasions so that he sent his polite regrets to Ryan at being "unable to attend."

The governor's letter follows:

> Dear Joe:
> I would surely be delighted to come to the annual affair of the Joseph P. Ryan Association on Saturday, May 20th if possible. As it happens, Mrs. Dewey and I have accepted an invitation to the marriage of Lowell Thomas's only son that week-end and we just can't possibly make it.
> It is mighty nice of you to ask me and I wish you would give my regards to all the fine people at the dinner.
> On behalf of the people of the entire state, I congratulate you and thank you for what you have done to keep the Communists from getting control of the New York waterfront. Be assured that the entire machinery of the Government of New York State is behind you and your organization in this determination.
> With warm regards,
>
> > Sincerely yours,
> > Thomas E. Dewey

This letter was written by a New York politician who had ridden to power on his reputation as a racket-buster when in the district attorney's office as they still were flourishing when he wrote the letter as governor. It was carefully written, sending regards only to the "fine people" at the dinner and ignoring the others.

To many the Ryan dinner was a symbol of either Ryan's or McCormack's power. But to Father Corridan it epitomized the moral corruption which, leechlike, was sucking away the life blood of the harbor. It sickened him,

Father Corridan says, to "see that same corrupt influence extended in recent years to some of the harbor's Catholic communion breakfasts."

"It was in early 1950," Father Corridan remembers, "that a Chelsea longshoreman, 'Happy' Donahue, came to me and asked for advice on how to run a longshore communion breakfast. I suggested three simple rules to protect the integrity of the occasion.

"First, the committee running the breakfast should be composed of strict rank-and-file longshoremen. Their chairman should be a man well over 60 known to have no political ambitions, a man respected by the longshoremen as a 'God-fearing' man.

"Second, the mass preceding the breakfast should be rotated among the waterfront churches, to help every pastor to build up his church, spiritually and materially.

"Third, at the breakfast itself, no union or company official should be seated on the dais.

"There is no differentiation at the altar rail," Father Corridan told Donahue, "and there should be no differentiation at the communion breakfast. Let them keep that for their political dinners."

On May 7, 1950, the first longshore communion breakfast was run, with honor given to much the same cast of characters as appeared at the Ryan dinners. What grieved Father Corridan, he says, was not the fact that many of those listed on the program as "Our Guests," were later revealed in the State Crime Commission hearings to be poor advertisements for virtue.

"It was the fact," Father Corridan says, "that independent of any Crime Commission revelations, the longshoremen knew the unjust dealings of those men on a daily basis for years. When one longshoreman said to me, 'Father, some of the biggest bums we have in the harbor, both in the union and in management, were honored at the breakfast this morning,' I shared in his bitter frustration. I recalled Pius XI's admonition:

> " 'For there are some who, while exteriorly faithful to the practice of their religion, yet in the field of labor and industry, in the professions, trade, and business, permit a deplorable cleavage in their conscience and live a life too little in conformity with the clear principles of justice and Christian charity.
>
> " 'Such lives are a scandal to the weak, and to the malicious a pretext to discredit the church.' "

Later in the early fall of 1950 Father Corridan was invited by a pastor in Newark to be the principal speaker at the first longshore communion breakfast in Port Newark. "I had to decline," says Father Corridan, "because I knew that the cochairmen of the breakfast, Pat Ferrone and Joe the Gent, business agents of the Newark I.L.A. locals, had just shaken down some fur importers for 70,000 dollars. A year or so later Joe the Gent had died in such circumstances that he had to be refused Christian burial."

The communion breakfast, however, that violated all the norms of religious decency, Father Corridan says, was the twenty-eighth communion breakfast of the United States Customs Service. It was held on March 24, 1952. A short time before, the New York State Board of Inquiry had published its report on the corrupt conditions which caused the 1951 wildcat strike.

Another Jesuit, Father Laurence J. McGinley, president of Fordham University, Father Corridan remembers, was asked to waive his rule of not speaking at communion breakfasts. Father McGinley consented to give a spiritual talk on the assurance there would be no political atmosphere in the occasion.

"That breakfast reeked with the cheapest kind of politics, as anyone could gather from reading the New York *Times* on the following day," Father Corridan says.

According to this *Times* report, Harry M. Durning, Collector of the Port and a speaker at the breakfast, "denied allegations that the New York waterfront is a racket-ridden community."

"Referring to newspaper and magazine articles that pictured the New York waterfront as a haven for criminals and racketeers, Mr. Durning said they were part of a widespread campaign to drive business away from New York to other seaports. He characterized the whole idea as an effort to knock down the port for selfish reasons."

The New York *Times* account went on to say that Edward F. Cavanagh, Jr., Commissioner of the city's Marine and Aviation Department, was another government official who spoke in similar tenor at the breakfast.

"The Commissioner took sharp issue with 'individuals who, with little or no knowledge of the facts and, for purposes of their own, find the New York waterfront a cesspool of iniquity,'" the *Times* narrative ran. "'I have no illusions about the political aspects of the situation,' Mr. Cavanagh said. 'Of course, with millions of dollars going to our allies there are legislators who are anxious to see their states get the business.'

"Mr. Cavanagh admitted that certain types of crime have existed along the waterfront, but suggested that further facts be obtained before any conclusion was reached."

At the time of that breakfast, attacks on Big Bill McCormack, as "Mr. Big" of the waterfront, were beginning to be spread through magazines and newspapers. Mr. McCormack was on the dais. Mr. Durning asked him to stand up and take a bow. McCormack obliged. Then the Collector of the Port continued:

> "Bill is a very able man, a religious man, a family man, and a patriotic American who has worked on the port for 40 years. New York City and the country at large are under obligation to him, not only for what he did during the war years, but what he did during the administration of Mayor La Guardia, Mayor O'Dwyer, and Mayor Impellitteri."

Mr. Durning had praise, too, for Joseph P. Ryan, as president of the International Longshoremen's Association. Durning said he had known Ryan as he had known McCormack for about 30 years. Ryan, he continued, was also a very good friend of his, although he did not always see eye to eye with him. He predicted that there would be some improvements worked out in regard to problems involving longshoremen. Then he asked two United States district attorneys, Myles J. Lane of Manhattan and Frank J. Parker of Brooklyn, who also were seated on the dais, to stand up. Both men did.

If there were any corruption on the waterfront, Mr. Durning said, "these two outstanding public-spirited citizens would start proceedings."

"If religion is on the decline as a moral influence in the lives of many people, breakfasts such as these, as much as the corrupt conditions on the waterfront, are a cause," Father Corridan says.

PART VI

THE MAFIA

WHILE THE TRIAL of the Apalachinites, as well as the multiple inquiries preceding the trial, provided no legal evidence as to the true purpose and proceedings of the conclave, official speculation holds that Apalachin was the site of a Grand Council of the Mafia.

"It has been speculated . . . that the gathering was a meeting of the so-called 'Mafia,' of which at least eight of the participants are identified, in various *law enforcement agency files,* as leading members," noted the Reuter report.

The sedate *New York Times* announced in headlines "27 Apalachin Men Indicted by U.S. in Drive on Mafia" (*New York Times,* May 25, 1959). The lead sentence declared that "the Federal Government moved yesterday to smash what it called the largest crime syndicate in the United States—a branch of the Sicilian underworld organization, the Mafia."

"Although the Federal Bureau of Narcotics is certain that the private party (at Apalachin) was, in reality, a meeting of the *Mafia* Grand Council, today it is still far from proving it. Such is the veil of secrecy that surrounds the *Mafia,*" comments Judge John M. Murtagh, Chief Magistrate of the City of New York (Murtagh and Harris, Sara, *Who Live in Shadow,* p. 80).

In his very knowledgeable *Treasury Agent,* Andrew Tully entitles the Apalachin chapter, "The Mafia Meets."

"The *Mafia* is very real indeed," states Frederic Sondern in the Preface to his *Brotherhood of Evil,* "and has been for a long time, to Commissioner Harry J. Anslinger of Narcotics, Chief U. E. Baughman of Secret Service" and to others. The first chapter of this book, subtitled "The Mafia," is headed "A Grand Council Meets," a dramatic description of the gathering at Apalachin.

Anslinger himself writes the Foreword to the book to vouch that "the author is qualified to tell this story . . . for he knows what he is talking about at first hand." Commenting on organized crime, Anslinger insists that "the core of this army are the *mafiosi.* Like the Communists, they have discipline, cohesion, and a philosophy. These are no ordinary hoodlums; they are far more menacing and have been for a long time."

In his *King of Crime, Journal-American* reporter Dom Frasca entitles his chapter on Apalachin, "The Grand Council." And he notes in opening that "a *mafia* crime convention is very much like a businessman's convention" (p. 171).

Testifying before New York's Joint Legislative Committee on Government Operations, John T. Cusack in his capacity as southeastern area District Supervisor of the Narcotics Bureau stated his opinion that the meeting at Apalachin was not the first such gathering. There were others: Binghamton in 1956, Chicago in 1954, Florida in 1953 and 1952, Cleveland in 1928. "We of the Federal Narcotics Bureau call these *Mafia* meetings," stated Cusack.

In the minds of several government agencies, then, the Mafia, if not a proven fact, is certainly a working hypothesis. And for most crime reporters, the gathering at Apalachin was a meeting of Mafia's Grand Council.

Apalachin was the second time in a decade that Mafia was listed as top crime. At the opening of the decade (1951) the Senate Crime Investigating Committee, chaired by Estes Kefauver, concluded that "behind the local mobs which make up the national crime syndicate is a shadowy, international criminal organization known as the Mafia, so fantastic that most Americans find it hard to believe it really exists" (*Crime in America*, p. 15). The excerpt entitled "The Kefauver Conclusion" is the official statement of the Senate Investigating Committee on the role of the Mafia.

At least a full decade before Kefauver, the Narcotics Bureau developed an active interest in the Mafia. Testifying in 1957, Cusack announced that "the Narcotics Bureau has been interested in the Mafia, as such, for approximately eighteen years, carrying the government's official concern back to 1939" (quoted in *Brotherhood of Evil*, p. 42).

And a half century before that, in 1890 to be exact, the city of New Orleans was aflame over the crimes of the Mafia. That year, a grand jury probed into the mortal shooting of New Orleans' Police Chief David Hennessey to find that "the extended range of our researchers has developed the existence of the secret organization styled 'Mafia.' The evidence comes from several sources fully competent in themselves to attest its truth, while the fact is supported by the long record of blood curdling crimes, it being almost impossible to discover the perpetrators or secure witnesses." (*Mafia*, Ed Reid, quoted on p. 102.)

Now, seventy years after the grand jury indictment of New Orleans, it can still be said of the Mafia that although there is an even longer "record of blood curdling crimes" attributed to the Mafia by "fully competent sources," the very fact that it is so difficult to "discover the perpetrators or secure witnesses" leaves the Mafia legally a still unproven fact.

The Mafia—whose existence is assumed by some government agencies—is a rare "secret" society whose existence is truly secret.

A "secret" society such as the Masons is really not a secret at all, for, whatever its privy rites may be, its existence is a public matter. A revolutionary organization, such as the Communist Party, may have secret agents, meetings, and operations, but as a party its existence is not denied nor unprovable in a court of law. But of the Mafia it may be said, as Reuter did say in his Apalachin report, that while "its membership and organization have been the subject of many books and reports," such documents were "based almost entirely upon information short of legal evidence." This circumstance "permits of reasonable inference or speculation but . . . no official findings can be properly made."

While the existence of the Mafia is still legally conjectural, theories of its existence can not be ignored, especially in view of testimony such as that of Cusack of the Narcotics Bureau that "on the basis of our official investigations that extend over a 30 year period, we have amassed conclusive evidence of the existence of the Mafia, and consider this secret international society a threat. . . ."

To ignore it is impossible, yet to pursue it is to stir up a political hornet's nest. The events surrounding the New Orleans' "Mafia" trials and lynching in 1890 led to a rupture of diplomatic relations between Italy and the United States. The findings of the Kefauver Committee in 1951 led to charges that the Tennessee senator was prejudiced against Italians. The trial of the Apalachinites—all of Italian ancestry—led defense counsel to charge prejudice. Shortly after the trial, an organization of Italo-Americans was composed to defend the good name of the Italians in the American community, fearing that the trial would be fuel to anti-Italian prejudice.

For this reason, any public discussion of this sensitive matter has had to be prefaced by a separation of the two terms—Mafia and Italian.

Sondern, in the introduction to his *Brotherhood of Evil*, stresses that "the mafiosi, singularly insidious though they are, make up a minute fraction of the many hundreds of thousands of Americans of Sicilian birth or extraction, the great majority of whom are honest people engaged in conventional pursuits. The reader is asked to remember that the terms Mafia and Sicilian are not synonymous. The latter group must be protected against the stigma which is growing and will continue to grow in the course of many investigations into the Mafia that are now under way."

The sensitivity of the Italian community about the Mafia is not without parallel in other times and places, with other ethnic groups. In the mid-twenties, when Arnold Rothstein was boss of New York's underworld and the roster of criminality from 1890 to 1930 was studded with names like Monk Eastman (Edward Osterman), Kid Dropper (Nathan Kaplan), Little Augie (Jacob Organ), Kid Twist (Max Zweibach), Legs Diamond, Johnny Spanish, Jake Zelig, Lepke, and Gurrah, the Jewish community was embarrassed and sought to minimize or rationalize the freak known as "the Jewish gangster." Before the turn of the century, when the New York underworld was dominated by names like Red Rocks Farrell, Googy Corcoran, Slops Connolly, Piker Ryan, Bull Hurley, Dorsey Doyle, Mike Lloyd, Big Josh

Hines, and Baboon Connolly, the Irish of New York were viewed by many as "criminal by nature."

In the underworld, as in our society generally, there have been ethnic trends: the rise and fall of various national groups reaching out for supreme power. Since the thirties, the top names in the underworld are Italian in origin, just as in New York, for instance, they were Jewish in a previous period, Irish in a period before that, and—in other cities and times—predominantly Polish, Bohemian, and German. And in still other times and places good old American families like the James boys, the Grahams, the Youngers, the Daltons, the Barkers, the Floyds, and Bill Bonney and a hundred other autochthonous sobriquets put their brand on gangs.

Confusion about mafia arises from the fact that the word itself originally meant two allied but different things: first an attitude, and then a group of men. The word is "not found in Italian writing before the Nineteenth Century," according to Gaetano Mosca. (*Encyclopedia of the Social Sciences* article on Mafia.) In sharp contrast to both the lurid journalism on Mafia and the shocked denial of Mafia, the scholarly piece by the great Italian sociologist, Gaetano Mosca, contained in the excerpt entitled "The Mafia in Italy" offers a calm, prosaic account of the word, the movement, and its development in Sicily. Traina's Sicilian-Italian dictionary (1868) defines it as a neologism denoting any sign of bravado, a bold show. Montillaro's dictionary (1876) defines it as a word of Piedmontese origin equivalent to gang (camorra). Both meanings of the term—attitude and gang—are recorded here.

The *Oxford English Dictionary* (1933) also notes both meanings: "In Sicily, the spirit of hostility to the law and its ministers prevailing among a large portion of the population and manifesting itself frequently in vindictive crimes. Also the body of those who share in this anti-legal spirit (often erroneously supposed to constitute an organized secret society for criminal purposes.)"

Writing in 1902, Mosca insisted that "the Mafia is not, as is generally believed one vast society of criminals, but is rather a sentiment akin to arrogance which imposes a special line of conduct upon persons affected by it. The mafioso considers it dishonorable to have recourse to lawful authority to obtain redress for a wrong or a crime committed against him" (quoted in *Oxford English Dictionary* under "Mafia").

Mussolini's chief of Police, Cesare Mori, who was charged with a massive drive against the Sicilian Mafia in the late 1920's, is in basic agreement with Mosca. "Many people suppose that the Mafia is an association, in the sense of being a vast aggregate organized and incorporated on regular principles, although the outward forms are more or less masked or hidden. I have often been asked what signs of recognition among themselves the *mafiosi* have, what is their hierarchy, what the rules of admission, what the system of appointing chiefs, what the secret laws, the methods of administration and of dividing the profits, and so on: *but in reality nothing of this kind exists.* (Italics mine) It has happened at certain times and in certain districts that the *mafiosi* habitually met in groups which had all the characteristics of true association, with regular and, of course, secret statutes, concealed badges and marks of recognition, definite hierarchies and elections of chiefs; but these were exceptional cases, or cases of a special and sporadic nature. The Mafia, as I am describing it, is a peculiar way of looking at things and of acting which, through mental and spiritual affinities, brings together in definite, unhealthy attitudes men of a particular temperament, isolating them from their surroundings into a kind of caste. It is a potential state which normally takes concrete form in a system of local oligarchies closely interwoven, but each autonomous in its own district. There are no marks of recognition; they are unnecessary. The *mafiosi* know one another partly by their jargon, but mostly by instinct. There are no statutes. The law of *omerta* and tradition are enough. There is no election of chiefs for the chiefs arise of their own accord and impose themselves. There are no rules of admission. When a candidate has all the necessary qualifications, he is absorbed automatically: and he is automatically expelled, or, if need be, done away with, if he loses them." (Pp. 39–40.) (Some Mori critics insist that as Mussolini's chief of police Mori blew up the Mafia menace to cover wholesale arrests and deportations of antifascist radicals.)

On the surface, it appears that the views of Mosca and Mori and, if you wish, the *Oxford English Dictionary,* are quite contrary to those of our Narcotics Bureau, and the crime writers—carrying unofficial official endorsement —who allegedly base their conclusions on government files. And yet, once we build the necessary semantic bridge, the gap is traversable.

Ordinarily when we speak of an *organization* we refer to a "corporate" body with a written charter. We expect to find a written statement of purpose, a constitutional design, a regularized method of choosing officers, a prescribed mode of initiation or admittance, and a processed method of exit or disassociation. But there are "organizations" that are essentially "corporate" bodies without any of these written or spoken relationships. A family is one such. A juvenile gang is another. The Mafia, according to Mori, is still another. It is composed of men—relatively few in number whether in Sicily or America—with a common attitude. It has a hierarchy, resting on power and personality, serving without title, risen to one level or the other by its own devices. It "initiates" its "members" (who are neither "initiated" nor "members") in a gruesome process of trial by ordeal and fire alongside of which the usual process called "initiation" is an infantile piece of tomfoolery. It has a system of severance for individuals, but the "member" who chooses to leave on his own finds that the severance pay is death.

To use Mori's phrase, the Mafiosi compose "a caste," with an internal hierarchy. The Mafia is far less formal, less subject to due process, than a society such as the Masons, Oddfellows, or Knights of Columbus. But without the trappings of "a society" it is far more cohesive than formalized organizations. The kinship that formal fraternities try to arrive at by ritual, the Mafia attains effortlessly—through common attitude, environment, and deeds.

According to some writings, there are evidences of formal organization as well as formal ties. "I pledge my honor to be faithful to the Mafia, like the Mafia is faithful to me. As this saint and a few drops of my blood were burned, so will I give all my blood for the Mafia, when the ashes and my blood will return to their original status."

Writers describe dialogues conducted in shibboleths to enable one Mafioso to recognize another, like the Masonic high sign. There are also descriptions of lurid initiation rites with the letting of blood and the wetting of figures.

Whether these oaths and passwords and rites are universal and current is highly doubtful. Certainly the shibboleths cannot be worth very much if they are known to our government agencies and if their content is published in a widely circulated book. And while the oath and the rites of entry may have been practiced here or there at one time or another, there is reason to doubt the universality of the practice. Before a man can rise in the underworld to any post where he will be entrusted with vital secrets he is put through an apprenticeship of carrying through muggings, sluggings, killings, and standing up silently through a third degree of grilling by the police. After this kind of "initiation," an oath and a pin prick certainly appear superfluous and anticlimactic. If the rites do exist today, they are pure embroidery, doing more to conceal than reveal the true nature of the Mafiosi.

One of the reasons why there are contradictory descriptions of the Mafia arises from the fact that, to begin with, the Mafiosi were not part of a monolithic organization. The mafia was, to use the language of the *Encyclopaedia Britannica*, "a form of criminality." These mafiosi operated in bands. Some of them might have had their rites and rituals. Others did not. Some bands operated in alliances. Others did not. What brought them all under one banner was "a sentiment," an attitude toward one another and toward society. The section entitled "The Mafia" is another of the items which describes without passion the nature of the criminal phenomenon.

Where did the Mafiosi come from?

Although it is commonly agreed that the Mafia had its origins in Sicily, apparently nobody knows exactly or even inexactly just when.

Sometime in the ninth century, according to *Life*'s story on the Mafia, "an underground organization evolved to conduct war against Arab invaders. The name Mafia was bestowed on it later."

A more popular story dates the Mafia rather exactly from March 30, 1282, when a young Sicilian called upon his people to drive out the French oppressors, because of the rape of his intended bride, with the cry of *Morte alla Francia* ° ("Death to France"). (One writer translates this as "death to *all the* French," a novel transliteration for "alla.") To this was added *Italia anela* (Italy cries). The initials of the mnemonic slogan read: M-A-F-I-A. This is the most romantic, the most popular, and the most unfounded explanation of the society's origins. The only verifiable aspect of the tale is a three-day massacre of French elements on the island by the native Sicilians.

The Narcotics Bureau dates the Mafia back to more recent times: the latter part of the eighteenth century. At that time, the society was put together to combat the Bourbons.

Obviously, the three separate explanations—dating the origin of the Mafia at separate points from the ninth to the eighteenth century—are vastly inconsistent. And yet they may be logically consistent if one does not confuse a movement with its form, an historic drive with its organized expression. If the Mafia is thought of as a social expression rather than an Order of the Elks, the character of the phenomenon as well as the uncertainty of its birth date become clear.

Perhaps the easiest way to understand the phenomenon referred to in Italy as the Mafia is to think of Sicily as living under the chaotic conditions of the American frontier and to think of the "Mafia" as a collective and generic term to cover our free-wheeling gun-slingers—both good guys and bad guys—of the wild west. One difference: our frontier was brief, while Sicily was torn with conflict, conquest, upheaval, suppression and struggles for more than 2000 years.

(In the brief sketch of Sicilian history that follows the focus is on those factors that created disorder. A more complete canvas would include the story of Sicily's parliament prior to England's, the reputed "mother of parliaments," and the story of Syracuse, one of the great centers of ancient learning. Just as the full story of the U.S. is not the story of the frontier or of organized crime, so the story of the forces producing the Mafia spirit is hardly the full story of Sicily.)

Sicily is an island of some ten thousand square miles so situated in the Mediterranean, off the coast of Italy, as to be a natural stepping-stone for expanding empires, reaching out from Africa to Europe and from the Orient to the Straits of Gibraltar.

For nearly two thousand years Sicily was overrun by conquerors and invaders and torn by inner conflict. In language that any child can under-

---

° If this is what the young Sicilian cried out, he must have been a rare linguist, for the Italian used above was virtually unknown as a language in the Sicily of 1282.

stand, the Book of Knowledge—in the days before World War II—stated plainly that, "Occupied in turn by Greeks, Carthaginians, Romans, Franks, Goths, Byzantines, Saracens, Normans, Angevins, and Aragonese, Sicily has had *the most eventful history* of all Europe."

There was never a dull moment. When the Greeks first came to the island about 800 B.C. they found it divided with Siceli in the east, with Sicani in the center, and with people of a Trojan origin in the west. The Greeks also found that Phoenicians had established little tyrannies and amassed great wealth. The Hellenization of the island, however, was interrupted by the armies of Hamilcar from Carthage. In 480 B.C. Hamilcar was defeated, but a few years later his grandson, Hannibal, returned with an army to capture Himera—the city where Hamilcar was killed—and to slaughter three thousand of its inhabitants for vindication. The Carthaginian victory was not complete, however, since only part of the island was conquered. For generations, East and West were divided and at war in a ceaseless struggle of regions, cultures, and classes. In the third century of the Christian era, Roman power moved into Sicily. But by the fifth century, the vandals invaded Sicily from Africa and, in 476, ceded most of the island to Odoacar, the "barbarian king of Italy." When the Roman Empire fell apart, Sicily fell to Byzantium, only to pass in 703 to the Arabs, and to be overrun in 1060 by the Normans.

The year 1282 is a turning point in Sicilian history, although not for the romantic reason of rape revenged commonly mentioned in Mafia folklore. That year there was an uprising against Charles of Anjou, who was colonizing the island with French. "On the outbreak of the revolt a parliament at Palermo offered the crown to Peter III of Aragon, who became Peter I of Sicily." It took twenty years of warfare for this Aragonese dynasty to be established.

In the centuries that followed, Sicily became the plaything of Papal, feudal, and dynastic politics. When Napoleon overran southern Italy, Sicily fell into a state of near anarchy. When Sicily finally became an integral part of Italy, it still remained a troublesome spot. In the late 1920's Mussolini assigned Mori to break Sicilian resistance, an action that the latter carried through by lumping Mafiosi and antifascists together as criminals and condemning them in mass trials. Even today, there is a sizeable and passionate movement in Sicily for independence from Italy.

There has never been a dull moment in Sicily. But at what precise moment in "this eventful history" the Mafia arose, nobody can really say.

Nor is the date vital, for if the Mafia as an "organized movement" issued from the mafia as a "social attitude" then the exact date of *organization* is less important than the circumstance that produced the *attitude*. This circumstance was the repeated conquest and enslavement, conflict and disorder that marked Sicilian history. The intensity and continuity of these disturbances is only hinted at broadly in our sketchy history of Sicily. Each conquest took many years. Parts of the island were subjugated while other parts revolted. For each conqueror, maintaining power was as difficult as, if not more difficult than, attaining power.

Out of such a caldron, it was inevitable that individuals and bands of men should arise with little or no respect for established "law and order." These men must have seen the order change too often to hold it sacred. They must have seen "law" written with the sword and knew that it could be rewritten with the stiletto. Yesterday's ruler could become today's serf and, by the same twist of the fist, today's servant could become tomorrow's master. What claimed to be "government" was an alien force imposing fealty by a violence that provoked counterviolence.

Amidst such disorder, the spirit of mafia flowered, with persons and groups arising to dispute power, to check oppression, to raid and pillage, to extort and exploit, to harass the stronger and harness the weaker—to be a law unto itself. Amidst intermittent anarchy and foreign rule, where else is true law and swift justice if not in one's own fist! The relationship between mafia-minded bands and government was essentially the same as that between Robin Hood and the Sheriff of Nottingham, as that between the Irish Republican Army and the British Crown, as that between a juvenile gang and the city cop. The band lives outside the law by its own code, with its own courts and enforcers.

The Mafia is alleged by some writers to have found its origins in a struggle for Sicilian liberation. While there can be no doubt that people, as individuals and bands, motivated by the "mafia" sentiment of lawless hostility, probably preyed on their wealthy foreign oppressors, made life miserable for the tax-collectors, and may even have joined in localized or more island-wide upheavals, there is no evidence that a "mafia," as an organized movement, ever played a major role in the efforts to liberate Sicily. This is particularly true prior to the nineteenth century—when the concept of the "mafia" as "organization" is virtually unknown.

"Mafia was never a vast association of malefactors with a hierarchy of leaders and ramifications throughout Sicily," notes Mosca. "In this respect it differed sharply from the highly unified Neopolitan Camorra, with which it had no relationship except that of similar criminal objectives. Mafia consisted rather of many small autonomous associations, each active over a limited district. Each association was a *cosca* (Sicilian dialect: *tuft*), generally having a membership of twelve to fifteen although some were larger. There was no election of chiefs, authority being wielded by members long addicted to crime, who directed the movements of younger associates, superintended dealings with victims and divided booty. Insubordination and especially misappropriation of booty were considered violations of mafist honor and punished sometimes with death. The relations between neighboring *cosche* might be cordial or so antagonistic that difficulties would have to be settled by shooting. The great majority of mafist murders grew out of rivalry between *cosche* or members of one *cosca*."

Here Mosca is describing the social phenomenon not really peculiar either to Sicily or Italy, although the prolonged disorder and anarchy of the Mediterranean island may have been particularly fertile soil for this growth. What Mosca calls the *cosca*, we call the gang. The *capo mafioso* is the gang leader who holds power by taking it and wielding it. The gang demands discipline—do what you're told and keep your mouth shut. And the great— although not exclusive—killings arise from fratricidal warfare inside a gang or between gangs. While Mosca describes this briefly in the *Encyclopaedia of the Social Sciences* as it applies to Sicily, Herbert Asbury depicts exactly the same phenomenon in his *Gangs of New York, Gem of the Prairies* (Chicago), and *Barbary Coast* (San Francisco) as it existed in three great American cities long before any Italian names appeared prominently on the criminal roster.

Even the famous code of *omerta*—with its great wall of silence—is not peculiarly Sicilian. It is the universal code of the underworld, the inner government of the outlaw—whether he be criminal, patriotic, revolutionary or delinquent. The only aspect that is distinctly Sicilian is the word itself— *omerta*—generally believed to be derived from *uomo* ("man") and meant to refer to a kind of "manhood" where one stands up for himself with fist or pistol.

Describing the evolution of *omerta* in Sicily, Mori writes:

"In its original meaning *omerta* also implies exemption from the common law: as such it embodies the pride of all rebels against injustice and tyranny, in every age and country, besides a particular view of questions involving personal honour. It is easy to understand, then, that *omerta*, in its original sense, has always exerted a special influence over the masses, for the masses love the man who can take the law into his own hands to revenge an injury better than him who can forgive."

The five rules of *omerta*, according to Ed Reid in his very readable book *The Mafia,*° are:

1. Reciprocal aid in case of any need whatsoever.
2. Absolute obedience to the chief.
3. An offense received by one of the members to be considered an offense against all and avenged at any cost.
4. No appeal to the state's authorities for justice.
5. No revelation of the names of members or any secrets of the association.

These rules might very well have been written for the Three Musketeers

---

° The same rules appear in *Chambers Journal* of 1892.

(one for all and all for one), for the Industrial Workers of the World (an injury to one is an injury to all), for the Irish Republican Army, the Mau Mau, the Hatfield's and McCoy's, or for any street corner gang engaged in warfare against another gang or against the "authorities." These are the standard rules of the "we's" versus the "they's," of the tribe against the world, of the hostile subculture against the reigning civilization. These may be the rules of "mafia," but they are also the rules of every underworld gang that ever survived beyond its first illegal deed.

The fantasy of the Mafia is enlarged by references to their secret language, a dialect that is virtually a code. This assertion, like so many of the others about the Mafia, is a half-truth. The secret code and gestures of the Mafia are no more mysterious than the argot and costume of the Parisian apache or the San Francisco beatnik or Harlem's cats.

Commenting on this aspect of the Mafia, Mosca writes that "while it is untrue that members of the various *cosche* used conventional words and gestures to recognize one another, they did have peculiar mannerisms, including pronunciations of certain words, frequent use of others, and a certain furtive and shuffling expression. To any experienced Sicilian these betrayed connection with a *cosca*."

"They use a certain jargon, intonation and gesticulation of their own," noted a magazine profile of "The Mafiosi" in 1892 (*Chambers Journal,* reprinted in *Living Age,* July–Sept. 1892). "For instance, the word for prison is *cullegia* (college); for manacles, *curuna* (rosary); for sword, *statia* (steelyard)."

In the modern development of the Mafia, there are three landmarks: first, the appointment of mafia, "strong men," to administer the latifundia at the time of Napoleon's invasion of southern Italy: second, the reorganization of the Mafia *cosche* to gain respectable fronts after the police offensive of the late nineteenth century; third, the use of the franchise by the Mafia to elect its friends after the extension of the suffrage in 1882 and again in 1912.

When Napoleon invaded Southern Italy, "lawless conditions led the owners of large estates to place their lands in charge of energetic ruffians who exercised almost despotic powers over a terrorized peasantry," records the *Britannica.* These "energetic ruffians" were mafiosi, men with the necessary strength, moral and physical, to establish and enforce their own law. These *compieri,* akin to the foremen and bosses of our frontier lumber camps and railroad gangs, were in time much more than administrators of the latifundia ruling a docile labor force. The *compieri*—generally the local strong man backed by a mafist gang—could now dictate terms all around, to his "superior" as well as his "inferiors." He became middleman, adjudicator, judge, ward heeler, learning to hold an iron fist under a velvet glove.

"The contiguity of the estates," continues the *Britannica,* "enabled these men to form an organization which gradually became very extensive and powerful, so much so that in time it turned against the land-owners themselves. The members of the organization were not very numerous, but, bound by close ties of fellowship and capable of any crime, they compelled the land-owners to employ persons of their choice, fixed the compensation they claimed for their services, and the rents and price of the lands and of the crops to be sold at open auction, and effectively hindered all efforts likely to interfere with their interests."

A second landmark in Mafia development came at the end of the nineteenth century after an attempt by Prefect of Police Malusardi to break the back of the creature by exiling several hundred Sicilians "against whom precise evidence was lacking" to coastal islands. This led to the reorganization of the *cosche* who "perfected their methods of operation" (Mosca). One aspect of this change was the decision of Mafia members to practice "a trade from which they appeared to live" (Mosca). As the Mafia moved into the twentieth century it learned the great skill of modern organized crime, the *ars celare artem.*

This more sophisticated and businesslike *modus operandi* probably developed first in the urban areas, as distinct from the rural. As early as 1892, one report noted that "there is a distinction between the Mafiosi of the mountains and those of the seashore, especially those of the commercial cities. In the mountains, the crimes are of a ruder sort—stealing and slaughtering cattle, incendiarism and other outrages; along the coast and in the cities, the alliance works with fraud, extortion, and assassination, with a cunning skill that attains to the perfection of a fine art."

This early distinction in Sicily foreshadows parallel and similar distinctions in other times and climes, the shift from rural to urban gangs, from Jesse James to Arnold Rothstein—neither of whom, incidentally, was Sicilian.

A third landmark in the development of the Mafia occurred after the first important extension of the franchise in 1882, when the outlaw reached out through the ballot to become the law. "In some communes," according to Mosca, the mafists "dominated political elections." This movement was hastened and extended by the universal suffrage adopted in 1912. The poorest classes, although not themselves mafists, "yielded . . . to mafist threats and supported candidates endorsed by mafists. The *cosche* required their legislative tools to obtain for their members permission to carry weapons, to intercede with the police in their favor and to serve them in other ways" (Mosca).

What then was the mafia as Sicily knew it?

The mafia was the spirit of contempt and hostility toward established law and order. In this spirit, men arose who felt it was not only their need but also their duty to take the law in their own hands. Such men joined in bands for a variety of lawless acts—revolutionary, patriotic, vindictive, criminal. These bands—each with its own name, its own allegiances, its own leader —were all infected with the outlaw spirit, the temper of mafia. While each of these bands had its own brand name, such as Fratellanza, Amoroso, Stop-paglieri, Mala Vita, etc., the generic term to describe this vast body of "bad men" was mafia.

These mafia bands were strongest when and where government was weakest. In times of war and revolution, they flourished. With their portable little governments, they were indispensable in times of breakdown, such as attended the Napoleonic invasion, in administering large estates.

While these bands warred among themselves, like rival unions over a jurisdiction or competing business over the market, they established relationships toward the "outside" world to give them a common character and cohesiveness. Out of such common needs, there developed loose alliances, thrown together at "the great cattle fairs" where they gathered to "adjust their reciprocal interests" (Littell's *Living Age,* p. 573).

In the mountainous, more rural areas, the mafia specialized in straight pillage, particularly in cattle rustling. In the coastal—more urban—areas, they specialized in extorting a regularized tribute. When faced with a police crackdown, the methodology shifted to the more businesslike approach, polished off with respectable fronts.

To gain immunity and power, the mafia entered into alliances with politicians.

While this development was proceeding in Sicily, a parallel and almost identical development was proceeding in the United States—with virtually no Italians in it. On the open frontier of our West and on the internal frontier of our slums, there arose "bad men," tough guys, operating solo and in gangs. Where government was weakest—as on the frontier or in the corrupt cities— the gangs were strongest. While these gangs all had their own names—James Boys and Plug Uglies, Daltons and Whyos, Youngers and Dead Rabbits— they were all part of an outlaw world.

Although these gangs were separate entities, they evolved a system of treaties and alliances, working out jurisdictions and cooperative actions. In periods when lawlessness swept the nation or a portion of it, as in the New York draft riots, the post-Civil War period, and the Prohibition Era, these gangs became more powerful.

On the open frontier—rural America—the gangs specialized in direct pillage and spoliation, especially cattle-rustling and train robberies. On the internal frontier—urban America—the gangs specialized in "the rackets," robbery on a retainer basis. And when faced with legal crackdown, the citified gangster turned to smoother methods, glossed with a businesslike front.

Finally, to continue operation without hindrance, the criminal-politician concordat was concluded.

When the mafia came to America in the post-Civil War period, organized crime was well on its way. The mafia was just another strand, albeit a mighty one, in the garroting rope of American crime.

At first mafia elements operated almost exclusively within the "little Italies" of America. Then they entered into warfare against the other ethnic gangs. Then they merged. And then they became the dominant element in the merger.

While lurid journalism has made "organized crime" and "mafia" synonymous, this is a dangerous distortion of both the origin and nature of the underworld. Organized crime in America is not an import, "Made in Sicily." It is American, risen out of a native matrix of lawlessness, different but not dissimilar from that of Sicily. The underworld is not an Italian organization, but a vast syndicate of many ethnic and native groups.

The final three excerpts in this section—by Daniel Bell on "The Myth of the Mafia," by a California Crime Commission on "L'Unione Siciliano," and by Turkus and Feder on the victory of "L'Unione versus the Mafia"— are separate attempts to describe and evaluate the role of this much-discussed phenomenon in American crime.

Bell argues that there is no institution like the Mafia, engaged in a criminal "plot." He prefers to find sociologic roots for the recurrence of Italian names in high gang circles in recent decades.

The California Crime Commission shares a theory with Turkus that the Mafia is a thing of the past, supplanted by a more Americanized outfit, composed of younger men who preferred interethnic merger to the moustached, old-worldish, sectarian Mafia.

While all three of these essays—for different reasons—deny the existence or the supremacy of the Mafia, all three are curiously in agreement; namely, that a sociologic trend has produced an era in organized crime in America with a predominance of names, coming, at this moment, from one ethnic group.

If this conclusion is placed against the total background of organized crime in America, then the loosely used term "mafia" falls into place: one ethnic tile—large and spatially blatant—in the giant mosaic that has included the many races and people who composed our culture. In the past the finger pointed at the Yankee, the Irish, the Jewish, the Reb. Today it points at the Italian. At whom will the accusing finger point tomorrow?

Section 38 **THE KEFAUVER CONCLUSION**

From Third Interim Report, Special Committee to Investigate Organized Crime in Interstate Commerce, 82d Cong., 1st Sess.

The structure of organized crime today is far different from what it was many years ago. Its power for evil is infinitely greater. The unit of organized crime used to be an individual gang consisting of a number of hoodlums, whose activities were obviously predatory in character. Individual gangs tended to specialize in specific types of criminal activity such as payroll, or bank robbery, loft, or safe burglary, pocket picking, etc. These gangs normally confined their activities to particular areas of the country or particular communities. Occasionally their activities were aided and abetted by law-enforcement officials. The crooked sheriff who aids the outlaws is as much of a stock character as the fearless "law man" who makes justice triumph.

New types of criminal gangs have emerged during prohibition. The huge profits earned in that era together with the development of twentieth century transportation and communication, made possible larger and much more powerful gangs, covering much greater territory. Organized crime in the last 30 years has taken on new characteristics. The most dangerous criminal gangs today are not specialists in one type of predatory crime, but engage in many and varied forms of criminality. Criminal groups today are multipurpose in character engaging in any racket wherever there is money to be made. The modern gang, moreover, does not rely for its primary source of income on frankly predatory forms of crime such as robbery, burglary, or larceny. Instead the more dangerous criminal elements draw most of their revenues from various forms of gambling, the sale and distribution of narcotics, prostitution, various forms of business and labor racketeering, black-market practices, bootlegging into dry areas, etc.

The key to successful gang operation is monopoly of illicit enterprises or illegal operations, for monopoly guarantees huge profits. In cities that gangland has organized very well, the syndicate or the combination in control of the rackets decides which mobsters are to have what rackets. In cities which have not been well organized, the attempt by one mobster to take over the territory or racket from another mobster inevitably breeds trouble, for modern gangs and criminal syndicates rely on "muscle" and murder to a

far greater degree than formerly to eliminate competitors, compel cooperation from reluctant victims, silence informers, and to enforce gangland edicts.

Modern crime syndicates and criminal gangs have copied some of the
organizational methods found in modern business. They seek to expand their
activities in many different fields and in many different geographic areas,
wherever profits may be made. We have seen evidence of the operation of the
Costello-Adonis-Lansky crime syndicate, whose headquarters is in New
York, in such places as Bergen County, N. J., Saratoga, N. Y., Miami, Fla.,
New Orleans, Nevada, the west coast of Havana, Cuba. We have seen evi-
dences of operations of the other major crime syndicate, that of Accardo-
Guzik-Fischetti, whose headquarters is in Chicago, in such places as Kansas
City, East St. Louis, Miami, Nevada, and the west coast.

Some indication of how modern crime syndicates operate and how they
open new territory is apparent from the facts described under the city story
of Chicago elsewhere in this report in relation to the extraordinary testimony
of Lt. George Butler of the police department of Dallas, Tex. Lieutenant
Butler was approached by a member of the Chicago mob by the name of
Paul Jones. According to Butler, Jones stated that he was an advance agent
of the Chicago crime syndicate and was prepared to offer the district attorney
and the sheriff $1,000 a week each or a 12½-percent cut on the profits if the
syndicate were permitted to operate in Dallas under "complete protection."
Jones also stated that syndicate operations were conducted by local people
who "front" for the Chicago mob. The syndicate, according to Jones, controlled such cities as St. Louis, Kansas City, New Orleans, and Little Rock.
In addition the syndicate had connections in every large city, and if Jones
ran into trouble anywhere, money and help would be forthcoming.

Lieutenant Butler advised his superiors, and on instructions, played
along with Jones and indicated that the Dallas police were interested in his
propositions. Jones, therefore, brought Pat Manno, a notorious Chicago syndicate mobster and a partner of Guzik and Accardo, who was labeled as the
fifth man in the syndicate, to Dallas to talk matters over with Butler and
Sheriff Guthrie, who had been apprised of the situation. Recordings of the
conversation between Lieutenant Butler, Sheriff Guthrie, Manno, and Jones
were made. Manno stated that he had been in the policy business in Chicago
for 17 years and was interested in opening up operations in Dallas. He stated
that the Chicago syndicate was definitely interested in coming into Dallas
and that he, as representative of the syndicate, was looking the town over
to see if they could operate it in collaboration with the police. The work of
the Dallas Police in this connection was most commendable.

There are many other criminal gangs and criminal groups throughout
the country that have more than a local importance. For instance, the Klein-
man-Rothkopf-Polizzi group has operated in many different Ohio counties as

well as in the Newport and Covington area of Kentucky, in Nevada, and in Miami, Fla. Members of the Detroit gang have operated in Miami, Saratoga, and Kentucky. Individual gangsters and gangs in different parts of the country have also frequently worked in close and profitable relationship with each other, particularly in gambling casinos where often members of several gangs participate on a systematic basis. Outside gangs coming into an area will often use local hoodlums and local gangs.

It is apparent, as Narcotics Commissioner Anslinger testified before the committee, that the leading figures in organized crime do business with each other, get together in places like Miami and Hot Springs and on occasion do each other's dirty work, when a competitor must be eliminated and an informer silenced, or a victim persuaded. Commissioner Anslinger did not think that the activities in one part of the country occur as a result of instructions given in other parts of the country as a general rule. In some cases "it is pretty well organized in that particular way but I wouldn't say that one section of the country controls another section." What happens, Mr. Anslinger testified, is that leading mobsters throughout the country "confer together or talk to each other, deal with each other." He agreed with Mr. Halley's characterization that "they confine their dealings pretty well to the family."

As we have seen one of the major areas in which leading gangs cooperate is in enforcing each other's edict, silencing informers, persuading potential victims through intimidation, violence, and murder. It is obviously far more difficult for local law enforcement officials to detect the work of outside gangsters than the products of their local talent.

Modern gangland operations on any sizable scale cannot be carried on without protection. The gangs have unbelievable cash assets available for this purpose, moreover. Much of the moneys of criminal gangs and syndicates are invested in legitimate enterprises which presents special dangers to our economy and our people.

The Mafia, the committee is convinced, has an important part in binding together into a loose association the two major criminal syndicates as well as many minor gangs and individual hoodlums throughout the country. Wherever the committee has gone it has run into the trail of this elusive, shadowy, and sinister organization. Because of its importance to organized crime in this country, data on the Mafia will be presented in some detail.

The Mafia was originally one of many secret societies organized in Sicily to free the island of foreign domination. The methods used for securing secrecy of operations, unity of command, intimidation and murder, and the silencing of informers, were adopted by a criminal group that became the Mafia after the Bourbons were driven from Sicily.

According to historians and the most authentic research material available, the following is the history of the Mafia:

The various secret organizations in Sicily were fused into a single group known as the Fratellanza or the "Brotherhood" which sometime later became known as the Mafia. Initiates and new members of this organization took solemn oaths never to reveal the secrets of the group under any circumstances and never to divulge the names of fellow members, even under torture. This secret association was organized in groups of 10 members. Each group had a leader. The group leaders were known to each other but not to the members of the various groups. The group leaders reported to the provincial chief who in turn reported to the supreme chief in Palermo, a very wealthy and influential man.

This organization grew enormously in Sicily after 1860. Smuggling, cattle stealing, extortion, and shake-downs were its major criminal activities. The administration of justice was so openly defied by this organization that many attempts were made by law-enforcement agencies in Sicily to deal with it. Although many arrests were made, law-enforcement agencies found it extremely difficult to break the power of the Mafia. The arrested members of this organization would not talk. Witnesses of various crimes committed by members of the Mafia were intimidated and were afraid to testify. Political influence was used to protect Mafia members charged with crime. Good legal talent was always available for their defense. The various drives against the Mafia in Sicily which were made by Italian Governments from the 1870's down to Mussolini's time, were therefore largely ineffective in destroying the Mafia. However these drives had the effect of causing large numbers of Mafia members to migrate to the New World and many of them came to this country.

As early as the 1880's, New Orleans was the focal point of Mafia activity. According to Pasquale Corte, the Italian consul in New Orleans, large numbers of escaped Italian criminals settled there. These and other desperados grew rich and powerful upon the profits of robbery, extortion, assassination. Most of the victims were fellow countrymen who failed to pay the sums demanded by Mafia leaders.

The Mafia in New Orleans overreached itself when it ordered the murder of a popular police officer, David Hennessy. After he was murdered, a dozen Mafia leaders were arrested. None were convicted after a trial marred by the intimidation of witnesses and jury fixing. The defendants, however, who had been held in jail on other charges, were lynched by a mob of aroused New Orleans citizens. After these lynchings the power of the Mafia in New Orleans was temporarily broken.

The Mafia became established in other cities besides New Orleans. Moreover, like many other underworld organizations, it grew rich and powerful during prohibition in the sale and distribution of alcoholic beverages. In addition both during prohibition and since that time this organization has entered every racket promising easy money. Narcotics, pinball machines, slot machines, gambling in every form and description are some of its major activities at the present time.

Many of the individuals suspected of connection with the Mafia operate behind legitimate fronts. The olive oil, cheese, and the export and import businesses are some of the favorite fronts for Mafia operations. They offer a cover, particularly, for narcotics operations. They also help explain interstate, and international contacts between persons suspected of Mafia connections.

Mafia operations in this country have been described by the Narcotics Bureau as follows:

> It is almost inevitable that the Mafia should take an important part in American criminal rackets. Here is a Nationwide organization of outlaws in a sort of oath-bound, bloodcemented brotherhood dedicated to complete defiance of the law. Where personal advantage or interests are concerned, here is a more or less permanently established network, an organized maze of underground conduits, always ready and available when racket enterprise is to be furthered. The organization is such that a member in one part of the country can, with perfect confidence, engage in any sort of illicit business with members in any other section of the country. Most helpful to the Mafia has been the attitude on the part of many law-enforcement officers in connection with its murders. These are sometimes passed over lightly on the theory these cases are just hoodlums killing off one another and that it is not a matter on which to waste police time and energy.

The ruthless elimination of competitors from enterprises which Mafia leaders decide to take over, the ruthless elimination of persons who have weakened in their Mafia loyalties, failed to carry out Mafia orders, or who have informed against the Mafia, has left a trail of murder from Tampa to San Francisco. This is well illustrated by the following comments of the Narcotics Bureau:

> Joseph Sica and Alfred Sica of California are satellites of Anthony Rizzoti, alias Jack Dragna, and closely allied to members in New York and New Jersey from where they went to California several years ago. In 1949, a narcotics case was developed against the Sicas, principally upon the testimony of one Abraham Davidian who made purchases of narcotics from them, sometimes in lots costing more than

$15,000. Early this year, while the case was pending for trial, Davidian was shot to death while asleep in his mother's home in Fresno.

Another west coast case of great importance was developed in 1944. This concerned a New York-California-Mexico smuggling ring in which Salvatore Maugeri and others were convicted. During the course of the investigation, a narcotics agent working undercover learned that one of the ring with whom he was negotiating, Charles "Big Nose" LaGaipa, of Santa Cruz, Calif., was in bad odor with some of his criminal Mafia associates. LaGaipa disappeared. He never has been found. His car was recovered with blood on the seat and brain tissue on the dashboard.

One Nick DeJohn, active in the narcotics traffic in Chicago, and Thomas Buffa, active in the narcotics traffic in St. Louis, transferred their activities to California. A short time later, evidently for trying to muscle in, both were killed. Buffa died from shotgun fire. DeJohn's body was found in an automobile with wire twisted around the neck.

A member of this combine named Ignazio Antinori went to Havana frequently to obtain narcotics for middle western members of this organization. The leader was Joseph De-Luca.* * * On one occasion, Antinori, in return for $25,000, delivered a poor grade of narcotic. The middle western group gave him 2 weeks in which to return the money. At the end of that period, having failed to make good, he was killed in Tampa by shotgun fire in 1940. Evidently the middle western group ordered the Tampa leader to do this job. Thereafter his two sons continued in the traffic. After considerable investigation, we arrested DeLuca, Antinori's two sons, Paul and Joseph, and many others involved in 1942. The testimony of one of the defendants, Carl Carramusa, served to assure conviction of all defendants. The sentences meted out to these vicious murderers were shockingly low. In the case of Joseph DeLuca, who got 3 years, the court ordered that he not be deported on recommendation of the district attorney. After the leader, DeLuca, had served 1 year, he was paroled. Carramusa had moved to Chicago to escape vengeance by the combine. One morning, in 1945, as he was repairing a tire in front of his home, he was killed by a shotgun blast before the eyes of his 15-year-old daughter. His murder remains unsolved, but it unquestionably was the work of the Chicago members of the combine on orders from the Kansas City group. The neighbors of Carramusa who could have furnished information remained silent because of fear. This is the same pattern which follows all of their activities. Witnesses in narcotic cases against members of this combine refuse to testify knowing that they will be marked for death.

The committee found it difficult to obtain reliable data concerning the extent of Mafia operation, the nature of the Mafia organization, and the way it presently operates. One notable concrete piece of evidence is a photograph of 23 alleged Mafia leaders from all over the United States, arrested in a hotel in Cleveland in 1928. When arrested, the group possessed numerous firearms. Among those arrested were Joseph Profaci of New York, Vincent Mangano of New York, and "Red" Italiano of Tampa. Profaci, who is considered by the experts to be one of the top leaders of the Mafia, was questioned about this meeting at a closed committee hearing. At first, he asserted that he was in Cleveland in connection with his olive-oil business. Then after admitting that he had no olive-oil business in Cleveland before 1935 or 1936, he was unable to give a satisfactory explanation of his presence at the Cleveland convention.

Almost all the witnesses who appeared before the committee and who were suspected of Mafia membership, either denied that they had ever heard of the Mafia, which is patently absurd, or denied membership in the Mafia. However, many of these witnesses readily admitted knowledge of and associations and friendships with suspected Mafia characters in other parts of the country. A notable exception is Tony Gizzo, who testified in a closed hearing that he had heard that James Balestrere was the leader of the Mafia in Kansas City. Gizzo changed his testimony at the open hearing. Another notable exception is Philip D'Andrea who said that the Mafia was freely discussed in his home when he was a child, and that he understood it to be a widely feared extortion gang. On the basis of all the evidence before it, plus the off-the-record but convincing statements of certain informants who must remain anonymous, the committee is inclined to agree with the opinion of experienced police officers and narcotics agents who believe:

1. There is a Nation-wide crime syndicate known as the Mafia, whose tentacles are found in many large cities. It has international ramifications which appear most clearly in connection with the narcotics traffic.

2. Its leaders are usually found in control of the most lucrative rackets in their cities.

3. There are indications of a centralized direction and control of these rackets, but leadership appears to be in a group rather than in a single individual.

4. The Mafia is the cement that helps to bind the Costello-Adonis-Lansky syndicate of New York and the Accardo-Guzik-Fischetti syndicate of

Chicago as well as smaller criminal gangs and individual criminals throughout the country. These groups have kept in touch with Luciano since his deportation from this country.

5. The domination of the Mafia is based fundamentally on "muscle" and "murder." The Mafia is a secret conspiracy against law and order which will ruthlessly eliminate anyone who stands in the way of its success in any criminal enterprise in which it is interested. It will destroy anyone who betrays its secrets. It will use any means available—political influence, bribery, intimidation, etc., to defeat any attempt on the part of law-enforcement to touch its top figures or to interfere with its operations.

The Mafia today acts closely with many persons who are not of Sicilian descent. Moreover, it must be pointed out most strongly that the Mafia group comprises only a very small fraction of a percentage even of Sicilians. It would be most unfortunate if any inferences were erroneously drawn in any way derogatory to the vast majority of fine law-abiding citizens of Sicilian and Italian extraction.

Section 39 **THE MAFIA IN ITALY**

> From "Mafia" by Gaetano Mosca, *Encyclopaedia of the Social Sciences.*

MAFIA. The Sicilian word mafia is not found in Italian writings before the nineteenth century. Traina's Sicilian-Italian dictionary (1868) defines it as a neologism denoting any sign of bravado, a bold show; Mortillaro's dictionary (1876), as a word of Piedmontese origin equivalent to gang (*camorra*). Neither definition is exact. The word is employed by Sicilians in two different although related senses: on the one hand, it is used to denote an attitude which until recently has been fairly widespread among certain classes of Sicilians; on the other, it signifies a number of small criminal bands.

Mafia describes the attitude which assumes that recourse to legal authority in cases of persecution by private enemies is a symptom of weakness, almost of cowardice. It is an exaggeration of the sentiment, more or less common in Latin countries, that appeal to law against offenses involving personal insult, for instance adultery, is unmanly and that the duel is the proper means of recovering lost honor. Sicilian circles affected by mafist psychology held that many offenses must be avenged by personal action or by that of relatives and friends. Common theft, for example, was considered a sign of lack of respect indicating that the thief did not fear vengeance.

The mafist attitude, of which there were many degrees, was common in western Sicily and almost unknown in the eastern provinces, particularly Messina and Syracuse. It was practically non-existent among educated people as well as among the large class of sailors and fishermen and rare among all urban classes. It was most firmly rooted among peasants and large landowners.

By no means all people with such sentiments were actual or potential criminals. The great majority violated no law. When a person sharing mafist sentiments had relations with criminals he was usually actuated by a desire to prevent offenses against himself and not to commit them against others. The most serious consequence of such a tendency was the fact that refusal to report offenses to constituted authorities, which would have been contrary to the mafist moral law of *omerta,* prevented the capture of criminals by the state and thus facilitated the formation and activities of bands of malefactors.

Mafia was never a vast association of malefactors with a hierarchy of leaders and ramifications throughout Sicily. In this respect it differed sharply from the highly unified Neopolitan Camorra, with which it had no relationship except that of similar criminal objectives. Mafia consisted rather of many small autonomous associations, each active over a limited district. Each association was a *cosca* (Sicilian dialect; *tuft*), generally having a membership of twelve to fifteen, although some were larger. There was no election of chiefs, authority being wielded by members long addicted to crime, who directed the movements of younger associates, superintended dealings with victims and divided booty. Insubordination and especially misappropriation of booty were considered violations of mafist honor and punished, sometimes with death. The relations between neighboring *cosche* might be cordial or so antagonistic that difficulties would have to be settled by shooting. The great majority of mafist murders grew out of rivalry between *cosche* or members of one *cosca.* While it is untrue that members of the various *cosche* used conventional words and gestures to recognize one another, they did have peculiar mannerisms, including pronunciations of certain words, frequent use of others, and a certain furtive and shuffling expression. To any experienced Sicilian these betrayed connection with a *cosca.*

The *cosche* engaged chiefly in cattle rustling, extortion and occasional kidnaping for ransom. Often an ally of the *cosca* would offer to recover stolen cattle for the owner, and if such an offer were accepted the cattle would soon be found wandering about the countryside and the "friend" would be indemnified for his "expenses" to the extent of a third or a half the value of the cattle. In regions where agriculture was intensive, a tribute system prevailed. Every landowner or tenant paid to the *cosca* an annual tax higher than the combined imposts of the state, province and commune. Refusal to pay was punished by destruction of trees and vines and the slaughter of livestock. Letters demanding the deposit of a sum of money at a designated place or its consignment to a designated messenger were a method generally used by novices. Kidnaping of wealthy individuals for ransom fell into disuse some twenty years ago because of its difficulty. No woman or baby has been kidnaped for a decade, and no kidnaped person has been killed for three or four. The police have generally suspended efforts to discover the kidnapers until the victim has been freed. A *cosca* through more or less veiled threats would often induce a landowner to entrust the marketing of produce to one of its members or to lease his estate to persons in their confidence. In the first case small thefts by novices not associated with the *cosca* were prevented, a part of the produce being appropriated as payment by the *cosca* itself. In the second case a rebate, often half the lease price, was extracted.

In cattle rustling, the most common offense, two *cosche* collaborated. Stolen oxen and sheep would be dispatched to a commune fifty or more kilometers away, secretly butchered and consumed. Stolen horses and mules were sometimes sent as far as Tunis, where the mafists had connections with Sicilian emigrants. *Cosche* also have had close relations with criminal bands in the United States whose members were ex-mafists. A letter sent from America to a notorious Sicilian mafist announced a murder committed during its transit. The murder of a New York City police lieutenant, Petrosino, at Palermo in 1909 was perpetrated in cooperation with mafist criminals in America.

About 1878 Prefect of Police Malusardi, in whom the minister of the interior vested authority over all Sicily, exiled to the coastal islands several hundred criminals against whom precise evidence was lacking. Later, however, the *cosche* reorganized and perfected their methods of operation, and most of their members practised a trade from which they appeared to live. The government was long powerless to stop their crimes. Although the mafist chiefs were fairly well known, the police could offer no evidence but popular report. Few persons dared appear against the criminals. Even when a chief could be identified he could prove an alibi, and the youths who actually had perpetrated offenses were unknown. When the latter were arrested they rarely informed on those who had ordered them to commit an offense, for they would then not only be condemned but would also forfeit mafist honor and the help customarily given by the *cosca* to captives of the police.

But the chief obstacle to legal action was the political influence of the mafists, who in some communes dominated political elections. This power developed after the first important extension of the franchise in 1882 and increased after universal suffrage was adopted in 1912. The poorest classes, now given the vote, were by no means most largely represented in the *cosche;* but because of ignorance and fear they yielded most easily to mafist threats and supported candidates endorsed by mafists. The *cosche* required their legislative tools to obtain for their members permission to carry weapons, to intercede with the police in their favor and to serve them in other ways. The question of public safety in Sicily was repeatedly discussed by the chamber and all ministers of the interior instructed the prefects of police to make no compromise with crime. More ministers, however, also recommended support of the parliamentary candidacy of a mafist tool, and the prefects often carried out the second instruction while ignoring the first.

During recent years the mafist attitude has weakened. Immediately after the World War the general confusion and the ambitions of the younger members of the *cosche* to gain control led to a recrudescence of mafist activities and a series of murders within the *cosche.* Beginning about 1925, the Fascist government undertook a rigorous war against the mafia. In this struggle it was aided by the weakening of mafist sentiments resulting from the wider diffusion of culture and of material comforts and the more frequent contacts with the continent which followed upon the improvement of transportation and communication. The government pushed the fight with vigor and success, inducing victims to give sufficient proof to bring about many arrests and convictions. The Fascist system of appointing members of the legislature prevents mafist influence on elections. Today conditions of public safety in Sicily may be considered normal.

Section 40   **THE MAFIA**

From the *Encyclopaedia Britannica.*

MAFIA, a word of uncertain origin, used to designate a specific form of criminality which arose on the great landed estates (*latifundia*) of Sicily as a result of bad government during a long period of the island's history, and more especially during the disorders consequent on the Napoleonic invasion of South Italy. Lawless conditions led the owners of large estates to place their lands in the charge of energetic ruffians who exercised almost despotic powers over a terrorized peasantry. The continguity of the estates enabled these men to form an organization which gradually became very extensive and powerful, so much so that in time it turned against the land-owners themselves. The members of the organization were not very numerous, but, bound by close ties of fellowship and capable of any crime, they compelled the land-owners to employ persons of their choice, fixed the compensation they claimed for their services, and the rents and price of the lands and of the crops entrusted to their protection. Their activities soon extended to the neighbouring towns, they made it practically impossible for lands or crops to be sold at open auction, and effectively hindered all efforts likely to interfere with their interests. On the other hand, fierce quarrels of all kinds arose among them leading to terrible acts of revenge; whence the formation of bands of outlaws, at feud among themselves, and all the crimes consequent on outlawry: robbery, rapine, extortion.

A complicated code of traditions regulated the *mafia*, based on so-called *omerta* (from Sicilian *omu*, man), the obligation never, under any circumstances, to apply for justice to the legally constituted authorities, and never to assist in any way in the detection of crime committed against oneself or others. Absolute silence was required and enforced by ruthless reprisals, the right to avenge injuries being reserved to the victims or their families. Like the Camorra (q.v.), the Mafia was soon powerful in all classes, and even the commander of the royal troops acted in collusion with it. In Sept. 1892, about 150 Mafiusi were arrested at Catania, but the only result was to drive some of the members abroad, with disastrous results to other countries. In Oct. 1890 David Hennessy, chief of police in New Orleans, was murdered. Subsequent legal inquiry proved the crime to be the work of the Mafia, which had been introduced into the United States 30 years before. In May 1890 a band of Italians living in New Orleans had ambushed another gang of their fellow countrymen belonging to a society called *Stoppaghera*. The severe police measures taken brought the vengeance of the society upon Hennessy. Eleven Italians were indicted on suspicion of being implicated in his murder; but the jury was terrorized and acquitted six. On March 14, 1891, a mob led by well-known New Orleans citizens broke into the gaol where 19 Italians were imprisoned and lynched 11 of them.

Since 1870 the Italian Government has endeavoured with varying and scant success to rid Sicily of the *mafia*, which continued however to be tolerated by local authorities as affording a ready means to unscrupulous candidates to secure a majority at the political or administrative elections. The abnormal conditions consequent on Italy's participation in the World War (1915–18) led to an alarming revival in these criminal activities. When the Fascist Government took office (Oct. 1922) it undertook to root out this evil, and used its exceptional powers to identify, capture and bring to trial the leaders and their accomplices. This led, in 1927, to a series of trials at Termini Imerese (prov. of Palermo) and Palermo. The accused, in batches of as many as 150 at a time, were brought before the courts and their victims, reassured by the energetic police measures taken to ensure their safety, gave evidence against them. The leaders, found guilty of a long series of atrocious crimes, received life sentences, and exemplary punishment was meted out to their accomplices.

Section 41   THE MYTH OF THE MAFIA

From *The End of Ideology* by Daniel Bell, 1959.

The mobsters were able, where they wished, to "muscle in" on the gambling business because the established gamblers were wholly vulnerable, not being able to call on the law for protection. The senators, however, refusing to make any distinction between a gambler and a gangster, found it convenient to talk loosely of a nationwide conspiracy of "illegal" elements. Senator Kefauver asserted that a "nationwide crime syndicate does exist in the United States, despite the protestations of a strangely assorted company of criminals, self-serving politicians, plain blind fools, and others who may be honestly misguided, that there is no such combine." The Senate committee report states the matter more dogmatically: "There is a nationwide crime syndicate known as the Mafia. . . . Its leaders are usually found in control of the most lucrative rackets in their cities. There are indications of a centralized direction and control of these rackets. . . . The Mafia is the cement that helps to bind the Costello-Adonis-Lansky syndicate of New York and the Accardo-Guzik-Fischetti syndicate of Chicago. . . . These groups have kept in touch with Luciano since his deportation from the country."

Unfortunately for a good story—and the existence of the Mafia would be a whale of a story—neither the Senate Crime Committee in its testimony, nor Kefauver in his book, presented any real evidence that the Mafia exists as a functioning organization. One finds police officials asserting before the Kefauver committee their *belief* in the Mafia; the Narcotics Bureau *thinks* that a world-wide dope ring allegedly run by Luciano is part of the Mafia; but the only other "evidence" presented—aside from the incredulous responses both of Senator Kefauver and Rudolph Halley when nearly all the

Italian gangsters asserted that they didn't know about the Mafia—is that certain crimes bear "the earmarks of the Mafia."

The legend of the Mafia has been fostered in recent years largely by the peephole writing team of Jack Lait and Lee Mortimer. In their *Chicago Confidential,* they rattled off a series of names and titles that made the organization sound like a rival to an Amos and Andy Kingfish society. Few serious reporters, however, give it much credence. Burton Turkus, the Brooklyn prosecutor who broke up the "Murder, Inc." ring, denies the existence of the Mafia. Nor could Senator Kefauver even make out much of a case for his picture of a national crime syndicate. He is forced to admit that "as it exists today (it) is an elusive and furtive but nonetheless tangible thing," and that "its organization and machinations are not always easy to pinpoint." *
His "evidence" that many gangsters congregate at certain times of the year in such places as Hot Springs, Arkansas, in itself does not prove much; people "in the trade" usually do, and as the loquacious late Willie Moretti of New Jersey said, in explaining how he had met the late Al Capone at a race track,

* The accidental police discovery of a conference of Italian figures, most of them with underworld and police records, in Apalachin, New York, in November 1957, revived the talk of a Mafia. *Time* magazine assigned a reporter, Serrell Hillman, to check the story, and this is what he reported: "I spent some two weeks in New York, Washington and Chicago running down every clue to the so-called Mafia that I could find. I talked to a large number of Federal, state and local law enforcement authorities; to police, reporters, attorneys, detectives, non-profit civic groups such as the Chicago Crime Commission. Nobody from the F. B. I. and Justice Department officials on down, with the exception of a couple of Hearst crime reporters—always happy for the sake of a street sale to associate the 'Mafia' with the most routine barroom shooting—and the Narcotics Bureau believed that a Mafia exists as such. The Narcotics Bureau, which has to contend with a big problem in dope-trafficking, contends that a working alliance operates between an organized Mafia in Italy and Sicily and a U. S. Mafia. But the Bureau has never been able to submit proof of this, and the F. B. I. is skeptical. The generally held belief is that there is no tightly knit syndicate, but instead a loose "trade association" of criminals in various cities and areas, who run their own shows in their own fields but have matters of mutual interest to take up (as at the Apalachin conference). At any rate, nobody has ever been able to produce specific evidence that a Mafia is functioning."

In early 1959, Frederic Sondern, Jr., an editor of the *Reader's Digest,* published a best-selling book on the Mafia, *Brotherhood of Evil,* but a close reading of Mr. Sondern's text indicates that his sources are largely the files of the Narcotics Bureau, and his findings little more than a rehash of previously publicized material. (For a devastating review of the book, see the *Times Literary Supplement,* London, June 12, 1959, p. 351.) Interestingly enough, in May, 1959, Alvin Goldstein, a former assistant district attorney in New York, who had prosecuted racketeer Johnny Dio, conducted a crime survey of California for Governor Pat Brown and reported that he found no evidence of the existence of a Mafia in California.

"Listen, well-charactered people you don't need introductions to; you just meet automatically."

Why did the Senate Crime Committee plump so hard for its theory of a Mafia and a national crime syndicate? In part, they may have been misled by their own hearsay. The Senate committee was not in the position to do original research, and its staff, both legal and investigative, was incredibly small. Senator Kefauver had begun the investigation with the attitude that with so much smoke there must be a raging fire. But smoke can also mean a smoke screen. Mob activities is a field in which busy gossip and exaggeration flourish even more readily than in a radical political sect.

There is, as well, in the American temper, a feeling that "somewhere," "somebody" is pulling all the complicated strings to which this jumbled world dances. In politics the labor image is "Wall Street" or "Big Business"; while the business stereotype was the "New Dealers." In the field of crime, the side-of-the-mouth low-down was "Costello."

The salient reason, perhaps, why the Kefauver Committee was taken in by its own myth of an omnipotent Mafia and a despotic Costello was its failure to assimilate and understand three of the more relevant sociological facts about institutionalized crime in its relation to the political life of large urban communities in America, namely: (1) the rise of the American Italian community, as part of the inevitable process of ethnic succession, to positions of importance in politics, a process that has been occurring independently but also simultaneously in most cities with large Italian constituencies—New York, Chicago, Kansas City, Los Angeles; (2) the fact that there are individual Italians who play prominent, often leading roles today in gambling and in the mobs: and (3) the fact that Italian gamblers and mobsters often possessed "status" within the Italian community itself and a "pull" in city politics. These three items are indeed related—but not so as to form a "plot."

Section 42 L'UNIONE SICILIANO

From Final Report, Special Crime Study Commission on Organized Crime, California, 1953.

To mention the so-called Mafia is to venture into a region of underworld groups who have obtained an extraordinary degree of security through the discipline of secrecy from which there has been little deviation. Based as it is on the cohesive force of common national origin, it plays an important and unique part in criminal activity in the United States. Today it is inaccurate to refer to this organization as "The Mafia." It is now known as "L'Unione Siciliano." Confusion arises because of its origin in the ancient Sicilian Mafia, which was a feared and powerful force during the years when immigration from Italy to the United States was at its peak. Originally a semi-revolutionary and benevolent society, it degenerated here into a criminal gang. This organization is generally considered the most sinister and powerful criminal organization in the world. It has headquarters on at least two continents. Its centers of organization are far from California, and the Commission makes no claim to have developed by its own efforts any important information concerning it. However, some few words concerning the organization are necessary and appropriate in order to give true significance to the activities of its branches and members in California. According to a memorandum supplied to us by the Federal Bureau of Narcotics, L'Unione Siciliano in conception and organization is attributed to the old Sicilian Mafia or Black Hand Society. It was organized over 30 years ago in the United States by one Joe La Porta now in his early fifties and a resident of the Bronx. La Porta and many of his colleagues fled from Palermo, Sicily, at the time Mussolini ordered a concerted drive on the Mafia Society throughout Sicily. Joe La Porta and many other Mafia Society members took refuge in New York City and in the Bronx. It was here that L'Unione Siciliano was first formed and La Porta conceived the idea of conducting criminal enterprises behind the disguise of small business operations.

The first of these business fronts were a number of Italian coffee shops. These were followed by distributors of candy, olives, olive oil, cheese and fruit and later by such businesses as undertaking parlors, small garment factories and many others. Today, successful members of the Sicilian underworld are still using the same technique and are operating behind the façade of very large businesses.

L'Unione Siciliano, it is said, expanded rapidly throughout the United States during the 1930's. Its expansion was accomplished by the formation of various Italo-American clubs, all bearing different names, but all secretly connected with the parent body. The criminal activities of L'Unione Siciliano cover all major illegal enterprises, according to the memorandum from the Bureau of Narcotics. It had national control of bookmaking activities through the seizure of the so-called wire service by the Capone Syndicate, and it is the principal organization, if not the only one, in the narcotics, prostitution and counterfeiting rackets in nearly all parts of the United States. It has even secured control of certain labor unions.

According to the Narcotic Bureau's memorandum, membership in L'Unione Siciliano is open to both criminal and noncriminal persons. The society has learned that its greatest opportunity lies in political activities, and in recent years, much of its money and attention have gone into this field.

At first this was largely confined to using the tremendous funds from the rackets for the purpose of bribing law enforcement officers, judges, juries, civil service employees and legislators. More recently, it is claimed that these resources are being used in political campaigns in the support of candidates who will further the society's interests. The memorandum lists a number of such cases.

The membership in L'Unione Siciliano is no longer confined exclusively to persons of Italian origin, although they retain control of its very secretive governing councils.

The widely separated origins and extensive travel of many of the persons connected with the Nick De John case, while they do not in themselves reveal the hand of L'Unione Siciliano, do show the very close associations in large cities from one end of the country to the other. Certainly the murder of Nick De John, on May 7, 1947, underlines the necessity for constant vigilance to ward off the infiltration of hoodlum gangs and continued alertness to the activities of the members of L'Unione Siciliano. De John, whose strangled corpse was found concealed in the trunk of his automobile, was a rich and powerful figure in the Chicago underworld syndicates, including the infamous Capone gang. He was a nephew of Vince "The Don" Benevento, an important Chicago hoodlum who was assassinated on September 21, 1946, near Lake Zurich, Illinois. Benevento, in addition to his other activities, was proprietor of a cheese merchandising business, a fact of some significance because of the interest of several of De John's San Francisco associates in the Sunland Sales Company, a San Francisco cheese and olive oil distributing firm. Benevento, De John and many of the individuals with whom they were identified in Chicago, were commonly accepted as members of L'Unione Siciliano. With this background, De John's appearance in San Francisco a few months before his assassination was discovered by the police to have been regarded with some fear by the city's Sicilian underworld. Frank Scappatura, a part owner of the Sunland Sales Company, Leonard Calimia, its sales manager, Tony Lima, an olive oil and cheese salesman, Mike Abati, and Sebastiano Nani, a hoodlum from Brooklyn, were indicted for De John's murder. Scappatura and Lima were never apprehended. The prosecution of the others, hampered by typical reticence on the part of the gang members and victims alike, and crippled by perjury, came to naught. It became plain, however, that those implicated in the De John killing had associated in a criminal organization extending all over the world. Its members were engaged in illegal gambling and the narcotics traffic, and possessed criminal records in places as far-flung as New York, Chicago, Kansas City, Florida, Pennsylvania, Toronto, Montreal and Ohio. From all of these places, police records coupled them with L'Unione Siciliano, and in several instances with large narcotic distribution rings.

There can be little doubt that Jack Dragna and his gang of associates, such as the Sicas and the Adamos of Los Angeles, and the Matrangas, Dippolitos and Le Mandris of San Bernardino County, were all connected with the notorious L'Unione Siciliano. Certain papers seized by the Los Angeles police on February 14, 1950, from the Dragnas definitely tend to confirm this view. Several small address books were taken from the gangsters. The names listed read like a Who's Who of the Mafia in the United States. Some of them are regarded as among the most powerful and dangerous professional criminals in the Country. They also contained, of course, the usual sprinkling of names of police officers, district attorneys, investigators, bail bond brokers, lawyers and lobbyists. That these acquaintances were business rather than social is indicated in many instances by Dragna's canceled checks, the payees of which were often known gangsters. The seized papers also showed that gangster funds are being invested in certain legitimate businesses, such as clothing, fruit, wine, olive oil and importing.

The Dragna gang is discussed here, not because it is any more important than other criminal groups, but because it is typical and illustrative.

At the time of the publication of the Standley Commission's Third Progress Report, in which the existence and origin of the Dragna gang was first publicly exposed, the ruthless methods of gangster retaliation were made realistically clear with the murder of Abraham Davidian in Fresno on February 28, 1950. Although Davidian was not killed in the Los Angeles area, the events which led to his death had their origin in that community. Davidian, a short period before his death, had attempted to establish himself in the illicit narcotic trade and had testified before a federal grand jury in Los Angeles concerning his purchase of heroin from a wholesaler whom he identified as Joe Sica, a former member of the Dragna gang and a close associate of several other hoodlums who were identified as members of L'Unione Siciliano.

Davidian, although not one who could be classified as a member of the society, had broken the code of silence concerning gang activities. Underworld rumors that Davidian was marked for assassination as a result of his testimony were brutally confirmed. He was killed at his mother's home while sleeping on the sofa in the front room by assassins who left no clues of their identity. The conspiracy case against Sica and others was subsequently dismissed with the removal of this principal witness.

Perhaps of all the law enforcement agencies throughout the State of California, the Los Angeles Police Department is more acutely aware of the dangers of the mere existence of members of L'Unione Siciliano in its community and the plague which the society visits upon the citizens. It has been gratifying to this Commission to see the active work done by the Los Angeles Police Department to control and combat this menace. Chief of Police Parker and Captain James Hamilton, who heads the Intelligence Unit of the Los Angeles Police Department, have continuous studies and investigations under way to discover the positions and activities of leaders of L'Unione Siciliano and hoodlums in the Los Angeles area who are suspected of membership. As a result of their interest in the gangland killings of the past and present, and in order to further study the Mafia, the Los Angeles Police Department has prepared a survey report entitled "Gangland Killings, Los Angeles Area, 1900–1951." This is a good picture of the rackets, illustrating the problem that the department has to contend with, and is typical of the problems which confront other law enforcement agencies. The survey report deals with some 57 murders which have been committed in the Los Angeles area from the year 1900 to 1951. It is true that so-called Mafia killings are surrounded with the secrecy which has proved to be most difficult to penetrate. However, the study of these crimes over the years shows a definite pattern, the repetition of which in case after case cannot be laid to coincidence.

Section 43   L'UNIONE vs. MAFIA

From *Murder Inc.* by Burton B. Turkus and Sid Feder, 1951.

It has become popular in recent years to "expose" Unione as the single society ruling all crime in these United States. The evidence and recorded history paint a different picture of the facts. No one who really knows anything at all about the sharp clannishness of mob bosses with respect to nationalities and creeds would ever attempt to attribute to any one group the control over the whole. Besides, if one such unit had all crime in this country under its power, is it not reasonable to assume that somewhere along the line, some law agency—federal, state, county or municipal—would have tripped it up long before this? No single man or group ever was so clever, so completely genius, as to foil all of them forever. Powerful, Unione is; murderous, unquestionably. But it always has been just one strong link among the many links in the national chain of crime. Actually, the Syndicate loves to have the theory expounded that there is a supreme irrevocable individual authority. Then, the directors of crime know that not too much heat will generate under their cozy rackets.

Even more serious, however, is the popular pastime of lumping Italian crime groups under one heading with interchangeable names. The most recent example of such misconception was that achieved by the Kefauver

Senate Crime Investigating Committee. Mafia, the Committee said officially, is "also known as the Black Hand and the Unione Siciliano." With no attempt to dim the work done by the Senators, I should like to point out that Unione is no more Mafia than man is the ape. In fact, as a factor of power in national crime, Mafia has been virtually extinct for two decades. Unione, meantime, has grown fat on felony. The evidence is incontrovertible. Court records prove it. The chief difference between the two lies in Unione's co-operation with other mobs, a characteristic entirely foreign to the clannish Mafia.

The inclusion of the headline-catching label of Black Hand as a synonym for either or both is even farther afield. In fact, striking evidence of this was found by the New York Police Department—and as far back as forty-four years ago! At the turn of the century, Black Hand was a fashionable form of extortion, aimed at honest, hardworking immigrants. The name grew out of menacing letters, each signed by a crude drawing of a black hand and demanding money, under threat of death, kidnap or mutilation of the selected victim's children. The letters became so prevalent that Police Commissioner William McAdoo assigned a squad to investigate.

The story of Italian criminal societies in this country begins shortly before the turn of the century, when old-world gangsters of Mafia and Camorra crept into America. Picking up where they left off at home, these brutal bandits preyed primarily on their decent newly-arrived countrymen, to whom tales of the dread Camorra and Mafia were still very real.

As the years passed, the infants who had migrated with their families grew up. So did the first generation spawned in the new world. They went to American schools and learned American ways—particularly the ways of the environment in which they grew. Many rose to eminence. Others followed the easier way. These fledgling felons differed from their older criminal countrymen in that the new world taught them it was possible to work together with others, even if they were not of the same blood. Eventually, they began to resent the elders. A contemptuous hatred was born. They referred to the elders of Mafia as "The Handlebar Guys" and "The Moustache Petes," because most of them were adorned with flowing moustaches that were reasonable facsimiles of coat hangers. The resentment stemmed, mostly, from the clannishness of the elders, their adamant refusal to associate with any but their own Sicilian-born tribesmen, and their continued preying on their own immigrant countrymen. Those were the ways of Mafia.

As they grew up, the new element—this Americanized faction—acquired sufficient strength to set up its own version of a mob, dealing not in comparatively puny extortions from immigrants with limited resources, but pointing toward bigger money crime. It was the first spark of Unione. All—old and new—were, however, generally grouped for descriptive purposes as "The Italian Society."

Ruling over the oldsters of Mafia in the early days was a greedy, sadistic character widely known as Lupo the Wolf, or just plain Lupo, since that means Wolf in his native tongue. Born Ignazio Saietta, he crossed the Atlantic after murdering a man in Italy, and here he found new fields of endeavor. In the late teens and very early twenties, his organization had a hand in such juicy pies as the Italian lottery, narcotics and extortions from immigrants— all accompanied by assorted bombings, blackmail and murder. But the money did not come fast enough for Lupo the Wolf. So, he took to paying off with money he manufactured himself. For that, the Government sentenced him to thirty years. President Harding commuted his sentence after a few years, but when Lupo showed virtually no signs of having reformed, he was sent back to finish out the full term. Many men died trying to move in as his successor.

In early Prohibition days, bootleggers hijacked their liquor from bonded government warehouses or acquired it from these same warehouses through official medicinal permits which they had the foresight to steal or obtain from "friendly" connections.

Like any business catering to the public taste, they ran into the normal problem of supply and demand. One man might get ten cases of bourbon, for example, and have a good customer who insisted on Scotch. Another might have Scotch, but needed bourbon for a steady-paying speakeasy client. The businessmen set up an exchange on the street curbs of a certain neighborhood in lower New York to barter for their requirements. Trading stolen government whiskey right out in the open was not, however, the height of their audacity. They actually set up their curb exchange on the very streets surrounding police headquarters!

It was here, on the scene of the bootleggers' curb exchange, that Giuseppe Masseria entered the picture. He was short and chunky and a gunman dating back to 1907. He just walked in, and declared himself the downtown boss, succeeding Lupo the Wolf. Through the next two years, Giuseppe proceeded, by conquest, to back up his claim. Since the head man of the Society is always "the boss," he soon took to calling himself "Joe the Boss." However, one Umberto Valenti, a bootlegger, was ambitious for the leadership, himself. He oiled up his pistol and sallied forth, abetted by aides and associates. Many shooting matches followed.

Joe the Boss called a peace conference in an East Side spaghetti house. Joe did not advise Valenti that he had two aides stationed a block away. The huddle over, the enemies strolled out together, like long-time friends. Masseria's hired hands joined them at the corner, and the shooting began. They chased Valenti across the street. One of them fired the entire clip from his pistol at the ambitious bootlegger's fleeing back. Valenti made it to a taxicab; even got the door open. Then he fell on his face.

Unopposed now as The Boss, the little man who could dodge bullets ruled for the next nine years. Joe was just as clannish as his predecessors—still for Mafia supreme—but he was not entirely averse to having his assistants form friendships with outside outfits. He was still a loner in principle, but his ideas were sufficiently modified, so that during his regime, the groundwork for Unione was laid.

Giuseppe Masseria came to count more and more on Lucky's mob know-how. Luciano blossomed out as racketeer, trigger and first assistant to the head man of the secret society. But Lucky did not think in Giuseppe's old-country way—the way of the "Moustache Petes." He became allied with a group that ruled the rum-running of the Atlantic Coast, from Maine to Virginia. There were associations with Frank Costello and his good right arm, Dandy Phil Kastel, a bucket shop and securities thief who still handled Frank C.'s tremendous New Orleans operations. And there was Charley (King) Solomon, the Boston boss, and Longy Zwillman, the New Jersey nabob. From these alone, it is obvious there were other gangs and other ganglords besides Mafia on the scene.

As the unpopularity of Prohibition brought louder public cry for repeal, a new type of businessman boss rose to power. This new order was realistic. It recognized the danger in indiscriminate shooting and gang warfare, and the limitations in the clannish every-man-for-himself mode of doing business. The idea began to spread among the sub-leaders who, like Lucky, had grown up in American ways. With Joe the Boss dealing entirely on the executive level, these moderns were the operational bosses, and they instituted changes. The trend was all toward less inter-gang rivalry and attendant blood-letting. Joe the Boss couldn't see it. He was not against friendships, but "combinations" did not appeal to Joe. He was still old school enough to be basically isolationist.

"An outfit runs on its own and knocks off anybody in the way," was his set credo.

Nevertheless, crime was moving toward co-operation, if not yet organization. Lepke and Gurrah already had a co-op of sorts going—an association with Buggsy Siegel's murderers. Lepke and Gurrah did the extortion and the organization stuff in industry; the Bug & Meyer Mob handled the enforcement.

Joe the Boss enjoyed Lucky's company. Although modern in his ideas on crime, Charley had an old world flair for living. He still has. So, when he invited Joe to Coney Island for dinner one unseasonably warm April day in 1931, The Boss looked forward to it.

Lucky called for a deck from the house. They played and they talked for about forty-five minutes. Scarpato's was completely empty now, except for the help sweeping up in the kitchen. It was then Lucky excused himself. He walked slowly between the rows of white cloths, and disappeared into the men's room.

It is too bad he took so long washing his hands, he explained. He missed it when impeachment proceedings were carried out against Joe the Boss. It seemed there must have been three voters. They came in while Lucky was away washing his hands—as he explained—and he missed it all. More than twenty bullets were sprayed around the premises. The passing years and the easy life must have robbed Joe of his agility, for five of them were buried in him.

Two factions still remained in the Society, despite Masseria's demise. They were still the old and the new; opposite poles in their ways of thinking. The so-called "Greaser" crowd—the Handlebar Guys—would not see the modern trend. With Lucky now the top man, though, the new held the upper hand. For the first time, Unione emerged as the dominant factor. Still, Mafia had to be reckoned with. Even with Joe the Boss gone, there was capable leadership, notably Salvatore Marrizano, or Maranzano. He headed the "Moustache Petes"—the oldsters—who were not yet convinced.

The rackets czar sought out his friend Lucky. Always one of the more respected counsels in the national underworld, Lepke had a plan all thought out. Lucky, he asserted, was blind to reality in this matter.

"You think this is a fight in the clothing business?" he challenged. "Open your eyes, Charley. Marrizano is out to take over the Italian Society again."

A most persuasive salesman was Lepke, with soft cow-eyes and a smooth, modulated voice. He convinced Lucky. Luciano decided it was time to settle this intra-mural rivalry once and for all. All the Greaser crowd would have to go. Not only in New York, either—but all over the country. And Marrizano was the No. 1 candidate. The day for the cleanup was set for September 11, 1931. It has long been known as "Purge Day" in Unione. All of the mob leaders in and around New York, in and out of the Society, pledged Lucky shooting co-operation.

An unusually mixed group of five men strode into Marrizano's office suite in the Grand Central Building that September afternoon. Leader of the party was Bo Weinberg, ace of Dutch Schultz's crack crew of killers. Police files say that those with him included a top assassin of the Bug & Meyer Mob; a fellow named Murphy and another named Allie, who were known as friends of Longy Zwillman, the Jersey magnate, and an unidentitfied fifth man. Incidentally, this Allie was later found full of bullets on a road leading to Troy, N. Y.

Twelve men were in Marrizano's outer office. The five flashed police badges and mumbled something about a raid. Almost docilely, the twelve who were there permitted themselves to be lined up against a wall. Then, while part of the invading party stood guard, the others barged into Marrizano's private inner office, shot him and cut his throat. Its mission accomplished, the quintet departed.

The day Marrizano got it was the end of the line for the Greaser Crowd in the Italian Society—the finish of "The Moustache Petes"—and a definite windup to Mafia as an entity and a power in national crime. For, in line with Lucky's edict—which had been inspired by Lepke's persuasiveness—some thirty to forty leaders of Mafia's older group all over the United States were murdered that day and in the next forty-eight hours! It was a remarkable example of planning and accomplishment that this mass extermination of Mafia executives across the country has never, as far as I have been able to learn, been linked, one with another. Had the connection been established then, in 1931, and Unione's position uncovered, there would now be none of the erroneous conception, grown so popular through the years, of classifying Mafia and Unione as one and the same.

They are, actually, no more the same than are the Democratic and Republican Parties. There is strong evidence on the subject. It was a matter of sworn court testimony during the Dewey rackets investigations in the late thirties. J. Richard (Dixie) Davis, the notorious attorney for Dutch Schultz and so many moblords, turned State's evidence and revealed that Bo Weinberg told him of the Purge in the Italian Society which left Mafia dead and Unione and Lucky as the surviving might and strength in every sense of the word.

Even more irrefutable evidence was provided as recently as 1944, directly from an insider—an eagle-beaked one-eyed thug named Ernest Rupolo, who is known as The Hawk and who describes his trade as an assassin for hire. Only out of prison a year, after doing nine years for one shooting, The Hawk was arrested for another. Almost eagerly, he pleaded guilty, stating that he had been hired for $500 for the job. Stubbornly, he refused to name his employers—until the Court threatened him with a sentence of forty to eighty years. That changed his mind. He supplied information that broke four murder cases. He involved Vito Genovese, then and now accredited with being a national power in Unione.

The Hawk went into the background and modernization of the Italian Society of crime, and supplied the clincher to the exploded myth. Unione, he declared flatly, is the self-appointed successor to Mafia. Since 1931, any similarity has been purely imaginative.

With its opposition and their antiquated methods erased, Unione spread like a high tide of scum to all corners of the country. The moderns who took over even accepted as blood brothers some members not of the same nationality or extraction. This must be final proof of the schism betweeen Mafia, with its deadly code of Omerta and its clannish ways, and Unione, with its modern-day methods of co-operative endeavor in crime. The old order would as soon have a polecat as a non-Sicilian on its rolls.

Like all heads of Unione, Lucky acquired the emblematic title: The Boss. And from far off Italy, in spite of his exile, he continues a powerful factor—if not absolute ruler of the order—to this day.

These early developments have been chronicled, since it is from Masseria's demise and the purge of Mafia, and Lucky's resultant coronation, that modern gangdom—Murder, Inc., the national crime organization—may be traced. When Joe the Boss bowed out, the old order packed up and went with him.

AT WHOM will the accusing finger point tomorrow?

The underworld of tomorrow is composed of the juvenile gangs of to-day. Indeed, the adult gangster is merely the adolescent hood grown up. From street-corner society arise the young tribes, engaged in horseplay, violence, petty thievery; they follow a leader; they swear eternal fealty; they war for jurisdiction. Inevitably, they evolve into adulthood, continuing the pattern of group action, with its code of internal relations and its negative code of external relations. From each generation issue new gangs, supplying fresh recruits to the underworld.

Although every age—including the present—is shocked and horrified by the rise of the juvenile mob, there has been no period in American history without its youth gangs. More than a hundred years ago, two leaders of the Daybreak Boys, a river gang, were hanged. One of these, Nicholas Saul, was twenty years old and the other, William Howlett, was nineteen. By that time they were already hardened criminals, having joined the gang when they were sixteen and fifteen years old. Others in the gang had joined at ten and twelve years of age.

Almost a hundred years later, two Brooklyn lads—Happy Maione and Abe (Kid Twist) Reles—merged their gangs to compose the skeleton of Murder Inc. Both had just attained their majority. Yet, at one and twenty, they were mob leaders with a following and a long record of crime behind them.

In the early 1930's, Frederic Thrasher noted that "a striking fact which bears directly upon the relation of juvenile delinquency to mercenary crime is the early age at which professional criminals, gangsters, gunmen, and racketeers begin their criminal careers" (*Crime for Profit*, p. 128).

And thirty years later, in the 1960's, our great metropolises are stunned by the recurrence of senseless violence inflicted by young gangs on one another and on innocent prey. Stung by the vicious character of these outbreaks, J. Edgar Hoover was moved to insist that the term "juvenile delinquency" was too apologetic for what he preferred to brand as "teen-age brigands."

The evolution of the street-corner clan into an organized gang, as well as the rise of the truant engaged in petty thievery to a criminal overlord engaged in finance, is a case of ontogeny recapitulating phylogeny as the development of gang and individual recapitulates the history of organized crime from Bowery brawler to Apalachin aristocrats.

It is the youth that gives the American underworld its eternal life. "After a grim set of public enemies are disposed of," wrote Frederic Thrasher, "there is always a new list equally long recruited from the younger lieutenants supplied from the extensive ranks of young hoodlums." What was true in the 1930's is true in the 1960's, guaranteeing the underworld with an institutional longevity extending far beyond the natural life span of its more mortal leadership.

The youth gang provides the underworld with a dynamic—a grim sort of democratic dynamic: the revolutions of the young versus the old; the rise of new ethnic groups to challenge formerly dominant strains; a resultant return to violence and to primitive push: a disruption of existing patterns of underworld-above-world ententes and the establishment of new criminal-political relationships.

The criminal youth gang is not coterminous with juvenile delinquent. Not every JD is a member of a gang and not every gang is delinquent in character. There are free-lancing delinquents, coming from many social levels, impelled by economic or emotional poverty to commit crimes. These free-floating transgressors, like their lonely counterparts in the adult criminal world, represent a nuisance but not an organized menace to society. On the other hand, there are gangs of boys who run in a pack, for the very innocent reason that they enjoy the animal warmth of the herd. These, too, may be found in all social strata, huddling together in the traditional patterns of their class. And though roughhouse and hazing are habitual, they need not be antisocial. The youth gang that imparts a dynamic to the world of organized crime is a special thing, the underworld in embryo, a deeply embedded aspect of our culture linking the generations of gangdom in America.

The young hoods represent an inevitable oedipal threat to the presiding potentates of the underworld. The top men in organized crime prefer anonymity and respectability; to untie all ties with the past. But they find themselves genetically bound to their occupational children, unable to disown parenthood and unable to purge the up-coming generation of the father's murderous impulses.

Consider the plight of the one-time outlaw who has "arrived." His ill-gotten gains are now well invested. What Karl Marx called the "primitive accumulation" of capital was completed by this mob mogul many years ago in the usual ugly manner of initial aggrandizement. In the style of the modern underworld, the mogul invested his money through a "trustee" or "trustees," to confound the Bureau of Internal Revenue and to compile a respectable pedigree for his legitimate enterprises. Now this elder statesman of crime is more or less ready to go straight and steady all the way. But he is prisoner of his past.

The contract between the mogul and his trustee is by word of mouth—the usual contract in the underworld, observed more punctiliously than most written instruments in the legal world. A man's word is as good as his bond in the underworld because violation of a contract is not corrected by "damages" but by death. The bargains of organized crime are written in the invisible ink of blood. To enforce the contract between original investor and administrator of the living estate, the old mogul must have a "gun" at his command. And this "gun," for the man who has arrived at respectability, is not a shooting iron but an executioner ready to do the old man's bidding.

The "old man," then, is constantly subject to a double double-cross: by his trustee and by his janissary. Of these two, the latter is the key man, the decisive person for keeping the intended establishment intact. If the trustee double-crosses, then the janissary can set things right by threat or by a "hit," the underworld term for the executioner's act. But if the janissary turns against his master, perhaps in a compact with the trustee, then the old man is a "has-been."

The janissary, almost needless to say, is invariably a younger man, still foolish enough to play with fire and virile enough to have a taste for the kill. This young hood, symbol of the new generation, is the ultimate irony in the development of the underworld. He does to the "old man" what the "old man" in his day did to other powers: entering the establishment as a servant prepared to do dirty work, he takes over the household and consigns the master to the dustbin.

But even this newest of the potentates must face his challenge—not by a younger man in his own strain but by an outside youth of a foreign clan. These "outside youths" are presently referred to by the more settled "organization man" as the "indians." The latter are usually of a new ethnic group, the most recent arrivals to the inner frontier of the slum. They have their own gangs, with a common racial or national origin, with their own costumes, their own argot, their own loyalties, their own locale, and their own hatreds. They learn the ways of the outlaw in the stimulating sport of street fighting. They organize their neighborhood clubs, easily evolved into political clubs. They learn their way with the police, develop "pull," elect friends, and defeat enemies. And they turn to crime—first stick-ups and then regularized racketeering.

Starting in a small way in their rackets, operating among their own people as "runners" for the big "bankers," as sluggers for the big respectables, as small fry for the big fish, they soon come to claim equality. In our democratic society, these new ethnic groups demand their fair share of the criminal proceeds, their rightful status in the world of crime. Indeed, one prominent political leader of a minority group in New York stated quite bluntly that his people were being discriminated against in the bookie and numbers rackets by being held down to positions of "runners" and the like while older ethnic groups held on to the banker posts in the rackets. This spokesman for America's most marked minority demanded equality for his people!

Equality—eventually superiority—is rarely attained in the underworld, however, by the open plea of political leaders for legal equality in the illegal world. Fair footing is attained with the unfair fist. The process of "muscling-in" begins all over again—a robbery in a protected store, extortion from protected businessmen, violent attacks on the protecting agency. The jungle war is on again.

The older ethnic groups, with economic power and political influence, tend first to subdue the "indians" with financial and governmental power. The "indian" is arrested and hailed into court—fingered by the established underworld. Police are glad to co-operate because the "indian" is a disturbance, a source of violence, a disruption to old ties, a threat to the monthly stipend. The cop-on-the-beat, whose philosophy is not to eliminate but to control crime in his precinct, can honestly feel that he is a pillar of virtue when he acts on the tip of the "syndicate" to eliminate an independent.

But this attempt to wipe out the indian by "due process" is bound to fail, just as it failed twenty and thirty years ago in containing the present powers of crime. The new ethnic groups are just as contemptuous of the law as their other-tongued precursors. What is more, the new population group is now electing its own public officials, laying its own crooked lines of courthouse contact, learning to put in the fix, rearing its own lawyers, getting its own judges. In the final analysis, the war of the jungle beast is fought out in jungle fashion, with the victory going to the youngest and the hungriest. Once more, youth is triumphant—giving the underworld new life and vigor.

The first excerpt in this section, entitled "The Idle Boy," was a description of the metropolitan delinquent written when this century was young: before television and psychoanalysis were widespread, before Bosnia and Korea, before the A and H bombs had made life cheap. This magazine piece is only one from a vast literature on the rising wave of youth delinquency, appearing periodically through the decades, with each of these timely items sounding the alarum against the menace. This 1913 excerpt is full of local color, transient references, dated language, yet by the simple transposition of a few terms, this description of the idle boy of half a century ago is an adequate portrayal of the delinquent today. Even in this early piece, the relationship between the young potential and the old professional is noted. Out of "the ancient den of thieves, older than the living memory of man" where the yegg and the "banker of criminals" reigned came the new cadets of crime.

The second excerpt, "A Training School for Crime," leaps across a half century to New York City in the 1960's. Here, in a brief newspaper account on the arrest of twenty-two persons accused of belonging to a crime-school gang, is the outline of an organized system whereby the overlords of crime provide on-the-job training to the young apprentices, with a curriculum covering robbery, murder, and—as always and above all—how to enforce silence.

The third excerpt is "A Street Scene," a current newspaper description of a modern "delinquency area," one of several such avenues in a great metropolis. This brief, colorful, frightening sketch of a crowded, decaying block in mid-Manhattan is more than the portrayal of a poverty-stricken street, just a few yards from some of the richest dwellings in the world. Emerging from these few sharp contours is the outline of a community separated economically, socially, legally from the greater city of which it is a part. 100th Street between First and Second Avenue is a casbah, a civilization within a civilization, where flatfeet fear to tread, where the law ends, where the typical American is a stranger, an outsider, and the object of suspicion. The block is marked-off territory, where a corner lamp illuminates a scrawl on a wall, reading: "Gypsys: Nick, Pee Wee, Count, Honey Boy, Youngster, Fat Man, Little Joker, Beaver, Sunny, all of 100 St." Here is a street on which the gang has already put its brand.

Not every name on the Gypsy roster is a gangster-to-be. Within the young gang, a process of differentiation sets in, as some find jobs, get married, move into other neighborhoods. A process of natural selection operates within the gang to choose those who can and will make crime a career.

Some insight into this process of selection is revealed in the excerpt entitled "A Youth Looks At Gangs." Here a former member of a street gang is describing his development—and also the fate of his former friends. Those who escape the gang are described as having "gone social." The term—coming out of the gang itself—provides a key clue to the relationship between the children of the casbah and the world around them. The outside world is a thing called "society." To get into it is to have "gone social." And to do so is to break with your own heritage—your block, your pals, your people. To go "social" is to fit into the other world, that outside world, that world of the law and the squares. And while such departure is permissible, although even that takes some special arranging, the act of going "social" is hardly the deed of the hero.

The street gangs from which come the great individuals and armies of organized crime are separated from the dominant civilization of which they are nominally a part by a triple barrier: by age, by poverty, by ethnic difference. Each of these barriers further separates the delinquent subculture from its surrounding society. Each of these barriers is both a point of separation and a point of friction. Behind these barriers arise the gangs of today and the organized criminals of tomorrow.

Youth breeds revolt—against parent, against the older generation, against authority, the status quo, and the present that for the youth is already a thing of the past. Whether this revolt springs from the individual's urge to challenge the parent, from one generation's need to replace another, or from both, the inevitable clash of age groups is age-old.

The revolt is less defiance than assertion. The ties to parent and parental world are not severed; but new ties to peers and the world of peers are established. At some point, the youth no longer turns to grownups for approval, warmth, and security; he turns for acceptance, affection, and certainty to his colleagues—gang, club, clan. The school tie rates with the family tie. The frat is household for many. And in street-corner society the gang —commonly referred to as "the family"—is often headed by a leader called "daddy-o."

Where family ties are strong, the youth will tend toward behavior patterns with his peers that do not too strongly and visibly strain familial relations. But even in the best of families youth will have its secret world, a world to be shared with friends and not with family, especially not with the elders in the family who just would not understand. In families where family ties are weak or nonexistent, the private and secret world of the youngster may form without inhibition, expressing the animal urges and fantasies of the gang.

The degree of discontinuity between this secret world of the youth and the world of the adult depends upon a variety of factors. One factor that sharpens the break between young and old is a rapidly changing civilization. The youth literally grows up in a different world: his heroes in movie, TV, radio, song, and even politics are not the heroes of father and mother. The values vary; the concept of self and of responsibility to others varies; the place of the individual in society varies. The world of the young varies—and varies directly as the speed of social movement.

In an interesting section of his *America as a Civilization*, Max Lerner compares the American youth-gang with the playing fields of Eton. This excerpt sees the gang as an inherent, troublesome, not necessarily totally negative aspect of our culture. Yet whatever judgmental values one may attach to the gang, it is part of growing up.

But this is a growing up that implies a clash of groups, that foreshadows friction, that produces conflict. Sometimes the conflict is soft and legal and sometimes the conflict is loud and illegal. In some strata, the conflict is settled by economic competition, in others, by political rivalry and sometimes by gang warfare. And where a youth group—with its inner understandings and loyalties—is engaged in vigorous combat (whatever the reason or manner) it tends to close ranks and to form ties that bind for a lifetime.

Poverty breeds revolt—and where a gang of youth is raised in poverty, it is doubly destined to organize against the older outer world. To the struggle of young versus old is added the further dimension of poor versus rich. The world becomes two worlds; the world of "we" versus the world of "they." The "they" may mean many things; the rich and the virtuous, the cops and the courts, the folks on the other side of the tracks or other side of the street. The "they" represents money, power, and the dress and manners that go with these posts of status. The "they" is a thing to imitate in burlesque, for to imitate in reality is futile. The "they" is the enemy in an undeclared war.

While "they" is vague, the "we" is definite. It is the gang—with a group name and with individual given names. The "we" is a tight band agreed to despise the world into which it can not enter. The "we" creates itself *sui generis* to demonstrate its disdain for all that went before and all that surrounds it. Each member of the gang is given a name, a real name, not some derivative of ancient Hebrew, Greek, Latin, or Anglo-Saxon. The name has meaning; it is descriptive, it is the person as he really is. Fat Man, Blackie, Cock-eye, Honey-boy. His family name goes lost. The gang affiliation is family enough.

The slum youth-gang is engaged in a curious kind of class struggle. Where Karl Marx spoke of "class consciousness," the gang thinks in terms of gang loyalty. Where the "class movement" acts through collective bargaining and strikes, the gang acts through thievery and "bopping." Where the social revolutionary dreams of "changing the system," the gang acts to "beat the system." The slum gang is rebel without a cause, seeking a place in the sun—even in the courts—for the gang.

In the slum, family ties also tend in many cases to be weak. Father and mother may work. Families are large—and children unattended. The "street corner" becomes the home; the candy store becomes the chapel. The older gangster becomes a father figure.

Within the gang, multiple relations develop. The central relationship is that between leader and follower, but it is not the sole relationship. A total and basic ethic prevails within the group—an ethic of reciprocity. Its motto: "You do for me and I do for you." The ethic is not derived from "above" or "outside" as a set of duties based on some eternal moral law. The ethic of reciprocity is the ancient law of the primitive tribe, of the herd, of the jungle. It is a system of mutual aid and defense, standing above all other laws and codes. The ethic of reciprocity means aid in a fight, sharing poverty, and—above all—a refusal ever to betray any member of the gang to the "enemy."

"Street Corner Society," by William F. Whyte, is a classic study of the relationship within the gang and between the gang and its immediate community. The excerpt entitled "The Gang and the Individual" is a brief summary of Whyte's findings. Although Whyte's study centers around the formation and habit of the slum gang—the street-corner boy—inevitably the book examines the ties between the young gang and the underworld— with its further business and political connections.

The excerpt by Dr. Albert Cohen, entitled "The Delinquent Subculture," sees the youth gang as "a delinquent solution" to a status problem. The gang is composed in the bowels of a slum subculture. Unable to achieve status in the traditional manner, the gang creates its own standards—its new concept of true status. And within the framework of these standards, the gang finds heroism and virtue, camaraderie and communal security. The gang sets its own styles—a special language, a peculiar costume, an inverted snobbery. The gang becomes the aristocrat standing on his head!

The revolt of youth and the revolt of the poor find a final and third reinforcing dimension in the revolt of the ethnically segregated. Whether this "segregation" is imposed by the community or by self is less important in this context than the fact of separated existence. Segregation separates the "inner" group from the law, the mores, the standards of the larger, "outer" community. At the same time this tightens loyalties within the segregated group as it confronts the outside world. In the poor, ethnically segregated community, the youth gang grows up behind a triple wall of youth, poverty, and ethnic diversity. This very isolation makes it a hard, tough component not easily dissolved by the forces of the outer world.

In New York in the 1960's the accusing finger begins to point at the Puerto Ricans, who are going through the forced evolution of the other ethnic groups before them. In a remarkably sober, thoughtful, and insightful address to the Fordham University School of Business, Reverend Joseph P. Fitzpatrick, S. J., Associate Professor of Sociology, brings the story of the "delinquent culture" up-to-date in an attempt to "break the old tribal practice of blaming everything on the newcomers." This address appears as the section, "Crime and the Immigrant."

The juvenile gang, then, develops as a culture within our culture. The first great "civilizing force" directed by the total society at taming this unruly group—namely, the school—is of minimum value. Truancy becomes for many youths the first crime. If attendance is compelled, the school becomes a blackboard jungle. The second great "civilizer," the reform school, becomes a place of criminal learning. The settlement house is an avenue of entry to the outer world for the boys who want to go "social," but it is an object of scorn for those who proclaim their own status and status symbols.

The delinquent culture becomes an inner frontier, raising barbarians in our midst, strange and hostile to our larger civilization. Out of this culture comes the young gang that in adulthood becomes part of organized crime in America, either by absorption or by conquest.

Organized crime, then, is not a thing of the past; nor is it a tamed beast for the present; it is a powerful, ever renewed social force with which America will have to contend for many years to come.

Section 44 **THE IDLE BOY**

From "The Idle Boy" by George K. Turner, *McClure's,* 1913.

Month after month the United States Army officer and the New England school-teacher, who were directing the New York police five years ago, looked into their card catalogues and maps of crime and saw a significant thing. From one small spot on the East Side of New York crime arose and spread all over the city, like pestilence from a swamp.

Around Chatham Square and the lower Bowery were the ancient dens of thieves, older than the memory of living men. There was the saloon of the old pickpockets, the yeggs' dingy meeting-place and post office, kept by the "dope fiend" and banker of criminals, from which the tramp burglars started out to break country safes all over the United States. There were the nightly "hang-outs" of the misshapen lumps of beggars, the noisy rendezvous of the paid ruffians and professional murderers. A few blocks to the west were the resorts of the Italian bombmen and counterfeiters and "white slavers"; a few blocks to the east, the coffee rooms, from which the young pickpockets and "cadets" and prostitutes sallied forth to invade the regions of the prosperous upper West Side. It was the center of the underworld of the city, never yet disturbed.

From time to time an impulse came to Commissioner Bingham and his deputy, Woods:. Why not smash the nests of this thing? Why not destroy the holes from which, year after year, crime had crawled out and spread over the city? The moment this was proposed, the detective force—and the best and most conscientious men on it—protested.

"Don't do it," they said anxiously. "Don't! You'll make the greatest mistake of your life. You've got your thieves there now all together under your hand. If you scatter them, where will you find them?"

It was a cry of alarm from the deepest convictions of the old police. They were destroying the old hunting-grounds of the detectives, tearing the heart out of the old traditions of the New York police force for handling crime. But underneath that honest protest, always distinct, was the sullen resistance of the Police System.

"Hands off our man-hunting grounds," said the police; "for the sake of the work of the department first—if not, hands off anyway."

This immemorial Police System stood around them, listening, threatening, thwarting, and defeating them. What was the thing? They asked themselves, as thousands of other men have done. The average policeman is a good fellow, certainly as honest as the average man in his circumstances. And yet, there they were, surrounded at their headquarters and at their chief agencies by men of evil purpose. Why should the body of police continually put at their head the men who made the System? It was not long before they found the main clue. The average patrolman, as a matter of fact, had small chance to become an officer in the department. There was an inherited aristocracy of crookedness which rose, generation after generation, to take the higher offices of the force.

The significant fact they saw was this: three-quarters of the police officers at the head of the department had started their careers on the force as plain-clothes men, operating at the centers of the underworld. They were sometimes members of the old detective bureau, but more often the plain-clothes agents of the notorious old-time officers of the police—the graduates of the man who gave the Tenderloin its name, of the chief who opened the town and threw away the key. These men had been chosen plain-clothes agents for obvious reasons: they were quick-witted, safe, and crooked; they alone had the political influence and the money needed to buy promotion in dishonest police administration; they alone had had that close observation and training, in the work of the higher grades, which placed them at the head of examinations for promotion in the administrations that were honest. The average patrolman had no chance for advancement in competition with these men of the "System."

Over a long period of years this Police System has established its traditions, which it hands down from one generation to another. These traditions form a strange code of ethics. Thieves, according to this code, should be caught—if it is not too hard work—and not licensed to operate for money. Money may be taken from citizens who want their stolen goods recovered, but it is only the more crooked detectives who take the money of thieves. Yet "stool-pigeons" must be employed as spies upon other criminals, and for this privilege they must have the right to operate in their minor specialties and get a living for themselves. Saloonkeepers and gamblers may be taxed for the privilege of breaking the law. They are a part of the "necessary evil" in a great city, as is prostitution.

Concerning the tax upon prostitution, the tradition of the System is a little different. This is "blood-money"—"dirty money." It is always taken, but some officers let the plain-clothes agents keep it. They give it up, not on moral grounds, but because there is a wide-spread superstition that this graft is unlucky. A number of men in the System (their names are familiar in the force) who took it have had a great deal of trouble in their families. But some one takes this money, always.

Gradually the management of the New York police began to sense the situation. And, as they watched, crime and vice and criminals kept boiling up from the same old stews on the East Side.

General Bingham was an obstinate and headstrong man.

"By ged," said Bingham, slamming his fist down on his desk—and his lower lip quivered and his pointed mustache stood out straight,—"we're going after 'em, and we're going after 'em all."

He started first to smash the district with the ordinary police force. Nothing happened, except explanations.

"No explanations!" said Bingham. "What I want is results. You're off that job."

Finally, instead of leaving vice to be handled by patrolmen, its suppression was delegated to specialists. This was not, indeed, a part of the theory of the Bingham administration, but it gradually became, in fact, its practice. The suppression of vicious resorts was first made the responsibility of the inspector in a particular district; but inspectors were moved along until one man was found who could be trusted to pound them. And afterward this man was moved from one district to another for the same purpose. He had become a specialist.

In addition, the ex-schoolmaster, Deputy Woods, with the aid of special squads, moved against the ancient dens around Chatham Square. Evidence was secured, new methods were devised for outwitting the sharp corps of lawyers under constant retainer by the various departments of the underworld, and the dives of Chatham Square, whose doors had never closed, day or night, for generations, were shut—and shut to stay.

There was no doubt of the success of this method. The handling of vice is exactly like the handling of crime. It is not a patrolman's business; it is the work of a specialist—of a detective. Evidence must be secured by detective methods—for obvious reasons. Vice is a business carried on by a body of persistent violators of the law, exactly as the great bulk of crime is carried on by professional criminals. And it requires a specially trained body of men, who know its operations and its personnel, to watch it.

That the methods of the Bingham administration were successful was shown by the growing chorus of threats which rose from the whole underworld. Word came from every direction:

"We'll get you yet."

The slum politicians were busy howling day and night for the Police

Commissioner's head. And finally, through the minor incident of photographing a juvenile offender for the detectives' gallery, the crisis came, and the first modern administration of the New York police was forced to a sudden end. At bottom, the fact was that the great forces of the underworld, with their endless ramifications, were too strong to be resisted. They "got" the Bingham administration of the New York police in exactly the same way and for the same reasons that the underworld and their politicians in Paris are credited with having "got" Lepine, the world-famous chief of the Paris police, this last winter.

Now, the Bingham administration, composed of educated and intelligent men, had taken control of the police of the greatest city on the continent in blank ignorance of police work. Their ignorance, plus their intelligence, was the exact reason why they reformed it. They examined from the foundation up an organization built upon the traditions and customs of the great body of uneducated men who form police departments, and made it over into an entirely different thing. And they demonstrated thoroughly the fact that American police should be commanded, not by a man who has risen within its ranks, but by a man of an entirely different mental training, who will introduce into the structure the methods of administration common to all really modern institutions.

These pioneers in police work had followed out, in their development of new methods, the simple, logical processes of an orderly, trained mind. They had brought modern organization and system to the suppression of crime in the detective bureau, and, passing beyond this, they had applied exactly similar methods to dealing with vice.

But meanwhile they had reached the ultimate limits of police work under the old idea of it, and had touched a problem far deeper than the police could go. They had reached the system of the schools of the underworld, the source from which came up the constant stream of criminals which was discharged upon the city through the dens they were breaking up in Chatham Square and Second Avenue and Mott Street. To carry the campaign further, there must be recruited still another mental and moral force from outside the ranks of the police.

The theorist and reformer knows very little of the unfailing sources of criminals; he lives in another and less populous world than the one from which they come. But every common patrolman understands it—for he has seen it all his life. And for this very reason—strange as it may seem—the handling of the thing must be taken from the province of the patrolman and given to the reformer, who is now just beginning to see this huge social problem, the recruiting of the criminal classes—that old evil whose roots grow far down into the awful idle nights and Sundays in the three-room tenements.

When any intelligent person stops to think of this thing, it is clear enough. The young human animal shut up idly in three or four crowded rooms causes a situation intolerable both to himself and to the adults with him. He drifts naturally, often he is driven bodily by his parents, out to the city streets. And there he learns the old unwritten lessons of the night schools of the pavements of New York.

The ingenuity of the young boy pitted against the problem of making a city street a playground is one of the most extraordinary things in a great city. Founded upon the elements of familiar outdoor games, he has invented or adapted half a dozen ways of amusing himself. A tin can is a football, a flight of stone steps and the sidewalk a baseball bat. And most elaborate systems count the score. Nothing could be more clever or more pathetic than the efforts of the boy to overcome the limitations of the city street. But, in the end, the street defeats him. The limitations of space turn him unwillingly but certainly from active athletic sports to gambling.

Within the last fifteen or twenty years a new game, by its perfect adaptation to city conditions, has become the most popular pastime of the young boys of big cities. It is the dice game of craps—as old, probably, as the world, but here always the Negro game—very possibly brought from Africa. At any rate, the Negro gambler, coming up from the South with his "bones," has taught it to the whole country. It has become, in the last decade or two, a pre-possession of the boys of the tenement districts in New York. Marbles and tops and baseball have their seasons—they demand more space than is accessible. But a pair of "bones" in a boy's pocket, a group on the corner of the sidewalk, and a gang of boys is embarked for hours of excitement in one of the oldest fascinations of the race. It is the game of all seasons and of any place. Surpassing all others, this African Negroes' gambling game is now the almost universal pastime of the boy of great cities.

The extent and vitality of public gambling in the great city is a constant surprise to most men who were bred elsewhere. Generations of gamblers are educated, almost inevitably, on the sidewalks of New York and Chicago under existing conditions. And every generation of boys passes on the traditions to its juniors. Children of four or five are taught to "roll the bones" for their older brothers; by the time they are six or seven they know the somewhat complicated count, and in a year or two more they have made their own investment of a couple of cents, asked for the dice in the little newspaper shop around the corner, and are embarked in playing for their own pennies.

Now, the thief, as any city policeman will inform you, is almost invariably a gambler. This may seem odd, at first. But, if you know the city, you know that gambling and thieving almost necessarily go together. There is nothing more natural; for, from the dim edge of babyhood, the thief has stolen to gamble. There is a continual course in the education of crime in New York City, nicely adjusted upward from the first kindergarten lesson in craps to the electric chair.

This desperate juvenile game of craps is a fight to the finish; it usually ends only when all parties except one in the contest are cleaned out financially. And the natural result is a general foray of a good-sized group of boys for the purpose of replenishing their resources. The petty pilfering in a great city is constantly evident even to the most casual observer. Every now and then the passer-by sees children scurrying back into a side street with bundles of wood or coal; and everywhere throughout the boundaries of New York there is the scratching of the fingers of juvenile thieves. A great share of their thieving is stimulated by the driving necessities of the popular pastime of the juvenile world which requires financial stakes.

Cement bags are very desirable—they bring two cents apiece; bags of kindling-wood, taken from demolished buildings, have a market value in the tenement districts of ten cents; small bags of coal grabbed from wharves are quoted at about the same price. This fuel, the ice from the docks in summer, and vegetables from hucksters' carts always find a ready and constant market among the poorer foreign tenement population—and no questions asked.

So sure is this source of income that boys sometimes conduct a regular little business delivering stolen coal and ice. On the extreme West Side of New York, gangs have made a practice of delivering groceries on Saturday on a regular route. They visit tenements, taking orders at a scale of prices about half the retail grocer's rates; go out in a group to grocery stores and steal enough to fill these orders; take the cash from their customers; and spend the entire afternoon devoting the proceeds to a crap game, from which one boy emerges with the entire sum. So, as naturally as they breathe, generations of gamblers are bred in the great city; and, just as naturally, the child who is destined to be a thief is always sure to be a gambler.

A great proportion of the boys of a city could not, if they would, make their living as professional gamblers or thieves. At fourteen or fifteen they must go to work. And thus they leave the social and political organization of their localities to the Idle Boy—that great social force which dominates to such an extent the recreations and politics of the great city. The Idle Boy—whether he becomes a professional politician or a professional thief—continues his education through a common and well defined course of training.

The professional thief—and most thieves, like most prostitutes, are nearer twenty than thirty—continues his education in gambling and thieving simultaneously. His favorite "hang-out" is not the liquor saloon—according to the old-time popular belief; it is the cheap pool and billiard parlor, or, in rarer cases, a small cigar store with its rear gambling-room. The pool parlor, as every detective in the city knows, is the great grammar school of thieves and gamblers.

Pool itself is a promising field for gambling; the surface of the pool-table makes an excellent place for the game of craps, and soon the pool parlor has added special crap-tables and equipment for other gambling games. It is a little gambling center; and the older boys find that gambling in its higher courses is exactly as stimulating to thievery as is the kindergarten on the sidewalks.

The Idle Boy, who loafs about these places while other boys of his age are working, must have money. Gambling demands it; he needs it to maintain the sartorial effects that are required by the traditions of his set. The pool parlor and little gambling place become the centers at which young thieves originate and pass on methods of crime. And in an exceedingly short time that curious product of new environment, the modern city thief, is sent out into practical life.

He is a soft-handed youth who carefully maintains a code of dressing of his own—a particular hair-cut, fine-striped suits, deep-cuffed trousers. In his way, he is as vain and scrupulous of his appearance as an eighteenth-century fop. As a matter of fact, he is a most important social figure, with widespread social and political responsibilities.

Very few people realize how far the destinies of a great city are taken charge of by the Idle Boy. The one place where votes form naturally in bunches, ready to the hand of the professional politician, is in the gangs of youths just coming into manhood, into which a large part of New York and Chicago and other cities naturally divide themselves. And the apprentice politician who takes charge of them is, naturally, the Idle Boy, who is developing the physical and social traits of a leader. The more crooked the gang, the more votes it will cast; and, by natural sequence, the "wise boys" graduate successively to take charge of city governments.

It is the Idle Boy, also, who takes over the social life of the city. Dances and "rackets" are his by right of leadership. In the teens the instinct of sex-hunting develops in the gang, and is directed by the Idle Boy. Everywhere to-day there is universal skepticism over the possible continence of the male population before marriage. In the crowded city tenement districts there is small question that nearly all boys begin their sexual experience in their teens.

The little girls are forced into the streets exactly as the boys are; and, in the boys' minds, they come to be divided roughly into "good girls" and "bad girls." The "good girls," it is stated, are those that "their folks make come in by ten o'clock at night." They are the girls, in other words, whose parents take some care of them.

With the girls, as with the boys, the main trouble is the awful nights and Sundays in the tenements—the restlessness of youth against the bars of circumstance. It is on Sundays that the police must put out their "strong-arm" squad to beat down the wild boys, with half savage manners, who "rough-house" the city transportation lines. Special policemen must go here and there to break up the crap games, run by the larger boys for bigger stakes, which are the regular Sunday morning institutions of the tenement districts. And all day in summer, and all the afternoons in winter, the boys and girls give up Sundays to their own "rackets" or their Sunday matinee dances.

The promoter of these dances and country excursions is still the Idle Boy, backed, generally, by a syndicate of intimates. In summer-time they run their trips and dances in the suburbs—their dollar "beer-rackets," with dancing, and unlimited free beer, in some sordid "summer garden" or park, where a few dejected shrubs or a couple of papier-mache palm trees work Sundays as a forest. In some cases, in Philadelphia and New York, suburban farms rent their grounds and buildings complete on Sundays to these picnic dancing parties. The Idle Boy is in charge of a great share of these entertainments, and he tends always to drag the institution down to his own level. The dance, to him, is a sex hunt.

The girls of the tenements dance early. The sidewalk dance around the street-piano is one of the commonest games of their childhood, and they wait anxiously for the time, in their middle teens, when the etiquette of juvenile society first considers them of age to go to public dances. After nightfall, from September to June, all young New York is dancing. There are now nearly six hundred licensed public dance-halls, and their attendance runs nightly into tens of thousands and on Saturday nights and Sunday afternoons into hundreds of thousands of boys and girls in their teens and early twenties. Every year in the past decade there has been a growth in the popularity of the public dance. In the last three or four years, since the arrival of the "nigger" dances and the "rags" and the "turkey trots," dancing has become a public obsession. Like the gambling game of craps,—which has supplanted or changed the habits of boyhood from the traditions of sport of northern Europe to the games of the negro,—this new dancing is a curious recrudescence, apparently originating from the same source as the gambling game. The "nigger" dance seems to find its main origin in the crude and heathen sexual customs of middle Africa, afterward passing through the centers of prostitutes in large cities, where the contributions of city savages, from Paris to San Francisco, have been added to it.

This "nigger"-dancing craze, moving from the South and West to the East, has swept the city populations of America like an epidemic. In most of its many variations, it is not taught by dancing academies with any concern for their reputations or their licenses. But its steps are passed from one person to another, from the youths to the children, until it has gone through the country with the thoroughness of a great popular song. In its simpler and grosser forms, it is the easiest kind of dancing ever introduced—being merely a modified form of walking. Thousands of people who never learned the older dances have picked this up, and the popularity of dancing has been widened tremendously by the fact. Even little children dance the grotesque steps upon the sidewalk.

The promoter of cheap dances has never before had such a public for his enterprises, and never before has dancing been such a provocation to immorality. The recent trend has been entirely toward the ideals of the Idle Boy. Around him centers the organization for sex-hunting of the boys who are seeking the "bad girls"; for strangers in the hall, he and his assistants are constant sources of information on the same subject. The natural instinct of the man to test and tempt the woman is solidified in the dance-hall into what is, for all practical purposes, a perfect system.

The Idle Boy is the hero as well as the leader of these affairs. The swashbuckler type, who develops into the ruffian and gunman, has all the charms of masculine audacity suited to impress the immature and romantic female mind. And this and the amiable juvenile worship of reckless courage all feeds his ambition to "go the limit" in any crime he undertakes. The dressy pickpockets, who are naturally clothed in a manner suitable to their public walk in life, are also most attractive to feminine taste; and in a very short time the personal alliance is formed between the flashy or weak "bad girl" and the Idle Boy, in the inevitable semi-marital relation of the criminal and the prostitute.

And so, by gradual and natural steps, the solidarity of the criminal world is built up. The gambler is a thief, the thief is a "cadet"; the prostitute part wife, part business partner, part slave of her man. And the vice promoters and the slum politicians and the crooked policemen are all a part of the same class.

It was the last focus of this criminal world—the place in the city where all the graduates of the schools found their gathering-places—that Bingham, as New York Police Commissioner, had attacked. And for doing this the underworld, in turn, had broken him.

And then, with the fall and disorganization of the Bingham police force, and the advent of a new city administration, all the underworld and its women ran wild, until it worked its own destruction, and brought down with it its old ally, the Police System, through the killing of the famous professional gambler, Rosenthal, by professional murderers in the hire of a New York police officer.

The attention of the city of New York, and of the nation, was centered by this event upon the police and their alliance with the criminal classes.

What is a policeman, and what is his capability and proper sphere? the entire country asked itself.

In the course of the investigations in New York, the Municipal Research Bureau, acting with the Aldermanic Committee, took the statistics concerning the men who entered the New York police force in 1912. Of 421 appointed, four out of every five were born in New York City. The average age on entering the force was twenty-four years, and about two out of every three were unmarried. Only two of the 421 had an education reaching through a high school; the remainder had gone no further than the grammar grades. They were drawn from a great variety of occupations—more than a quarter of them from positions like those of drivers and motormen, concerned with the traffic of the public streets; and nearly all of the remainder were drawn from work of a grade somewhat above that of the common laborer. Only about ten per cent had been in clerical positions. About one third of these men had been arrested, nearly all for the minor offenses in which active city-bred youths of their class are most apt to be concerned— the commonest charge being that of disorderly conduct.

The police, in short, are drawn from the boys brought up on the streets of New York. They know the poorer population as no reformer can ever know it; for they are a part of it.

In the older police force, the patrolman was assigned, whenever possible, to the district he grew up in. And, to some extent, he is still. To the patrolman observing an offense, some one has said, the practical question far too often is: "Shall I take my friend's money or send him to jail?" In the home district he is, naturally, everybody's friend. And, wherever he may be, the people in shady occupations are using every means, direct and indirect, to get upon a friendly footing with him.

Now, a class with the viewpoint and the associations of the patrolman could scarcely be expected, in any case, to originate methods of handling the great and delicate policies required for dealing with vice and crime in a great city. As a matter of fact, the police force has never originated any movement toward improvement in administering the law—especially in that greatest of all questions, the suppression of criminal immorality—of its own accord. This has always been the province of the outsider—of the reformer with the up-country ideals of human conduct.

Out of this source has arisen, in the last few years, another movement toward both a more rational and a more human treatment of crime and vice in great cities. From this, it may be hoped, will soon come the complete idea of a new police.

The present old-time idea of a police force is built upon the ideals and traditions of generations of constables and watchmen. At its best, it follows, through the rule-of-thumb processes of a class untrained in modern organization, the business of taking finished offenders, largely for committing crimes against property, and letting pass, as venal offenses, the "necessary evils" (according to its code of reasoning) of vice, and gambling, and the breaking of the liquor law.

An outline of the new police that American cities must have can be gathered from a consideration of the Bingham experiment in New York and the still broader reforms now being formulated and worked out in other large cities.

The new police will put the patrolman into the place for which he is eminently fitted—the position of general neighborhood watchman and guardian. He will be trained for this not too easy work in police schools.

Modern commercialized crime, with its specialists, criminal and legal, will be met by the specialization of the detective force, helped by the most modern systems of following crimes and identifying criminals.

Vice and excise offenses and gambling will be handled in much the same way. They are carried on by perfectly well known operators; they should be followed by specialists. It is definitely determined, in every mind that has any knowledge on the subject, that the underworld is a unit which can not, by its nature, be dissected into artificial parts. The only way to arrest the thief, without arresting the gambler or the "cadet," would be to split the individual offender in half, arbitrarily arrest the south side of him as a thief, and let the north side go as a gambler.

Then, still beyond the matter of mere administration of law, must come the more important function now generally proposed for the new police— the focusing of the best and soundest sentiment of the community upon the great question of public morals.

For a number of years past, private organizations like the Parkhurst Society and the Committee of Fourteen in New York have been working on the general problem of vice. In the past half dozen years this interest has quickened and extended. Local agencies in a great many of the cities of the country have been studying the question, and especially the relation of the unfortunate girl to it. One society, the American Vigilance Association, has become a general agency for conducting this work in widely separated cities.

From these movements, quite naturally, has developed a general interest in the personal life and diversions of the population from which criminal and vicious classes are drawn. One notable and most healthy expression of this has been seen in the movement, which has extended across the country, to offset the present wave of indecent dancing by offering opportunities, within the means of the poorest, for dancing under decent and attractive conditions.

And now the latest proposal is to consolidate all the movements of this type, in different cities, into general morals or public welfare commissions, which would, on the one side, bring the best sentiment of the community to bear upon the enforcement of the law by the police, and, on the other, consolidate the movements for breaking up the schools for criminals and prostitutes, which have developed in all our cities, through establishing means for satisfying the normal tendencies and activities of childhood and youth, which are now let loose to run wild toward destruction.

The exact method of relating this new representation of public sentiment to the police is a somewhat debatable matter. The plan is being worked out somewhat differently in different cities—in New York and Pittsburgh and Chicago and San Francisco. But there seems no doubt now that public conscience in different cities will find a means, in these commissions, to express itself effectively upon this whole great subject of public morals in cities; and that this will go far toward effecting a radical change long needed in urban police.

That a new police with new ideals must come in our cities, and must come soon, no one can doubt. This is not merely a question of new methods of organization; it requires a great social reformation. And the outbreaks of strange and barbaric crime in all the great cities of the world—in London and Paris as well as in New York—show that it is one of the greatest and most pressing questions of modern city life, which can not much longer be ignored.

Section 45   **A TRAINING SCHOOL FOR CRIME**

From *The New York Times,* 1960.

A Brooklyn crime school for youthful apprentices was uncovered yesterday in a large-scale police raid against a "junior Apalachin" syndicate. At least one boy was apparently killed in gangland style by the syndicate as an object lesson for informers.

The police rounded up twenty-two persons accused of belonging to the crime-school gang. They were accused of carrying out a series of burglaries in the last two years in which the loot might reach a total of $500,000.

The burglary ring was described as a try-out organization under the tutelage of established mobsters, who, the police said, offered education in murder as well as in theft.

Assistant Chief Inspector Raymond V. Martin, who led forty detectives in the mass arrests, said:

"This was a junior Apalachin group, being groomed for future activities in the crime syndicate."

The "Apalachin" reference was to the gangland meeting in Apalachin, N. Y., on Nov. 14, 1957. The police picked up sixty men at the meeting, including many with long underworld records. Twenty were found guilty in Federal Court for conspiracy in not divulging why they were at the gangland conference. Some are free on bail, and others are in jail pending appeal.

Chief Martin said that he was not prepared at this time to identify the top mobsters responsible for the burglary ring and crime school but that he would name them later. He declared that most of the money realized in the sales of merchandise stolen by the apprentice gang went to top underworld figures.

The crime school gang was uncovered during an investigation of the gangland murder of a 17-year-old Brooklyn youth two months ago. He was slain a few hours before he was scheduled to appear as a defendant in court.

The victim, Vincent Graffeo of 1860 West Fifth Street, Brooklyn, was thrown from a car, beaten and shot five times on June 3. He had been arrested in February on a charge of possessing burglary tools and was scheduled to appear in Special Sessions Court.

Graffeo was believed to have been a member of a burglary ring. The police speculated at the time that he had been murdered to prevent exposure of other members of the ring. He had been arrested again a few weeks after the first arrest. That time he was seized with another youth while loading $40,000 worth of stolen men's clothing into a station wagon in Queens.

The police said that Graffeo was a member of the burglary ring but that he had aroused the suspicions of other members who were afraid, apparently, that he meant to tell all he knew about the gang.

According to the police, the youthful apprentices roamed the five boroughs and extended their operations into White Plains. The members were said to have centered on supermarkets, television repair shops and clothing stores. Their burglaries, according to the police, would bring them $500 for a single theft. The receivers, also in the ring, would pass the stolen goods to higher crime echelons, where the value often went to $10,000 or more.

The police said that the slaying of Graffeo had apparently been ordered not only to keep him quiet but also to give other members of the school a "practical lesson" in the techniques of gangland murder for stool pigeons.

Section *46* **STREET SCENE**

From *The New York Times,* 1960.

Around 8 o'clock on a hot summer evening the sun's rays, striking across town, light up East Harlem's decaying building fronts and turn the lines of fire-escapes into a fine, gilt tracery.

Once the sun sets, however, it grows much darker there than in most other parts of the city. It is because the buildings do not light up. The twenty-five-watt bulbs inside the tenements barely turn their windows a faint yellow.

The streets of El Barrio ("the neighborhood") as its residents call it, harbor the city's highest rate of juvenile delinquency.

In one ten-block area, bounded by Ninety-ninth and 104th Streets, and by First and Third Avenues, 158 of every 1,000 children under 16 years old have been in trouble with the law.

A policeman or youth worker in the area, if asked for an off-hand guess as to which is the worst single block, would probably name 100th Street between First and Second Avenues.

This block paradoxically is not a center for any of East Harlem's three major fighting gangs. It is, however, one of the most heavily hit by juvenile narcotics addiction, which has to some extent replaced gang activity as the major cause of concern to youth workers.

Offenses ranging from persistent truancy, through vandalism and theft, to assault and narcotics "pushing," make up this block's delinquency roster. Because of its narcotics record, it has acquired the nickname, among some of its teen-agers, of "Business Street."

It is the block that Gov. Mark Hatfield of Oregon, who was in New York City last summer, asked to visit. After some police reluctance, the Governor was finally taken on one quick walk down the street. A police captain in plain clothes walked beside him. A radio car waited at each end of the block.

It is a block where policemen, from the Twenty-third Precinct, responding to the familiar call to turn off a fire hydrant that children have opened, have been known to come in fours. Two turned off the water, while the other two watched the rooftops with drawn pistols.

It is a block where a stranger is almost immediately spotted and, by many, distrusted.

It is, as well, one of the city's most heavily populated blocks. Four thousand persons are estimated to live in its twenty-six tenement buildings.

Ash-gray, standing six stories tall, their crumbling walls reek of decayed garbage. Late last Saturday night they resounded to a hubbub of talking, laughing, calling out. Radios turned up high shook out Caribbean rhythms. Glass crashed occasionally in the cool, relatively quiet rear courtyard.

The sidewalks were jammed three or four deep in some places. Under the three street lamps, men sat around tables playing dominoes. Infants slept in baby carriages. Youths and young girls called to each other continually.

Seven and 8-year-old girls, in starched, pastel-colored frocks, shot about in all directions like bright pinwheels.

"These people, they don't stay home, they're always in the street," said a policeman disgustedly.

"It's like doing time. You feel better in the jail yard than in the jail cell," said a youth worker who was accompanying a reporter on a tour of the neighborhood.

A former war counselor for a fighting gang in the area, Tomi Enah —it is not his real name—is finishing parole after spending six years in jail for wounding a man in a shooting.

Tomi, a man in his late 20's with an air that combines gaiety and severity, is well known to the youth on the block. In a black hallway two forms moved suddenly from the darkness and hugged him, squealing.

"Tomi I love you!" said one, a blond girl in red blouse and shorts, who seemed no more than 11, although she was 14. Her companion, darker, was of the same age and appeared equally a child.

"You going to church tomorrow Cinny?" Tomi asked the first.

"Ah, Tomi, you know we can't cross that block," Cinny answered.

"Oh that's right," he said. "Be good anyway, will you?"

"Sure Tomi."

He explained that the girls belonged to the Conservative Frenchies, a relatively peaceful club that had become embroiled with the Arabian Queens, a similar group near by.

"Cinny has to go fight with them Sunday to settle it," he said. The girls would use fists, pins, nail-files, maybe a knife.

He pointed to two boys, about 14, sitting side by side on the curb in the darkness. Their eyes were closed, their heads were falling forward jerkily.

Tomi, who once used heroin himself, said:

"They're hooked. They start off with wine. Then they start waking up feeling sick and go to yerba (marijuana). Somebody offers them tecata (heroin) and they snort it. Pretty soon they've got a golden nose. Then they find it's cheaper to shoot it in their arm. Their car, their clothes, their house—all go into their arm, their golden arm."

Tomi had carefully disarrayed the reporter's clothes, had shown him how to walk, had given him a bag of potato chips to appear "natural." But after a few rounds of the block, he advised leaving.

"They're beginning to wonder about you," he said.

"They" were groups of lounging youths who did not stare directly but glanced half around at the passers-by, voices exploding suddenly twenty yards back, a young man who passed quickly, almost brushing by.

"On this block you can be a Puerto Rican, a Negro, but until they know just who you are and what you're there for, you're in trouble," Tomi explained.

Later the reporter returned with a photographer and three detectives attached to the Youth Division. The detectives, husky young men, walked tensely, one hugging a wall, one at the edge of the sidewalk, one in the middle of the street. They watched the rooftops.

The group was as conspicuous as a bass drum in a string orchestra. When the photographer began taking pictures, lights began going out, loungers drifted away. Two groups of men ran by, each carrying a table with a domino game on it.

Five bottles crashed into the street near by. One breaking close to a stoop, cut two women on the legs. The detectives went to the roofs but found nothing.

By 2 in the morning the street was quiet. A car sped through, hit a bump and dropped a taillight cover. Someone shouted after it. The driver stopped the car, reversed, sped backward down the block, recovered the lost item and sped off toward First Avenue.

A Sanitation truck passed, spraying water. Empty beer cans, piled three and four deep, bobbed and dipped in the gutters. A corner lamp illuminated a scrawl on a wall:

"Gypsys: Nick, Pee Wee, Count, Honey Boy, Youngster, Fat Man, Little Joker, Beaver, Sunny, all of 100 St."

Section 47 **A YOUTH LOOKS AT GANGS**

From "A Youth Looks at Gangs" by Gay Talese, *The New York Times*, 1959.

A tall, bony youth with thin fingers, alert eyes and a face scarred by somebody else's razor relaxed long enough yesterday to discuss what it was like to lead a juvenile gang, quit and reform.

The narrator was a 21-year-old East Harlem youth who gave up all the grim power and jungle prestige he had earned as the leader of a tough New York gang for a $45-a-week job as a clerk in a luggage firm. Sometimes he wonders why.

"Why did you quit?" he was asked after work yesterday.

"I got tired of bopping," he said. "I wasn't getting what I was looking for any more in bopping."

"What were you looking for?"

"Fun, excitement, to be constantly doing something. Last year I quit because I got interested in other things."

"Like?"

"Girls," he said. "That's one of the main reasons guys quit. They get married early in East Harlem."

"Why?"

"They get involved early. Mature fast sexually."

"Do these marriages work?"

"Not in the cases I know," he said, lighting a cigarette. "Hey, you're not going to use my name in this, are you?"

"No."

He re-lit his cigarette, ran his fingers through his pompadour, and said it was often difficult to quit a gang. Some gangs beat up quitters, he said, and others "froze you out"—would not talk to the quitter.

"When do most boys quit?"

"At about 19 or 20. Although I know a guy who's 35 and he's still bopping. He's suspected of supplying his gang with guns."

"Do some boys get nostalgic for the old gang and return?"

"It's rare. But often guys will return to talk about the old days. If our gang gets beat up, the old guys always say: 'If I was in the gang it wouldn't have happened.' The older guys always think they were heroes, or some-thin'. You'd think they killed 10,000 Viceroys.

"In fact, one guy from our gang who's now studying at Columbia, occa-sionally comes back to our block and brags all the time."

"How do gangs keep informed of other gangs' activity?"

"You hear about it in schools, and we all read the papers. In fact, one gang has a guy who clips all gang news from the newspapers. When gangs get their names in the papers they buy 'em like mad."

"Why did you join a gang in the first place?"

"I wanted to get a rep."

"Did you?"

"Yeah, I'm pretty good with my hands. I used to box amateur. I never carried a gun or knife. I been in the hospital only once—that's when six other guys jumped me. I was stabbed eight times. That's how I got the scars on my chin and head."

He said he was born and grew up in East Harlem and had joined the gang at 14. The gang, he said, was made up of light-skinned Puerto Ricans and operated in the area from 100th to 107th Street between Fifth and Third Avenues. Dark-skinned Puerto Ricans, he said, were usually ex-cluded.

Gang life agreed with him, he said, until he wanted to marry. He now has one child.

"Would you let your son join a gang?"

"Not if I can help it," he said.

"What has happened to the forty boys you had in your gang two years ago?"

"About half of them are now put away—arrested for bopping or on a weapons charge. About ten have gone on to worse things—taking drugs, or selling it, or gone into prostitution. The other ten have 'gone social.'"

"Meaning?"

"That means they either get married, or go back to school, or look for a job, or join a social club in the neighborhood, and hang around with other boys who have quit fighting gangs.

"That's what I've done—gone social. You go to a friend on the Youth Board, and they arrange for you to see other gangs, and you tell them you're out of the gang. This means you can walk in their territory.

"Sometimes the other gangs won't let you quit—because maybe they're waiting to get revenge on your gang, and they want to get you too."

"What is your ambition now?"

"I'm hoping to be an executive some day. I'd like to be the boss of a lot of people."

He is going to high school at night and after his marriage he moved into another neighborhood at his wife's request.

Many former gang members are among his friends. Sometimes they bowl on Friday nights.

"How has life treated you since you left the gang?"

"Well, it's tough right after you quit a gang. You have all these new responsibilities. You have to obey laws. You have to respect other people. Life gets complicated. Used to be I didn't care about nobody."

"Have you told your employer you belonged to a gang?"

"No."

"Do you feel it could hurt your chances?"

"Yes. With most of the papers playing up gangs the way they are. But some of the Youth Board men, who are the biggest help we have, have been in gangs. Floyd Patterson (former heavyweight boxing champion) was in a gang."

"Is it tougher outside the gang than in?"

"At the start," he said, and he ran his hand through his pompadour again.

Section 48   THE GANG AS AMERICA'S ETON

From *America as a Civilization* by Max Lerner, 1957.

Thus the young American grows up to see life as a cornucopia spilling its plenty into the lap of those who are there to take it. Within the limits of his family's income, and sometimes beyond it, there are few things denied to the growing son and daughter. Their attention is focused on what they can *get*, first out of their parents, then out of life. The growing girl learns to get clothes and gifts from her father and later from her husband. The boy fixes his attention on a succession of artifacts, from a toy gun and an electric train to a car, preferably a convertible. Their levels of aspiration stretch to infinity. Often the parents are blamed for this pliancy and indulgence, yet it is also true that the culture, with its sense of plenty, contains the same principle of infinite possibility. It tells the boy that if only he wants something hard enough, even the Presidency of the nation, he can achieve it. This spurs his striving but it also sets unrealizable goals, since his capacities may not equal the tasks he sets himself, or his class and status handicaps may be too crippling. Thus he misses the sense of security which one gets from the compassable. No limits are set to his goals, and often he reaches for incompatible sets of goals. Rarely does he learn the tolerance of deprivation or the recognition of limits which are a matter of course in less dynamic cultures and which exact a lesser psychic toll than the sense of infinite possibility.

Such an oceanic sense of possibility has its elements of strength for the boy or girl in growth. The feeling of impasse that so many of the youth of Europe have, in cul-de-sac economies where the job chances are narrow and they feel they must break through doors shut against them, does not crop up often in America. It is hope and not hopelessness that runs like a repeated chord through the growing-up years. They are the years in which heroisms are dreamed, tight-lipped resolutions made, values first crudely formulated. The emotional life awakens in all its tumbling confusion, the imagination ranges far, the lights and shadows of the moral life are accented, the shapes of good and evil take on their most intense forms. Anything is possible, and everything is fraught with far-reaching meanings. There is a sense of limitless potentials, of obstacles to be overcome by a surpassing display of energy and talent. At home, as in school, the archetypal prizes held up are the big ones and the stories told are the success stories. There is a constant demand for vitality, in season and out, regardless of whether it is charged with meaning. The emotional dangers that the young American runs are not those of apathy or despair but of anxiety about success or failure. He finds it hard to keep from wondering whether he is swift and strong enough to win in so exacting a race. Even within the minority ethnic groups, with their residual sense of status restrictions, the young American feels the pressure to succeed within the standards of the minority mold, or even to break out of it—especially to break out of it. And if he fails he cannot assign the failure to his goals or society but only to himself.

Growing up with the assumption that he will "make his mark" and "knock them dead," he is rarely allowed to forget that he lives in an expanding civilization in which he must accomplish "bigger and better" things. Just as he is enveloped by the sounds of cars, trains, planes, so the symbols investing his life are those of speed and movement, violence and power—the symbols of competitive drive. They don't have to be preached to him: they come through the culture-in-action. He picks them out of the air—from how his family behaves, from what his teachers and schoolmates say and what he reads and hears, from the men and careers held up to him for emulation.

Asked for more than he feels he can fulfill, he comes in turn to ask more of his family and milieu than they can fulfill, with a resulting insecurity and bleakness of mood. He turns to his age peers to find with them the expressiveness and sense of kinship not to be found among their elders. Their families

may be too protectively concerned with providing for their children's outward wants to be able to gauge their inner nature with wisdom. An adult
society, with churches that seem distant and "preachy" and with spinster-
staffed schools that seem only an extension of the nursery, offers little that
exacts loyalty or heroism from young people who are hungry for both. Their
hunger arises from the fact that when they are torn away from the primary
ties to their parents there is no corresponding growth in their confidence
of their own strength. They yearn for the sense of belonging which will
restore those primary ties, and they attach them now to agencies of their own
peers.

Into this vacuum come the teen-age activities, some of which amuse the
elders, while others worry them. Among the first are the hero worship of the
gods of popular culture, the love affair with the TV screen, the calf-love
obsessions that turn the teen-agers "girl crazy" or "boy crazy," the jazz or
jive madness that "sends" them. Less amusing are escapades of bored baby-
sitters that break into the headlines, or the sexual antics of the high-school
"non-virgin" clubs which shock parents and teachers without jolting them
into an understanding of their emotional sources.

There is a passage in Thomas Wolfe's *You Can't Go Home Again* describing "the desolate emptiness of city youth—those straggling bands of boys of
sixteen or eighteen that one can always see at night or on a holiday, going
along a street, filling the air with raucous jargon and senseless cries, each
trying to outdo the others with joyless catcalls and mirthless quips and
jokes which are so feeble, so stupidly inane, that one hears them with strong
mixed feelings of pity and shame." Wolfe asks "what has happened to the
spontaneous gaiety of youth," and answers that these youngsters "are without innocence, born old and stale and dull and empty . . . suckled on darkness, and weaned on violence and noise." In his *Studs Lonigan* novel sequence
James Farrell shows similarly the social violence and cultural emptiness
which condition the emotional bleakness of a boy's life on the city streets.

Yet in his formative years the city boy, especially from the working class,
learns more—bad and good—from the gang than from any other group
except the family. The gang is a group on the margin between rebellion and
crime, forming a clannish community in play and war against parents, elders,
teachers, police, and rival gangs. Sometimes it is a harmless effort of normal
youngsters in a disturbed and impressionable life phase to huddle together
for human warmth, sometimes it is a desperate attempt to channel floating
aggressions. The gang brings into the emotional vacuum of the boy's life a
structure of authority which makes demands on loyalty, on spartanism in the
face of adversity, even on honor and heroism of a sort; above all, on a sense
of acting together. That is where the boy learns crudely and even brutally
the mystery of sex, the warmth of friendship, and the heady sense of prestige

gained not through class position but through strength and natural leadership. It is ironic that the lack of effective codes in the larger society should leave the gang codes as the only substitutes: or perhaps these are only negative parallels of the middle-class codes from which the boys (most of them coming from the lower classes) feel themselves shut out as from an Eden; and so they turn the Eden upside down into a Hell. But even the gang codes prove tawdry and worse as the gangs move over the margin into the pathology of violence and rape and crime.

Not many young Americans follow them that far. But most of them look back to the adventures of their all-male peer groups as their time of expressiveness. It may be that the gang gatherings on city street corners, the loitering counter at small-town drugstores, and the crossroads taverns in the rural areas where you smoke and buy cokes and play the juke boxes are for American boys the playing fields of Eton.

Section 49   **THE GANG AND THE INDIVIDUAL**

From *Street Corner Society* by William F. Whyte, 1943.

The corner-gang structure arises out of the habitual association of the members over a long period of time. The nuclei of most gangs can be traced back to early boyhood, when living close together provided the first opportunities for social contacts. School years modified the original pattern somewhat, but I know of no corner gangs which arose through classroom or school-playground association. The gangs grew up on the corner and remained there with remarkable persistence from early boyhood until the members reached their late twenties or early thirties. In the course of years some groups were broken up by the movement of families away from Cornerville, and the remaining members merged with gangs on near-by corners; but frequently movement out of the district does not take the corner boy away from his corner. On any evening on almost any corner one finds corner boys who have come in from other parts of the city or from suburbs to be with their old friends. The residence of the corner boy may also change within the district, but nearly always he retains his allegiance to his original corner.

Home plays a very small role in the group activities of the corner boy. Except when he eats, sleeps, or is sick, he is rarely at home, and his friends always go to his corner first when they want to find him. Even the corner boy's name indicates the dominant importance of the gang in his activities. It is possible to associate with a group of men for months and never discover the family names of more than a few of them. Most are known by nicknames attached to them by the group. Furthermore, it is easy to overlook the distinction between married and single men. The married man regularly sets aside one evening a week to take out his wife. There are other occasions when they go out together and entertain together, and some corner boys devote more attention to their wives than others, but, married or single, the corner boy can be found on his corner almost every night of the week.

His social activities away from the corner are organized with similar regularity. Many corner gangs set aside the same night each week for some special activity, such as bowling. With the Nortons this habit was so strong that it persisted for some of the members long after the original group had broken up.

Most groups have a regular evening meeting-place aside from the corner. Nearly every night at about the same time the gang gathers for "coffee-and" in its favorite cafeteria or for beer in the corner tavern. When some other activity occupies the evening, the boys meet at the cafeteria or tavern before returning to the corner or going home. Positions at the tables are fixed by custom. Night after night each group gathers around the same tables. The right to these positions is recognized by other Cornerville groups. When strangers are found at the accustomed places, the necessity of finding other chairs is a matter of some annoyance, especially if no near-by location is available. However, most groups gather after nine in the evening when few are present except the regular customers who are familiar with the established procedure.

The life of the corner boy proceeds along regular and narrowly circumscribed channels. As Doc said to me:

> Fellows around here don't know what to do except within a radius of about three hundred yards. That's the truth, Bill. They come home from work, hang on the corner, go up to eat, back on the corner, up to a show, and they come back to hang on the corner. If they're not on the corner, it's likely the boys there will know where you can find them. Most of them stick to one corner. It's only rarely that a fellow will change his corner.

The stable composition of the group and the lack of social assurance on the part of its members contribute toward producing a very high rate of social interaction within the group. The group structure is a product of these interactions.

Out of such interaction there arises a system of mutual obligations which is fundamental to group cohesion. If the men are to carry on their activities as a unit, there are many occasions when they must do favors for one another. The code of the corner boy requires him to help his friends when he can and to refrain from doing anything to harm them. When life in the group runs smoothly, the obligations binding members to one another are not explicitly recognized. Once Doc asked me to do something for him, and I said that he had done so much for me that I welcomed the chance to reciprocate. He objected: "I don't want it that way. I want you to do this for me because you're my friend. That's all."

It is only when the relationship breaks down that the underlying obligations are brought to light. While Alec and Frank were friends, I never heard either one of them discuss the services he was performing for the other, but when they had a falling-out over the group activities with the Aphrodite Club, each man complained to Doc that the other was not acting as he should in view of the services that had been done him. In other words, actions which were performed explicitly for the sake of friendship were revealed as being part of a system of mutual obligations.

Not all the corner boys live up to their obligations equally well, and this factor partly accounts for the differentiation in status among them. The man with a low status may violate his obligations without much change in his position. His fellows know that he has failed to discharge certain obligations in the past, and his position reflects his past performances. On the other hand, the leader is depended upon by all the members to meet his personal obligations. He cannot fail to do so without causing confusion and endangering his position.

The relationship of status to the system of mutual obligations is most clearly revealed when one observes the use of money. During the time that I knew a corner gang called the Millers, Sam Franco, the leader, was out of work except for an occasional odd job; yet, whenever he had a little money, he spent it on Joe and Chichi, his closest friends, who were next to him in the structure of the group. When Joe or Chichi had money, which was less frequent, they reciprocated. Sam frequently paid for two members who stood close to the bottom of his group and occasionally for others. The two men who held positions immediately below Joe and Chichi were considered very well off according to Cornerville standards. Sam said that he occasionally borrowed money from them, but never more than fifty cents at a time. Such loans he repaid at the earliest possible moment. There were four other members with lower positions in the group, who nearly always had more money than Sam. He did not recall ever having borrowed from them. He said that the only time he had obtained a substantial sum from anyone around his corner was when he borrowed eleven dollars from a friend who was the *leader* of another corner gang.

The situation was the same among the Nortons. Doc did not hesitate to accept money from Danny, but he avoided taking any from the followers.

The leader spends more money on his followers than they on him. The farther down in the structure one looks, the fewer are the financial relations which tend to obligate the leader to a follower. This does not mean that the leader has more money than others or even that he necessarily spends more— though he must always be a free spender. It means that the financial relations must be explained in social terms. Unconsciously, and in some cases consciously, the leader refrains from putting himself under obligations to those with low status in the group.

The leader is the focal point for the organization of his group. In his absence, the members of the gang are divided into a number of small groups. There is no common activity or general conversation. When the leader appears, the situation changes strikingly. The small units form into one large group. The conversation becomes general, and unified action frequently follows. The leader becomes the central point in the discussion. A follower starts to say something, pauses when he notices that the leader is not listening, and begins again when he has the leader's attention. When the leader leaves the group, unity gives way to the divisions that existed before his appearance.

The members do not feel that the gang is really gathered until the leader appears. They recognize an obligation to wait for him before beginning any group activity, and when he is present they expect him to make their decisions. One night when the Nortons had a bowling match, Long John had no money to put up as his side bet, and he agreed that Chick Morelli should bowl in his place. After the match Danny said to Doc, "You should never have put Chick in there."

Doc replied with some annoyance, "Listen, Danny, you yourself suggested that Chick should bowl instead of Long John."

Danny said, "I know, but you shouldn't have let it go."

The leader is the man who acts when the situation requires action. He is more resourceful than his followers. Past events have shown that his ideas were right. In this sense "right" simply means satisfactory to the members. He is the most independent in judgment. While his followers are undecided as to a course of action or upon the character of a newcomer, the leader makes up his mind.

When he gives his word to one of his boys, he keeps it. The followers look to him for advice and encouragement, and he receives more of their confidences than any other man. Consequently, he knows more about what is going on in the group than anyone else. Whenever there is a quarrel among the boys, he hears of it almost as soon as it happens. Each party to the quarrel may appeal to him to work out a solution; and, even when the men do not want to compose their differences, each one takes his side of the story to the leader at the first opportunity. A man's standing depends partly upon the leader's belief that he has been conducting himself properly.

The leader is respected for his fair-mindedness. Whereas there may be hard feelings among some of the followers, the leader cannot bear a grudge against any man in the group. He has close friends (men who stand next to him in position), and he is indifferent to some of the members; but, if he is to retain his reputation for impartiality, he cannot allow personal animus to override his judgment.

The leader need not be the best baseball player, bowler, or fighter, but he must have some skill in whatever pursuits are of particular interest to the group. It is natural for him to promote activities in which he excels and to discourage those in which he is not skilful; and, in so far as he is thus able to influence the group, his competent performance is a natural consequence of his position. At the same time his performance supports his position.

The leader is better known and more respected outside his group than are any of his followers. His capacity for social movement is greater. One of the most important functions he performs is that of relating his group to other groups in the district. Whether the relationship is one of conflict, competition, or cooperation, he is expected to represent the interests of his fellows. The politician and the racketeer must deal with the leader in order to win the support of his followers. The leader's reputation outside the group tends to support his standing within the group, and his position in the group supports his reputation among outsiders.

The leader does not deal with his followers as an undifferentiated group. Doc explained:

> On any corner you would find not only a leader but probably a couple of lieutenants. They could be leaders themselves, but they let the man lead them. You would say, "They let him lead because they like the way he does things." Sure, but he leans upon them for his authority. Many times you find fellows on a corner that stay in the background until some situation comes up, and then they will take over and call the shots. Things like that can change fast sometimes.

The leader mobilizes the group by dealing first with his lieutenants. It was customary for the Millers to go bowling every Saturday night. One Saturday Sam had no money, so he set out to persuade the boys to do something else. Later he explained to me how he had been able to change the established social routine of the group. He said:

I had to show the boys that it would be in their own interests to come to me—that each one of them would benefit. But I knew I only had to convince two of the fellows. If they start to do something, the other boys will say to themselves, "If Joe does it—or if Chichi does it—it must be a good thing for us too." I told Joe and Chichi what the idea was, and I got them to come with me. I didn't pay no attention to the others. When Joe and Chichi came, all the other boys came along too.

Another example from the Millers indicates what happens when the leader and his lieutenant disagree upon group policy. This is Sam talking again:

One time we had a raffle to raise money to build a camp on Lake Blank (on property lent them by a local businessman). We had collected $54, and Joe and I were holding the money. That week I knew Joe was playing pool, and he lost three or four dollars gambling. When Saturday came, I says to the boys, "Come on, we go out to Lake Blank. We're gonna build that camp on the hill."

Right away, Joe said, "If yuz are gonna build the camp on the hill, I don't come. I want it on the other side."

All the time I knew he had lost the money, and he was only making up excuses so he wouldn't have to let anybody know. Now the hill was really the place to build that camp. On the other side, the ground was swampy. That would have been a stupid place. But I knew that if I tried to make them go through with it now, the group would split up into two cliques. Some would come with me, and some would go with Joe. So I let the whole thing drop for a while. After, I got Joe alone, and I says to him, "Joe, I know you lost some of that money, but that's all right. You can pay up when you have it and nobody will say nothin'. But, Joe, you know we shouldn't have the camp on the other side of the hill because the land is not good there. We should build it on the hill."

So he said, "All right," and we got all the boys together, and we went out to build the camp.

Disagreements are not always worked out so amicably. I once asked Doc and Sam to tell me who was the leader of a corner gang that was familiar to both of them. Sam commented:

Doc picked out Carmen. He picked out the wrong man. I told him why he was wrong—that Dominic was the leader.

> But that very same night, there was almost a fight between the two of them, Dominic and Carmen. And now the group is split up into two gangs.

Doc said:

> Sometimes you can't pick out one leader. The leadership may be in doubt. Maybe there are a couple of boys vying for the honors. But you can find that out.

The leadership is changed not through an uprising of the bottom men but by a shift in the relations between men at the top of the structure. When a gang breaks into two parts, the explanation is to be found in a conflict between the leader and one of his former lieutenants.

This discussion should not give the impression that the leader is the only man who proposes a course of action. Other men frequently have ideas, but their suggestions must go through the proper channels if they are to go into effect.

In one meeting of the Cornerville S. and A., Dodo, who held a bottom ranking, proposed that he be allowed to handle the sale of beer in the club-rooms in return for 75 per cent of the profits. Tony spoke in favor of Dodo's suggestion but proposed giving him a somewhat smaller percentage. Dodo agreed. Then Carlo proposed to have Dodo handle the beer in quite a different way, and Tony agreed. Tony made the motion, and it was carried unanimously. In this case Dodo's proposal was carried through, after substantial modifications, upon the actions of Tony and Carlo.

In another meeting Dodo said that he had two motions to make: that the club's funds be deposited in a bank and that no officer be allowed to serve two consecutive terms. Tony was not present at this time. Dom, the president, said that only one motion should be made at a time and that, furthermore, Dodo should not make any motions until there had been opportunity for discussion. Dodo agreed. Dom then commented that it would be foolish to deposit the funds when the club had so little to deposit. Carlo expressed his agreement. The meeting passed on to other things without action upon the first motion and without even a word of discussion on the second one. In the same meeting, Chris, who held a middle position, moved that a member must be in the club for a year before being allowed to hold office. Carlo said that it was a good idea, he seconded the motion, and it carried unanimously.

The actions of the leader can be characterized in terms of the origination of action in pair and set events. A pair event is one which takes place between two people. A set event is one in which one man originates action for two or more others. The leader frequently originates action for the group without waiting for the suggestions of his followers. A follower may originate action for the leader in a pair event, but he does not originate action for the leader and other followers at the same time—that is, he does not originate action in a set event which includes the leader. Of course, when the leader is not present, parts of the group are mobilized when men lower in the structure originate action in set events. It is through observation of such set events when the top men are not present that it is possible to determine the relative positions of the men who are neither leaders nor lieutenants.

Each member of the corner gang has his own position in the gang structure. Although the positions may remain unchanged over long periods of time, they should not be conceived in static terms. To have a position means that the individual has a customary way of interacting with other members of the group. When the pattern of interactions changes, the positions change. The positions of the members are interdependent, and one position cannot change without causing some adjustments in the other positions. Since the group is organized around the men with the top positions, some of the men with low standing may change positions or drop out without upsetting the balance of the group. For example, when Lou Danaro and Fred Mackey stopped participating in the activities of the Nortons, those activities continued to be organized in much the same manner as before, but when Doc and Danny dropped out, the Nortons disintegrated, and the patterns of interaction had to be reorganized along different lines.

One may generalize upon these processes in terms of group equilibrium. The group may be said to be in equilibrium when the interactions of its members fall into the customary pattern through which group activities are and have been organized. The pattern of interactions may undergo certain modifications without upsetting the group equilibrium, but abrupt and drastic changes destroy the equilibrium.

The actions of the individual member may also be conceived in terms of equilibrium. Each individual has his own characteristic way of interacting with other individuals. This is probably fixed within wide limits by his native endowment, but it develops and takes its individual form through the experiences of the individual in interacting with others throughout the course of his life. Twentieth-century American life demands a high degree of flexibility of action from the individual, and the normal person learns to adjust within certain limits to changes in the frequency and type of his interactions with others. This flexibility can be developed only through experiencing a wide variety of situations which require adjustment to different patterns of interaction. The more limited the individual's experience, the more rigid his manner of interacting, and the more difficult his adjustment when changes are forced upon him.

This conclusion has important implications for the understanding of the problems of the corner boy. As we have seen, gang activities proceed from day to day in a remarkably fixed pattern. The members come together every day and interact with a very high frequency. Whether he is at the top and originates action for the group in set events, is in the middle and follows the origination of the leader and originates for those below him, or is at the bottom of the group and always follows in set events, the individual member has a way of interaction which remains stable and fixed through continual group activity over a long period of time. His mental well-being requires continuance of his way of interacting. He needs the customary channels for his activity, and, when they are lacking, he is disturbed.

Doc told me this story:

> One night Angelo and Phil went to the Tivoli to see a picture. They didn't have enough money for Frank, so they had to leave him behind. You should have seen him. It's a terrible thing to be left behind by the boys. You would have thought Frank was in a cage. I sat next to him by the playground. Danny was holding the crap game in the playground. Frank said to me, "Do you think Danny would have a quarter for me?"
>
> I said, "I don't know. Ask him if you want to."
>
> But Frank didn't want to ask him. He asked me, "Do you think Long John has a quarter?"
>
> I said, "No, I know that Long John is clean." Frank didn't know what to do. If he had got the nerve up to ask Danny for the quarter right away, he could have run after the boys and caught up with them before they reached the theater. I knew that he would run if he had the money. But he waited too long so he wouldn't be able to catch up with them. It was nine-thirty when the crap game broke up. Frank went into the playground with me. He wanted me to ask Danny for something, but I told him to ask himself. He didn't want to. He said he thought he would go home, and he started, but then he came back. He asked us when we were going down to Jennings. I told him ten o'clock. We always go at ten now. He said that was too long to wait so he went home. Danny, Long John, and I went down to Jennings. We had been there about fifteen minutes when in walks Frank, and he sits down at a table next to us and starts reading the paper. Danny says, "What's the matter, Frank, no coffee?"
>
> Frank says, "That's all right. I don't feel like it."
>
> Danny says, "Go ahead, get your coffee." So Frank got coffee. We were ready to go before Angelo and Phil had

come in. I could see that Frank didn't want to leave, but he had to because you're supposed to go out with the man that takes care of your check. He walked home with us, and then I guess he went back to Jennings' to meet Angelo and Phil.

Frank had a very high regard for Danny and Doc, and at an earlier period he would have been perfectly happy in their company, but since Angelo had become the leader of the group he had seldom interacted with them and he had been interacting regularly and frequently with Angelo and Phil. When he was deprived of their company, the resulting disturbance was strikingly apparent.

A man with a low position in the group is less flexible in his adjustments than the leader, who customarily deals with groups outside of his own. This may explain why Frank was so upset by events of only a few hours' duration. However, no matter what the corner boy's position, he suffers when the manner of his interaction must undergo drastic changes. This is clearly illustrated in the cases of Long John's nightmares and Doc's dizzy spells.

Long John had had this trouble on certain previous occasions, but then the fear of death had gone, and he had been able to sleep without difficulty. He had not been troubled for a long period up to the time he experienced his latest attack. I do not know the circumstances surrounding the earlier attacks, but on this occasion Long John's social situation seemed clearly to explain his plight. He had become adjusted to a very high rate of interaction with Doc and Danny. While he did not have great influence among the followers in the Nortons, they did not originate action for him in set events, and he occasionally originated action for them. When the Nortons broke up and Doc and Danny went into Spongi's inner circle, Long John was left stranded. He could no longer interact with Doc and Danny with the same frequency. When he went over to Norton Street, he found the followers building up their own organization under the leadership of Angelo. If he was to participate in their activities, he had to become a follower in set events originated by Angelo. The members who had been below him in the Nortons were constantly trying to originate action for him. When his relationship with Doc and Danny broke down, he had no defense against these aggressions.

Doc brought about the cure by changing Long John's social situation. By bringing him into Spongi's inner circle, Doc reestablished the close relationship between Long John, Danny, and himself. In so doing, he protected Long John from the aggressions of the former followers. When Long John was once more interacting with Doc and Danny with great frequency, his mental difficulties disappeared, and he began acting with the same assurance, that had previously characterized his behavior.

Doc's dizzy spells came upon him when he was unemployed and had no spending money. He considered his unemployment the cause of his difficulties, and, in a sense, it was, but in order to understand the case it is necessary to inquire into the changes which unemployment necessitated in the activity of the individual. While no one enjoys being unemployed and without money, there are many Cornerville men who could adjust themselves to that situation without serious difficulties. Why was Doc so different? To say that he was a particularly sensitive person simply gives a name to the phenomenon and provides no answer. The observation of interactions provides the answer. Doc was accustomed to a high frequency of interaction with the members of his group and to frequent contacts with members of other groups. While he sometimes directly originated action in set events for the group, it was customary for one of the other members to originate action for him in a pair event, and then he would originate action in a set event. That is, someone would suggest a course of action, and then Doc would get the boys together and organize group activity. The events of Doc's political campaign indicate that this pattern had broken down. Mike was continually telling Doc what to do about the campaign, and I was telling him what to do about seeing Mr. Smith and others to get a job. While we originated action for him with increasing frequency, he was not able to originate action in set events. Lacking money, he could not participate in group activities without accepting the support of others and letting them determine his course of action. Therefore, on many occasions he avoided associating with his friends—that is, his frequency of interaction was drastically reduced. At a time when he should have been going out to make contacts with other groups, he was unable to act according to the political pattern even with the groups that he knew, and he saw less and less of those outside his circle of closest friends. When he was alone, he did not get dizzy, but, when he was with a group of people and was unable to act in his customary manner, he fell prey to the dizzy spells.

When Doc began his recreation-center job, the spells disappeared. He was once again able to originate action, first for the boys in his center, but also for his own corner boys. Since he now had money, he could again associate with his friends and could also broaden his contacts. When the job and the money ran out, the manner of interaction to which Doc was adjusted was once more upset. He was unemployed from the time that the center closed in the winter of 1939–40 until he got a W.P.A. job in the spring of 1941. The dizzy spells came back, and shortly before he got his job he had what his friends called a nervous breakdown. A doctor who had an excellent reputation in Eastern City examined him and was unable to find any organic causes to account for his condition. When I visited Cornerville in May, 1941, he was once again beginning to overcome the dizzy spells. He discussed his difficulties with me:

When I'm batted out, I'm not on the corner so much. And when I am on the corner, I just stay there. I can't do what I want to do. If the boys want to go to a show or to Jennings or bowling, I have to count my pennies to see if I have enough. If I'm batted out, I have to make some excuse. I tell the boys I don't want to go, and I take a walk by myself. I get bored sometimes hanging in Spongi's, but where can I go? I have to stay there. Danny offers me money, and that's all right, but he's been getting tough breaks. Last week he was complaining he was batted out and a couple of days later he offered me two dollars. I refused. I don't want to ask anybody for anything. Sometimes I say to Danny or Spongi, "Do you want a cigarette?" They say, "No, we've got some," and then I say, "All right, I'll have one of yours." I make a joke out of it, but still it is humiliating. I never do that except when I'm desperate for a cigarette. Danny is the only one that ever gives me money.

Before I got this W. P. A. job, I looked terrible. I eat here at home, but I can't expect them to buy clothes for me. I had one suit, and that was through at the elbow, and the cuffs had more shreds than a chrysanthemum. When I had to go places, I kept my overcoat on, or else I carried it over my arm to hide the hole in the elbow. And I was literally walking on the soles of my feet. You think I like to go around like that?

Lou Danaro has been after me to go out with him. He's got a new Buick—a brand-new Buick. That's pretty nice, you know. He wants me to get a girl, and we'll go out together. But I won't go. I'd have to play a secondary role. No, that's what you want me to say. I mean, I wouldn't be able to do what I want to do.

Last summer, they asked me to be chairman of the Norton Street Settlement outing. I worked with the committee, and all that, but the night before the outing the whole committee was supposed to go out to the camp and spend the night there. That was a big time. But I didn't go. I didn't have any money. Next morning I saw them off on the bus, and I said I would be out later. I went around and bummed a couple of bucks and drove up with one of the boys. I stayed a couple of hours, and then I came home. The chairman is expected to be active at one of those affairs.

> He is supposed to treat people—things like that. They think
> I'm shirking my responsibilities, but it isn't true. It's the
> money.
>   I have thought it all over, and I know I only have these
> spells when I'm batted out. I'm sorry you didn't know me
> when I was really active around here. I was a different man
> then. I was always taking the girls out. I lent plenty of money.
> I spent my money. I was always thinking of things to do
> and places to go.

Doc showed that he was well aware of the nature of his difficulties, but understanding was not enough to cure him. He needed an opportunity to act in the manner to which he had grown accustomed. When that was lacking, he was socially maladjusted. If he had been a man with low standing in the group and had customarily been dependent upon others to originate action for him in set events, the dependence which resulted from having no money would have fitted in with the pattern of his behavior in the group. Since he had held the leading position among his corner boys, there was an unavoidable conflict between the behavior required by that position and the behavior necessitated by his penniless condition.

The type of explanation suggested to account for the difficulties of Long John and Doc has the advantage that it rests upon the objective study of actions. A man's attitudes cannot be observed but instead must be inferred from his behavior. Since actions are directly subject to observation and may be recorded like other scientific data, it seems wise to try to understand man through studying his actions. This approach not only provides information upon the nature of informal group relations but it also offers a framework for the understanding of the individual's adjustment to his society.

Section 50 **THE DELINQUENT SUBCULTURE**

From *Delinquent Boys* by Albert K. Cohen, 1955.

The delinquent subculture, we suggest, is a way of dealing with the problems of adjustment we have described. These problems are chiefly status problems: certain children are denied status in the respectable society because they cannot meet the criteria of the respectable status system. (The delinquent subculture deals with these problems by providing criteria of status which these children *can* meet.)

We remarked earlier that our ego-involvement in a given comparison with others depends upon our "status universe." "Whom do we measure ourselves against?" is the crucial question. In some other societies virtue may consist in willing acceptance of the role of peasant, low-born commoner or member of an inferior caste and in conformity to the expectations of that role. If others are richer, more nobly-born or more able than oneself, it is by the will of an inscrutable Providence and not to be imputed to one's own moral defect. The sting of status inferiority is thereby removed or mitigated; one measures himself only against those of like social position. We have suggested, however, that an important feature of American "democracy," perhaps of the Western European tradition in general, is the tendency to measure oneself against "all comers." This means that, for children as for adults, one's sense of personal worth is at stake in status comparisons with all other persons, at least of one's own age and sex, whatever their family background or material circumstances. It means that, in the lower levels of our status hierarchies, whether adult or juvenile, there is a chronic fund of motivation, conscious or repressed, to elevate one's status position, either by striving to climb within the established status system or by redefining the criteria of status so that one's present attributes become status-giving assets. It has been suggested for example, that such typically working-class forms of Protestantism as the Holiness sects owe their appeal to the fact that they reverse the respectable status system; it is the humble, the simple and the dispossessed who sit at the right hand of God, whereas worldly goods, power and knowledge are as nothing in His eyes. In like manner, we offer the view that the delinquent subculture is one solution to a kindred problem on the juvenile level.

Another consideration affecting the degree of privation experienced in a given status position is the "status source." A person's status, after all, is how he stands in somebody's eyes. Status, then, is not a fixed property of the person but varies with the point of view of whoever is doing the judging. I may be revered by some and despised by others. A crucial question then becomes: "Whose respect or admiration do I value?" That *you* think well or ill of me may or may not *matter* to me.

Even on their "own" social level, the situation is far from simple. The "working class," we have repeatedly emphasized, is not culturally homogeneous. Not only is there much diversity in the cultural standards applied by one's own working-class neighbors and kin so that it is difficult to find a "working-class" milieu in which "middle-class" standards are not important. In addition, the "working-class" culture we have described is, after all, an ideal type; most working-class *people* are culturally ambivalent. Due to lack of capacity, of the requisite "character structure" or of "luck," they may be working-class in terms of job and income; they may have accepted this status with resignation and rationalized it to their satisfaction; and by example, by class-linked techniques of child training and by failure to support the middle-class agencies of socialization they may have produced children deficient in the attributes that make for status in middle-class terms. Nevertheless, all their lives, through all the major media of mass indoctrination—the schools, the movies, the radio, the newspapers and the magazines—the middle-class powers-that-be that manipulate these media have been trying to "sell" them on middle-class values and the middle-class standard of living. Then there is the "propaganda of the deed," the fact that they have seen with their own eyes working-class contemporaries "get ahead" and "make the grade" in a middle-class world. In consequence of all this, we suspect that few working-class parents unequivocally repudiate as intrinsically worthless middle-class objectives. There is good reason to believe that the modesty of working-class aspirations is partly a matter of trimming one's sails to the available opportunities and resources and partly a matter of unwillingness to accept the discipline which upward striving entails.

However complete and successful one's accommodation to an humble status, the vitality of middle-class goals, of the "American dream," is nonetheless likely to manifest itself in his aspirations for his children. His expectations may not be grandiose, but he will want his children to be "better off" than he. Whatever his own work history and social reputation may be, he will want his children to be "steady" and "respectable." He may exert few positive pressures to "succeed" and the experiences he provides his children may even incapacitate them for success; he may be puzzled at the way they "turn out." But whatever the measure of his own responsibility in accounting for the product, he is not likely to judge that product by unadulterated "corner-boy" standards. Even "corner-boy" parents, although they may value in their children such corner-boy virtues as generosity to friends, personal loyalty and physical prowess, are likely also to be gratified by recognition by middle-class representatives and by the kinds of achievement for which the college-boy way of life is a prerequisite. Even in the working-class milieu from which he acquired his incapacity for middle-class achievement, the working-class corner-boy may find himself at a status disadvantage as against his more upwardly mobile peers.

Lastly, of course, is that most ubiquitous and inescapable of status sources, oneself. Technically, we do not call the person's attitudes toward himself "status" but rather "self-esteem," or, when the quality of the self-attitude is specifically moral, "conscience" or "superego." The important question for us is this: To what extent, if at all, do boys who are typically "working-class" and "corner-boy" in their overt behavior evaluate themselves by "middle-class," "college-boy" standards? For our overt behavior, however closely it conforms to one set of norms, need not argue against the existence or effectiveness of alternative and conflicting norms. The failure of our own behavior to conform to our own expectations is an elementary and common-place fact which gives rise to the tremendously important consequences of guilt, self-recrimination, anxiety and self-hatred. The reasons for the failure of self-expectations and overt conduct to agree are complex. One reason is that we often internalize more than one set of norms, each of which would dictate a different course of action in a given life-situation; since we can only *do* one thing at a time, however, we are forced to choose between them or somehow compromise. In either case, we fall short of the full realization of our own expectations and must somehow cope with the residual discrepancy between those expectations and our overt behavior.

We have suggested that corner-boy children (like their working-class parents) internalize middle-class standards to a sufficient degree to create a fundamental ambivalence towards their own corner-boy behavior. Again, we are on somewhat speculative ground where fundamental research re-mains to be done. The coexistence within the same personality of a corner-boy and a college-boy morality may appear more plausible, however, if we recognize that they are not simple antitheses of one another and that parents and others may in all sincerity attempt to indoctrinate both. For example, the goals upon which the college-boy places such great value, such as intellectual and occupational achievement, and the college-boy virtues of ambitiousness and pride in self-sufficiency are not as such disparaged by the corner-boy culture. The meritoriousness of standing by one's friends and the desire to have a good time here and now do not by definition preclude the desire to help oneself and to provide for the future. It is no doubt the rule, rather than the exception, that most children, college-boy and corner-boy alike, would like to enjoy the best of both worlds. *In practice,* however, the substance that is consumed in the pursuit of one set of values is not available for the pursuit of the other. The sharpness of the dilemma and the degree of the residual discontent depend upon a number of things, notably, the intensity with which both sets of norms have been internalized, the extent to which the life-situations which one encounters compel a choice between them, and the abundance and appropriateness of the skills and resources at one's disposal. The child of superior intelligence, for example, may find it easier than his less gifted peers to meet the demands of the college-boy standards without failing his obligations to his corner-boy associates.

It is a plausible assumption, then, that the working-class boy whose status is low in middle-class terms *cares* about that status, that this status confronts him with a genuine problem of adjustment. To this problem of adjustment there are a variety of conceivable responses, of which participation in the creation and the maintenance of the delinquent subculture is one. Each mode of response entails costs and yields gratifications of its own. The circumstances which tip the balance in favor of the one or the other are obscure. One mode of response is to desert the corner-boy for the college-boy way of life. To the reader of Whyte's *Street Corner Society* the costs are manifest. It is hard, at best, to be a college-boy and to run with the corner-boys. It entails great effort and sacrifice to the degree that one has been indoctrinated in what we have described as the working-class socialization process; its rewards are frequently long-deferred; and for many working-class boys it makes demands which they are, in consequence of their inferior linguistic, academic and "social" skills, not likely ever to meet. Nevertheless, a certain proportion of working-class boys accept the challenge of the middle-class status system and play the status game by the middle-class rules.

Another response, perhaps the most common, is what we may call the "stable corner-boy response." It represents an acceptance of the corner-boy way of life and an effort to make the best of a situation. If our reasoning is correct, it does not resolve the dilemmas we have described as inherent in the corner-boy position in a largely middle-class world, although these dilemmas may be mitigated by an effort to disengage oneself from dependence upon middle-class status-sources and by withdrawing, as far as possible, into a sheltering community of like-minded working-class children. Unlike the delinquent response, it avoids the radical rupture of good relations with even working-class adults and does not represent as irretrievable a renunciation of upward mobility. It does not incur the active hostility of middle-class persons and therefore leaves the way open to the pursuit of some values, such as jobs, which these people control. It represents a preference for the familiar, with its known satisfactions and its known imperfections, over the risks and the uncertainties as well as the moral costs of the college-boy response, on the one hand, and the delinquent response on the other.

What does the delinquent response have to offer? Let us be clear, first, about what this response is and how it differs from the stable corner-boy response. The hallmark of the delinquent subculture is the explicit and wholesale repudiation of middle-class standards and the adoption of their very antithesis. *The corner-boy culture is not specifically delinquent.* Where it leads to behavior which may be defined as delinquent, e.g., truancy, it does so not because nonconformity to middle-class norms *defines* conformity to corner-boy norms but because conformity to middle-class norms *interferes with* conformity to corner-boy norms. The corner-boy plays truant because he does not like school, because he wishes to escape from a dull and unrewarding and perhaps humiliating situation. But truancy is not defined as intrinsically valuable and status giving. The member of the delinquent subculture plays truant because "good" middle-class (and working-class) children do not play truant. Corner-boy resistance to being herded and mar-shalled by Middle-class figures is not the same as the delinquent's flouting and jeering of those middle-class figures and active ridicule of those who submit. The corner-boy's ethic of reciprocity, his quasi-communal attitude toward the property of in-group members, is shared by the delinquent. But this ethic of reciprocity does not sanction the deliberate and "malicious" violation of the property rights of persons outside the in-group. We have ob-served that the differences between the corner-boy and the college-boy of middle-class culture are profound but that in many ways they are profound differences in emphasis. We have remarked that the corner-boy culture does not so much repudiate the value of many middle-class achievements as it emphasizes certain other values which make such achievements improbable. In short, the corner-boy culture temporizes with middle-class morality; the full-fledged delinquent subculture does not.

It is precisely here, we suggest, in the refusal to temporize, that the ap-peal of the delinquent subculture lies. Let us recall that it is characteristically American, not specifically working-class or middle-class, to measure oneself against the widest possible status universe, to seek status against "all comers," to be "as good as" or "better than" anybody, that is within one's own age and sex category. As long as the working-class corner-boy clings to a version, however attentuated and adulterated, of the middle-class culture, he must recognize his inferiority to working-class and middle-class college-boys. The delinquent subculture, on the other hand, permits no ambiguity of the status of the delinquent relative to that of anybody else. In terms of the norms of the delinquent subculture, defined by its negative polarity to the respect-able status system, the delinquent's very nonconformity to middle-class standards sets him above the most exemplary college boy.

Another important function of the delinquent subculture is the legitima-tion of aggression. We surmise that a certain amount of hostility is generated among working-class children against middle-class persons, with their airs of superiority, disdain or condescension and against middle-class norms, which are, in a sense, the cause of their status-frustration. To infer inclinations to aggression from the existence of frustration is hazardous; we know that aggression is not an inevitable and not the only consequence of frustration. So here too we must feel our way with caution. Ideally, we should like to see systematic research, probably employing "depth interview" and "pro-jective" techniques, to get at the relationship between status position and aggressive dispositions toward the rules which determine status and toward persons variously distributed in the status hierarchy. Nevertheless, depite our imperfect knowledge of these things, we would be blind if we failed to recognize that bitterness, hostility and jealousy and all sorts of retributive fantasies are among the most common and typically human responses to public humiliation. However, for the child who temporizes with middle-class morality, overt aggression and even the conscious recognition of his own hostile impulses are inhibited, for he acknowledges the *legitimacy* of the rules in terms of which he is stigmatized. For the child who breaks clean with middle-class morality, on the other hand, there are no moral inhibitions on the free expression of aggression against the sources of his frustration. Moreover, the connection we suggest between status-frustration and the aggressiveness of the delinquent subculture seems to us more plausible than many frustration-aggression hypotheses because it involves no assumptions about obscure and dubious "displacement" of aggression against "substitute" targets. The target in this case is the manifest cause of the status problem.

It seems to us that the mechanism of "reaction-formation" should also play a part here. We have made much of the corner-boy's basic ambivalence, his uneasy acknowledgement, while he lives by the standards of his corner-boy culture, of the legitimacy of college-boy standards. May we assume that when the delinquent seeks to obtain unequivocal status by repudiating, once and for all, the norms of the college-boy culture, these norms really undergo total extinction? Or do they, perhaps, linger on, underground, as it were, repressed, unacknowledged but an ever-present threat to the adjustment which has been achieved at no small cost? There is much evidence from clinical psychology that moral norms, once effectively internalized, are not lightly thrust aside or extinguished. If a new moral order is evolved which offers a more satisfactory solution to one's life problems, the old order usually continues to press for recognition, but if this recognition is granted, the apple-cart is upset. (The symptom of this obscurely felt, ever-present threat is clinically known as "anxiety," and the literature of psychiatry is rich with devices for combatting this anxiety, this threat to a hard-won victory. One such device is reaction-formation. Its hallmark is an "exaggerated," "dispro-portionate," "abnormal" intensity of response, "inappropriate" to the stimulus which seems to elicit it. The unintelligibility of the response, the "over-reac-tion," becomes intelligible when we see that it has the function of reassuring the actor against an inner threat to his defenses as well as the function of meeting an external situation on its own terms.) Thus we have the mother who "compulsively" showers "inordinate" affection upon a child to reassure herself against her latent hostility and we have the male adolescent whose awkward and immoderate masculinity reflects a basic insecurity about his own sex-role. In like manner, we would expect the delinquent boy who, after all, has been socialized in a society, to seek to maintain his safeguards against seduction. Reaction-formation in his case, should take the form of an "irrational," "malicious," "unaccountable" hostility to the enemy within the gates as well as without; the norms of the respectable middle-class society.

If our reasoning is correct, it should throw some light upon the peculiar

quality of "property delinquency" in the delinquent subculture. We have
already seen how the rewardingness of a college-boy and middle-class way
of life depends, to a great extent, upon general respect for property rights.
In an urban society, in particular, the possession and display of property are
the most ready and public badges of reputable social class status and are,
for that reason, extraordinarily ego-involved. That property actually is a reward for middle-class morality is in part only a plausible fiction, but in general
there is certainly a relationship between the practice of that morality and
the possession of property. The middle-classes have, then, a strong interest
in scrupulous regard for property rights, not only because property is "intrinsically" valuable but because the full enjoyment of their status requires
that status be readily recognizable and therefore that property adhere to
those who earn it. The cavalier misappropriation or destruction of property,
therefore, is not only a diversion or diminution of wealth; it is an attack on
the middle-class where their egos are most vulnerable. Group stealing, institutionalized in the delinquent subculture, is not just a way of *getting* something. It is a means that is the antithesis of sober and diligent "labour in a
calling." (It expresses contempt for a way of life by making its opposite a
criterion of status.) Money and other valuables are not, as such, despised by
the delinquent. For the delinquent and the non-delinquent alike, money is
a most glamorous and efficient means to a variety of ends and one cannot
have too much of it. But, in the delinquent subculture, the stolen dollar has
an odor of sanctity that does not attach to the dollar saved or the dollar
earned.

   This delinquent system of values and way of life does its job of problem-
solving most effectively when it is adopted as a group solution. We have
stressed in our chapter on the general theory of subcultures that the efficacy
of a given change in values as a solution and therefore the motivation to
such a change depends heavily upon the availability of "reference groups"
within which the "deviant values" are already institutionalized, or whose
members would stand to profit from such a system of deviant values if each
were assured of the support and concurrence of the others. So it is with delinquency. We do not suggest that joining in the creation or perpetuation of a
delinquent subculture is the only road to delinquency. We do believe, however, that for most delinquents delinquency would not be available as a response were it not socially legitimized and given a kind of respectability,
albeit by a restricted community of fellow-adventurers. In this respect, the
adoption of delinquency is like the adoption of the practice of appearing at
the office in open-collar and shirt sleeves. Is it much more comfortable, is it
more sensible than the full regalia? Is it neat? Is it dignified? The arguments
in the affirmative will appear much more forceful if the practice is already
established in one's milieu or if one senses that others are prepared to go

along if someone makes the first tentative gestures. Indeed, to many of those who sweat and chafe in ties and jackets, the possibility of an alternative may not even occur until they discover that it has been adopted by their colleagues.

This way of looking at delinquency suggests an answer to a certain paradox. Countless mothers have protested that their "Johnny" was a good boy until he fell in with a certain bunch. But the mothers of each of Johnny's companions hold the same view with respect to their own off-spring. It is conceivable and even probable that some of these mothers are naive, that one or more of these youngsters are "rotten apples" who infected the others. We suggest, however, that all of the mothers may be right, that there is a certain chemistry in the group situation itself which engenders that which was not there before, that group interaction is a sort of catalyst which releases potentialities not otherwise visible. This is especially true when we are dealing with a problem of status-frustration. Status, by definition, is a grant of respect from others. A new system of norms, which measures status by criteria which one can meet, is of no value unless others are prepared to apply those criteria, and others are not likely to do so unless one is prepared to reciprocate.

We have referred to a lingering ambivalence in the delinquent's own value system, an ambivalence which threatens the adjustment he has achieved and which is met through the mechanism of reaction-formation. The delinquent may have to contend with another ambivalence, in the area of his status sources. The delinquent subculture offers him status *as against* other children of whatever social level, but it offers him this status *in the eyes* of his fellow delinquents only. To the extent that there remains a desire for recognition from groups whose respect has been forfeited by commitment to a new subculture, his satisfaction in his solution is imperfect and adulterated. He can perfect his solution only by reflecting as status sources those who reject him. This too may require a certain measure of reaction-formation, going beyond indifference to active hostility and contempt for all those who do not share his subculture. He becomes all the more dependent upon his delinquent gang. Outside that the gang itself tends toward a kind of sectarian solidarity, because the benefits of membership can only be realized in active fact-to-face relationships with group members.

This interpretation of the delinquent subculture has important implications for the "sociology of social problems." People are prone to assume that those things which we define as evil and those which we define as good have their origins in separate and distinct features of our society. Evil flows from poisoned wells; good flows from pure and crystal fountains. The same source cannot feed both. Our view is different. It holds that those values which are at the core of "the American way of life," which help to motivate the behavior which we most esteem as "typically American," are among the major determinants of that which we stigmatize as "pathological." More specifically, it holds that the problems of adjustment to which the delinquent subculture is a response are determined, in part, by those very values which respectable society holds most sacred. The same value system, impinging upon children differently equipped to meet it, is instrumental in generating both delinquency and respectability.

Section 51 CRIME AND THE IMMIGRANT

From "The Puerto Ricans" by Rev. Joseph P. Fitzpatrick, S. J., 1960.

Newspapers tell us that delinquency is a serious danger in New York City. Indeed it is. But a far more serious danger would be a sense of panic in the minds of New Yorkers; a fear that our Fair City has begun to decay; a sense of pity that older and peaceful and prosperous times are being snowed under in a new phenomenon of teen-age crime, of slum living, and of poverty.

This would be a strange state of mind for New Yorkers to fall into, but there must be something in the heavy air of the Hudson or the East River that induces this illness in New Yorkers. They have been assigning their Fair City to the dust heap for the past hundred and fifty years, but it always seems to come out fairer than ever. And New Yorkers had another old tradition, something like a tribal practice, I suppose, of always blaming her recurrent ills on the latest strangers who arrived to populate her slums. It takes a bit of maneuvering to substitute Idlewild Airport for Castle Garden, but the New Yorkers look as if they are going to succeed in doing it. There are signs of life in the old lady yet. The Irish and the Germans, the Italians and the Jews have now become respectable. But it looks as if the Puerto Ricans will enable the old tradition to survive. For they are joining the company of all the great peoples who went before them; getting their initiation into the noble heritage of immigrants; by having all the crime and the ills of the city attributed to their coming.

The interesting thing about this strange infirmity that New Yorkers like to cherish is simply this: that the older and more peaceful and more prosperous times never existed. New York has always been a rough city; often a violent one. Turbulence and upheaval, conflict and adjustment, change and struggle have always been her way of life. That is what made her great. One contemporary judge wants us to slow things down to give the City time to catch up. New York has never had time to catch up. Wave after wave of new-comers kept driving the city onward; struggle and change have kept her on her toes. The City is great precisely because destiny never allowed her to take a rest. Effort and energy, challenge and striving have drawn from her mind and soul a constant burst of creativeness, of imagination, of drive that has made her what she is. I give you the quotation, for what it is worth, of an old friend of mine, a hard-bitten Irishman who spent his life in the excitement of the Stock Exchange—where New York was so very much New York. "Father," he said, "you are privileged to be living in New York these days. You are witnessing the greatest moments of the City's life."

The one simple prescription to cure this recurring dizziness is a sense of perspective, a realization that these are not the worst times of the City's history. They may be the best. Let's forget about Mayor Wagner for a few moments and listen for a while to the man who was Mayor of New York in 1825. Philip Hone never thought the city would last long enough to have a mayor in 1859 much less 1959. He wrote in his diary on Monday, December 2, 1839 as follows:

> One of the evidences of the degeneracy of our morals and of the inefficiency of our police is to be seen in the frequent instances of murder by stabbing. The city is infested by gangs of hardened wretches, born in the haunts of infamy, brought up in taverns, educated at the polls of elections, and following the fire engines as a profession. These fellows (generally youths between the ages of twelve and twenty-four) patrol the streets making night hideous and insulting all who are not strong enough to defend themselves; their haunts all the night long are the grog-shops in the Bowery, Corlear's Hook, Canal Street and some even in Broadway, where drunken frolics are succeeded by brawls, and on the slightest provocation knives are brought out, dreadful wounds inflicted, and sometimes horrid murder committed. The watchmen and police officers are intimidated by the frequency of these riots, the strength of the offenders and the disposition which exists on the part of those who ought to know better to screen the culprits from punishment.
>
> *Diary of Philip Hone, 1828–51* (N.Y.: 1936), p. 434.

This is a description of those more peaceful and prosperous days that modern New Yorkers long to have back again. One doesn't have to look very far to see who Philip Hone blames for the distress. According to him, the doom of the city was already assured by the worthless element that was there in abundance.

(These Irishmen) . . . are the most ignorant and consequently the most obstinate white men in the world, and I
have seen enough to satisfy me that, with few exceptions,
ignorance and vice go together. . . . These Irishmen, strangers among us, without a feeling of patriotism or affection in
common with American citizens, decide the elections of the
City of New York. . . . the time may not be very distant
when the same brogue which they have instructed to shout
'Hurrah for Jackson!' shall be used to impart additional
horror to the cry of 'Down with the natives!' *Id.*, p. 190.

Can you imagine what chances he would have of becoming Mayor today!
    Philip Hone was not by any means alone in his prejudices. John Pintard
was another outstanding man of those days, a very spiritual and generous
soul who spent much of his time raising funds for the building of St. Patrick's
Cathedral and for the support of Irish orphans. Pintard had doubts on many
things but he was a true New Yorker. He knew the city was going to the
dogs and he knew the reason why:

But the beastly vice of drunkenness among the lower labor-
ing classes is growing to a frightful excess, owing to the
cheapness of spirits and the multitudes of low Irish Catholics,
who, restrained by poverty in their own country from free
indulgence, run riot in this. . . . We have 3500 licensed
dram shops in this city, two or three on every corner; but if
we stop one half, . . . the consumers will all go to the other
corner. . . . as long as we are overwhelmed with Irish immigrants, so long will the evil abound. . . . Thefts, incendiaries, murders which prevail, all rise from this source.
    Letters of John Pintard (N.Y.: 1941), Vol. III, p. 51.

It is too bad that Philip Hone and Joseph Pintard did not tell us more
of the really peaceful, and orderly and prosperous days that came twenty
years later. Another generation had come; more immigrants had arrived;
the City was worse than ever. And who gets the blame? You guessed it. By
this time the United States Congress had become interested, just a little
prelude to Senator Hennings' visit. And we owe to them the following sketch
of New York in the 1850's.

It has been stated in the public journals that of the 16,000
commitments for crimes in New York City, during 1852, at
least one fourth were minors, and that no less than 10,000
children are daily suffering all the evils of vagrancy in that

city. In 1849, the chief of the police department of that city called attention to the increasing number of vagrant, idle and vicious children of both sexes growing up in ignorance and profligacy, and destined to a life of misery, shame and crime. . . . He stated that there were then 2,955 children of the class described, known to the police in eleven patrol districts, of whom two thirds were females between eight and sixteen years of age. Most of the children, as was stated at the time, were of German or Irish parentage, the proportion of the American born being not more than one in five.

Foreign Criminals and Paupers. Report from the Committee on Foreign Affairs, August 16, 1856 (U.S. 34 Congress, 1st session, House Report No. 359), pp. 16–17. Quoted in Edith Abbott, *Historical Aspects of the Immigration Problem* (Chicago: Univ. of Chicago Press, 1926), p. 621.

The good members of the House Committee did not confine themselves to New York. They thought on a national scale. It was not only New York City that was going to the dogs; it was the entire nation. However, they had spent enough time in New York City to catch the spirit of that strange tribal practice of finding the roots of all evil in the strangers to our land:

. . . The sources of this great moral evil may be almost wholly traced to the many vices of the foreign population, who afford no other examples to their children than habits of disorder, idleness and uncleanliness, and degrading vices of all kinds, and who exercise no parental authority whatever on them.

Id., quoted in Abbott, p. 621.

Really, if a New Yorker wants to get the spice of life, a real image, in vivid pictures, of what was going on; if he wants to know the names of some of these vicious children, and the methods of their trade, he can turn to that extraordinary bit of historical reporting that so many New Yorkers so quickly forgot: Herbert Asbury's *Gangs of New York.*

About this time, new rays of light began to appear in public statements. Crime, indeed, preoccupied everyone's mind, and its association with the immigrant poor was taken for granted; but as public officials began to look into the housing conditions of the time, they began to see the situation in new perspective:

That crime, in general, is on the increase in our community, is a melancholy fact, in spite of the prevalent taste for reading, the multiplication of means of education. . . . Where shall we look for the rankest development of this terrible combination, but in the hideous anomalies of civilization which are to be found in the tenant-house system? . . .

Report of the Select Committee Appointed to Examine into the condition of Tenant-houses in New York and Brooklyn (N.Y. State Assembly Document No. 205, 1857). Quoted in Abbott, p. 635.

The Committee had pointed out earlier who was living in these horrible slums. If I may quote a bit more:

But we must pass over without description hundreds of dilapidated, dirty and densely populated old structures which the committee inspected in different wards and which come under the head of re-adapted, reconstructed or altered buildings. In most of them the Irish are predominant, as occupants, though in some streets Negroes are found swarming from cellar to garret of tottering tenant houses. In this connection it may be well to remark, that in some of the better class of houses built for tenantry, Negroes have been preferred as occupants to Irish or German poor; the incentive to possessing comparatively decent quarters appearing to inspire the colored residents with more desire for cleanliness and regard for property than is impressed on the whites of their own condition. . . .

Id., quoted in Abbott, p. 635.

Make no mistake. This Committee had no particular respect for the foreign poor. They did not think good housing would enable good foreigners to remain good; rather good housing would enable Americans to reform the evil ways of foreign people. The tribal practice had been given a new tone; but they were the same biased words.

As a surety we must, as a people, act upon this foreign element, or it will act on us. Like the vast Atlantic, we must decompose and cleanse the impurities which rush into our midst, or like the inland lake, we will receive the poison into our whole national system.

Id., quoted in Abbott, p. 636.

All this time, of course, while the Daybreak Boys were breaking the skulls of rival gangs or decent citizens, and while committee after committee spoke philosophically about the evil immigrant poor, hundreds of thousands of these supposedly evil immigrants were pushing their way courageously through poverty and exploitation, were working hard to bring up decent families against hopeless odds; were building their churches and schools; were laying the solid bricks, with human courage and human hope, of what was to be the greatest city of the world.

But the eighteen fifties passed. Came the Civil War, the draft riots, and after the Civil War, amidst the flowering of industry and commerce, the flowering again of those persistent elements of New York life: crime, slums and poverty. John Francis Maguire, a well-known Irish writer, came to observe how his fellow Irishmen were doing in America. Interestingly enough, he caught the fever of New York's writers very quickly. He found the City in a hopeless condition, with little indication that it would ever overcome the difficulties that faced it:

> The evil of overcrowding is magnified to a prodigious extent in New York. . . . There is scarcely any city in the world possessing greater resources than New York, but these resources have long since been strained to the uttermost to meet the yearly increasing demands created by this continuous accession to its inhabitants; and if there be not some check put to this undue increase of the population, for which even the available space is altogether inadequate, it is difficult to think what the consequences must be. Every succeeding year tends to aggravate the existing evils which, while rendering the necessity for a remedy more urgent, also render its nature and its application more difficult.
>
> John F. Maguire, *The Irish in America* (N.Y.: 1868), pp. 218–19.

There were less than eight hundred thousand people in New York when Maguire wrote. If the available space was altogether inadequate then, I wonder what he would say about the nearly eight million who live in the City today.

This, then, is part of the record of that old and peaceful and orderly life which so many New Yorkers long for when they read of the Royal Crowns and the Egyptian Kings. It was a life, like so much of New York's life, of crime and violence, of struggle and effort. But with it all, the strong, human, creative elements won out. New York has not become what it is without struggle; and if the struggle of the past gave us the greatness of the present, can we not expect that the struggle of the present will give us the even more impressive greatness of the future?

As we reach the time when my quotations end, about the year 1870, certainly we could say the City needed a rest. If only they could have stopped migrations to allow the city to catch up, to clear the slums, to eliminate the crime. And what happened? New ships appeared with new faces, bringing an even stranger babble of new tongues. The Italians and the Jews began to crowd in just about the time when the Irish and the Germans were finding themselves. Whereas the Irish may have brought 100,000 a year at some times; the new migration was to bring a million a year. New York had not seen the beginning of strangers. New challenge; new distress; new slums; new poverty; new crime; and hundreds of thousands of new immigrants to be blamed for it. The record need not delay us. Jacob Riis was around to write some of the record for us. *How the Other Half Lives* (America Century Series, N.Y.: Sagamore Press, 1957) is fortunately out in paperback. Read it for yourselves. Were things bad in 1870? They were worse in 1890. Riis tells us there were gangs on every corner (Riis, p. 164). Where did they come from? Here we have not only a new tune, but a new script. Riis saw what many an intelligent person had seen before him. The gang was not the product of evil foreigners. It was the product of life in New York; the by-product of generations lost in the confusion and bewilderment of the uprooting; the weak ones who fell by the wayside when they faced the shock of moulding a new way of life for themselves in a new world; the price we pay for a system that urges people of talent to advance socially and economically—some people are ground down in the process; the unfortunate resultant of a system in which parents of one culture will never fully understand the way of life of their children, and children will never fully understand the way of life of the parent; these are some of the things we began to see more clearly toward the close of the last century. But the record of history is eloquent: the crime that distressed the City, the slums and poverty that created such a constant burden on its life did not destroy the City's greatness; they were a part of the goad, the stimulus, the challenge that evoked the energy and effort that made the City great.

Now again we have crime; we have slums; we have poverty; and, now again, we face the traditional malady of the New Yorker: the lament that the City is going to the dogs; and the revival of the old tribal practice: of blaming our crime and poverty on the Puerto Ricans who now find themselves socially in the slot where the Germans and the Irish were a century ago.

INDEX

83-14667
Title II — ESEA

364.1
T

AUTHOR

52517

Tyler, Gus.

TITLE

Organized Crime in America

DATE	BORROWER'S NAME	ROOM NUMBER

52517

364.1
T

Tyler, Gus.

Organized Crime in America

83-14667

4-25-14
5-1-14

LOURDES HIGH SCHOOL LIBRARY
4034 W. 56TH STREET
CHICAGO, ILLINOIS 60629

DEMCO